INSTITUTE OF CORNISH STUDIES

Cornish Studies (second series) exists to reflect current research conducted internationally in the inter-disciplinary field of Cornish Studies. It is edited by Professor Philip Payton, Director of the Institute of Cornish Studies at the University of Exeter, Cornwall Campus, and is published by University of Exeter Press. The opinions expressed in *Cornish Studies* are those of individual authors and are not necessarily those of the editor or publisher. The support of Cornwall Council is gratefully acknowledged.

Cover illustration: Mebyon Kernow poster, early 1970s

CORNISH STUDIES

Second Series

TWENTY-ONE

'Coming of Age'?

edited by
Philip Payton

UNIVERSITY
of
EXETER
PRESS

First published in 2013 by
University of Exeter Press
Reed Hall, Streatham Drive
Exeter EX4 4QR
UK
www.exeterpress.co.uk

British Library Cataloguing in Publication Data
A catalogue record for this book is available from the British Library.

ISBN 978 0 85989 886 7

Typeset in Adobe Caslon by
Kestrel Data, Exeter

Printed in Great Britain by
Short Run Press Ltd, Exeter

Contents

Notes on contributors   vii

Introduction   1

1 Philip Payton: Cultural Entrepreneur for a Rhetorically   9
   Defined Space
   Matthew Spriggs (Australian National University)

2 The Unimportance of Being Cornish in Cornwall   17
   *Bernard Deacon (Institute of Cornish Studies, University of
   Exeter)*

3 Adjectival and Adverbial Prefixes in Cornish   33
   N.J.A. Williams (University College Dublin)

4 Visitations of Cornish Churches, 1281–1331   76
   Nicholas Orme (University of Exeter)

5 The Duchy of Cornwall and the Wars of the Roses: 104
   Patronage, Politics and Power, 1453–1502
   R.E. Stansfield (University of Lancaster)

6 Justifying Imperialism: English Representations of Ireland   151
   and Cornwall before and during the Civil War
   James Harris (University of Exeter)

7   The Duchy of Cornwall and the Crown: Disputes and   175
    Accommodation
    John Kirkhope (University of Plymouth)

8   Bishop Benson's Vision for Truro Cathedral and Diocese: 207
    The Umbrella and the Duck
    David Miller (Institute of Cornish Studies, University of Exeter)

9   Against Taxonomy: The Fairy Families of Cornwall   223
    Simon Young (Florence, Italy)

10 'Where there were two Cornishmen there was a "rastle"':   238
    Cornish Wrestling in Latin and North America
    Mike Tripp (University of St Mark & St John, Plymouth)

11 'The imprint of what-has-been': Arthur Quiller-Couch,   260
    Daphne du Maurier and the writing of *Castle Dor*
    Kirsty Bunting (Manchester Metropolitan University)

12 The Happy Chance of Jack Clemo   276
    Luke Thompson (University of Exeter)

13 Celtic Tradition and Regional Discontent: Cornish   288
    Nationalism Revisited
    Peder Clark (Birkbeck College, University of London)

14 Betjeman's Badge: Postscript for a Pan-Celtic Nationalist   321
    *Philip Payton (Institute of Cornish Studies, University of
    Exeter, and Flinders University, Australia)*

Bibliography: Philip Payton   329

Notes on contributors

Peder Clark is a public health trainee in south-east London. He has recently completed an MA in Contemporary History and Politics at Birkbeck College, University of London. His dissertation examined the roots and history of Cornish nationalism.

Bernard Deacon is Honorary University Fellow at the Institute of Cornish Studies, University of Exeter, where he was formerly Senior Lecturer in Cornish Studies. He has written extensively on Cornish topics and his most recent publications are a chapter in *Celts in the Americas* on 'Chameleon Celts: The Cornish in the Americas', an article entitled 'D'une ethnie à une nation? Les trois moments de l'identité Cornouaillaise moderne', which appeared in the Quebec journal *Bulletin Politique*, and a book – *The land's end? A Critique of Current Planning Policies*.

Kirsty Bunting is a Lecturer in English Literature at Manchester Metropolitan University with research interests in literary collaborations and archival studies.

James Harris graduated in 2012 from the University of Exeter's Cornwall Campus, where he read History, and is now studying for an MA in History at the University's Streatham Campus in Exeter. He divides his time between Lelant, Cornwall and Exeter.

John Kirkhope is a Public Notary and Chartered Insurer by profession. He has recently completed a PhD on the Duchy of Cornwall at the University of Plymouth, where he is also an Associate Lecturer.

David Miller was awarded the degree of Doctor of Philosophy in Cornish Studies at the University of Exeter in November 2012 for his thesis, entitled 'The Episcopate of Bishop Benson, 1877–1883 and the beginnings of the Truro Diocese and Cathedral: The Umbrella and the Duck'. He is a Canon of Truro Cathedral and Rector of the parishes of Helston and Wendron in Cornwall.

Nicholas Orme is Emeritus Professor of History at the University of Exeter, and an Emeritus Lay Canon of Truro Cathedral. He has written extensively on the history of the Church in medieval England, and on that of Cornwall, in particular in *Cornwall and the Cross* and *The Victoria County History of Cornwall*, Volume 2. His parallel study of *The Church in Devon* appeared in 2013.

Philip Payton is Professor of Cornish & Australian Studies at the University of Exeter (Cornwall Campus), where he is also Director of the Institute of Cornish Studies. During 2013 he was Visiting Fellow in the Institute of Advanced Study at the University of Warwick. He is also Adjunct Professor of History at Flinders University, Adelaide, Australia. His most recent book (edited with Helen Doe and Alston Kennerley) is *The Maritime History of Cornwall*, published by University of Exeter Press.

Matthew Spriggs is Professor of Archaeology and Head of the Archaeology Department within the School of Archaeology and Anthropology at the Australian National University, Canberra.

Robert E. Stansfield studied History at the University of Lancaster, and has also studied at the University of Copenhagen. His doctoral research was published as *Political Elites in South-West England, 1450–1500: Politics, Governance, and the Wars of the Roses* (2009), and his research focuses primarily on the political history of late-medieval and early modern Britain. He is Secretary of the Chetham Society, and Member of Council of the Lancashire and Cheshire Antiquarian Society.

Luke Thompson is a PhD student at the University of Exeter, focussing on the work and life of the clay country poet Jack Clemo. Recent work includes co-organization of the 2013 Jack Clemo Conference 'Kindling the Spirit', and co-editing the new nature and place magazine, *The Clearing*.

Mike Tripp retired recently as Head of Department of Sports Development and Outdoor Learning at the University of St Mark and St John (aka 'Marjon'), Plymouth, where he taught the history, politics and sociology of sport. He obtained his doctorate from the Institute of Cornish Studies, University of Exeter, in 2010 for his thesis 'The Persistence of Difference: A History of Cornish Wrestling'. He has contributed articles on wrestling to *The Oxford Companion of the Body*, *The New Dictionary of National Biography*, the *Encyclopedia of British Sport* and the *Encyclopedia of Traditional British Rural Sports*.

Nicholas Williams is Professor Emeritus in Celtic Languages, University College, Dublin. He has written extensively on the Celtic languages, in particular Irish, Manx and Cornish. With Graham Thomas he edited *Bewnans Ke: The Life of St Kea*, published by University of Exeter Press in 2007. His translation of *The Holy Bible* into Cornish appeared in 2011. His most recent volume on Cornish is *Geryow Gwir: The Lexicon of Revived Cornish* (2013).

Simon Young is a British historian based in Florence, Italy. He has previously written on the Irish *Peregrini*, and on the medieval British-Celtic colony of Britonia. At present he is preparing his sixth book, a work on the decline of fairy belief in nineteenth-century Britain and Ireland.

Introduction

Publication of *Cornish Studies: Twenty-One*, this present volume, represents the 'coming of age' of the current series. Perhaps, too, as Matthew Spriggs suggests in his evaluation of this editor's contribution to the field, it marks a wider 'coming of age' within Cornish studies as a whole. In the 1990s, as Spriggs remarks, *Cornish Studies* became the vehicle for the 'New Cornish Studies' and its twin progeny (as Bernard Deacon once described them), the 'new Cornish historiography' and the 'new Cornish social science'. Privileging issues of Cornish identity—seen to be its principal *raison d'être*—this 'New Cornish Studies' sought to escape the narrow confines of antiquarian local history and to create instead an interdisciplinary, international, comparative inquiry that would both learn from and contribute to broader academic debates across the academy.

Looking back, it was an impossibly ambitious agenda. Yet the rhetoric of 'New Cornish Studies' was so persistent and, for some at least, so persuasive, that its small but growing band of practitioners did manage to engage with an ever wider cross-section of disciplines. Political science, sociology, geography, cultural studies, literature, early modern history, contemporary history and other areas were soon co-opted under the 'New Cornish Studies' label, specialists in those fields encouraged to write for *Cornish Studies* but also to take Cornish perspectives into the heart of their own disciplines. This sustained advocacy—'cultural entrepreneurship, as Spriggs has it—bore fruit to the extent that each edition of *Cornish Studies* was soon oversubscribed with potential contributors, a veritable backlog of articles waiting their turn. But, perhaps more importantly, it also resulted in the regular appearance of Cornish studies articles in national and international journals, an occurrence that Spriggs describes as now 'commonplace'. Today, on those occasions when one allows the nostalgic luxury of looking back, it remains a delight to turn again to fondly remembered (and milestone) pieces such as Mark Stoyle's 'Pagans or Paragons?: Images of the Cornish during the English Civil War' in the *English Historical Review* in 1996, or Ella Westland's 'D.H. Lawrence's Cornwall: Dwelling in a Precarious Age' in *Cultural Geographies* in 2002, or Kerryn

Husk's 'Ethnicity and Social Exclusion: Research and Policy Implications in a Cornish Case Study' in *Social and Public Policy Review* in 2011.

More recently, argues Matthew Spriggs, the rhetoric has relaxed, the argument won, a 'coming of age' where it is no longer necessary 'to privilege theory over content' or to project 'the strident assertion of novelty'. As he puts it: 'The relevance of a Cornish studies perspective in a range of settings from biography to studies of modern British identities, and indeed of identities further afield, is now abundantly clear . . . To ignore this perspective is now merely a sign of poor scholarship'.

Perhaps; yet Bernard Deacon in his essay 'The Unimportance of Being Cornish in Cornwall' worries that the institutional base of Cornish studies may now be too narrow, too constrained, to maintain academic leadership over that range of disciplines. First delivered as the annual Caroline L. Kemp Memorial Lecture at the University of Exeter (Cornwall Campus), Tremough, in November 2012, Deacon's contribution takes its cue from Charles Thomas's inaugural lecture as Professor of Cornish Studies in 1973, given shortly after the foundation of the Institute of Cornish Studies, a joint project by the University of Exeter and the then Cornwall County Council. Entitled 'The Importance of Being Cornish in Cornwall', Thomas's lecture was intended as a clarion call, a warning that the survival of Cornwall and the Cornish—both threatened by widespread deleterious socio-economic change and environmental degradation—was now in question. Part of the role of the Institute, he suggested, was to address such issues. It was not to be some kind of 'Old Cornwall depot', he insisted. Instead, the Institute's 'official remit embraces the study of man [*sic*] in his Cornish setting, past, present and future'. Moreover, implicit in this was the assumption that 'Cornishness, the national consciousness and the national historic identity' were intrinsically worthy of study in their own right. 'Let there be no doubt about the official view here', he explained, 'in sponsoring and supporting the Institute of Cornish Studies, both your democratically-elected County Council and the University of Exeter, using rates and taxes to that end, have publicly committed themselves to such an assumption'.

In his lecture in November 2012, published here, Bernard Deacon returned to the questions raised by Charles Thomas nearly four decades before. Ostensibly, much had changed since the early 1970s. Yet despite a generally far more confident expression of Cornish identity, and a political environment in which devolution (even independence for Scotland, perhaps) was now the order of the day, Cornwall and the Cornish remained on the margin. As Deacon argued, 'even mentioning the Cornish and their right to exist can for some seem slightly distasteful. Liberal hackles rise and deeply buried embarrassments at a colonial past threaten to resurface'. Constant in-migration had continued to erode the proportion of Cornish-born, with second and holiday homes fuelling a manic house-building programme. Wilting under such pressure, there were those who sought national minority status for the Cornish in their own homeland, on the grounds that this would protect Cornish rights and interests against hostile intrusion.

Yet despite this gloomy picture, where for many policymakers, planners and developers 'being Cornish is supremely unimportant', Deacon observed that the number of individuals self-identifying as 'Cornish' had actually increased noticeably in recent years. The Cornwall Pupil Level Annual Schools Census (PLASC), for example, in 2006 indicated that 24 per cent of children were self-identified as 'Cornish'. This had risen to 30 per cent by 2008, and 41 per cent in 2011—at a time when the Cornish proportion of the population was apparently declining. As Deacon observed, 'ethnic boundaries are porous; people can and do change their ethnic identification'. Such complexities, Deacon continued, demand a critical Cornish studies fully engaged with contemporary Cornwall. Yet despite the rhetoric of 'New Cornish Studies', and especially its 'new Cornish social science', Deacon argues, Cornish studies has been increasingly boxed in by 'an epistemological tradition that equates Cornish studies with the study of times past'. In particular, he laments the Institute's 'institutional imprisonment at Tremough within an outpost of a History Department based at Exeter', and wonders who will provide the critical Cornish studies so necessary for the future.

Part of the answer, perhaps, is that the burgeoning range of Cornish studies achieved in recent decades has, in the manner described by Matthew Spriggs, given it a vibrant academic life beyond the confines of the Institute. The University of Plymouth, for example, as Deacon acknowledges, has produced important work on contemporary Cornwall—most recently from the pen of Kerryn Husk—and elsewhere in the academy, in the UK and beyond, individuals and clusters of scholars work on a variety of Cornish themes. The epistemological link with history is undeniable. Yet even here range and diversity is apparent, one recent trend being an increasing willingness by medievalists—hitherto often suspicious of the Cornish studies 'project'—to ply their wares alongside those of other Cornish studies practitioners. Maybe the sheer breadth of Cornish studies today—'what we now think of as the scope of Cornish studies', as Spriggs puts it—can give us sufficient confidence for the future. Perhaps, even, as Spriggs argues, 'we can shift from talking about "the new Cornish studies" simply to discussing modern Cornish studies'.

If so, then maybe *Cornish Studies: Twenty-One* does represent a timely 'coming of age', its pages carrying contributions from a wide variety of scholars, some associated with the Institute of Cornish Studies but others from sometimes far beyond. The Cornish language, as ever, remains within the purview of Cornish studies, and in his contribution N.J.A. Williams—incontrovertibly our leading Cornish language scholar—presents a *tour de force* on 'Adjectival and Adverbial Prefixes in Cornish', employing numerous examples from the traditional canon to further our knowledge of the historic language as well as to assist present day revivalists. Drawing his examples from the medieval and early modern texts, he reminds us that in this period much of Cornwall was Cornish-speaking, the language of ecclesiastical scholarship (the so-called 'Miracle Plays') as well as of the ordinary people. Many of his examples have religious contexts: for example, *der temptacon an teball ow hendas adam pur weare eave re gollas der avall an place glorious pur sure* 'through the temptation of the devil my grandfather Adam, he indeed has by an apple lost the glorious place surely'; and *War aga dewlyn y ze zerag Ihesus re erell aga fen y a sackye hag a gewsy pur debell worth Ihesus rag y anger* 'Upon their knees other came before Jesus; they shook their heads and spoke very wickedly to Jesus to annoy him'.

Nicholas Orme, a leading scholar of medieval Cornwall, in his article alights upon another important aspect of Cornish religious life in this period, the 'visitations' of 1281 and 1331. Regular inspections by the Church authorities, such visitations provide often extremely detailed information about individual churches, their buildings, vestments, books, and other properties and possessions. Much of this information is similar to that collected in visitations east of the Tamar. But sometimes there are specifically Cornish details. At Veryan, for example, the church possessed 'one little bell of St Symphorian', the patron saint, and Orme wonders whether this was of the 'Celtic' type, such as that of St Piran held at Perranzabuloe. At Altarnun a Life of St Nonn (the patron saint) and St David (her son, in Welsh hagiography) was appended to the 'ordinal' or guide to services. And at Perranzabuloe, most remarkable of all, were the relics of St Piran: his head (kept in a locked reliquary), his body (preserved in a shrine), his silver bowl, his copper bell, and his pastoral staff worked with silver, gold and precious stones.

Medieval Cornwall is also the subject of Robert Stansfield, who examines the Duchy of Cornwall during the Wars of the Roses, 1453–1502. Reflecting the increased academic interest in recent years in the Duchy of Cornwall, its constitutional status and its relationship with the territory of Cornwall, Stansfield attempts a forensic analysis of patronage, politics and power during this turbulent period. He describes a somewhat paradoxical picture, in which the Duchy ensured that Cornwall remained distinctly different from England and Wales, yet reflected the realm as a whole, even to the extent of presenting a microcosm of national politics and power. More complex still, he explains, was the role of the Duchy of Cornwall as a focus for Cornish loyalty and identity. However, such loyalty remained symbiotic. When, as in 1497 and 1549, the Crown was seen to have reneged on its responsibilities, the Cornish rose to restore their rights and privileges—in the process displaying that curious blend of loyalty and rebelliousness that was to characterize subsequent centuries.

The Cornish rebellions of 1497 and 1549 form part of the backdrop for James Harris's comparative examination of English representations of Ireland and Cornwall during the Civil War. Although the historical experience of Ireland and Cornwall varied widely during this period, both territories, Harris argues, were subject to an 'English imperialism' designed to bring them under England's sway. In justifying this imperialism, Harris adds, the English drew derogatory representations of their Celtic neighbours, representing them as a barbarous 'other' incapable of self-government and in need of civilization. Here Harris detects a parallel with Edward Said's famous study *Orientalism*, where much later similar English attitudes justified imperialism in the Middle East. Intriguingly, Harris also alights upon the Duchy of Cornwall, arguing that it was part of a structure that afforded Cornwall a subordinate junior partner role in the English state in the early modern period, one in which the Cornish sometimes acquiesced and against which at others they rebelled.

John Kirkhope, in his article, endeavours to uncover something of the precise nature of the Duchy of Cornwall, examining in particular its various territorial and constitutional disputes in the nineteenth and twentieth centuries. He discovers that such disputes were usually resolved by resort to opinion or arbitration, so that much of what the Duchy of Cornwall asserts has not been tested by a Court of Law. He notes too that the Duchy has usually asserted constitutional distinctiveness with an eye to economic advantage or to avoid paying fees or taxes. Thus the right to give consent to legislation and Crown Immunity—both claimed by some Cornish activists as evidence of Cornwall's constitutional distinctiveness—are actually devices of recent origin designed to protect the Duchy's finances. Nonetheless, Kirkhope concedes that in an important sense the 'The Duchy *is* Cornwall', and that the relationship between the Duchy and Cornwall today remains more intimate and intricate than many imagine.

Cornwall's nineteenth-century constitutional identity was also enhanced by the creation of a separate Anglican diocese, releasing Cornwall from its lengthy embrace by Exeter, and resulted in both the building of Truro Cathedral and the arrival of Edward White Benson as the first bishop in 1877. As David Miller shows in his article, Benson had a particular vision for the new diocese, and saw himself reaching out to and embracing all the people of Cornwall as part of his mission. There was a marked element of Cornish patriotism in this activity, including the use of the Cornish language in the civic welcome of the future Edward VI when he laid the foundation stone for the cathedral in May 1880. Benson also introduced the now famous Nine Lessons and Carols on Christmas Eve, borrowing from the successful Methodist 'hymn sandwich' service, as it was sometimes described. Yet, as Miller concedes, despite Benson's undoubted impact at Truro, he did not succeed in his aim of persuading many Cornish Methodists and other Nonconformists to join his Anglican renewal. In the opinion of one Baptist minister at the time, 'looking around this great Nonconformist county, we do not need a Bishop any more than a duck needs an umbrella'.

If the latter half of the nineteenth century in Cornwall was a time of Anglican renewal, it was also the moment when folklorists turned their attention to Cornish folklore. As Simon Young shows in his article, Robert Hunt, William Bottrell and others began their assiduous collection of Cornish folk tales, part of an upsurge in such interest in Europe generally but also a nascent antiquarian Celtic revivalism, akin to W. B. Yeats's 'Celtic Twilight' in Ireland. But Hunt was a scientific man, and in folklore as in any other field of endeavour he demanded taxonomic clarity, the necessity of distinguishing between types and creating categories. Young describes the process, noting Hunt's classifications, and discussing the extent to which his taxonomy influenced (or not) other, later writers, such as Bottrell. He detects in Bottrell a resistance to categorization—Bottrell was akin to the old 'droll tellers' whose stories he marshalled, and certainly was no scientist—which Young finds instructive. As he concludes, if Cornish folklore studies are to progress—and the current level of interest suggests there has indeed been a recent upsurge in academic inquiry—then we need to be wary of nineteenth-century over-categorization and, in his estimation, become a little more like William Bottrell and rather less like Robert Hunt.

Nineteenth-century Cornwall was also the era of the 'Great Emigration', when thousands of Cornish men and women left for distant lands, many—but by no means all—drawn by the ever-expanding international mining frontier. As Mike Tripp observes in his contribution, in the mining camps of Latin and North America, Cornish emigrants cultivated their separate identity—often for reasons of socio-economic advantage—and among the repertoire of Cornish cultural distinctiveness was Cornish wrestling. Tripp explains the particular characteristics of Cornish wrestling, and charts its fortunes across the Americas in the nineteenth and early twentieth centuries, including its recent revival as a part of a rekindling of interest in Cornish heritage. He examines the anatomy of Cornish wrestling in places such as Grass Valley in California and Iron Mountain in the Upper Peninsula of Michigan—where and when were matches held, who organized them and why, who participated, and so on. He finds, not surprisingly, that there were many close comparisons with wrestling 'at home' in Cornwall, yet in America Cornish wrestling developed its own characteristics—it sometimes coexisted alongside other styles in matches, for example, and was sometimes a means of playing out ethnic hostilities: especially when Cornish met Irish.

Turning to the twentieth century, literary representations of Cornwall have become ever more popular on the international stage. Among the most celebrated writers of twentieth-century Cornwall were Sir Arthur Quiller-Couch (or 'Q' as he was universally known) and Daphne du Maurier. They belonged to different generations (Q died in 1944, du Maurier in 1983), and Q was Cornish-born while du Maurier was not. Nonetheless, they shared much in common, including friendship, and after Q's death his daughter Foy persuaded du Maurier to complete Quiller-Couch's final, unfinished novel *Castle Dor*. The story of this 'collaboration' is told by Kirsty Bunting, who in her article examines the mixed and sometimes hostile reception that the completed novel received on publication in 1962. She unpicks the criticism levelled at *Castle Dor*—the 'quaintly Cornish' content, for example, or the inability of the prosaic everyday characters to match the mystique of their Tristan and Iseult models—and detects a wider discomfort with the controversial process of collaboration. She concludes with a plea for *Castle Dor* to be read for what it is, 'an epic romance', rather than for its mode of telling.

Equally controversial, in his way, was Jack Clemo, the blind and deaf poet of Cornwall's china-clay country. Luke Thompson, currently embarking on a biography of Clemo, looks afresh here at a formative moment in the poet's life—the 'happy chance' of his marriage to Ruth Peaty. As Thompson explains, Clemo considered himself destined for marriage, a conviction that he carried throughout life until, at last, he met his wife-to-be. In many ways, the couple was ideally suited, and both believed firmly that God had brought them together. It was a belief that both were prepared to declare to the wider world, a remarkable witness to Christian faith. Yet neither was prepared to admit that what might be best described as a Christian dating agency had helped to smooth the way, and in his sensitive and careful discussion of the evidence, Thompson pieces together this important evidence that for the first time allows us a clearer understanding of the dynamics of this important marriage.

Peder Clark, in his discussion of modern and contemporary Cornwall, turns his attention to Cornish nationalism. He alights upon Eric Hobsbawm's well-known assertion: 'The Cornish are fortunate to be able to point their regional discontents in the attractive colours of Celtic tradition, which makes them so much more viable'. In doing so, he subject's Hobsbawm's contention to sustained analysis, probing the nature of the 'nationalist imagination' and asking why, if Hobsbawm had been correct, Cornish nationalism has not yet been successful. Clark concedes that the Cornish fit the criteria for identification as one of A.D. Smith's *ethnie* but argues that Cornwall's dual or hybrid identity has retarded the development of nationalist sentiment. Indeed, contrary to Hobsbawm's assertion, Clark considers that adherence to 'Celtic tradition' has sometimes drawn Cornish nationalism into an electorally unattractive ethno-nationalism, while in-fighting and organizational uncertainty has held back the development of the various Cornish nationalist parties. Only recently, Clark argues, has Mebyon Kernow developed a competent, credible civic nationalism that might bring greater rewards.

Finally, the multiple 'Celtic identities' of the late poet laureate John Betjeman are revisited in a brief article that takes account of recently discovered evidence which, among other things, reveals Betjeman's relationship with Mebyon Kernow to have been closer than previously understood. It was a relationship that allowed him to claim common cause with the Cornish, part of his strategy to make public the Celtic affinities he cultivated so passionately in response to the uncertainties and ambiguities of his own personal identity.

Philip Payton

Professor of Cornish & Australian Studies, and
Director, Institute of Cornish Studies,
University of Exeter, Cornwall Campus

Adjunct Professor of History,
School of International Studies,
Flinders University, Adelaide, Australia

I

Philip Payton

Cultural entrepreneur for a rhetorically defined space

Matthew Spriggs

Taking up the reins of the Institute of Cornish Studies (ICS) from the Foundation Director, Charles Thomas, was always going to be a hard act for incoming Director Philip Payton in 1991.[1] The complexities of funding of the Institute, part of the University of Exeter but also financially supported by the then-Cornwall County Council, meant that the job was always going to involve political sensitivities. These were amplified at the time with—as ever—a (small-c) conservative dominated Council intent on holding the line against what they saw as 'extremist' Cornish nationalists. These latter, whether in reality extremist or not, were expecting strong academic support for their political agenda as of right. Add into the mix the internecine warfare of the Cornish language revivalists of at least three different factions, each in their way seeking academic endorsement. In these circumstances the hard act to follow would have seemed more like what we would call in Australia and in rugby circles more widely a 'hospital pass'.[2]

As Philip now prepares to hand over those reins himself, we know that he rose to all the various challenges with a mixture of gentle humour, Navy-derived strategic planning skills and sense of the need for a 'tight ship', and phenomenal intellectual productivity. But what qualified him to take on the key job in Cornish Studies in 1991?

Being Cornish on his mother's side, and doubtless a comparative Celtic perspective provided by his father's Irish ancestry, gave him an early interest in things Cornish, not dulled but in fact stimulated by his early years in Western Australia where he heard from schoolteachers of the contribution to mining in Australia of the 'Cousin Jacks' he was proud to realize were 'his' people.[3]

The Payton migration stream to Australia was reversed and he spent the rest of his school days in Sussex. Again, exile stimulated his Cornish interests and he was soon involved in Mebyon Kernow and publishing in *Cornish Nation* and *New Cornwall* in his teenage years. In 1972 he moved somewhat closer to Cornwall as a student at the University of Bristol, where he studied Politics and Economics, with some History thrown in. His 1975 Honours thesis was on 'The Ideology of Celtic Nationalism'.

This qualified him to take up postgraduate work at the University of Adelaide, where he completed a PhD in 1978 on 'The Cornish in South Australia: Their Influence and Experience from Immigration to Assimilation, 1836–1936'. Elements of the thesis contributed to his first two substantial monographs, *The Cornish Miner in Australia* (1984) and *The Cornish Farmer in Australia* (1987).[4] These books were also based on considerable post-thesis research and highlighted what remains a lasting theme of his work, the Cornish overseas.

Returning to the UK, Philip joined the Royal Navy as an education specialist, with numerous postings on shore and at sea, notably in *HMS Fisgard*, a shore station at Torpoint in Cornwall.[5] His penultimate teaching appointment was at the Royal Naval Engineering College, Manadon, in Plymouth. During this time he made the perhaps somewhat eccentric decision to undertake a second PhD at Polytechnic South West (now the University of Plymouth). This resulted in his 1989 thesis 'Modern Cornwall: The Changing Nature of Peripherality'. He left the Navy in October 1991 after 12 years service to take up his present position at the ICS. He continued, however, in the Royal Naval Reserve for a further 18 years, and retired as a Commander. He saw active service during this time in (among other places) the former Yugoslavia in 1993, attached to British Army peacekeeping contingents in Croatia and Bosnia-Herzegovina, and during the Iraq War in 2003 he had his first and last experience of war at sea in the aircraft carrier *HMS Ark Royal*. I do not recall *Cornish Studies* ever appearing late during this time, so editing must have continued in both foxhole and amphibious landing vehicle on occasion.

At some stage soon after his appointment to the ICS the decision was made to revive and revitalize what had been an in-house produced journal *Cornish Studies*, and to turn it into an annual edited volume published by University of Exeter Press. The first volume was published in late 1993.[6] With this current issue the series reaches its maturity after 21 years of Philip's editorship. The *Cornish Studies* new series (henceforth CS) has proved to be the major vehicle for publishing material across the broad canvas that is Cornish studies during this time, and has proved decisive for stimulating interest outside the Duchy in Cornish scholarship and its comparative value across a range of discipline and area interests. It is now commonplace to find Cornish studies papers gracing the pages of national and international journals, something very rare until the late 1990s except in antiquarian fields of enquiry.[7]

Philip's 1992 book, *The Making of Modern Cornwall: Historical Experience and the Persistence of "Difference"*, based on his 1989 thesis, served as a manifesto for novel approaches to studying Cornwall's story to be utilized. They were later crystallized as the 'new Cornish historiography' and 'the new Cornish social science', these pithy phrases of course emanating from the pen of Philip himself.[8] Inevitably, the claim of novelty can be debated; it was in part just 'a rhetorically defined space' as Bernard Deacon pointed out. It was perhaps not so importantly a new departure in terms of theory-driven research into the history and sociology of Cornwall, but rather a rallying cry for a greatly increased scholarly effort to address the full range of issues that could be included under the Cornish studies rubric.[9]

The publications to hammer home the point just kept coming: 1993 also saw the edited volume *Cornwall Since the War*, followed in 1996 by *Cornwall*, the first of Philip's trilogy of semi-popular books for Alexander Associates. It was billed on the dust jacket as 'the first full-length, fully-illustrated, comprehensive history of Cornwall to be written for a generation', and was followed by *The Cornish Overseas* in 1999 and *A Vision of Cornwall* in 2002. This last is a very personal book, Philip's vision of what Cornwall has been and what it could be. It is full of hope for a true devolution of political power to Cornwall, which always seems within grasp but, as subsequent history has shown us, is somehow never quite obtained. Also during that period there was the important *New Directions in Celtic Studies*, co-edited with Amy Hale in 2000, and his edited *Cornwall Forever! The Millennium Book for Cornwall*, appearing in the same year and aimed at younger readers.[10] In the 1993 to 2002 period Philip also produced some forty-three articles and reviews in refereed journals and as book chapters (see his Bibliography in this volume, pp. 329–37). They ranged in scope from the aftermath of the 1497 rebellions to the ideology of language revival, nineteenth-century Cornish politics, modern ethnicity and identity, and Naval history. These publications, along with the contributions by other scholars to CS, many of them reacting to the Payton *œuvre*, made 'the new Cornish Studies' a self-fulfilling prophecy.

By the end of 2002 there was a substantial corpus of easily-accessible new scholarly Cornish work across a range of disciplines, produced through or by the ICS. *Cornish Studies: Ten* of that year, largely review articles looking back on developments over the previous decade in studies of history, politics, social science, economics, language revival, archaeology and literature, took an appropriately critical rather than self-congratulatory view of the period. Philip's own contributions to the subject were suitably deconstructed. Questions were asked about whether Cornish studies had in fact really advanced in theoretical sophistication at a time when other regional studies had forged ahead and new perspectives had taken hold of a variety of disciplines. The—perhaps very Cornish—conclusion seemed to be generally that, yes, some progress had been made but much more remained to be done. Re-reading the articles today, a further decade on, their sobriety is impressive. It had indeed been a heady decade for Cornish studies and for its acceptance and visibility outside Cornwall, but no one was letting themselves get too carried away!

Philip's very productivity drew criticism from some of the local historians one might—following Le Roy Ladurie—call 'truffle hunters': 'addicted to their archives, and high-minded in their search for what they believe to be the truth. They usually know a great deal about very little . . . and deliberately eschew broad generalizations or speculative hypotheses, on the grounds that they are inconsistent with the exacting grounds of real scholarship'. Ladurie contrasted them with 'parachutists' who: 'range more audaciously across the centuries, and survey a broader panorama of the historical landscape . . . they venture wide (and sometimes wild) generalizations, they move rapidly from one topic to another, and their work relies on secondary resources rather than on detailed research'. I am grateful to Treve Crago's article in CS:10 for these Ladurie quotations.[11] In his contribution, Treve made the point that a historian does not have to be one or the other; in fact both types of historians are needed, hopefully combined in the same individual.

The accusation was that Philip was exclusively a 'parachutist'. Indeed, the criticism was sometimes extended, by those who had never actually read the annual volumes, to include any and all who published in CS. The criticism was unjustified, not least because there was much evidence among Philip's earlier writings of extremely detailed archival and newspaper research—he can certainly truffle hunt when he wants to.[12] But the main point was that he was seeking to introduce a more theory-driven historiography and social science into Cornish studies, where before there had often been a somewhat timid empiricism and an inability to generalize the value of research results. Inevitably, as theoretical fashions change, parts of a more theoretically-informed body of work are likely to seem somewhat naïve and superficial in retrospect. That was never the point, however. The aim was to act as exemplar and stimulus rather than last word in the creation of a truly 'new' Cornish studies. Philip's 1990s corpus needs to be viewed in that light. Some historians are also notoriously snooty about attempts to popularize research, and his 1996 *Cornwall* (reissued and revised in 2004 as *Cornwall: A History*) was a brilliant attempt to do just that and reach a wider audience.

The subsequent decade of Philip's editorship of CS (2003–2012) has seen less frenetic activity and a deeper mastery of his subject matter, with 'only' four major books and one shorter monograph and twenty-two other chapters or articles published. The themes of his articles include familiar ones of Cornish identity, the language revival, emigration and Australia's 'Little Cornwall' on Yorke Peninsula, but also new ones such as Cornish and Irish folklore, the ANZAC myth and history teaching in Australian schools, and—most notably—the field of biography. This latter topic has seen four entries on notable Cornishmen in the *Oxford Dictionary of National Biography* (John Basset, Robert Were Fox, Richard Trevithick and Arthur Woolf), and articles on A.L. Rowse and John Betjeman in CS.[13]

These latter two were 'tasters' for substantial biographies of these writers' ambiguous relationships with Cornwall: *A.L. Rowse and Cornwall: A Paradoxical Patriot* (2005) and *John Betjeman and Cornwall: 'The Celebrated Cornish Nationalist'* (2010). We can add to this impressive biographical corpus a shorter work about another writer with an even more ambiguous relationship to the Duchy: *D.H. Lawrence and Cornwall* (2009).[14] The Rowse volume was Philip's first book-length venture into biography, and even the most hungry 'truffle hunters' should be satisfied with its minute examination of the Rowse archive at the University of Exeter. Detailed examination of original documents and archival sources are also a feature of Philip's other publications during this decade, prominently displayed in his *Making Moonta: The Invention of Australia's Little Cornwall* (2007) and most recently in his *Regional Australia and the Great War: 'The Boys from Old Kio'* (2012).[15] This latter work brings together his growing interest in First World War studies and his enduring interest in Moonta and South Australia's Yorke Peninsula.

With these recent books and articles a new maturity is evident, not just in Philip's writing but in the 'New Cornish Studies' really coming of age. No longer is there a need to privilege theory over content, and no longer a need for the strident assertion of novelty that was a feature of much 1990s writing. The relevance of a Cornish studies perspective in a range of settings from biography to studies of modern British identities, and indeed of identities further afield, is now abundantly clear to anyone with eyes to see and ears to listen. To ignore this perspective is now merely a sign of poor scholarship.

It is in this connection that I label Philip, with what I hope is not seen as a pejorative title, as a 'cultural entrepreneur'.[16] He has made many original written contributions and has through his editing of CS 'packaged' much other ongoing research to create what we now think of as the scope of Cornish studies. He has assiduously 'sold' this package to the extent that what was once considered a very marginal product with only a few local customers is now well established as a brand in the worldwide academic marketplace. One success of Philip's writings and of his editing of the second series of CS is that one can now find almost as much academic Cornish studies published outside of its pages on a year-to-year basis as one can within it. That was certainly not the case in 1993 when he re-launched CS. Early on there was a lot of smoke and mirrors about 'the new Cornish historiography' and 'the new Cornish social science'. They did indeed constitute 'a rhetorically defined space' as Bernard

Deacon was constrained to admit.[17] It is Philip's great contribution, through his efforts and those of his close colleagues in or otherwise associated with the Institute, that we can now shift from talking of 'the new Cornish studies' simply to discussing modern Cornish studies.[18]

Notes and references

1. Simon Baker of University of Exeter Press approached me to write this appreciation and provided a recent curriculum vitae and biographical summary. These provided useful background information and the framework and many of the details for this article. Additional information was gleaned from the various Prefaces to Philip's books and from Chapter 1 'Origins and Explanations' in P. Payton, *A Vision of Cornwall* (Fowey, 2002), and from my own observations—largely from afar—of the Cornish scene. Bernard Deacon very kindly provided comments for an earlier draft of this article. I first met Philip soon after he took over as Director of the Institute and have benefited greatly from Deidre and his hospitality and conviviality over the years. I will not admit to checking any details against Philip's *Wikipedia* entry.
2. This rugby-derived term is defined in the Collins Online Dictionary as '1: A pass made to a team-mate who will be tackled heavily as soon as the ball is received. 2: A task or project that will inevitably bring heavy criticism on the person to whom it has been assigned.' (www.collinsdictionary.com/dictionary/english/hospital-pass), accessed 24 April 2013.
3. Payton, 2002, p. 4.
4. P. Payton, *The Cornish Miner in Australia: Cousin Jack Down Under* (Redruth, 1984); P. Payton, *The Cornish Farmer in Australia* (Redruth, 1987).
5. See P. Payton, *The Story of HMS Fisgard* (Redruth, 1983).
6. That this was not the original plan can be seen by a reference in P. Payton, *The Making of Modern Cornwall: Historical Experience and the Persistence of 'Difference'* (Redruth, 2002), p. 253 to a forthcoming article by Philip in 'Cornish Studies 17, 1992'. There never was a volume 17 in the first series of *Cornish Studies* and the article in question eventually appeared in P. Payton (ed.), *Cornish Studies* (second series) *Two* (1994), pp. 83–95.
7. Bernard Deacon first drew attention to this change in B. Deacon, 'The New Cornish Studies: New Discipline or Rhetorically Defined Space?' in P. Payton (ed.), *Cornish Studies: Ten* (Exeter, 2002), pp. 24–43. See in particular footnote 23. In a quick count I find at least twenty UK and International journals publishing papers on social science and recent historical aspects of Cornish studies; just over a quarter of the contributions to CS during the same period could broadly be classified within the field of social science. Payton, 1992, p. x, notes the significant influence on his ideas of the Cornish Labour History Group, convened by Bernard Deacon and the late Fred Harris at Murdoch House in Redruth in the 1980s, and from discussions with David Dunkerley and Adrian Lee at Polytechnic Southwest, later University of Plymouth.
8. Bernard Deacon, 2002, footnote 2, traces these phrases to P. Payton, *ICS Associates Newsletter 4* (May 1995), p. 5 and P. Payton, 'Introduction' in P. Payton (ed.),

Cornish Studies: Four (Exeter, 1996), p.1. My memory is that Philip had been trying out these phrases verbally on his friends and colleagues for some time before 1995. They took particular form during the seminar series he and Bernard Deacon organized at the Institute involving, among others, Amy Hale, Alan Kent and Ronald Perry.

9. See Bernard Deacon, 2002, for a blisteringly honest appraisal of the value of these terms, posing the question as to whether at the time they merely represented 'a rhetorically defined space'. Further valuable discussion is provided by several other papers in P. Payton (ed.), *Cornish Studies: Ten* (Exeter, 2002), especially those by Malcolm Williams and Colin H. Williams.

10. P. Payton (ed.), *Cornwall Since the War: The Contemporary History of a European Region* (Redruth, 1993); P. Payton, *Cornwall*, (Fowey, 1996) (revised and reissued as *Cornwall: A History* (Fowey, 2004); P. Payton, *The Cornish Overseas* (Fowey, 1999) (revised and reissued as *The Cornish Overseas: A History of Cornwall's Great Emigration* (Fowey, 2005); P. Payton, *A Vision of Cornwall* (Fowey, 2002); A. Hale and P. Payton (eds), *New Directions in Celtic Studies* (Exeter, 2000); P. Payton (ed.), *Cornwall For Ever! The Millennium Book for Cornwall* (Lostwithiel, 2000).

11. The Ladurie quotations come from Treve Crago, 'Defining the Spectre: Outlining the Academic Potential of the "Cava Movement"' in P. Payton (ed.), *Cornish Studies: Ten* (Exeter, 2002), pp. 252–65 (p. 263).

12. For example, see P. Payton, 1984, Philip's first substantial book. Pages 217–19 list the very extensive archival and early newspaper sources consulted for this history of the Cornish miner in Australia.

13. W.H. Tregellas, rev. P. Payton, 'John Basset (1791–1843)', *Oxford Dictionary of National Biography*, Vol. 4 (2004), pp. 264–65; P. Payton, 'Robert Were Fox (1754–1818)', *Oxford Dictionary of National Biography*, Vol. 20 (2004), pp. 676–77; P. Payton, 'Richard Trevithick (1771–1833)', *Oxford Dictionary of National Biography*, Vol. 55, pp. 354–58; E. I. Carlyle, rev. P. Payton, 'Arthur Woolf (1766–1837)', *Oxford Dictionary of National Biography*, Vol. 60, pp. 252–53; P. Payton, '"I was before my time, caught betwixt and between": A. L. Rowse and the writing of Cornish and British History' in P. Payton (ed.), *Cornish Studies: Eleven* (Exeter, 2003), pp. 11–39; P. Payton, 'John Betjeman and the Holy Grail: One Man's Celtic Quest' in P. Payton (ed.), *Cornish Studies: Fifteen* (Exeter, 2007), pp. 185–208.

14. P. Payton, *A. L. Rowse and Cornwall: A Paradoxical Patriot* (Exeter, 2005); P. Payton, *John Betjeman and Cornwall: 'The Celebrated Cornish Nationalist'* (Exeter, 2010); P. Payton, *D.H. Lawrence and Cornwall* (St Agnes, 2009).

15. P. Payton, *Making Moonta: The Invention of 'Australia's Little Cornwall'* (Exeter, 2007); P. Payton, *Regional Australia and the Great War: 'The Boys from Old Kio'* (Exeter, 2012).

16. For the concept of 'cultural entrepreneur' as used here see R.E. Burton, *A Passion to Exist: Cultural Entrepreneurship and the search for authenticity in Cornwall*, PhD thesis, University of Exeter, 2000, where Philip Payton is so labelled. The thesis is available online at: http://cornishidentity.blogspot.com/, accessed 28 April 2013. In the 'Conclusions' Burton defines cultural entrepreneurs as 'culturally active actors involved in the re-creation, re-interpretation and re-invention of identity'. I am grateful to Cara Sheldrake of the University of Exeter for this reference.

17. B. Deacon, 2002.

18. As Philip departs we can expect many more productive years of research and publication to come. Soon to appear as I write this is a massive co-edited volume, P. Payton, H. Doe and A. Kennerley (eds), *The Maritime History of Cornwall* (Exeter, 2013). Philip's regional studies interests are again to be broadened by *A History of Sussex*, the home of his teenage years, which is also soon to appear.

2

The Unimportance of Being Cornish in Cornwall

Bernard Deacon

Introduction

In 1973 at Cornwall Technical College, the first Director of the Institute of Cornish Studies, Charles Thomas, lectured on the importance of being Cornish in Cornwall. He outlined the historical origins of Cornwall, asked how we might spot that endangered species—the Cornish—and discussed the various pressures on Cornwall. In doing so he painted a gloomy picture and issued a stark warning. Unless there was 'a more effective approach . . . this little land of ours will end up scarcely distinguishable from the Greater London area, with undertones reminiscent of Blackpool or Skegness'.[1] At his inaugural lecture at Exeter, Professor Thomas was even blunter: 'there are not many real Cornish left, and not all that much left of real Cornwall'.[2]

Now, from the perspective of my swansong [Caroline L. Kemp Memorial] lecture at Cornwall's gleaming new university campus of Tremough, almost forty years and several booms and slumps further on, things are clearly different. Or are they? It is time to revisit Charles Thomas's analysis. I shall begin from the perspective that it is still important to be Cornish in Cornwall, before moving on to the implication that it is supremely unimportant. I want to pursue two of the same questions Charles Thomas posed in 1973. I intend to ask who the Cornish are and, like Charles, how many of us remain. I will then review what the rest of this century holds for the Cornish before finishing with some brief speculation on the role of a Cornish studies project in coming decades. What I do not intend to review are the origins of Cornwall or of Cornishness. Since the 1970s, that particular ground has been well tilled with general histories appearing written from a variety of perspectives. Readers are now able to acquire a better knowledge of the narrative of Cornwall's past, if not to agree on its causes and consequences.[3]

As some of you may guess from the title, my conclusion could well strike an equally gloomy note. This might to some extent be personal. It suddenly dawned on me the other day that I had gone from being an angry young man to a grumpy old man, with no apparent time spent in between. It is too easy to draw the conclusion that we—and by we I mean the Cornish people—seem doomed to re-live our past. Small victories flicker before being extinguished within larger defeats. New passions excite us, only to melt into air, squashed by a structural juggernaut that steadily marches us mind-numbingly onwards. Being Cornish can easily seem irrelevant in a context of global warming, widening economic inequality and cynical political man-oeuvrings. Yet belonging to and identifying with a place has proved to be stubbornly persistent, surviving modernity and going on to a new lease of life in conditions of post-modernity. We live in an ever-changing world, made and unmade by the dizzying impact of trillions of dollars seeking temporary, sometimes very temporary, havens in their voracious hunt for profits. In this world people desperately search for moorings that can anchor them to communities and to deeper moral values than mere consumption. A search for certainties can, of course, produce a deeply conservative reaction, as we scurry back to basics and haul up the drawbridge, until we realize that our basics are built on sand and the tides of our economic system will soon make short work of any modern-day Canutes. But it can also produce a more hopeful, more realistic will to resist. For me, Cornishness has never been only or even mainly about preserving stuff but more about giving us the strength and the confidence to say this is what we want, this is where we live and struggle, this is the line that we will not allow 'them' to cross.

But who is this 'we' and how far does 'our' extend? In short, who are the Cornish? Charles Thomas was pretty pessimistic about this back in 1973. The 'true Cornish' he concluded, were already 'slightly in the minority'.[4] Others go a lot further. In an intriguing aside in his 2011 book on *Vanished Kingdoms*, Norman Davies mentions one case study dropped through lack of space. It was that of 'Kerno' [sic], 'decorated by reflections on the theme of cultural genocide'. Later, he is more explicit. While the Britons survived in Wales, we are informed that in Cornwall 'they did not'.[5] We have become used to read-ing historians who tell us that we no longer exist but it is still a slightly odd feeling, akin to reading your own obituary. If indeed we have not survived, then clearly this whole lecture is pointless. Being Cornish in contemporary Cornwall is irrelevant because there is no such thing beyond an attachment to a mere place on the map.

I assume Davies is equating being Cornish with speaking the Cornish lan-guage. But, as Charles Thomas rightly pointed out in 1973, 'the knowledge of the existence of a separate language, as distinct from a full knowledge of that language itself, is probably sufficient . . . to foster a sense of otherness'.[6] We do not have to be able to speak Cornish to feel Cornish; just as we do not have to be a fisherman or a bal maiden to be Cornish. Cornishness cannot be reduced to such simplistic cultural or economic determinism. Yet neither is it so nebulous that it is impossible to quantify. So let us return to the question of how many of us there are, whether quaint survivals, angry rebels or both.

Quantifying the Cornish

Just to ask that question is to step into a minefield. While Catalans, Basques and Scots gird themselves for their final push for self-determination, even mentioning the Cornish and their right to exist can for some seem slightly distasteful. Liberal hackles rise and deeply buried embarrassments at a colonial past threaten to resurface. The simplest way of defining who is Cornish would be to assume that the category includes anyone born in Cornwall. This is also convenient as we have a benchmark in the 1951 Census. At that time 69 per cent of Cornish residents were Cornish born.[7]

Unfortunately since then no one has thought it important to count those born in Cornwall or, more precisely, those whose mother lived in Cornwall at their time of their birth, as hospitalization of births in England was forced on the Cornish of the east and birthplace data became rather irrelevant. The last properly conducted survey that investigated details of place of birth was that of 1981/82 by Ronald Perry and others. Seven wards from St Just in the far west to St Stephen in Brannel in mid-Cornwall were sampled in a study of counter-urbanization.[8] The researchers discovered that 57 per cent of the people in these wards, which included a cross-section from the already predominantly non-Cornish Feock to the overwhelmingly Cornish St Stephen, had been born in Cornwall. Interestingly, one in five of these were return migrants.

But almost thirty years of further in-migration will have eroded this proportion of Cornish-born to under 50 per cent. Despite Cornwall Council's 'equality and diversity framework', which 'robustly' commits the Council to collect data for ethnic monitoring purposes, no similar scientifically acceptable survey of the proportions of non-movers, return migrants and incomers has taken place during the last quarter of a century. The 1983 survey implied a fall from around 70 per cent at the time of the 1951 Census to 55–60 per cent. As net in-migration did not start until the early 1960s, this had occurred in little more than twenty years, a drop of around 15 percentage points at a time when the population rose by 22 per cent. This in turn might suggest that for every one per cent rise in the population the proportion of native Cornish falls by around 0.7 per cent. Using this as our base we could calculate it will have fallen by maybe another 17 per cent, to be as low as 40 per cent now. We could but we should not. As the more numerate of you will no doubt quickly inform me, this method is nonsense, as at current rates of growth the numbers born in Cornwall would become zero by around 2095. That could only happen if one of those enduring myths about Cornwall—that all in-migrants are retirees—were correct and no one was ever born in Cornwall. In fact, the age profile of in-migrants is skewed more towards those of working—and therefore child-bearing age—than is that of the native population. These in-migrants will therefore have children who will in turn replenish the stock of those who qualify as Cornish by the simple criterion of birthplace. So, unless out-migration has become heavily skewed towards the non-Cornish, as people arrive on a sunny whim and leave in sodden desperation, the percentage of Cornish by this definition will at some point stabilize even with continuing high rates of gross migration. Nonetheless, after five decades of mass migration the proportion of the population born and brought up in Cornwall is likely to be somewhere around 40 per cent.

Qualifying the Cornish

But this is where the problems begin. Unprepared to accept such a simple definition, there has been, since the 1960s, an excessive concern to define who is or is not 'truly' Cornish. For Charles Thomas this meant having both parents born in Cornwall. I am quite happy with this, but that is because I qualify. If you do not qualify, then other definitions are always possible. For the late Fred Trull, being Cornish was a matter of proving the presence of ancestors in Cornwall back in the days of the 1508 Charter of Pardon. I am not sure how many achieved this feat, but my attempts to trace my family back soon foundered on the reefs of serial illegitimacies well before I had reached 1800.

This rejection of the idea that anyone can be Cornish—that if a kitten is born in an oven it does not make it a pasty—runs deep. A desire to patrol the ethnic boundaries helps us to explain the surge of interest among the Cornish in family history since the 1970s. We strive to root ourselves in our land, proudly displaying our genealogies as credentials of Cornishness, credentials that can only be extended to those beyond the chosen people after many years, indeed generations, if not centuries, of residence. Such an over-exclusivity is hardly surprising in the face of the demographic growth since the 1960s that has wreaked profound social changes, not the least in the way we speak. But it remains a sign of a lack of confidence and goes hand in hand with an over-nostalgic Cornishness. This in turn stems from a preservationist trope that has dominated discussions of Cornishness since the antiquarian impulse of the early eighteenth century at least.[9] By all means *cuntelleugh an brewyon ez gerez, na vo kellez terveth* [collect the fragments that remain, so that nothing is lost] but an over-concentration on the rear-view mirror leaves us in danger of failing to spot the scat-up that is coming right at us over the horizon.

We might call this the we-belong-to-do-it-this-way syndrome. It was nicely illustrated by a letter to the London *Guardian* in March about the Tory/Liberal Democrat Government's vindictive tax on pasty-eaters.[10] The chattering metropolitan classes were sagely informed that 'a true Cornishman or Cornishwoman eats an oggie cold'. Really? The implication of this debatable assertion is that nothing must ever change from the days when our great grandfathers took their pasties down the mines with them for their crowst. Comforting perhaps in the face of unstoppable change but a slight overstatement when we note the number of pasty shops in our towns doing a roaring trade in hot (or even tepidly warm) pasties. It is all very well us saying *na ra gara an vor goth rag an vor noweth* [do not leave the old road for the new road]. Remembering the past with pride and affection has its place but nostalgia for a world that is gone can be counter-productive. If we can only do things in the way that we have always belonged to do them, how will we ever find the new ways necessary to build a Cornwall that is not driven primarily by external agendas?

From minority to majority status: reversing the discourse of decline

That said, despite the predictions of the doom-mongers of the 1970s, we find that both Cornwall and the Cornish have survived and in many ways are stronger than before. Different, certainly. More confident in some ways, more explicit, more 'in your face' perhaps. Here we meet the paradox of modern Cornwall. As the quantity of Cornish has declined in relative terms, the quality of Cornishness (and indeed *its* quantity too) has been enhanced. We are now used to the ubiquitous St Piran flags fluttering in the gentle westerly gales, forgetting how as recently as the 1970s flying this black and white icon was something only done by consenting adults in private. 'Cornish' has become a marketable brand; supermarkets sell a choice of Cornish beers. The Cornish language, or at least a revived version of it, is more visible and is backed by a (now fast diminishing) pot of public money. Even the good old pasty is re-branded as something 'cool', if often re-heated. Sanitized and hi-tech reminders of our heritage are scattered around the landscape courtesy of heritage lottery funds and European grant money. We may not care too much for the banal 'dumbing down' that seems to be a necessary accompaniment of this progress from pasties to pastiche. But Cornishness—in the sense of Cornwall being a different and special place—survives, albeit in a new guise and in many ways seemingly more secure now than forty or fifty years ago. And yet, it is also hard to shake off that distinct feeling that the Cornish themselves still teeter on the brink of extinction. Are we not *lawetha an darraz po marth ledrez* [locking the door when the horse has been stolen]? The ways of our parents and grandparents are no more, soon to be as curious and foreign as the lives of those medieval peasants who spoke our former language. We may be more culturally confident but we are still granted little or no political respect, or even awareness of our right to exist. We are still casually ignored, blatantly patronized and persistently misunderstood. We are still being asked to look on helplessly as the landscapes that were the playgrounds of our youth disappear under the houses and roads of a new population.

But wait. If I am right and around 40 per cent of the population is Cornish born, then why does a recent doctoral thesis on Cornish ethnicity conclude that the proportion of ethnically Cornish in Cornwall is not 40 per cent at all but more like 25 per cent?[11] And why is this figure in fairly close agreement with the 2007 Quality of Life survey conducted for Cornwall County Council, which in turn reinforced the evidence from parish surveys which also suggest a proportion of Cornish somewhere between 25 and 30 per cent? The reason is simple. These surveys measure the proportion of those 'who self-identify as Cornish'. The problem then occurs when this group of what we might call 'consciously Cornish' people is wittingly or unwittingly confused with the native Cornish. The two are not the same.

There is considerable confusion over the word 'Cornish', and who or what qualifies. Two uses of the term are possible. The first rests on an objective reference to things that are Cornish because they happen to be located in or associated with Cornwall. This applies to artefacts such as the pasty, geographical features such as beaches, cliffs or settlements, or people, such as the native Cornish. The second use invests the term with more subjective meaning. In this case a pasty is not Cornish just because it is baked in Cornwall. Instead, the concept of a Cornish pasty invokes other things such as memories of home, family meals, or even a proud mining history. When it comes to people, this second, more subjective meaning encompasses those who would claim a Cornish ethnicity. This might include some but not all of the native Cornish, and of course could include others who are not native Cornish by my earlier definition of birthplace.

Until now, whether calculating the quantity of objective or subjective Cornish, the obvious conclusion to draw is that not only are the Cornish a national minority within the state in which they are governed but, unlike the Scots or Welsh, we are a national minority in our own homeland.[12] This has led to a situation where those who wish to see more protection for the remaining Cornish adopt a minority rights discourse. Their argument is that as the Cornish become a minority, the danger of marginalization increases.

A non-Cornish majority is able to impose its views and shape the land to suit their own convenience. More generally, the slow erosion of Cornwall's native population has resulted in community fragmentation, if the conclusion of researchers at Sheffield University in 2008 is right and rapid population growth undermines community resilience and cohesion.[13]

Yet, I want to suggest that a minority status for the Cornish is not at all inevitable. Indeed, classifying the Cornish as a minority group plays right into the hands of those who think that being Cornish in Cornwall is unimportant, and is a dangerous game in a society that at least pays lip service to democratic forms. For the Cornish do not comprise some unchanging essential category. In reality, ethnic boundaries are porous; people can and do change their ethnic identifications. Change is the only thing we can rely on. But it is too easy to forget that change can operate in different and perhaps contradictory directions. While the proportion of native Cornish changes only slowly, the proportion of consciously Cornish could change relatively quickly. Indeed, since 2006 something strange and unexpected has happened. The Cornwall Pupil Level Annual Schools Census (PLASC) collects information about the subjective ethnicity of schoolchildren, that of children of primary age being supplied by parents. Every year the percentage of Cornish children has increased, even as the native Cornish decline. In the first survey of 2006 the proportion of self-identified Cornish children in our schools was 24 per cent. By 2008 this had risen to 30 per cent. Last year (2011) as many as 41 per cent said they were Cornish. The PLASC surveys are evidence of a greater willingness of children and their parents to choose to define themselves as Cornish and give rise to the strong possibility that the proportion of self-consciously Cornish, as opposed to native born and bred Cornish, is increasing and could soon comprise a majority again. This evidence is backed up by a small scale survey in 2008 which tried to measure the relational aspect of identity.[14] It found that 41 per cent of those questioned felt either 'Cornish and not English' or 'more Cornish than English'. Another 14 per cent felt 'equally Cornish and English' while 43 per cent were more English than Cornish. This illustrates the polarization of identities that has taken place. More of us are now more likely to define ourselves as Cornish as opposed to English and only a small minority as both.[15] Given the mass in-migration of the past half-century these data also imply that at least some in-migrants must be choosing to define themselves as Cornish in addition to, or instead of, English.

The important point here is why settle for minority status in Cornwall when we still retain the possibility of claiming majority status? With 40 per cent native Cornish, a growing proportion of whom are now asserting their Cornishness, together with an unknown but presumably growing number of incomers who are prepared to identify themselves as Cornish, we still have a window of opportunity—a chance to build on the cultural resurgence of the past twenty years and demand our right to retain Cornwall as the homeland of a distinct people. If we allow the Cornish to be labelled as a minority group, an interesting historical relic consigned to the museum shelves and the local histories, then we give up a critical weapon in the struggle to obtain the right to make our own decisions about how we live and what sort of Cornwall we want here—in Cornwall.

If, in contrast, Cornwall is regarded as the homeland of a majority group of Cornish people, and that majority becomes revitalized and more self-aware, then we can more easily demand recognition and respect from central and local government as well as from European levels of governance, which seem more sympathetic to our case. However, this is a window of opportunity that is in danger of being closed if the political/bureaucratic plan succeeds to increase the population growth rate again. Inducting a new population into awareness and respect for the unique heritage of the place they have chosen to reside in becomes ever more difficult as Cornwall becomes less distinctively 'Cornish'. Less Cornish in terms of the environment around us; supermarkets, housing estates and industrial units tend to look the same whether they are in Cornwall, Canterbury or Caithness. And less 'Cornish' in terms of its society. The decline in the proportion of native Cornish has to be stabilized and reversed—and soon if we are to have any chance of retaining a Cornwall that is still in some way recognizably Cornish.

The future of Cornwall—and the unimportance of being Cornish

It is time to turn from who the Cornish are to what the future holds for them. Here, the picture is considerably more depressing. I have argued that while the Cornish are at present a minority this fate is not necessarily predetermined. A cultural resurgence—seen in areas as diverse as music, literature and drama and sporting activities—shows that Cornishness is alive and kicking.[16] Yet that nagging doubt persists. Can the latter really thrive if the proportion of native Cornish in Cornwall continues to decline? And here we meet those who think it is unimportant to be Cornish in modern Cornwall. *Bewnans Kernow*, which represents sixty-five Cornish cultural organizations, when submitting its views on Cornwall Council's Local Plan, containing its planning policies for the next twenty years, pointed out that 'Cornwall has a unique demographic environment which entails a special care and responsibility for maintaining the homeland of this ethnic group in a sustainable fashion'.[17] They pointed to Article 16 of the Framework Charter for the Protection of National Minorities, something ratified by the UK in 1998, endorsed by Cornwall County Council in 2007 and reaffirmed by Cornwall Council in 2011, which states that 'all parties shall refrain from measures which alter the proportions of the population in areas inhabited by persons belonging to national minorities'.

But not a word appears in the Council's Equality and Diversity Assessment of its Local Plan about this rather important matter. So what more generally does the Local Plan have to say about the Cornish or about the responsibility of the Council to protect and sustain this ethnic group? The short answer is nothing at all. Earlier this year a draft of the Local Plan made no mention of the Cornish people as such in any of its 366 pages of consultation documents. In fact it seemed a bit embarrassed altogether about using the word 'Cornish'. It only resorted to 'Cornish' four times as an adjective—'the Cornish context', 'Cornish language', 'Cornish World Heritage Site' and 'Cornish average'. This echoes a curious predilection among bureaucrats to use the term Cornwall as an adjective rather than Cornish—as in the odd phrase 'Cornwall towns' (rather than Cornish towns) which found its way into a previous structure plan. To some extent this reflects a wider tendency—Cornwall cottages, Cornwall media for example, although never Cornwall pasties.

In 1973 Charles Thomas noted that 'certain sections of the local government machine are, probably without realizing it, committed to courses of action that could destroy Cornishness for ever'.[18] In this respect it appears that little has changed. Cornishness may be able to survive in a context of demographic turnover. But it may not. And it would certainly be easier to envisage its survival in a context of a stable population which supplied the breathing space which many of us have repeatedly called for since the 1970s.[19] However, we have had nothing like a stable population in Cornwall for a considerable time now.[20] Indeed, population rose from 1961 to 2011 by 57 per cent in Cornwall, compared with 21 per cent in England, 15 per cent in Wales and less than 2 per cent in Scotland. When compared with English counties, we find that just seven of the forty-six experienced a faster rate of growth and these are all clustered on the edge of the London labour market in an arc running from Cambridgeshire and Buckinghamshire through Wiltshire and around to Sussex.

This demographic growth is important not just for the ability to be Cornish in Cornwall. The really over-heated growth occurred at just that period in the 1970s and 1980s when the Institute of Cornish Studies was in its enthusiastic first blaze of youth. The rate of growth in the resident population of Cornwall is in fact slowly—too slowly—declining. The growth in the twenty years from 1971 to 1991 was 87,000. From 1991 to 2011 that growth fell to 63,000. Fitting a trend line projection for the next twenty years would result in a further fall to 53,000. As councillors ponder their Local Plan, in a rational world, therefore, they might have been expected to reduce the expected housebuilding rate to match this gradual slowdown in population growth. However, they are doing nothing of the sort.

In the twenty years from 1991 to 2011, according to the Council's own data, 41,320 houses were added to Cornwall's housing stock. The latest iteration of the Council's Local Plan aims at a housing target of 48,500, voted through in November 2012 by the Cabinet by four votes to three, with up to three councillors abstaining. The closeness of the vote hints at growing doubt on the part of councillors as they begin to realize that something is not quite adding up here. But, deluged by their officers with distinctly dodgy data and apocalyptic warnings about annoying the Secretary of State, urged on by a powerful developers' lobby, and encouraged by a neo-liberal political consensus unable to see beyond the next housing boom, they look determined to hand over decisions about the timing and quantity of housebuilding to developers.[21] In the process they irresponsibly ignore the pleas of such groups as *Bewnans Kernow* for that much-needed but constantly deferred breathing space.

Our gurus of growth at County Hall/Lys Kernow stubbornly stick to their script. The Consultation Draft of the Local Plan stated that this number of houses resulted from 'the level of need that comes from the number of new households that come from our existing communities, young people leaving home, family break-up, older people living longer, and through an expected level of migration into or back into Cornwall'.[22] What the Council is claiming here is that household size is falling as the result of a number of social changes and that demand remains high due to net in-migration.

Navigating the Boscoppa Triangle

With the benefit of hindsight and the 2011 Census results we can test out these assertions. Much to the consternation of Cornwall's planners, mean household size in the 2000s was virtually stable, falling from 2.285 in 2001 to 2.272 in 2011. This means that just 1,250 houses, or 5 per cent of those built from 2001 to 2011, were in fact required to meet increased longevity, young people forming new households, family break-up and the like among the existing population. Another 14,350 houses, or 58 per cent of the total, would have been sufficient to house the flow of in-migrants, a flow that was incidentally far lower than that predicted by the Council as Cornwall's growth rate slipped below that of Avon, Dorset and Wiltshire, though still higher than Devon and Somerset.

But you might notice that we have a mystery here. We seem to have our own version of the Bermuda Triangle—let us call it the Boscoppa Triangle—as 9,340, or 37 per cent, of the houses built in the last decade appear to have disappeared into thin air, surplus to the requirements of either household change or demographic growth. This Boscoppa Triangle has other implications. In England, for every 1,000 rise in the population in the 2000s, 421 houses were built; in Wales every 1,000 rise was accompanied by 517 more houses. But here in Cornwall for every 1,000 growth in our numbers we need to build 765 houses. Let us put it another way. In Cornwall we have a build rate that, relative to population growth, is 82 per cent higher than that in England. Only in Cambridgeshire and Lincolnshire were more houses built in the ten years after 2001 in relation to the 2001 census population. And both had population growth rates in that decade well above Cornwall's (13 per cent and 10 per cent respectively, compared with our 6.5 per cent).

The Boscoppa Triangle is actually rather easily explained. The number of missing houses is almost identical to the growth in the number of second and holiday homes in Cornwall. Strange then, that Cornwall Council chooses to emphasize factors that account for only 5 per cent of the houses built as the reason we have to build so many while usually completely forgetting to mention the demand from those they now prefer to call 'temporary residents'. Our housing growth rate, therefore, has to be maintained at an artificially high rate and we have to consume our countryside at a faster rate than elsewhere in order to fuel the growth of the holiday home sector. There are bigger issues here than Cornishness. Continuing this rate of building growth not only irresponsibly threatens environmental diversity and landscapes but is also likely to reverse the long-term fall in the population growth rate. This must strike any rational observer as deeply unsustainable behaviour. Even allowing for the way our housing stock is being siphoned off by temporary residents, if a rate of 48,500 houses every twenty years is maintained for another century we are looking at a possible increase of population from its current 535,000 to 900,000 by 2100.

In 1976 County Council planners estimated that in order to 'maintain the physical characteristics of Cornwall' its ideal population capacity would be 430,000.[23] We are well on our way to more than doubling that—and with hardly any public debate, as the issue of planning policy remains stuck in the arcane sidings of a technical planning discourse. Meanwhile, a smokescreen of housing need and jobs growth—or indeed any kind of growth at all—is manufactured in order to divert our attention from the long-term consequences. I do not have time to delve into the reasons for this. But you will be able to read more about the financial and ideological imperatives that drive the growth fixation in my *The land's end: The Great Sale of Cornwall*, due to be published in 2013.

In 1973 Charles Thomas spoke of the circular logic of more population, more roads, more land given over to housing and greatly increased tourism, to bring more income and so on in a never-ending cycle.[24] Although forty years of such logic has left us at the bottom of the UK wages league, policy-makers remain stuck in a mindset that insists we need more houses to bring more jobs to be filled by more in-migrants who will live in the new houses linked by the new roads along which will drive all the new people . . . and so on, and so on. We live in the midst of a giant Ponzi scheme which is sacrificing our environmental and cultural capital for illusory benefits peddled by a political class that has lost its will to live and a regeneration project and mandarin class that has lost all touch with reality.

Charles Thomas pulled no punches in 1973. The Cornish had a 'shocking environmental record' while local councils were 'short-sighted' and 'stuffed with builders, developers and those engaged in the tourist industry'.[25] The tourist trade came in for special condemnation, the annual influx having reached 'nightmare proportions'. Would the 'residents of Cornwall', Charles asked, 'consent to be exploited on an ever-increasing scale by that 11 per cent of the population whose livelihood is tourism'?[26] That proportion is now 14 per cent and the answer is, sadly, yes. As we have seen, tourism is directly implicated in the artificially high rate of housebuilding and loss of agricultural land in Cornwall. It stimulates demand to move temporarily or permanently to Cornwall, despite Cornwall's economic unattractiveness. It helps weave the fabric of a low-wage, flexible labour, non-unionized economy and high rent housing market. Tourist numbers have grown from three to five million since 1973 and the sector remains over-influential, despite intermittent calls since the 1980s to diversify the economy. The tourist trade's domination of public discourse and the ubiquitous dissemination of this discourse by an uncritical local media drown out alternative ways of organizing our economy.

While little seems to have changed in relation to tourism, attitudes towards the environment remain surprisingly complacent despite awareness of our effect on climate change. Recently, I sat through two hours of a Cornwall Council Planning Policy Advisory Panel meeting that was discussing the Local Plan housing targets. The environmental consequences of current growth rates were hardly raised. Truffling around in the statistics of affordable housing, job creation and demographic projections, councillors seem to have lost all capacity to think through the consequences of policy decisions.[27] Any hints of vision were largely bleached out, replaced by an arid, mechanical and soulless debate, restricted and regulated by an ideological self-policing. All in all, a fine example of that old Cornish saying *nag ez goon heb lagaz na kea heb scovarn* [there is no down without an eye nor hedge without an ear].

Reasons to be cheerful?

In 1973 Charles Thomas looked to two areas for inspiration. The first was the environmental lobby. He suggested that environmentalists automatically believed that 'the convenience of those in Cornwall must be put first'.[28] Cornwall's voters were urged to 'bring about the election of councillors who are committed to put the environment first' and who believe that Cornwall should be governed in 'the long-term interests of all the inhabitants, not the immediate convenience of the temporary residents'. This is still a valid position and provides us with useful criteria when considering one of our now rare opportunities to vote for local councillors in May 2013.

But, just as democracy is becoming a distraction from the business as usual of 'sustainable' development, we ought to be a little less sanguine forty years on about the environmental lobby. Take *Our Cornwall*'s campaign this year (2012) for a more sustainable planning policy. This was enthusiastically supported by some, notably Friends of the Earth and most, though not all, members of the CPRE. But, despite several invitations to sign up in support, neither Greenpeace nor the Green Party felt able to. Indeed, when Camborne Town Council debated whether to support *Our Cornwall*'s call to Cornwall Council to reduce its housing target, the sole Green Party councillor joined with the Labour Party in voting against.

The second bright spot in the firmament of 1973 was the presence of a 'national consciousness', created and fostered by a revivalist movement that had toiled thanklessly among Cornwall's Celtic remains since the end of the nineteenth century. It was this national consciousness that had produced the Institute of Cornish Studies and kept Cornishness alive. Here one could find the core of those who believed that being Cornish in Cornwall was important. Yet, would people be so positive about the role of Cornish revivalism these days? An explicitly national consciousness, as opposed to a Cornish conscious-ness, remains marginal and is likely to remain so in a context of continuing population turnover. Although until recently we had half a dozen MK councillors [reduced to four in the May 2013 elections], and although the party is taken more seriously than in the 1970s, it is still marginalized in both media and society.[29] Meanwhile, the revived Cornish language, now officially recognized and funded, finds itself in the dubious embrace of government.[30] But government funding has the paradoxical result of fossilizing the language in its strange blend of high modernism and twee medievalism. Street signs proliferate based on fifteenth-century syntax but written in an orthography that never existed when the language was actually spoken by more than a handful. This guarantees that the Cornish language remains just as obscure now to the bulk of the population as it was back in the 1940s when Morton Nance was practicing his elvish script on the back of invitations from his stockbrokers to purchase shares.

For some of us, being Cornish is still important, although the ways of performing that Cornishness have changed considerably since the 1970s. For others being Cornish is supremely unimportant. So, finally, is Cornish studies still important? In 1973 Charles Thomas spent a lot of time assessing the 'present national malaise in Cornwall' and its 'internal social crisis'.[31] In an echo of this, the second Director of the Institute of Cornish Studies, Philip Payton, called for a 'new Cornish social science' in the early 1990s.[32] This would make contemporary Cornwall the subject of its researches. In practice though, just as the more dynamic and vibrant elements of the broader Cornish cultural movement can be found on its margins—music rather than language, for example—so has work on contemporary Cornwall been largely left to the periphery of Cornish studies. By periphery I am here thinking of Plymouth University in particular, with its body of quantitative work on housing, migration and ethnicity. In its institutional phase, the ambitions of a new Cornish social science were doused by an epistemological tradition that equates Cornish studies with the study of past times. Combine that with institutional imprisonment at Tremough within an outpost of a History Department based at Exeter, and those of us in the core of Cornish studies were able to offer disappointingly small purchase on contemporary Cornwall and its tribulations since 1973.

And yet a critical contemporary Cornish studies is now even more vital. In a world of complacent and anodyne press releases and the hyped-up promises of the marketing departments, someone has to speak truth to power. Someone has to ask what exactly 'transforming knowledge' means on the ground. Somebody has to think beyond the box of neo-liberal politics that drains democracy of meaning and hands policy-making over to the interests of a small minority. If I can slightly rephrase the question Charles Thomas posed in 1973: 'does Cornwall really exist solely for the benefit of Wain Homes, Sainsburys, the Inox Group or the Duchy of Cornwall?' A critical Cornish studies is still important. Although the questions remain—who will provide it? And how?

Notes and references

1. Charles Thomas, *The Importance of Being Cornish, in Cornwall* (Redruth, 1973), p. 16.
2. Charles Thomas, *The Importance of Being Cornish* (Exeter, 1973), p. 16.
3. Narrative Cornish histories have appeared since 1973 from a range of perspectives, including John Angarrack, *Breaking the Chains: Propaganda, Censorship, Deception and the Manipulation of Public Opinion in Cornwall* (Camborne, 1999); Bernard Deacon, *Cornwall: A Concise History* (Cardiff, 2007); Roy Green, *The National Question in Cornwall* (London, 1980); Philip Payton, *The Making of Modern Cornwall* (Redruth, 1992) and *Cornwall: A History* (Fowey, 2004); David Riley, *King Arthur's Realm: A History of the Kingdom of Cornwall* (Ilfracombe, 2004). It is disappointing therefore to see how often historians beyond the Tamar and others still resort to Frank Halliday's *A History of Cornwall*, despite this originally being published in 1959.
4. Thomas, *The Importance of Being Cornish, in Cornwall*, p. 12.

5. Norman Davies, *Vanished Kingdoms: The History of Half-Forgotten Europe* (London, 2011), pp. 9, 43.

6. Thomas, *The Importance of Being Cornish, in Cornwall*, p. 10.

7. Ibid., p. 12.

8. Ronald Perry, Ken Dean and Bryan Brown (eds), *Counterurbanisation: Case Studies of Urban to Rural Movement* (Norwich, 1986), p. 84.

9. See Simon Naylor, *Regionalizing Science: Placing Knowledges in Victorian England* (London, 2010).

10. The *Guardian*, 26 March 2012.

11. Kerryn Husk, 'Ethnic Group Affiliation and Social Exclusion in Cornwall: Analysis, Adjustment and Extension of the 2001 England and Wales Census Data', unpublished PhD thesis, University of Plymouth, 2012.

12. For the implications of this see Kerryn Husk, 'Ethnicity and Social Exclusion: Research and Policy Implications', *Social and Public Policy Review* 5.1 (2011), pp. 7–25.

13. See Danny Dorling et al., 'Changing UK: The way we live now', available at http://sasi.group.shef.ac.uk/research/changingUK.html.

14. Joanie Willett, 'Cornish Identity: Vague Notion or Social Fact?' in Philip Payton (ed.), *Cornish Studies: Sixteen* (Exeter, 2008), pp. 183–205.

15. In this respect Cornwall resembles the Basque Country or Wales, rather than Scotland, Catalonia or Brittany where dual identities are more common—see data presented in Lieven de Winter, Margarita Gómez-Reno and Peter Lynch (eds), *Autonomist Parties in Europe: Identity Politics and the Revival of the Territorial Cleavage* (Barcelona, 2006).

16. See, for example, Merv Davey, '"As is the manner and the custom"; folk tradition and identity in Cornwall', unpublished PhD thesis, University of Exeter, 2011; Alan Kent, *The Theatre of Cornwall: Space, Place, Performance* (Bristol, 2010) and the refreshing contemporary novels of Myrna Combellack, Alan Kent and N.K. Phillips.

17. Jane Howells, 'Preliminary Report on the Cornwall Council Core Strategy Preferred Approach Equality Impact Assessment (Bewnans Kernow, 2012), p. 15.

18. Thomas, *The Importance of Being Cornish, in Cornwall*, p. 14.

19. For example, Bernard Deacon, Andrew George and Ronald Perry, *Cornwall at the Crossroads* (Redruth, 1989).

20. For a study of this growth and its effects, see Katarzyna Kowalczuk, 'Population Growth in a High Amenity Area: Migration and Socio-Economic Change in Cornwall', unpublished PhD thesis, University of Plymouth, 2010.

21. For a good exposé of the contradictions of neoliberalism, see Colin Crouch, *The Strange Non-death of Neoliberalism* (Cambridge, 2011).

22. Cornwall Council, *Planning Future Cornwall* (Truro, 2012), p .8.

23. Cornwall County Council, *Structure Plan Policy Choice Consultation Document* (Truro, 1976), p. 76

24. Thomas, *The Importance of Being Cornish, in Cornwall*, p. 18.

25. Ibid., p. 14.

26. Ibid., p. 20.

27. The unsustainability of current growth policies are more generally explained by Tim Jackson, *Prosperity Without Growth: Economics for a Finite Planet*, (London, 2009). For a more pessimistic take on the incompatibility of capitalism and the

environment, see Joel Kovel, *The Enemy of Nature: The End of Capitalism or The End of the World?* (London, 2007). There is little evidence that any of our councillors have read or are even aware of these books.

28. Thomas, *The Importance of Being Cornish, in Cornwall*, p. 20.
29. Bernard Deacon, Dick Cole and Garry Tregidga, *Mebyon Kernow and Cornish Nationalism* (Cardiff, 2003).
30. For recent work on the revived language, see Anina Carkeek, 'Cornish Language Revival: Attitudes, Behaviour and The Maintenance of an Ethnic Identity' unpublished PhD thesis, University of East Anglia, 2009; Andrew Donaldson, *Linguistic Minorities in Rural Development: A Case Study of the Cornish Language and Cornwall* (University of Newcastle, 1999); Dave Sayers, 'Reversing Babel: Declining linguistic diversity and the flawed attitudes to protect it', unpublished PhD thesis, University of Essex, 2008.
31. Thomas, *The Importance of Being Cornish, in Cornwall*, p. 13.
32. See Introductions to the series *Cornish Studies*, edited by Philip Payton.

3

Adjectival and Adverbial Prefixes in Cornish

N.J.A. Williams

Speaking of the adjective in Cornish Nance says:

> In the positive degree this normally follows the noun: **cümyas tēk**. In cases where the adj. comes first it may be considered as compounded or hyphenated with the noun, **pür, brās, cot, cam, gow, gwȳr, gwan, tebel, drōk, fals, hager, hȳr**, are oftenest so used (CfA: 11).

Nance says that the preceding adjective is 'compounded or hyphenated' with the noun. 'Prefixed' is perhaps a better term.

As we shall see, Nance in his list has omitted some further adjectives that may precede their noun. Moreover he does not mention that the behaviour of prefixed adjectives may vary. Most, though not all, can be used after a noun, so that, for example, one can say *hyr-penys* 'long abstinence' but also *termyn hyr* 'a long time'. Many can also be used predicatively. For example, one can say *camwyth* 'evil deeds' but also *henna nyns yw cam* 'that is not wrong'. Other adjectives can also be prefixed to verbs and thus acquire adverbial function, e.g. *drok dywethe* 'to end badly', *tebel fara* 'fare badly'. Still others, when prefixed change their sense, e.g. *gwan* 'weak' but *gwan hanow* 'evil name', and *pur* 'pure, utter' but *pur tha* 'very good'. Further a number of English borrowings can be prefixed to adjectives and verbs, e.g. *overdevys* 'overgrown' and *bad-ober* 'bad work, crime'. Finally there remains the question of how far prefixed adjectives lenite the initial consonant of the word to which they are attached.

Let us look at the prefixed adjectives in turn to see how each one is used in the traditional language.

Adjectival Prefixes in the Cornish Texts

drok-, drog- 'bad, evil, wicked'

This commonly functions as an adjective prefixed to its noun:

*A out warnes **drok venen** worto pan wrussys cole* 'damn you, evil woman, that you paid attention to him' OM 221–22

*pan rellens remembra ha lamentya aga pehosow haga **drog bewnans** esans ow ledya* 'when they remember and lament their sins and their evil lives which they were leading' TH 6a

*mar ny fystyn pup huny why as byth **drog vommennow*** 'if everyone does not hurry, you will get evil blows' OM 2323–24

*Ser duk me a weyl tevdar ha parcel a **throk coscar** pur thevrey orth y sewa* 'Sir duke, I see Teudar and a group of evil fellows indeed following him' BM 2358–60

*In meth an lader arall **drok zen** os kepar del ves* 'The other thief said, "you are an evil man as you have been"' PA 192a

*Thymmo heb mar, te **drog-den**, ny vethyth gowr* 'To me indeed, you evil man, you will not be a husband' BK 2960–61

*Gans an ezewon war hast **drok zewas** a ve dyzgtys* 'By the Jews in haste an evil drink was got ready' PA 202a

*vyngens re'n geffo amen ha **drok thyweyth*** 'may he suffer vengeance, amen, and an evil end' RD 2085–86

*A **throg thewath** re wyrwhy!* 'May you die an evil death!' BK 473

*yma eff ow dysky fatell ra **drog gerryow** ha **drog prederow** deservya condemnacion* 'he teaches that evil words and evil thoughts will deserve condemnation' TH 9

*pan ello ow corf yn pry guyth vy rak an joul **drok was*** 'when my body goes into the earth, protect me from the devil, the evil fellow' RD 1563–64

*kemereugh corf a'n **drok was** vgy ow flerye gans blas yw myligys* 'take the body of the evil fellow that is stinking with an accursed odour' RD 2159–61

*gallas genaf ve **droag lam** poran rag an ober na* 'I have suffered an evil fate precisely for that deed' CW 1687–88

*kepar hag ef on crousys ha dre wyr vreus quyt iuggys rak agan **drok ober** kens* 'like him we are crucified and by true judgement condemned for our evil deeds ere now' PC 2900–02 *kepar dell ra an laddron, advltrers, denlath, hag oll an **drog pobill** erell* 'as the thieves do, adulterers, murderers and all the other evil people' TH 24

*Gallas Lucifer **droke preve*** 'Lucifer, the evil snake, has gone' CW 335

*them shape ow honyn ytama why a weall omma treylys **drog pullat** ha brase* 'to my own shape, behold me, you see me transformed, an evil fellow and a great one' CW 925–27

*So rag an wyckyd han **drog requestys** ma eff a ve grevously rebukys ha reprovys* 'but for these wicked and evil requests he was grievously rebuked and reproved' TH 46a.

Drok-, *drog-* may also be prefixed to verbs and verbal nouns, as is clear from the following examples:

*dre laha y coth dotho **drok dywethe*** 'by law he ought to meet an evil end' PC 1827–28

*me a'm bues gallos i'n bys ha'm yskerans a **throkfar*** 'I have power in the world and my enemies will fare badly' BK 1411–12

*gueyt an harlot na scapyo **drok handle** del om kyry pan gyffy dalhen ynno* 'make sure that the scoundrel does not escape mistreatment, as you love me, when you get your hands on him' PC 990–92

*hy re ruk ov delyfrya mes a preson mam kerra le mayth ena **drokhendelys*** 'she has delivered me from prison, dearest mother, where I was being mistreated' BM 3758–60

*y thadder yw **drok tylys** pan y'n lathsons dybyte* 'his goodness has been badly repaid since they have killed him without mercy' RD 3096–97.

The jussive particle *re* may separate *drok-* and the verb *fara* 'to fare' as can be seen in: *A, harlot, **drog re fary** gans the govanscosow gow!* 'Oh scoundrel, may you fare badly with your lying excuses!' BK 459–60.

In the above examples *drog-* often lenites initial *b* and *gw*, and it may also lenite *d* > *th*. It seems, however, that initial *p* is not usually lenited after *drog-*. We thus find the following: *drok pyn* 'evil torment' PC 2108, 2726; *drog pys* 'badly paid, angry' PC 3089; *drok pryson* 'evil prison' RD 2002; *drok pobyll* 'evil people' BM 1325; *drog pobyll* 'idem' TH 18, 25, 29a, 40, 40a; *drog pobill* 'idem' TH 24, 24a x 2, 25 x 4, 31a x 3; *droke polat* 'evil fellow' CW 769; *drog pullat* 'idem' CW 927; *drog polat* 'idem' CW 1441, 1485; *drog prederow* 'evil thoughts' TH 9; *droke preve* 'evil snake' CW 335. Indeed I can find no example anywhere of *drok-*, *drog-* leniting following *p* > *b*.

This prefixed *drok-, drog-* is thus the ordinary way of saying 'badly' in Cornish. The adverbial particle *yn* is never attested with *drog* itself. *Yn ta* 'well' is common in the texts, but **yn trog* 'badly' is wholly unattested. The only attested example of 'badly' not involving a prefixed adverb in Cornish is probably *rag eff a recevyas Corf Dew* **warlerth badd maner** 'for he received the body of God badly' SA 65a.

Drok, drog is also used as an adjective predicatively with parts of the verb *bos* 'to be'. Particularly common is the use with the pronominal forms of the preposition *gans* to mean 'be sorry, regret' (all our examples of this latter idiom contain the first person singular):

> *mar* **pue drok** *a oberys trogh yhy gans the glethe* 'if what I did was evil, cut her with your sword' OM 291–92

> *a ihesu whek re iovyn* **drok yv** *gyne na venta kammen tryle yn maner tek* 'dear Jesus, by Jove I regret that you will not convert nicely at all' PC 1291–94

> *thomas ty yv me a grys an gokye den yn beys ha henna* **yv drok** 'Thomas, you, I believe, are the silliest man in the world and that is bad' RD 1453–55

> *thomas ty yv muskegys hag yn muscokneth gyllys* **drok yv** *gynef vy lemmyn* 'Thomas, you are mad and sunken in insanity, I regret' RD 1127–29

> **Drog yv** *genef gruthyl den* 'I regret having created man' OM 917

> **drok yv** *gynef bones mar lyes enef ow mos the'n nef* 'I am sorry that so many souls are going to heaven' RD 298–300

> **drog yv** *gena doys oma* 'I regret coming here' BM 457

> **Drog o** *the gan owth owtya* 'Evil was your song as you yelled' BK 27.

Drok, drog is also used in adjectival phrases of the kind *drog y gnas, drog aga gnas* 'evil natured'. There are two instances in PC:

> *arluth lauar dyssempys thy'nny mars yv both the vreys ha bolenegoth a'n tas my the wyskel gans clethe nep vs worth the dalhenne scherewys* **drok aga gnas** 'Lord, tell us immediately whether it is your wish and the Father's will that I should strike with a sword those who are seizing you, evil their nature' PC 1137–42

> *a peue den* **drok y gnas** *ny alse yn nep maner pur wyr cafus mar mur ras rak sawye tus dre vn ger* 'had he been a man of evil nature, he could not in any way indeed have had such great grace to cure people by a single word' PC 2969–72.

In the Cornish texts *drok*, *drog* also functions as a noun 'evil, disease', for example in the following examples:

ol en da han **drok** *kepar ze ihesu bezens grassys* 'for all the good and the evil alike let Jesus be thanked' PA 24d

kyns yn ta ef a ylly tus a bup **drok** *ol sawye* 'ere now well he could cure people of all ill' PA 194b

kemys **druk** *vs ov cothe ha dewethes hag avar yma ken thy'm the ole* 'so much evil is occurring both late and early, I have reason to weep' OM 628–30

gul **drok** *thy'so ny vynna* 'I will not do you any harm' RD 1815

gothvos ynweth decernya omma ynter **drok** *ha da yv ov ewnadow pup vr* 'also to be able to distinguish here evil from good is my desire always' BM 28–30

an wethan ma ew henwys gwethan gothvas **droke** *ha da* 'this tree is called the tree of the knowledge of evil and good' CW 375–76

ha why ra boaze pocara Deew a cothaz Da ha **Droag** 'and you shall be like God knowing good and evil' Rowe

Nessa, urt an Skavaoll Crack-an-codna iggava setha war en Cres an awles ewhall (cries tutton Harry an lader) heb **drog** *veeth* 'Next, because of the precarious stool he sits on in the middle of the high cliff, called the hassock of Harry the thief, without any harm' BF: 12

Na tedna ny en Antoll, buz gwitha ny vrt **droag** 'Do not lead us into temptation, but deliver us from evil' BF: 55.

Drok, *drog* is not generally used, however, as an attributive adjective after its noun. There are no examples of **den drog* 'evil man', **benen throg* 'evil woman', **pollat drog* or **ober drog* 'evil work' for example. The only exception to this rule that I can find is the following from BM:

Nefra cosker ongrassyas menogh a ra bostov bras neb tebel dorne pan vo grueys mas **hap drok** *orthugh a skyn gase farwel me a vyn molleth du in cowetheys* 'Ever an ungracious crowd will often make great boast when some evil trick is done. But an evil fortune will descend upon you. I shall take my leave. God's curse on the company' BM 1282–87.

Note: this one example is slighty doubtful, however, for a number of reasons. The noun *hap* is not otherwise attested in Cornish, although *parhap* 'perhaps' occurs twice (OM 1352, CW 661), moreover the usual word for 'but' in BM is *sav*, not *mas*. It is not impossible that the original text here was something like: **par hap drok orthugh a skyn* 'perhaps evil will fall upon you'. In which case we would have no example in Cornish of *drok* after the noun it qualifies.

In Middle Breton, as in Cornish, the word *drouc* can be used either as a noun meaning 'evil, wickedness' or as a prefixed adjective in such compounds as *drouc-preder* 'evil thought', *drouc-speret* 'evil spirit' and *drouc-ober* 'evil deed'. *Drouc* does not seem to be used after the noun it qualifies. In Welsh *drwg* 'bad, evil' can also be a noun meaning 'evil, wickedness' and an adjective 'evil, wicked'. When prefixed, it often appears as *dryg-*, e.g. *drygddyn* 'evil person', *drygliw* 'bad colour, stain' and *drygair* 'bad name, ill report'. *Drwg* can also, however, be used after its noun, e.g. in such expressions as *dydd drwg* 'evil day', *ffrwyth drwg* 'evil fruit'. Notice incidentally that Welsh exhibits vocalic alternation in *drwg* by itself but *dryg-* in compounds. Such alternation is absent from both Breton and Cornish.

The Irish congener of *drok* is *droch-*, which is a prefixed adjective only, e.g. *drochétach* 'poor clothes', *drochmenma* 'bad mood, dejection', *drochduine* 'evil person', etc. *Droch-* cannot be used predicatively, nor as a noun. It would seem therefore that the common Celtic usage was to prefix the reflexes of **druko-* to the noun qualified. The Welsh syntax of allowing *drwg* to follow its noun seems not to be favoured in the other insular Celtic languages, though we may have one example in Cornish.

tebel- 'evil, wicked'

This word seems to be a learned borrowing from Latin *debilis* 'weak, poor'. When used as a noun it means 'devil, evil one':

> *besy yw zys bos vuell ha seruabyll yth seruys manno allo an **tebell** ogas zys bonas trylys* 'it is vital for you to be humble and diligent in your service so that the devil may not be turned near towards you' PA 19cd

> *poken yma an **tebell** war agan dalla* 'or the devil blinds us' TH 51

> *der temptacon an **teball** ow hendas adam pur weare eave re gollas der avall an place gloryous pur sure* 'through the temptation of the devil my grandfather Adam, he indeed has by an apple lost the glorious place surely' CW 2133–36

> *hedre vo yn the herwyth fythys nefre ny vethyth gans **tebeles** war an beys* 'while you carry it never will you be overcome by evil ones in the world' OM 1464–66

hag y res gover fenten marth erhyth thotho hep fal may hallo tus ha bestes ha myns a vynno eve may whello an **debeles** *ov gueres menough thethe* 'and a stream of spring will flow, if you bid it without fail, so that man and beast and whoever wishes may drink, so that the evil ones may see my frequent help to them' OM 1845–50

Tebelas 'devils, evil ones' Bodewryd MS: 99.

Tebel and *yn tebel* are both used adverbially to mean 'severely, wickedly, horribly':

hag ena ij an scorgyas **yn tebel** *gans ij scorgye ha hager fest an dygtyas corf ha pen treys ha dewle* 'and then two scourged him horribly with two scourges and very grimly they treated him, body and head, feet and hands' PC 130cd

War aga dewlyn y ze zerag Ihesus re erell aga fen y a sackye hag a gewsy pur **debell** *worth Ihesus rag y angre* 'Upon their knees others came before Jesus; they shook their heads and spoke very wickedly to Jesus to annoy him' PA 195ab.

The commonest use of *tebel-* is as an adjective prefixed to a substantive:

Out warnas, **tebal-venyn!** 'Damn you, evil woman!' BK 1210

a **teball benyn** *heb grace ty ram tullas ve heb kene* 'O evil woman without grace, you have deceived me without cause' CW 854–55

an dragon yv **tebelvest** 'the dragon is a nasty animal' BM 4128

Inweth **teball vewnans** *a thora dampnacion thyn rena vgy ow teball vewa* 'Also evil life brings damnation to those who live wickedly' TH 16a

sav ny vyn awos trauyth gage y **tebel crygyans** 'but he will not for anything forsake his evil belief' PC 1813–14

tebel den *ef mar ny fe ny ny'n drosen thy'so gy* 'had he not been a wicked man, we would not have brought him to you' PC 1975–76

Gans gloteny ef pan welas cam na ylly y dolla en **tebell el** *a vynnas yn ken maner y demptye* When he saw that he could not seduce him by gluttony the devil tried to tempt him by another means' PA 13ab

ena wy a gyff in lel guas ovth eria heb question esel yv then **tebel el** 'there you will find indeed a fellow defiant without question; he is a limb of the devil' BM 967–69

*Inna yth ew scriffes fatell rug an wyly serpent an **tebell ell** dos the eva* 'in it is written that the wily serpent, the devil came to Eve' TH 3

*yma agys yskar an **teball ell** kepar ha lyon ow huga* 'your enemy the devil is like a roaring lion' TH 3a

*Fy the Jovyn, **tebel-el**! Henna ew dyowl pur* 'Fie to Jove, an evil angel! He is an utter devil' BK 134–35

*rag ef o **tebel ethen** neb a glewsys ov cane* 'for he was an evil bird that you heard singing' OM 223–24

*martesyn y a yll skynnya in myschew an parna may teffans ha tenna re erell dre aga **teball examplis** ha gwrythyans* 'perhaps they can descend into mischief of that kind so that they may draw other people by their bad examples and deeds' TH 25a

*me ny'th sense guel es ky denagh the **tebelvryans*** 'I will not esteem you more than a dog; deny your evil deeds' BM 3501–02

*maras yns fur y a nagh in vr na **tebel wythres*** 'if they are wise then they will renounce evil deeds' BM 4122–23

*pan rens y ry thotheff **teball gyrryow**, eff ny re aga **theball** gortheby* 'when they used wicked words against him, he did not answer them wickedly' TH 23

*skettyaf the ben ha'th coloven theworth the scoyth gans the gonha kepar ha goyth, te mab hora, **tebal-voran**!* 'I will smash your head and your skull from shoulder and neck like a goose, you son of a whore, an evil hussy!' BK 2159–65

*The'n cans myl deawl reg yllough ha byner re thewellough, why, na **tebal nawothow**!* 'May you go to the hundred thousand devils and may you never return, you nor bad news!' BK 744–46

*Aron whek pyth a cusyl a reth thy'm orth am vresyl a son a'n **debel bobel*** 'Dear Aaron what advice do you give me against the dispute of the murmuring of the wicked people?' OM 1813–15

*moyses kemer the welen ha ty ha'th vroder aren arag an **debel bobal** guask gynsy dywyth an men* 'Moses, take your staff and you and your brother Aaron before the wicked people strike with it twice the rock' OM 1841–44

*yssyw hemma trueth bras bos the corf ker golyys gans **tebel popel** ogh ogh* 'what a great pity this is that your dear body has been wounded by evil people, alas, alas!' PC 3182–84 *an falge dragon* **tebel preff** *ny gara gueles y grueff desawer vest yv honna* 'the treacherous dragon, evil reptile, I do not wish to see its face; it is a noisome beast' BM 4133–35

tebel seruont *a leuer mar serf ef bad y vester ke the honan ha gura guel* 'a wicked servant says, if he serves his master badly, "Go thyself and do better"' PC 2283–85

me yv vexijs anhethek gans **tebel speris** *oma* 'I am continuously vexed by an evil spirit here' BM 2630–31.

Notice that the compound *tebel-el* is used by several writers to mean 'devil'. Variously spelt *tebel el, tebell el, tebell ell, teball el, tebell el,* this expression is attested twenty-three times in the texts.

Tebel- is also prefixed to verbs where it bears adverbial sense as 'badly, wickedly, severely':

Inweth teball vewnans a thora dampnacion thyn rena vgy ow **teball vewa** 'Also evil living brings damnation to those who live wickedly' TH 16a

a ihesu gouy ragos mar **tebel dyghtys** *the vos* 'O Jesus, alas for you so wickedly treated!' PC 2633–34

Ay re **deball dowethy** 'Oh, may you end badly!' CW520

mar calla y **tebelfar** *drefen y voys sur heb mar erbyn fay crist dyspusant* 'if I can, he will fare ill because of course he is powerless against the faith of Christ' BM 2281–83

darne ov fobyl yv marov ha me **tebelwolijs** 'part of my men are dead and I am badly wounded' BM 2489–90

pan rens y ry thotheff teball gyrryow, eff ny re aga **theball gortheby** 'when they used wicked words against him, he did not answer them wickedly' TH 23

Ha pan ruga suffra myrnans, ny rug eff aga latha y, naga **theball henwall** 'And when he suffered death, he did not kill them, nor call them evil names' TH 23

Whath kyn feva lyas tyrmyn assays ha **teball pynchis**, *whath an feith a rug prevaylya woteweth* 'Yet though it was often tried and badly afflicted, still the faith prevailed in the end' TH 34.

When prefixed *tebel-*, as can be seen from the examples above, usually lenites *b > v* and *gw > w* in the next word. *Tebel-* also appears on occasion to lenite initial *p-* to *b-*.

As has been noted above, *yn trog* 'badly' is unattested in traditional Cornish. 'Badly' must be expressed by either *drog-* or *tebel-* prefixed to its verb. Rarely *tebel* is used adjectivally after the noun it qualifies:

rag dewes mar nystevyth yn certan y a dreyl fyth hag a worth **dewow tebel** 'for if they do not get drink certainly they will change allegiance and will worship evil gods' OM 1816–18

ham kyke yv **escar teball** *pur ysel me an temper* 'and my flesh is an evil enemy; I shall tame it full low' BM 162–63

prest an **ezewon debel** *ze Ihesus esens a dro* 'always the wicked Jews were about Jesus' PA 140d

Re an **ezewon tebell** *a leuerys heb pyte a wottense ow kelwel hely zozo zy wyze* 'Some of the wicked Jews said without pity, "Behold he is calling on Elijah to preserve him."' PA 203ab.

In all these four cases above the word *tebel*, *tebell*, *teball* is in final position in the line and is necessary for rhyme. We can assume that *tebel* was not usually put after its noun in the spoken language.

gwan-, gwadn 'weak, bad'

Gwan 'weak' as a prefix means 'evil, bad, poor (in quality)':

surely ymowns in **gwan cas,** *mas y a rella gans speda ha in du tyrmyn repentya ha gull penans* 'surely they are in a bad position, unless with haste and in due time they repent and do penance' TH 32a

Ellas emperour debyta mar mennyth oma latha flehys bythqueth na pehes yma dywhy **guan cusel** 'Alas, merciless emperor, if you will here kill children that never sinned, yours is wicked advice' BM 1591–94

Arte Iudas ow tryle **gwan wecor** *nyn geve par ny yl den vyth amontye myns a gollas yn chyffar worth ihesus ef a fecle* 'Again Judas turning—as a bad dealer he had no equal; no one can compute how much he lost in the transaction—to Jesus he spoke falsely' PA 40ac

Ha genz hedna, an **guadn-gyrti** *genz a follat a dhestriaz an dên kôth en guili* 'the wicked wife with her peramour killed the old man in the bed' AB: 252a

Ha nessa metten an **guadn-gyrti**, *hei a dhalasvaz dho 'uîl krei* 'And the next morning the wicked wife, she began to make an uproar' AB: 252a

pew vs in agan mysk ny mas eff a gylwe y gentrevak hay kyscristian foole vncharitably bo nampith a throg ha **gwan hanow** *arell?* 'who among us does not call his neighbour and his fellow Christian a fool uncharitably or some other unpleasant and evil name' TH 28a

moy ew ow **gwan oberowe** *hag inwethe ow fehasowe es tell ew tha vercy dew thym tha ava* 'greater are my evil deeds and also my sins than is your mercy to forgive me, O God' CW 1169–72

henna o **gwan obar** *gwryes* 'that was an evil deed done' CW 1268

nefra ny wren rejoycya mes pub ere oll ow murnya heb ioy vyth na lowena der tha **wadn ober** *omma* 'never shall we rejoice but always will be lamenting without any joy or happiness through your evil deed here' CW 1272–75

henna o **gwadn ober** *gwryes* 'that was an evil deed done' CW 1679

Me yv parys arluth da sav **guan revle** *yma oma na yllyn lefya kyn moys* 'I am ready, my good Lord, but this is a bad rule that we cannot have lunch before departing' BM 3924–26

yth ombrovas **gwan dyack** *mayth of poyntyes za bayne bras* 'I have proved myself a poor manager, so that I am condemned to great torment' CW 920–21.

In the two examples from AB *guadn-gyrti* is a compound of *gwan, gwadn* and *gwreg ty* 'house-wife' (seen in CF: 14), where *gw-* remains unlenited after *gwadn*. In *gwan wecor* (< *gwecor, gwycor* 'dealer') on the other hand *gwan-, gwadn-* appears to lenite following *gw > w*. There is no evidence that *gwan-, gwadn-* mutated *c > g*.

I have no examples of *gwan-, gwadn-* prefixed to verbs. *Gwan, gwadn* is, however, used adjectivally after its noun, e.g.

du assus lues **den gvan** *sawys genogh in bys ma* 'God, how many weak people have you cured in this world!' BM 757–58

lues **den guan** *in bys ma pur guir eff a confortyas* 'many weak people in this world in truth he comforted' BM 4480–82

in nomine patris et filij virtu crist rebo yly a **dus gvan** *dygh in tor ma* 'in the name of the Father and the Son may the virtue of Christ be a salve, O weak men, for you at this time' BM 555–57

Gwyr 'true'

Gwyr 'true' is used as a predicative adjective:

guyr yv y vones arluth ha'y ober a pref henna 'true it is that he is lord and his works prove that' PC 213

mester genough ym gylwyr hagh arluth henna yv **guyr** 'I am called master by you and lord and that is true' PC 873–74

reys yv bos **guyr** *an awayl* 'the gospel must be true' PC 924

ru'm fay **guyr** *yv agas cous* 'upon my faith, what you say is true' PC 1345

ty a yl y atendye bos **guyr** *ow cous kettep ger* 'you can observe that what I say is true, every word' RD 477–78

hep dout mars yw **guyr** *henna me a vyn mos alemma* 'without doubt if that is true, I shall go from here' RD 1236–37

ha na ylla possibly bos **gwyre** 'and it cannot possibly be true' TH 20

Gweyr *ew henna, by my sowl!* 'That is true, by my soul!' BK 767

dr' erama creege hedna tho bose **gweer** *eu skreefez enna* 'that I believe what is written there to be true' BF: 31.

Pur wyr means 'very truly, in very truth':

yn clewsons ow leuerell **pur wyr** *y fenne terry an tempel cref* 'they heard him saying very truly that he would destroy the mighty temple' PA 91ab

Kayphas **pur wyr** *a sorras hag eth pur fol yn vr na* 'Caiaphas very truly became angry and went quite mad then' PA 94a

ytho bethyth mylyges **pur wyr** *drys ol an bestes* 'therefore you shall be accursed very truly above all animals' OM 311–12

otte omma ve kunys ha fast ef gynef kelmys **pur wyr** *a das* 'behold here it is, firewood and it tied tightly by me very truly, O father' OM 1299–301

nep re ordenes y lathe **pur wyr** *y fythons dampnys the tan yfarn droka le* 'whoever have ordered that he be killed very truly will be condemned to the fire of hell, dreadful place' PC 3092–94

rak **pur wyr** *dasserghys yw* 'for very truly he has risen' RD 1004

yth egen yn cres almayn orth vn prys ly yn **pur wyr** *pan fuf gylwys* 'I was in the middle of Germany at lunch very truly when I was summoned' RD 2148–50 *my a wor* **pur wyre** *yn ta py ma an mester trygis* 'I know well very truly where the master lives' BM 38–39

yn ov scole ny ve bythqueth zyso gy **pur wyre** *cowyth yn discans nag yn dader* 'in my school there has never been anyone like you very truly in learning and goodness' BM 204–06

yma pensevyk an gluas dysplesijs **pur guir** *genas* 'the prince of the country is displeased with you very truly' BM 489–90

yma duk oma in vlays drehevys sur er the byn ha ganso **pur guir** *ost brays* 'a duke here in the country has risen surely against you and with in very truly a huge host' BM 2301–03

lues den guan in bys ma **pur guir** *eff a confortyas* 'many weak persons in this world he comforted very truly' BM 4480–81

Christ mab an ughella Tas ew Du **pur wyer** 'Christ the son of the most high Father is God very truly' BK 170–71

Pur wyer *ny'th car neb lyes rag the debal-vanerow* 'Very truly quite a lot of people do not love you because of your evil ways' BK 1064–65

Nu'm ankevyr ve **pur wyr** *hedre vo nef in e le* 'I shall not be forgotten very truly, as long as heaven remains in its place' BK 1471–72

The leud desyr a'm cuth **por wyer** 'Your lewd desire grieves me very truly' BK 2952–53

Por wyer *o'm gallos ema kekeffrys gul drog ha da* 'Very truly it is in my power to do both evil and good' BK 3112–13

heb dallath na dowethva **pur wyre** *me ew* 'very truly I am without beginning nor ending' CW 2–3

ty a thebar in tha wheys theth vara **pur wyre** *nefra* 'you will eat your bread very truly in the sweat of your brow for ever' CW 949–50

vnna a gyke pub huny gans peagh **pur wyre** *ew flayrys* 'in it everyone of flesh very truly stinks with sin' CW 2247–48

der temptacon an teball ow hendas adam **pur weare** *eave re gollas der avall an place gloryous* 'through the temptation of the evil one my grandfather Adam very truly has lost through the apple the glorious place' CW 2133–36.

Pur wyr (*pur guir, purguir, pur wyre, pur wyer, pur weyr, pur weare, por wyr, por wyer*) is very common in traditional Cornish. I have counted 188 examples.

Gwyr is also frequently used as a noun meaning 'truth':

gwyr *re gwesys yredy yn meth crist mygtern oma* '"You have spoken truth," said Christ, "I am a king."' PA 102d

lauar **gwyr** *zymmo vn ger mar sota mab den ha du* 'tell me truth, one word, if you are man and God' PA 129c

yma thy'mmo mur dysyr a wothfes ortheugh an **guyr** 'I have a great desire to know the truth about you' RD 194–95

guyr *a geusyth ievody* 'you speak truth indeed' RD 653

tav ty wrek gans the whethlow ha cous **guyr** *del y'th pysaf* 'silence, you woman, with your stories and speak truth as I beg you' RD 901–02

agan arluth yw marow ellas **guyr** *a lauaraf* 'our Lord is dead, alas; I speak truth' RD 907–08

me a leuer an **guyr** *thy's* 'I will tell you the truth' RD 1061

Rag purgacion theworth pegh a thee dre neb menes eral pella ys an gothfas an **gwyre** 'For purgation from sin comes by other means more than the knowledge of the truth' TH 14

thea tirmyn pedyr bys in dith hethow an **gwyr** *a ve derives a thorne the thorne* 'from the time of St Peter until the present the truth was transmitted from hand to hand' TH 48

why a levar **gwyre** *benyn vas* 'you speak truth, good woman' CW 675

tha thew nyng eis otham vythe awoos cawas agen pythe me a wore **gwyre** 'God has no need to receive our wealth, I know as truth' CW 1132–34

devethys tha baradice me a wore **gwyre** *yth oma* 'I know as truth that I have come to paradise' CW 2129–30

E ve welcumbes, me ore **gwir** 'He was welcomed, I know as truth' Tonkin.

A frequent use of *gwyr* as a noun is seen in the expression *the wyr* 'truly, indeed':

y won **the wyr** *dev an tas re sorras dre wyth benen* 'I know truly that God the Father has become enraged through the work of a woman' OM 255–56

lemyn my a wor **the wyr** *bos ov thermyn devethys* 'now I know truly that my time has come' OM 2343–44

crys my **the wyr** *the thasserghy* 'believe that truly I have risen' RD 868 *na nyl susten na pegans ny yllen dendyl* **the guir** 'neither food nor income could I earn indeed' BM 696–97

der an sperys sans kerra concevijs y fue **the guir** 'through the most beloved Holy Spirit he was conceived truly' BM 858–59

settys rag th'agan dyseysya me a wor **the wyr** *e vos* 'I know that he is ready truly to discomfit us' BK 2240–41.

This nominal sense of *gwyr* can also be seen in the expression *yn gwyr* 'in truth, truly':

gans luas y fons gwelys **en gwyr** *ze zustynee bos mab du neb o lezys* 'by many they were seen indeed to testify that it was the son of God who had been killed' PA 210cd

Onan ha try on **yn gvyr** *en tas ha'n map ha'n spyrys* 'One and three we are indeed, the Father and the Son and the Spirit' OM 3–4

yma ken thy'm the ole daggrow gois **in gvyr** *hep mar* 'I have reason to weep bitter tears of blood indeed' OM 630–31

tyr segh yn guel nag yn pras mar kefyth **yn gvyr** *hep gow ynno gueet in ta whelas bos the'th ly ha the'th kynyow* 'if indeed you find dry land in field or in meadow without doubt be careful to seek food for your lunch and for your dinner' OM 1137–40

pan pyn a gotho thotho lauar **en guyr** *thy'm certan* 'what punishment would be fitting for him, tell me truly for sure' OM 2233–34

dew vody tha ough **yn guyr** 'you are two good people indeed' OM 2461

an nyl torn y fyth ro hyr tres aral re got **in guyr** 'at one moment it is too long, at another moment too short indeed' OM 2548–49

drethos the gy y fyth ol ny **yn guyr** *sawys* 'through you all, we, indeed will be healed' PC 295–96

sur ol the wovynnadow ty a fyth **yn guyr** *hep gow* 'surely all your requests you will indeed have without falsehood' PC 599–600

ov hanov **in guir** *heb mar yv costyntyn the nobil* 'my name indeed of course is Constantine the noble' BM 1155–56

me a wor **in guir** *heb mar benytho arluth ath par pur thefry nygyn bethen* 'I know truly of course that we will not have a lord like you ever indeed' BM 4266–68

In gweyr heb mar, henna ew laver kymmyn 'Truly of course, that is a common saying' BK 757–58

hy ew esya tha dulla es adam in gwyre yn ta 'she is easier to deceive than Adam well truly' CW 472–73.

Note: Nance mistakenly took the collocation *yn guyr* in the texts to stand for *yn* the adverbial particle (which is followed by mixed mutation) + *guyr* as an adjective. He thus rewrote *yn guyr* as *yn whyr 'truly', a form which is unattested. *Yn guyr* means 'in truth', not 'truly'. Nance's *yn whyr is a mistake.

Gwyr is occasionally used as an attributive adjective after its noun:

hag ow bostye y bos ef cryst guyr vn vap dev a nef 'and boasting that he was true Christ, the only son of the God of heaven' PC 1576–77

nynsus ger guir malbe dam wath in ol the daryvays 'there is still not a true damn word in all you say' BM 864–65

me, myghtern Cragow, Corssyth, gans Arthor in quarel gwyr a vith paris corf ha pyth 'I, Corsyth, king of Cracow, with Arthur in true contention will be ready body and wealth' BK 1462–64

An lavar kôth yu lavar guir 'The old saying is a true saying' AB: 252

Enna ew ol guz dega gwir 'That is all your true tithe' Gwavas, LAM: 244.

As an attributive adjective, however, *gwyr* is most usually prefixed to its noun with lenition of the following initial consonant:

dre guyr vrus sur y cothe dotho gothaf bos lethys 'by rightful judgement surely he ought to be killed' OM 2237–38

certan guyr vres yv honna 'that certainly is rightful judgement' PC 515

eugh sacryfyeugh in scon yn meneth the'n tas a'n nef hag ol agas gvyr thege 'go, sacrifice quickly on the mountain to the Father of heaven with all your true tithe' OM 438–40

my a'th worth gans ol ov nel y'm colon pur trewysy hag a offryn thy's whare warbarth ol ov gvyr thege yn gorthyans thys y lesky 'I will worship you with all my strength in my heart very seriously and will offer you straight away together all my true tithe to burn it for you as worship' OM 510–14 *rag bos a abel* **gvyr thege** *ef a'n gefyth yn dyweth an ioy na thyfyk nefre* 'because there is a true tithe from Abel, he will get in the end the joy that never ends' OM 515–17

dvn yn vn rew scon hep lettye er byn ihesu neb yv **guyr dev** *ow tos the'n dre* 'let us go in a group soon without delay to meet Jesus, who is true God, coming to the town' PC 239–42

ellas bythqueth kyns lemmen y vos **guyr dev** *ny wythen* 'alas, we never knew before now that he was true God' PC 1913–14

Nyng es **gwyer Thew** *saw onyn* 'There is no true God but one' BK 194

e vos **gwyer Thew** *ne brevith bys venytha, te pen cog!* 'you will not ever prove that he is true God, you blockhead!' BK 230–31

Try personne eternal yns hag un **gwyer Thew** *byttygyns* 'They are three eternal persons and one true God nonetheless' BK 253–54

me re peghes marthys trus **guyr gos** *dev pan y'n guyrthys* 'I have sinned wondrous perversely when I sold the true blood of God' PC 1505–06

Martesyn te a lavar, fattellans bos gwyer? e vosama ow gweles an shap, an not an **gwyer gois** *agen arluth Christ?* 'Perhaps you will say, how can they be true? That I see the shape and not the true blood of our Lord Christ?' SA 62a

na ve y vose **guir sans** *mar lues merkyl dyblans byth ny russe* 'were he not a true saint, he would not have done so many manifest miracles' BM 2051–53

Meryasek del oys **guir sans** *lemen prest sav ov bevnans* 'Meriasek, as you are a true saint, now readily save my life' BM 2175–76 .

John Boson writes *Deiu guir* 'true God' BF: 55, and Gwavas writes *an Deu guir* 'the true God' LAM: 238. Earlier writers write *guyr dev* without lenition, and *gwyer Thew* with it. The lenited form is almost certainly correct. In revived Cornish 'true God of true God' of the Nicene creed has been translated as *gwyr Dew a wyr Dew*, for example in LPK: 23. In the light of the three instances of *gwyer Thew* in BK, this should perhaps now be emended to *gwyr Dhew a wyr Dhew*.

Hager 'ugly, foul'

This is used as an adjectival prefix:

*Kensa, vrt an **hagar auall** iggeva gweell do derevoll warneny* 'First because of the storms he causes to rise up against us' BF: 9

***Hager awell**, ha auel teag* 'Bad or foul weather, and fair weather' ACB: F f verso

*hena o **hagar vargayne*** 'that was a grim bargain' CW 791

***hager vernans** an par-na ef a'n gefyth* 'a hideous death like that he will get' RD 1984–85

*yn beys na allo den vyth gul **hager vernans** thy'mmo rak ow colon ow honan gans ov hollan me a wan* 'lest anyone in the world inflict a hideous death on me I will pierce my own heart with my knife' RD 2040–43

*ny rebue tus ongrasyas ha re vsias **hager gas** raffna ladra pur lues feyst* 'we have been graceless people and have used a foul case to ravage, to rob very many indeed' BM 2142–44

*yma ov tegensywe **hager gowes** war ov feth* 'a foul shower is threatening upon my faith' OM 1079–80

*ha saw ny gynes yn weth na'n beyn mar **hager thyweth** na mar garow* 'and save us with you as well that we do not have such a foul death and so violent' PC 2894–96

*govy na vuma war kyns **hager dyweth** yv helma* 'alas I was not aware before; this is an ugly death' BM 4099–100

*An **hagar musi** na ens vâze* 'The evil girls they are not good' BF: 58

*martezen (amedh ev) ma nebònen en nessa tshei, a 'ryg uelaz agen **hager oberou*** 'perhaps, he said, there is someone in the next house, who has seen our evil deeds' AB: 252a

*Ase rusta **hager prat**!* 'What a nasty trick you have played!' BK 84

*rag henna scon yz eth ef ze wrek pylat mayz ese han tebel el **hager bref** yn y holon a worre war y mester venions cref y to Ihesus mar laze* 'therefore quickly he went to Pilate's wife where she was, and the devil, foul reptile, put in her heart that severe vengeance would come upon her husband if he were to kill Jesus' PA 122bd

*Lebben an **hagar-breeve** o moy foulze avell onen veth ell an bestaz an gweale a reege an Arleth Deew geele* 'Now the evil serpent was more false than any one of the beasts of the field which the Lord God had made' Rowe

*henna vea **hager dra*** 'that would be a foul business' CW 259

*Gallas genaf **hager dowle*** 'I have suffered a nasty fall' CW 420.

Rowe uses the expression *hagar-breeve* five times. This is, of course, exactly the same word as *hager bref* in PA and it indicates that *p* is lenited to *b* after *hager* in this word at least; though *p* is unmutated in *hager prat*. It seems *b* becomes *v* after in *hager vernans* and *hagar vargayne*; *c* is lenited in *hager gas* and *hager gowes* while *t* is lenited in *hager dra* and *hager dowl*. The differing treatment in *hager thyweth* and *hager dyweth* is noteworthy.

Hager may be used predicatively:

*gouy vyth rak edrege bos mar **hager** ow gorfen* 'alas for regret that my end is so foul' PC 1529–30

***hager** lower os me avow* 'you are fairly hideous, I admit' CW 480

*blewake coynt yw ha **hager*** 'he is oddly hirsute and ugly' CW 1586.

It is also very rarely used after its noun:

*Ay a vynta ge orth mab dean pan vo gwryes a **slem hager** occupya rage sertayne ow rome* 'Do you wish that man, when he has been made of foul slime, should occupy my place indeed?' CW 254–56.

fals, falge 'false, perfidious'

This is used as a prefixed adjective:

*Me, Hirtacy, mightern Partys, a veth iwys orth Arthor, an **fals brathky*** 'I Hirtacy, the king of the Parthians, indeed will venture against Arthur, the treacherous cur' BK 2636–39

*pan faryng vs y'n temple gans ihesu an **fals brybor*** 'how are things in the temple with Jesus, the false vagabond?' PC 374–75

*An **fals brybours** dre bur tholowrs ru'm grug muscog* 'The false vagabonds by sheer affliction have driven me mad' BK 747–49

*Mar kowsyth moy a Arthor o'm goith ve, te **fals bribor**! neffra ny thibbryth bara* 'If you speak more of Arthur in my presence, you false vagabond! never shall you eat bread' BK 3185–87

*Yma in pov **falge cregyans** ov cul dym angyr an iovle* 'There is in the country a false belief that is giving me the devil's anger' BM 1161–62

*ihesu parde a nazare an **fals crystyon*** 'Jesus by God from Nazareth, the false Christian' PC 1111–12

*na ny gotha thetha settya in rag na mentenya **fals discans** thyn bobill* 'nor should they set out nor maintain false teaching for the people' TH 32a

*nyns a den vyth vynytha a'n keth re-na the'n tyr sans marnas calef ha iosue rag y the vynnas gorthye **fals duwow** erbyn cregyans* 'no one of those same will go to the Holy Land except Caleb and Joshua because they wanted to worship false gods contrary to belief' OM 1879–82

*Gwayt e worthya pub termayn ha nagh Astrot ha Jovyn ha'th **fals duwaw** in pub tu* 'Take care to worship him always and deny Astrot and Jove and your false gods on every side' BK 221–23

***Fals du** ema ow conys* 'He worships a false god' BK 399

*dyllyrf thy'nny baraban ny ol a'th pys dre the voth ha crous ihesu an **fals guas** yntre dismas ha iesmas* 'deliver to us Barabas, we all beseech you by your will and crucify Jesus, the false fellow, between Dismas and Jesmas' PC 2484–87

*Out warnogh wy **falge guesyon*** 'A curse upon you, you false fellows' BM 3803

*a **fals harlot** gowek pur* 'O false villain, utter liar' RD 55

*Te **falge horsen** nam brag vy* 'You false whoreson, don't threaten me' BM 3491

*my re gyrhas thy's the dre mab adam a[n] **fals huder** may hallo genen trege* 'I have fetched home to you the son of Adam, the false deceiver' OM 564–66

*re fethas an **fals ievan** hythyw ter-gwyth yn certan* 'he has conquered the treacherous demon three times today' PC 154–55

*rak **fals iudas** nep a'm guerthas ogas yma* 'for false Judas who has betrayed me is near' PC 1101–02

*ty re worthyas war nep tro an **fals losel*** 'you have worshipped on some occasion the false scoundrel' PC 2692–93 *gorreugh an **fals nygethys** gans abel a desempys the yssethe* 'put the false renegade immediately to sit with Abel' OM 914–16

*lauer thymmo ty lorden ay covs ty **falge negethys*** 'speak to me, you churl, of his words, you false renegade' BM 776–77

*da vye kyns dos sabovt dyswruthyl an **fals profes*** 'it would be good before the Sabbath comes to destroy the false prophet' PC 561–62

*Bethow ware a **fals prophettys*** 'Beware of false prophets' TH 19a

*Na'ra chee boaz **faulz teaze** bedn tha contrevack* 'Thou shalt not be a false swearer against thy neighbour' Rowe

*iudas ny gosk vn banne lymmyn dywans fystyne thu'm ry the'n **fals yethewon*** 'Judas is not seeping at all but is hastening immediately to betray me to the false Jews' PC 1078–1080.

It should be noted that as a prefix *fals-* does not appear to lenite a following consonant. *Fals* sometimes follows its noun:

*a pe danvenys thetha rag dyswruthyl der cletha an **anfugyk fals** na'm car* 'were he sent to them to destroy by the sword the false wretch who loves me not' BK 2722–24

*Modreth kyns ol y fynhas ahanowgh an darivyas, an **fykyl fals*** 'Modred first of all wanted account of you, the false hypocrite' BK 3264–66

***Iudas fals** a leuerys trehans dynar a vone en box oll bezens gwerthys* 'False Judas said, "Three hundred pence of money—let all the box be sold."' PA 36ab

*ha gwra avoydya talys nowith ha fanglys termys, ha bostow a **sciens fals*** 'and avoid new stories and fancy terms and boasts of false science' TH 18a

*a **dus fals** y redozyean purre laddron yn pow* 'from false men they had come, the veriest thieves in the country' PA 90d.

Fals- is sometimes used adverbially before a verb:

*ha genes mollat pup plu drefen **fals brugy** map dev map maria* 'and be accursed in every parish because you have falsely judged the Son of God, the son of Mary' RD 2198–200.

Otherwise 'falsely' is expressed in Cornish by the English borrowing:

*trueth vye den yw gulan **falslych** y vones dyswrys* 'it would be a shame for an innocent man that he should be falsely killed' PC 2437–38 *ef a whylas ihesu Cryst myghtern a nef ha **falslych** y'n iuggyas ef gans cam pur bras* 'he sought Jesus Christ, the king of heaven, and falsely he judged with very great injustice' RD 2261–64

*Mar pe oll an epscobow an bys re an par na, kepar dell esta se **falsly** ow reportia y the vos, pandra rug an sea postall a rome theth hurtya ge* 'If all the bishops in the world were like that, as you falsely report that they are, in what did the apostolic see of Rome hurt you?' TH 48.

*Yn fals 'falsely' is unattested.

Cam 'crooked, wrong'

Cam is an adjective meaning 'crooked, wrong'. It can be used attributively after its noun:

*A **consler cam**, pyth ew cusyl orth an wrusyl?* 'You crooked adviser, what's to be done against the insubordination?' BK 967–69

*ny vyn an vyl **harlot cam** awos an bys dywethe* 'the crooked scoundrel won't die for all the world' PC 2914–15

*a molath then **horsen kam** ha thage inweth gansa* 'Oh, a curse on the crooked scoundrel, and on you too with him' CW 806–05

*me a wra then **horsen cam** boos calassa presonys* 'I will make the crooked villain be more harshly imprisoned' CW 2037–38.

Cam is also used as a noun meaning both 'crooked person, criminal' and 'wrong, crime':

*syttyough dalhennow yn **cam** a leuer y vos map dev* 'seize the miscreant who says he is the son of God' PC 1125–26

*ma stryf yntre an thev **cam** ny wrons vry my the crye* 'there is a dispute between the two scoundrels; they don't care that I am calling' PC 2248–49

*ha falslych y'n iuggyas ef gans **cam** pur bras* 'and falsely he judged him with very great injustice' RD 2263–64

*A wek wegov agys mam thywhywhy y fye **cam** boys lethys am govys vy* 'O sweet sweets of your mother, for you it would be a crime to be slain for my sake' BM 1653–55 *yth ogh kerhys dymovy repreff na* **cam** *nygis beth* 'you have been brought to me; you will suffer neither reproof nor wrong' BM 1769–70

byth ny ra **cam** *the neb den gallus an iovle pup termen dretho a veth confundijs* 'never does it wrong to anyone; the power of the devil will always be confounded thereby' BM 2031–33

thynny prest y fye **cam** *mar ny rellen y gorthya* 'for us it would ever be a sin if we did not worhsip him' BM 3755–56

ymowns ow kull inivri ha **cam** *the crist* 'they commit hostility and wrong to Christ' TH 17a

a rug agan savyour, a supposta, inivry ha **cam** *an parna then stall po cheare an scribys han phariseis* 'did our Saviour, do you suppose, show hostility and wrong of that kind to the stall or chair of the scribes and the pharisees?' TH 48a

ha'm bos parys the sconya pub **cam** *der weras Jesu a'n prennas tyn* 'and that I am ready to reject all wrong by the help of Jesus who redeemed us dearly' BK 2028–30

"Eth esough why ow cul **cam** *thotho ef suer," e meth a* '"You do him wrong surely indeed" he said' BK 2232–33

Marya, an gwelha mam, in cheryta ragaf pys, ma'm bo gevyans ol a'm **cam** 'Mary, the best of mothers, in charity pray for me, that I may receive pardon for all my wrongdoing' BK 2827–29.

Cam- has been used as a prefix meaning 'crooked, wrong' since the Old Cornish period. One of the earliest compounds is the word *camniuet* 'yris uel arcus [rainbow]' OCV §436. The second element is *-niuet*, probably the plural of *nef* 'heaven'. The same word appears in Late Cornish as *Cabm-thavaz* (ACB: F f), where *cam* has been pre-occluded to *cabm-* and the second element has apparently been reshaped on the basis of the word *davas* 'sheep'. This is presumably as a result of the association of the rainbow with 'fleecy' clouds.

Here are some further compounds containing *cam-* as the first element:

An avel worth y derry wose my thy's th'y thefen ty re **gam wruk** *eredy* 'By plucking the apple after I had forbidden it to you, you indeed have sinned' OM 279–81

ty a **gam wruk** *yn tor-ma mes a egip agan dry* 'you did wrong now bringing us out of Egypt' OM 1646–47

ny the **gamwul** *y won guyr* 'I know truly that we have done wrong' PC 1065 *rak ty th'y* **gam worthyby** *ty a vyth box trewysy* 'because you answered him impertinently, you will get a nasty slap' PC 1268–69

yn ta ef re'n dyndylas pan **cam worthybys** *cayfascafus drok hag yfle grath* 'well he has deserved it, to reeive harm and revenge since he answered Caiaphas impertinently' PC 1402–04

ha gava tha ny gon **Kabmoth** [i.e. *cabmweyth*] 'and forgive us our tres-passes' Keigwin

camhinsic *injuriosus* 'injurious' OCV §306

camhinsic *injustus* 'unjust' OCV §403

henno myrnans in crowsse, dre paynys an parna gans **cammensyth** *procurijs* 'that was death on the cross by pains of that sort procured by injustice' TH 15

eff a suffras lyas kynde ha sorte a **kammynsoth** 'he suffered many kinds and sorts of injustice' TH 15a

tav se the vyn ty phelip rak pur wyr ty a **gam dip** *warnotho ef* 'silence your mouth, you Philip, for in truth you are mistaken about him' RD 995–97

may whrussons **cam dremene** *sur y vyllyk an prys* 'when they sinned surely they will curse the time' OM 337–38

as wrussough **cam tremene** 'how greatly you have sinned' RD 40

yma an apostyll pedyr ow leverall omma an very cawsse praga vgy tus ow **camvnderstondia** *scripture* 'the apostle Peter explains here the very cause that people wrongly understand scripture' TH 18.

It should be noted that *camhinsic* 'unjust' in Old Cornish and *cammensyth*, *kammynsoth* 'injustice' in Tregear are all based on *cam-* and the root **hins*, **hens* (Welsh *hynt* 'way', Breton *hent* 'way'). The simplex **hins*, **hens* is unattested in Cornish. Notice also that Lhuyd uses the expression *kabmdybianz* 'mistaken opinion' AB: 223, which is based on the verb seen in Tregear's *ty a gam dip*.

Cowl 'completely'

As an independent adverb *cowl* 'completely' usually appears as the disyllabic *cowal*:

vynytha ny efyth coul marrow **cowal** *ty a vyth* 'never will you drink soup; you will be completely dead' OM 2701–02 *ty a verow sur* **cowal** *awos the thev nay vestry* 'you will die completely in spite of your God and his power' OM 2737–38

er the pyn cousaf **cowal** *marth a'm bues a'th lauarow* 'I shall speak against you completely; I am astonished at your words' PC 2391–92

syns war the keyn an grous pren yma lour the saw thy'so pur **cowal** *ty a ynny* 'bear on your back your cross; sufficient for you is your burden—completely you will go on it' PC 2586–88

A'n mor the gela **cowal** *pur theffry ef a'n ystyn* 'from one sea to the other indeed it encloses entirely' BK 1199–200.

When used as a prefix the form is either *cowl-* or *col-*:

nebas lowre a vyth an gwayne pan vo genas **cowle comptys** 'little enough will the gain be when you have reckoned it all fully' CW 794–95

aban omma **cowle dyckles** *hag a paradice hellys me a vyn dallath palas* 'since I am entirely without resources and driven from paradise, I shall begin to dig' CW 1031–33

pur wyr leskys ef a vyth rag **cowlenwel** *both the vrys* 'in truth it will be burnt to fulfill the desire of your heart' OM 433–34

cresseugh **collenweugh** *kefrys an nor veys a dus arte* 'increase, also fill the earth with people again' OM 1211–12

yn lyfryow scryfys yma bos **collenwys** *lowene a ganow a'n fleghys da* 'in the scriptures it is written that joy is fulfilled from the mouths of good children' PC 435–37

lemyn na fo ol ow bouth **cowlynwys** *thy'mmo lemyn sav the voth the gy arluth bethens gruys yn pup termyn* 'now let not all my will be fulfilled for me, O Lord, but let your will be done at all times' PC 1037–40

y vothe re bo **collenwys** *genan ny pub pryes* 'may his will be fulfilled by us always' CW 2471–72.

ha penvo hy **cowle devys** *hy a vyth pub eare parys tha thone an oyle a vercy* 'and when it is fully grown it will ever be ready to bear the oil of mercy' CW 1938–40.

Lel 'loyal, true'

Lel 'loyal, true' is sometimes used predicatively after a noun:

> *travyth ny wreth gorthyby er byn* **dustenyow lel** 'you do not answer anything against reliable witnesses' PC 1317–18

> *hag ena gwrewh aga lyskye dowt dew genow tha1 serry mar ny wreen* **oblacon leall** 'and there burn them lest God be angry with you if we do not make true oblation' CW 1073–75

> *moyses mar sos* **profus lel** *rys yv thy'so dyogel ry dour thy'nny the eve* 'Moses, if you are a true prophet, you must give us water to drink' OM 1799–801

> *bersabe ov* **fryes lel** *rys yv gruthyl dyogel both agan arluth sefryn* 'Bathsheba, my faithful spouse, indeed it is necessary to do the will of our sovereign lord' OM 2187–89

> *guel yv vn den the verwel ages ol an* **bobyl lel** *the vos keyllys ru'm laute* 'upon my word better it is for one man to die than for the faithful people to be lost' PC 446–68

> *the vroder ov* **servont lel** *prag nagvsy ef genes* 'your brother, my loyal servant, why is he not with you?' OM 572–3

> *eugh ow dew el thu'm* **seruons lel** *yn pryson evs* 'go my two angels to my loyal servants who are in prison' RD 315–16.

More usually, however, *lel* is prefixed to both nouns and verbs. Here are some examples of prefixed *lel* as both an adjective and an adverb:

> *rak certan kemmys a'n crys ha a vo* **lel vygythys** *sylwel a wra* 'for certainly as many as believe him and are duly baptised he will save them' RD 1142–44

> *a pedar byth da the cher faste the gy the vreder yn* **lel grygyans** 'O Peter, be of good cheer; do you confirm your brothers in the true faith' RD 2367–69

> *henna yv an* **lel cregyans** *del deske sans eglos dyn ny* 'that is the true faith as holy church teaches us' BM 1319–1320

> *yth eseff prest ov cresy y vos* **lel du** *genys ay vam maria* 'I believe firmly that he is true God born of Mary his mother' BM 834–36

> *ef re thyndyles yn ta gothaf mernens yn bys-ma mara pethe* **lel iuggys** 'he has deserved to suffer death in this world, if he is properly judged' PC 1342–44

*del on ny the **lel bobil** devethys yth on warbarth rag enour* dis ha gorthyans 'as we are your loyal people we have come together for your honour and worship' BM 1173–75

*scryffes yma thym pub tra a thallathfas an bys ma may fova **leall recordys*** 'I have written everything from the beginning of this world that it may be truly recorded' CW 2171–74

*nefre me ny fanna cur marnes a vn ena sur du roy thym y **lel revlya*** 'never do I wish for a cure but of one soul surely; God give me to rule it rightly' BM 2845–46

*enoch yth ew owe hanowe **leal servant** than drengis tas* 'Enoch is my name, loyal servant to the Father, the Trinity' CW 2094–95

*der thowgys e tathorhas e honnyn par del vynnas, ha'y **lel servantes** dyspernys* 'through godhead he arose as he himself desired and his his loyal servants redeemed' BK 311–13

*Jesu Christ, mab Marya, roy thym gras the'th **lel-servya!*** 'Jesus Christ, son of Mary, grant me grace to serve you faithfully' BK 781–82

*me a goth in pur thefrye gorthya dew an **leall drengis*** 'I ought in very deed worship God, the true Trinity' CW 1955–56.

It is clear from *lel vygythys*, *lel grygyans*, *lel bobil* and *leall drengis* that lenition where possible was customary after *lel-*.

Lun, leun, luen, lene 'full, complete'

*ha the wull **lene amyndys** ha pe sufficiant raunsyn rag pehosow* 'and to make full amends, and to pay a sufficient ransom for sins' TH 12a

*the kekemmys na'm guello hag yn perfyth a'n cresso ow **len benneth** me a pys* 'for as many who do not see me but believe perfectly my full blessing I shall request' RD 1554–56

*pesef agys **leun vanneth*** 'I beg your full blessing' BM 211

*Meryasek welcum yn tre ham **luen vanneth** y rof zys* 'Dear Meriasek, welcome home and my complete blessing I give you' BM 216–17

*Tays ha mab han speris sans wy a bys a **levn golon*** 'Father and Son and Holy Spirit, you will beseech with your whole heart' PA 1a *mar pesy a **leun golon** whare sawijs y feze del vynna crist y honon* 'if he prayed with a full heart, straightway he would be healed, as Christ himself wished' PA 25cd

*ha henna sur my a greys a **luen colon** pur theffry* 'and that I believe surely indeed with my whole heart' OM 1263–64

*a thev a nef the pysy a **luen colon** gueres ny* 'O God of heaven—I beseech thee with all my heart—help us' OM 1607–08

*a bur fals dyscryggygyon tebel agas manerow na gresough a **luen golon** bos an tas dev hep parow* 'O you false unbelievers, wicked your ways, that you do not believe with all your heart that the Father is God without equal' OM 1855–58

*gorthyans the'n tas arluth nef a'm **luen golon** my a bys rag **luen gallosek** yw ef* 'glory to the Father, lord of heaven, I pray with all my heart, for he is wholly powerful' OM 2087–89

*pyiadow a **luen colon** a wor the ves temptacion na vo troplys y enef* 'pray with the whole heart puts temptation to flight that his soul be not troubled' PC 24–26

*gaf thy'm lemmyn yn tor-ma a **luen golon** me a'th pys* 'forgive me now at present, I beg you with the fullness of my heart' PC 1445–46

*me a'n pys a **luen golon** yeghes thy'mmo a thanfon* 'I will beg him with all my heart to send me good health' RD 1715–16

*ha fasta sy the vreder yn **luen grygyans*** 'and confirm your brothers in full faith' RD 1163–64

*eua war an beys meystry **luen gummyas** yma thy'mmo* 'Eve, I have mastery, full licence over the world' OM 409–10

*Me, Ethyon, duk Boecy, war the enmy a rys gans **lune devocyon*** 'I, Ethyon, duke of Boethia, will attack your enemy with full devotion' BK 2673–76

*rak me a wor lour denses marnes dre an **luen dvses** omma ny sef* 'for I know that much manhood will not stand here except through the full divinity' RD 2514–16

***luen dyal** war ol an beys ny gemeraf vynytha* 'full vengeance upon all the world I shall never take' OM 1233–34

*rag why re sorras an tas m'agys byth **luen edrege*** 'for you have angered the Father so that you will have full regret' OM 346–47

Dev a ros thy's an naw ran rag bewe orto certan dre y **luen grath** *ha'y versy* 'God gave you the nine parts to live on indeed through his full grace and his mercy' OM 493–95

guelas ow map y carsen a tas dre the **luen weres** 'I should like to see my son, O Father, by your full help' RD 442–43

Lowena ha **lune-rowath** *theso war ver lavarow* 'Joy and complete respect to you in few words' BK 1578–79

ihesu kyn wruk the naghe **luen tregereth** *me a pys* 'Jesu, though I did deny you, I beg full mercy' RD 1147–48
Lowena ha **lun yehas** *thu'm arluth ha gormolys* 'Joy and full health to my lord and praise' BK 2677–78.

It is apparent from the above examples that *a luen golon* was the customary way in Middle Cornish of saying 'with all one's heart'.
Lun- is not infrequently prefixed to verbs:

a'n beth the vos datherghys y **luen crygy** *me a wra* 'that you have risen from the grave, I will believe it fully' RD 481–82

yn wlas-na ow **len grysy** *tus yv tanow* 'in that land few men believe fully' RD 2461–62

pyv penagh a **len grysso** *yn weth bysythyys a vo a vyth sylwys* 'whoever believes fully and shall be baptised, will be saved' RD 2467–68

reys yv thy's ynno crysy ha **luen fythye** *yn teffry* 'you must believe in him and trust fully' OM 1508–09

rag y gerensa eff Du en tas ew **lene pacifies***, satisfies ha greis contentys gans mab den* 'for his sake God the Father is fully pacified, satisfied and made content with man' TH 10a

Maria mam ha guerhes me a vyn the **luenbesy** 'Mary, mother and virgin, I will beseech thee fully' BM 3591–92

E coyth thotha gothvas gras ha'y **lunworthya** *pub termyn* 'One should give him thanks and worship him fully always' BK 321–21

ha gans ow ru in ow thermyn me a'th **luenworth** 'and with my royal power in my time I worship thee fully' BK 1224–26.

Mur, muer 'great, grand'

Mur is sometimes used as an attributive adjective after its noun:

*ystyn quaral na relha erbyn Myghtern **Bretyn Veor*** 'lest he extend a quarrel agains the King of Great Britain' BK 1423–24

***laddron mur** us in pov ma lues den ov tustruya* 'there are great robbers in this country destroying many people' BM 2059–60

*rag y fynner mara kyller gans **paynys mer** ow dyswul glan* 'for one will, if possible, destroy me utterly by torments' PC 2600–02

***Trueth mur** yv ahanas* 'It is a great pity for you' BM 1992

*indelle te a alse gul **worschyp mur** theth nesse* 'thus you could provide great honour for your relatives' BM 2039–40.

It is also commonly used as a noun in the expression *mur a* 'much of, many of':

*anotha y ma notyes **mur a zadder** yn povma* 'much goodness is noted of him in this country' BM 188–89

*yn y golen fast regeth **mur a gerense** worzys* 'into his heart much love has gone towards you' PA 115c

*the vap den y tysquethas pur wyr **mur a kerenge*** 'to mankind he showed indeed much love' RD 2637–38

*may hillyn gwelas ha percevya fatell esa the crist **mer a garensa** worthan ny pan ruga suffra kymmys paynys ragan ny* 'so that we can see and perceive that Christ showed much love towards us when he suffered so many torments for us' TH 15a

***mur a onour** te a fyth te yw mygtern cvrvnys* 'much honour you shall have; you are a crowned king' PA 136c

*Mab marya **mur a beyn** a wozevy yn vr na* 'The son of Mary then suffered much pain' PA 54a

*hen o zozo **mur a bayn*** 'that was for him much anguish' PA 137d

*agys sperys sur an pren in anken ha **mur a beyn*** 'their spirit will pay for it indeed in misery and great torment' BM 1893–94

*serpent rag aga themptya **mer a bayne** es thyes ornys* 'serpent, for having tempted them much pain is ordained for you' CW 906–07 *my a re gans* **mur a ras** *whare lemyn strokyas vras* 'I will give quickly now with much grace great blows' PC 2715–16

mear a rase *thewhy sera* 'much thanks to you, sir' CW 702

Ko anberra der e derggawe gen **mear a worianze** 'Go into his gates with much worship' BF: 39.

It is also extensively used as a prefixed adjective:

ena ty a yl dysky martegen the vrys **mur dader** 'there you can learn, if it be minded, great goodness' BM 60–1

yma notijs sur ha covsis **mur thadder** *an keth den na* 'there is noted indeed and spoken much goodness of that same man' BM 2772–74

Ihesu crist **mur gerense** *ze vab den a zyswezas* 'Jesu Christ showed great love to mankind' PA 5a

iouyn roy theugh **mur onour** 'may Jove grant you great honour' PC 1712

The'n tas dev yn **mur enor** *war y alter my a wor grugyer tek hag awhesyth* 'To God the Father in great honour I place upon his altar a fine partridge and a skylark' OM 1201–03

my a's guyth gans **mur enour** *na vo harth den yn bys-ma kyn fe myghtern py emprour aga gorra alemma* 'I shall keep them with great honour so that no one in the world, be he even a king or an emperor, will be bold enough to remove them from here' OM 2051–54

Lowena thys corf heb par ha **mer honour** 'Joy to you, O person without peer' BK 72–73

try person in idn dewges ow kysraynya bys vickan in **mere honor** *ha vertew* 'three person in one godhead reigning together forever in great honour and power' CW 6–8

kyn fena lethys marow dre **mur peyn** *ha galarov ny'th tynahaf bynary* 'though I be killed dead by great torment and affliction, I will not ever deny you' PC 905–07

yn **mur payn** *pan y'th welaf ellas dre kveth yn clamder the'n dor prag na ymwhelaf* 'in great pain when I see you, alas for anguish in a faint why do I not fall down?' PC 2592–94

hag ena ow brodar cayne me an gweall ef in **mer bayne** 'and there my brother Cain, I see him in great torment' OM 1831–32

*Arluth a **ver ryelder**, the arghadow a vith gwrys* 'O Lord of great majesty, your command shall be done' BK 402–03

*Arluth ker thy's **mur worthyans** rag hyr lour ev ov bewnans* 'Dear Lord, to you much worship for long enough is my life' OM 847–48

*lemmyn cryst agan arluth **mur worthyans** thys del theguth worth agan dry alemma* 'now Christ our lord great worship to you as is fitting, bringing us out of here' RD 149–51

*The crist ihesu **mur worthyans** ha thys meryasek nefra* 'To Christ Jesu much worship and to you, Meriasek, forever' BM 3846–47

*An arlythy kepar dell goyth a the deffry pen ow arloyth th'y anterya, gans melody ha **mer worthyans*** 'The lords as is fitting will go indeed to bury the head of my lord with melody and great respect' BK 2903–08

***mear worthyans** theis ow formyer ha gwrear a oll an beyse* 'much worship to thee, my creator, and maker of all the earth' CW 1415

***mere worthyans** than drenges tase* 'great worship to the Trinity, father' CW 1940

***meare worthyans** thyes arluth nef* 'much worship to thee, Lord of heaven' CW 2478.

It seems that there is indeed a syntactic difference between *mur a gerense* 'much love' and *mur gerensa* 'great love', though the meaning is effectively the same. *Mur* is also used adverbially before a verb and a verbal adjective:

*du asota **mur presijs** dres ol breten heb awer* 'My God, how greatly praised you are throughout all Brittany freely' BM 230–31

***Mearthysaysys** of drys pub gyst* 'I am greatly afflicted beyond all joking' BK 1227–28.

pur 'pure, very'

When it is used attributively after a noun *pur* means 'pure, utter'.

*ny eve cydyr na gwyn na dewes marnes **dour pur*** 'he drank neither cider nor wine nor drink except pure water' BM 1969–70

*a pegh golhys dre **goys pur** wy a fya tek sawys* 'were you washed in pure blood, you would be cured beautifully' BM 1496–97 *en ezewon a arme* **treytour pur** *y vos keffys* 'the Jews kept crying out that he had been found an utter traitor' 119c.

It is also used attributively before nouns with the sense 'pure, sheer':

eff a suffras lyas kynde ha sorte a kammynsoth ha paynys intollerabill ha turmontys yn y **pur** *ha innocent* **corffe** 'he suffered many kinds and sorts of iniquity and unbearable pains and torments in his pure and innocent body' TH 15a

eugh yn fen ze bylat agis Iustis rag me an syns **pur zen** *len* 'go quickly to Pilate, your justice, for I consider him a pure honest man' PA 113ab

yth esen dre **pur hyreth** *war the lergh ovth ymwethe* 'we were for sheer longing pining for you' RD 1169–70

a **pur voren** *plos myrgh gal ty a verow sur cowal awos the thev nay vestry* 'O utter dirty wench, disreputable girl, you will die inspite of your God and his power' OM 2736–38

Reys o zozo dysquezas ze **pur treytours** *a zewle* 'he was compelled to show his hands to utter traitors' PA 157a

dre **pur natur** *ha reson pan wreth hepcor an bevnens hep guthyl na moy cheyson a hugh an eleth ha'n sens ty a thue the nef thu'm tron* 'by pure nature and reason when you relinquish life without making any more ado you will come to heaven to my throne above the angels and the saints' RD 458–62.

It is commonly used adverbially before adjectives to mean 'very':

A vroder ov banneth thy's rag the gusyl yv **pur tha** 'O brother, my blessing to you, for your counsel is very good' OM 1827–28

saw yma thym ahanes dowte **pur vras** *a anfugye* 'but I have very great fear of you of mischief' CW 575–76

gonys a wreugh **pur vysy** *thy'm del hevel fossow da gans lym ha pry* 'you will make for me very busily as it seems sound walls with lime and mortar' OM 2448–50.

Interestingly, Tregear does not use *pur* to mean 'very'. Instead he uses the English word itself:

Du a wellas pub kynd a ruga gull, ha yth ens **very da** 'God saw everything that he had made, and they were very good' TH 3 *fatell rug agan savyour govyn worth pedyr* **very ernysch**, *mar sega eff worth y gara eff moy ys onyn arell an aposteleth* 'that our Saviour asked Peter very earnestly whether he loved him more than any other of the apostles' TH 43–43a

ny a ra whare persevya nag o offence bean mas **very grevaws** *ha poos* 'we will soon perceive that it was not a small offence but very grievous and serious' TH 4

S Hierom inweth in y epistill the Damasus yma ow settya in mes **very notably** *an primasie* 'St Jerome as well in his epistle to Damasus sets out the primacy very notably' TH 49

S Ireneus martyr benegas in weth, **very ogas** *eff a ve then tyrmyn an abosteleth* 'St Irenaeus, a blessed martyr also, he was very near to the time of the apostles' TH 18a

han kyth tra na a yll bos prevys **very pleyn** *dre an scripture* 'and the same thing can be proven very plainly by means of scripture' TH 42a

Pan danger ewa the reylya in moyha spytfully a ylly bos, ha gans **very vylle** *termes ow Jestia gansa* 'What danger is it to rail most spitefully as possible and with very vile terms to make mock of it?' TH 55a.

Tregear also uses the English word very to mean 'very, self same' in such expressions as *y very corffe* 'his very body', *an very gyrryow* 'the very words', and *an very substans* 'the very substance'. This usage is found in BK and CW as well.

Revivalists, when using the word *pur* as a leniting prefix meaning 'very', pronounce the word with the same vowel as *pur* 'clean', i.e. with a fronted long [y:]. This, I believe, is probably a mistake. There has always been good evidence that *pur* 'very' had a reduced vowel, which was either schwa or short *o*. There is one Late Cornish example of *per*:

Nenna e eath car rag Frink rag debre an Tacklow ewe **per trink** 'Then he went away to France to eat the things that are very bitter' LAM: 226.

In Late Cornish 'very' is also sometimes written *por*:

Eth o ve **por loan** *tha gwellas why a metten ma* 'I am very glad to see you this morning' ACB: F f *verso*

Rag fraga an arleth ni ewe deawe **por tha** 'For why our Lord is a very good God' BF: 39.

Moreover Lhuyd makes it clear that the vowel of 'very' was schwa or a rounded vowel. Under *Optimus* 'best' he gives the Cornish forms as *Guella & guel'ha*, *por-dha* AB: 108c. In his Cornish Grammar he has two entries: **Por, pur** *and* **pyr**, *Very;* **Por-dhal**, *Very blind* AB: 232 and *Of Quality*. **Por**, *Very;* **Por dha** *and* **pordha** AB: 249. Lhuyd's *pur* in the entry from AB: 232 he has presumably got from the Middle Cornish written sources. Lhuyd also cites the sentence *Yma e* **pyr** *havel dhys* 'He is very like thee' AB: 142b, where *pyr* is a Lhuydian spelling for *por*. In the preface to his Cornish grammar, Lhuyd in his own Cornish writes *por* 'very' eleven times, inter alia in *por dha* 'very well', *por Spladn* 'very clear' and *por uir* 'very truly' (AB: 222–24).

Although Nance did not realize that prefixed *pur-* should have a reduced vowel, he himself used prefixed *por* < *pur* in Unified Cornish *porres* 'dire necessity, urgency', which derives from *pur* + *reys* 'necessity'. This is common in the texts; here are a few examples:

rag an lahys zynny es a vyn y dampnye **porres** 'for we have laws that will of necessity condemn him' PA 32c

Mas lemmyn rys yv **porris** *batayles kyns ys coske* 'But now it is very necessary to struggle before we sleep' PA 51a

rag sustene beunans thy'n rys yw **porrys** *lafurrye* 'to sustain life it is essential for us to work' OM 682-83

Eff a res **purris** *bos y very corfe eff hay gois in dede* 'It must of necessity be his very body and blood' TH 52

An Tas ha'n Mab der reson **porrys** *ew Du* 'The Father and the Son by reason must be God' BK 264–65.

It is also possible that *por* < *pur* occurs in the adverb *poran* 'exactly', but the second element is not clear. The pronunciation of Middle Cornish *pur* 'very' as *por* has now been amply corroborated by examples in BK:

Mars eugh the Arthor **por** *wyr* 'If you go to Arthur very truly' BK 1357

por *theffry ny vith kerys neb mar te va re venowgh* 'in very truth nobody is loved if he come too often' BK 1600–01

Bethans **por** *war!* 'Let him be very wary!' BK 1739

por *gentyll ew ha'y uos presyus hag honorys a ve va guyw* 'he is very noble and his blood is precious and it was worthily honoured' BK 2014–17

Henna ew kowsys garow hag a golan stowt **por** *wyer* 'That is roughly spoken and from a proud heart very truly' BK 2404–05 *neffra ny vith da e ger, na vith **por** wyer* 'never will his word be good, it will not very truly' BK 2762–63

*ha **por** harth the'n senators trybut Bretayn presant a in dyscharg thymmo nefra* 'and very courageously to the senators Britain's tribute, present it to discharge my debt for ever' BK 2840–42

*The leud desyr a'm cuth **por** wyer* 'Your lewd desire grieves me in very truth' BK 2952–53

*Ny thebbra' boys na nu'm deg troys, ny raf **por** wyr* 'I shall not eat food, nor shall foot carry me, I shall not in very truth' BK 2967–79

*Me a ra, syra, **por** wyr* 'I shall, sir, very truly' BK 3028

*Mar ny vethaf curunys, in tan **por** doun te a lysk* 'If I am not crowned, in very deep fire you will burn' BK 3095–96.

On occasion the scribe of BK writes *pour* rather than *por*. This suggests that the word may sometimes have been pronounced with a long [u:]:

*Ow lester a ve lehan drys mor **pour** thown* 'My vessel was a stone slab across a very deep sea' BK 94–5

*Pan desefsan bos an lorden **pour** galarak, grassa the Christ a re an pyst* 'When I should have thought that the fellow would be very wretched, the idiot gave thanks to Christ' BK 719–23

***Pour** awherak ha prederak ove, by God!* 'Very wretched and anxious am I, by God' 77–80.

This pronunciation is perhaps attested in BM also: *Plos marrek **pour*** 'utterly dirty knight' BM 2444, although here *pour* comes after its noun.

Sans 'holy'

Sans 'holy' as an attributive adjective usually follows its noun, in the expression *speris sans, spyrys sans, spuris sans, Speres zance, Spiriz Sanz* 'Holy Spirit' PA 1a, OM 85, BM 212, TH 5a, BF: 41, 56, etc., Lhuyd also writes *skryptor zanz* 'holy scripture' AB: 223. When used in conjunction with *eglos* 'church', however, the adjective *sans* is always prefixed:

*yth esough ov kuthyl ges a thu hag e **sans eglos*** 'you are making mockery of God and his holy church' PC 332–34 *aspyen gvas gans pors poys mar kyllyn den* **sans eglos** 'let us look for a chap with a heavy purse, a man of holy church' BM 1875–76

hythyv an dus **sans eglos** *pan lafuryens rag benefys ware y feth govynnys py lues puns a yl bos anethy grueys* 'today the people of holy church, when they labour for a benefice immediately is asked how many pounds can be made from it' BM 2826–30

te neb vgy ow defya ydols yth esas ow robbya **sans egglos** 'you who defie idols you rob holy church' TH 14a

in ascra agan mam **Sans egglos** 'in the bosom of our mother, holy church' TH 41

an dus coyth auncient ow tochya an primacie, bo an vhell ordyr a **sans egglos** 'the old ancient people concerning the primacy, or the high order of holy church' TH 46

Onyn an **sans egglos** *ew gilwis Vigilius a martyr* 'One of holy church is called Vigilius, the martyr' SA 64.

Notice also that John Boson prefixes *zans* to *Carrack* 'rock' in *Ma canow vee wor Hern gen Cock ha Rooz Kameres en* **zans Garrack** *glase en Kooz* 'My songs is about herrings by a boat and net taken in the holy green rock in the wood' BF: 43.

The different position of *sans* in *Spyrys Sans* but *sans eglos* may be a reflection of the usage in ecclesiastical Latin, where 'Holy Spirit' is usually *Spiritus Sanctus* but 'holy church' is *sancta ecclesia*, e.g. in the Apostles' Creed: *Credo in Spiritum Sanctum, sanctam ecclesiam catholicam* 'I believe in the Holy Spirit, the holy catholic church'.

Hen 'old', coth 'old', hyr 'long', cot 'short', gow 'falsehood'

Hen 'old' is not common in Cornish, being replaced in most contexts by *coth* 'old'. It does, however, occur once as an attributive adjective after its noun:

duen alemma verement brays ha byen **tus hen** *guelhevyn an pov* 'lets us go hence truly, great and small, elders, nobles of the country' BM 2927–29.

It occurs as a prefixed adjective only in words for 'grandfather, forefather.' We thus find:

avus **hendat** 'grandfather' OCV §129

whath kenthew ow **hendas** *cayne pur bad dean lower accomptys* 'yet though my grandfather Cain is a very bad man enough accounted' CW 1446–47

haw **hendas** *cayme whath en bew* 'and my grandfather Cain still alive' CW 1480

cayne whath kenthota ow **hendas** 'Cain, yet though thou art my grand-father' CW 1660

Rag kepar maner dell rug eff temptia agan **hendasow** *ny Adam hag eva* 'For just as he tempted our ancestors Adam and Eve' TH 3a

Ny a rug peha kepar hagan **hendasow**, *ny a rug an pith nag o da na mytt ragan the wull* 'We sinned as our ancestors sinned, we did that which was not good nor meet for us to do' TH 9a

abavus **hengog** 'great-grandfather' OCV §130

cayne ow **hengyke** *ew marowe* 'Cain my great-grandfather is dead' CW 1702.

Coth as a prefixed adjective occurs only, it seems, in the compound *cothwas* 'old fellow, old man':

hemma yv an keth ihesu a leuer y vos map dev map iosep an **coth was** *gof* 'this is the same Jesus who says he is the son of God, the son of Joseph the old fellow of a smith' PC 1693–95

Gans gweras ahanowgh why ow eskar a vith lethis, an **coethwas**, *my nu'm bues dowt* 'With your help my enemy will be killed, the old fellow, I have no doubt' BK 3246–48.

Nance says *hyr* is commonly used as a prefixed adjective, but the only example known to him would have been: *crist ker regyn danvoneys oma prest theth confortya kynth eses ovt[h]* **hyrpenys** 'beloved Christ has sent us here always to comfort you, though you be doing long fasting' BM 3883–85. A further instance of prefixed *hyr* is now known from *Scon te a vyth gorthybys heb* **hyrwyge** 'You will soon be answered without long delay' BK 152–53. Here *hyrwyge*, which is not otherwise attested, is apparently a compound of *hyr* 'long' and **gwega* 'to wind, to meander'; cf. *gweg* 'bindweed, vetch'; Welsh *gwyg* 'vetch', Bret. *gweg* 'vetch'.

Cot 'short' as a prefix is attested only in one phrase:

an moar brase yn **cutt termyn** *adro thom tyre a vyth dreys* 'the sea in a short time shall be brought round my land' CW 88–89 *yma thymma hyrathe bras rag gothevas pandra vea in* **cutt termyn** *ages negys* 'I have a great longing to know in a short time what your business would be' CW 590–92.

I can find no other examples of *cot* in this or other compounds.

Nance lists *gow* as a prefixed adjective, but this is a mistaken, since *gow*- is a noun, not an adjective. When used as a prefix it is rare, for it seems to be attested twice only. The first instance is Old Cornish **gouleueriat** *falsidicus* 'liar' OCV §424; and the second, *yma ree ov leferel heb ty vyth na* **govlya** *delyfrys der varia fetel ywa dyogel* 'some are saying without an oath or perjury that he has been delivered safely by Mary' BM 3739–42.

Rag, therag 'before'

The prepositions *rag* 'before' and *thyrag* 'before' are sometimes compounded with *leverel* 'to say' to give *ragleverel, theragleverel* 'to predict, to mention beforehand':

An seth yw **rag leueris** *as gwyskis tyn gans mur angus war hy holon* 'the predicted arrow struck her sharply with great grief upon her heart' PA 224ab

Trega suer ew an Spurys a ve **thyrag leverys** 'The Spirit, which was mentioned before, is a presence' BK 268–69

yma ynweth S paull ow scriffa the timothe hay exortya eff ernyssly in study an scriptur haw ry thotheff gans oll an rema an rulle **the rag leverys** 'St Paul also writes to Timothy and earnestly exhorts him in the study of scripture and gives him with all these the rule mentioned above' TH 18a

dell ew **therag leverys**, *eff a asas thynny lays rag synsy* 'as has been mentioned before he left us laws to keep' TH 40.

Lhuyd uses the expression *raglaveryz* 'aforementioned' seven times in the preface to his Cornish grammar. Lhuyd may well have heard *raglaveryz* (cf. *rag leueris* in PA) or it may a coinage of his own on the basis of Welsh *rhagddywedyd* and *rhagfynegi* 'to foretell, to mention before'.

Prefixed adjectives and adverbs borrowed from English

Bad 'bad'

Bad 'bad' occurs four times in *Jowan Chy an Hordh* (JCH §§31–320 in the expression *bad-ober* 'bad deed, crime'. It is also attested in the phrase *warlerth **badd** maner* 'in a bad manner' SA 65a and ***bad** dean* 'bad man' CW 1447. In these two cases it is not certain that we are dealing with true compounds, since both may simply be undigested borrowings from English.

Chyf 'chief'

Chyf 'chief' is widely used in Cornish as a prefixed adjective:

*Na rug Du dynvyn y **chyff apostill** pedyr the the rome* 'Did God not send his chief apostle to Rome?' TH 46a

*Me yv **chyff arluth** rohan* 'I am chief lord of Rohan' BM 1936

*Ith off gelwys costentyn in rome **chyff cyte** an beys emperour curunys* 'I am called Constantine, crowned emperor in Rome, chief city of the world' BM 2513–15

*poran in Rome, neb ew an pen ha **chife cyte** an bys* 'in Rome to be exact, which is the head and chief city of the world' TH 47a

*ov benneth thy's belsebuk del ose pryns ha **chyf duk*** 'my greetings to you, Beelzebub, as you are prince and chief duke' PC 1925–26

*yma ov conys thyuwhy **chyf guythoryon** ol a'n gulas* 'you have working for you the chief workers of all the kingdom' OM 2330–31

*henew the leverell, may fo agan **chiff ioye** ha delite settys in du* 'that is to say that our chief joy and delight should be set on God' TH 21–21a

*Rag an ena, an pith ew an **chyff part** a vabden* 'For the soul, that which is the chief part of man' TH 12

*whath an rema ew an **chiffe partys** anetha vs omma ow folya* 'still those which are the chief parts of them follow here' TH 36

*An **chiff poynt** a ra den tyrry charite ew murdyr* 'The chief way in which a man can break charity is murder' TH 27.

It is clear from the first two examples above that Rome was regularly in Middle Cornish referred to as *chyf cyte an bys* 'chief city of the world'

over 'over'

The English borrowing *over* was used adverbially as a prefix before verbs:

Arthur a vyn e vettya in hast ha'y **oversettya** 'Arthur wishes to meet him in haste and to overcome him' BK 2393–94

eff a rug **ouerwelas** *an dignite han beautye a sans egglos* 'he oversaw the dignity and the beauty of holy church' TH 31

the kafus an cure ha the **ouerwelas** *ha gouerna y egglos bys gorfen an bys* 'to obtain the cure and to oversee and govern his church until the end of the world' TH 41a

why am gweall, **overdevys** *yth ama warbarth gans bleaw* 'you see me, I am overgrown with hair' CW 1507–09

overdevys *oll gans henna yth os gans bleaw* 'moreover you are all overgrown with hair' CW 1604–05

defalebys ove pur veare hag **overdevys** *gans bleawe* 'I am greatly deformed and overgrown with hair' CW 1665–66.

It is likely that *casula* **ofergugol** 'chasuble' OCV §789 is a compound of Old English *ofer* 'over' and *cugol* 'hood' < *cuculla*.

At first sight the English word 'open' seems to be a prefix in **opyn guelys** *yv omma nag us du mas ihesu ker* 'it is openly seen here that there is not God but beloved Jesus' BM 4152–53. It is more likely, however, that *opyn* is a free-standing adverb that happens to be placed immediately before the verbal adjective. The same adverb occurs immediately after the verbal adjective in *kerys oys purguir gans du* **prevys open** *oma yv theragon in teller ma* 'you are very truly loved by God; it is openly proven here in this place before us' BM 675–77.

Conclusions

Nance is largely correct when he lists as the commonest prefixed adjectives *pur, bras, cot, cam, gow, gwyr, gwan, tebel, drog, fals, hager, hyr. Gow*, as we have seen, is not an adjective. Nance does not, however, mention *cowl-, lel-, lun-, mur* nor *sans* as prefixes. Neither does he cite either of the borrowings *chyf-* or *over-*, both of which are used as prefixed adjectives in the traditional language. This latter omission is presumably the result of his customary purism.

The examples from the texts cited above give us an insight into how the various prefixed adjectives and adverbs were used in the traditional language.

Probably the most important points for us as revivalists to remember are the following:

(1) that *drog-* 'bad' and *fals-* 'false' almost invariably precede their noun or verb. They do not follow. Furthermore neither of the two adverbs **yn fals* 'falsely' nor **yn trog* 'badly' is attested in the traditional language. 'Falsely' in Cornish is either *fals-* or *falslych*; 'badly' is either *drog-* or *tebel-*.

(2) that *pur* 'very' was pronounced with a short *o* or schwa, and in the revived language should perhaps be written *por.*

Abbreviations and sources

AB = Edward Lhuyd, *Archæologia Britannica* (London 1707, reprinted Shannon, 1971).

ACB = William Pryce, *Archaeologia Cornu-Britannica* (Sherborne 1790, reprinted Menston, 1972).

BF = O.J. Padel, *The Cornish Writings of the Boson Family* (Redruth, 1975).

BK = Graham Thomas and Nicholas Williams (eds), *Bewnans Ke: The Life of St Kea* (Exeter, 2007).

BM = Whitley Stokes (ed.), *Beunans Meriasek: The Life of St Meriasek, Bishop and Confessor, a Cornish Drama* (London, 1872).

Bodewryd MS = Andrew Hawke, 'A Rediscovered Cornish-English Vocabulary', *Cornish Studies: Nine* (Exeter, 2001), 83–104.

CF = *The Charter Fragment*, text from E. Campanile, 'Un frammento scenico medio-cornico', *Studi e Saggi linguistici* 60–80, supplement to *L'Italia Dialettale* 26.

CfA = R. Morton Nance, *Cornish for All: A Guide to Unified Cornish* (revised edn), Federation of Old Cornwall Societies, (St Ives, 1949).

CW = Whitley Stokes, *Gwreans an Bys: The Creation of the World* (London 1864, reprinted Kessinger Publishing, Montana, 2003).

Keigwin = John Keigwin's translation of *Genesis* 1, from Gwavas collection, British Library Add. MS 28554.

LAM = Alan Kent and Tim Saunders (eds), *Looking at the Mermaid: A Reader in Cornish Literature 900–1900* (London, 2000).

LPK = *Lyver Pysadow Kemyn*, Diocese of Truro (1980).

OCV = Eugene V. Graves, *The Old Cornish Vocabulary* (PhD thesis, Columbia University, 1962).

OM = 'Origo Mundi' in Edwin Norris, *The Ancient Cornish Drama* (London 1859, reprinted New York and London, 1968), i 1–219.

PA = Harry Woodhouse (ed.), *The Cornish Passion Poem in facsimile* (Penryn, 2002).

PC = 'Passio Christi' in Edwin Norris, *The Ancient Cornish Drama* (London 1859, reprinted New York and London, 1968), i 221–479.

RD = 'Resurrexio Domini' in Edwin Norris, *The Ancient Cornish Drama* (London 1859, reprinted New York and London, 1968), ii 1–199.

Rowe = J. Loth (ed.), 'Textes inédits en cornique moderne', *Revue Celtique* 23, 173–200.

SA = *Sacrament an Alter*, text quoted from an unpublished edition by D.H. Frost (St David's College, 2003).

TH = John Tregear, *Homelyes xiii in Cornyshe* (British Library Additional MS 46, 397), text from a cyclostyled text published by Christopher Bice (s.l. 1969).

4

Visitations of Cornish Churches, 1281–1331

Nicholas Orme

Introduction

From about the thirteenth century, the Church authorities visited parish churches to inspect them. The only records of this process relating to Cornwall before the Reformation relate to the visitations of fourteen churches and one manor belonging to Exeter Cathedral, made by representatives of the cathedral in 1281 and 1331. These records are valuable in providing evidence about church fabrics, ornaments, vestments, and books long before such evidence can be gathered from other sources such as churchwardens' accounts. This article analyses the two sets of records, showing how they relate to diocesan legislation about parish churches, and concludes that while few churches were perfect in terms of their possessions, virtually all were able to carry out their functions. A complete translation of the records is provided.

The visitation of religious houses and parishes by the Church authorities was a regular practice by the thirteenth century, with the aim of inspecting their possessions or monitoring their activities. Archbishops, bishops, religious orders, cathedrals, and archdeacons all acted in this way, but in the case of Cornwall very few of their operations have left any records. Some exist in relation to the Cornish monasteries, and these have been listed and discussed in print.[1] For the parish churches, on the other hand, only two sets of visitation documents survive from before the Reformation, carried out by representatives of Exeter Cathedral in 1281 and 1331.[2] These visitations were limited to the fourteen churches and one manor in the county over which the cathedral had patronage or jurisdiction, but in the absence of comparable records, they are invaluable in giving us an insight into the likely state of churches and parishes more widely. They provide evidence about the condition of church buildings;

the ornaments, vestments, and books that churches possessed; and, especially in the case of the earlier visitation, the properties and revenues of the clergy: houses, glebes, tithes, and offerings.

The visitation of 1281 took place in June, and was undertaken by Richard de Brendesworth and Gilbert de Tyting[s], canons of the cathedral, on behalf of its ruling body, the dean and chapter. They visited eight places beginning with Veryan, presumably because they started from Penryn, the Bishop of Exeter's base in west Cornwall, after staying there at the bishop's manor house or at Glasney College. From Veryan they travelled in an anticlockwise loop to St Winnow (including the chapel of St Nectan), Altarnun, St Breward, St Issey, Perranzabuloe, Gwennap, St Erth, and finally the manor of Methleigh in Breage. The visitation of 1331 was carried out by a single cathedral canon, Richard Braylegh (later the cathedral dean), after Easter in 1331. He started at Altarnun having presumably travelled there from Exeter, and toured Cornwall clockwise, passing through St Winnow (including Boconnoc, Bradoc, and Respryn), Veryan, Gwennap, Constantine, Mullion, Sancreed, St Erth, Gwinear, Perranzabuloe (including St Agnes), St Issey, and St Breward. The difference in the places visited is explained by the fact that the cathedral had disposed of Methleigh by 1331, but had acquired the churches of Constantine, Gwinear, Mullion, and a greater stake in Sancreed since 1281.

Why do we possess only these two visitations of Cornish parish churches and chapels? The answer is that if bishops kept records of such matters, they have not survived. The main responsibility for inspecting churches, however, belonged to archdeacons: in this case the Archdeacon of Cornwall, who was expected to visit them annually either in person or through a representative. It may well be the case that the archdeacons made notes of what they found and ordered to be done, and the cathedral visitation of 1331 hints at this in the cases of Sancreed and Veryan.[3] Notes of a visitation survive from the archdeaconry of Totnes in Devon in 1342,[4] but these are the only such record from the diocese of Exeter before the Reformation, no doubt because archdeacons did not have facilities to keep permanent archives. The cathedral was better organized in that respect, hence the survival of its two visitation records for Cornwall and some others for its parishes in Devon. It is not known how often the cathedral clergy made visitations of the churches belonging to them. Allusions are made in 1331 to previous inspections of Gwennap and Mullion, although they may refer to ones carried out by the archdeacon, and visitation records survive for some of the cathedral's churches in Devon between 1301 and 1320. This makes it possible that such events took place in Cornwall more often, but equally there were probably special circumstances in both 1281 and 1331. On the first occasion, a new Bishop of Exeter, Peter Quinil, had just taken office. On the second, the Bishop, John Grandisson, had been in office for four years, but he—like Quinil—was a conscious reformer, and it looks as if both bishops were appraising their dioceses and anxious to ensure that its churches and clergy were functioning properly. They may well have asked the cathedral to take its share of this enterprise in the parishes that it owned.

The cathedral had power over its Cornish churches in two and sometimes three ways. First of all, it was patron of all the churches visited by the canons, except for Boconnoc and Bradoc which, although daughter churches of its church of St Winnow, had their own lay patrons. As patron, the cathedral appointed the clergy to all the other churches concerned. Secondly, it had a peculiar jurisdiction over the churches of Perranzabuloe (with the chapel of St Agnes) and St Winnow (including the churches of Boconnoc and Bradoc along with the chapels of St Nectan and Respryn). These churches and chapels had been removed from the ordinary administration of the diocese in the late twelfth or early thirteenth century, and were governed for most religious purposes by the cathedral authorities, not by the Archdeacon of Cornwall. All but one of the cathedral's remaining churches (Altarnun, St Breward, St Erth, Gwennap, and Veryan in 1281, to which Constantine, Gwinear, and Mullion were added by 1331) formed part of the archdeaconry and came under the archdeacon's supervision. The exception was St Issey, which was a peculiar under the control of the bishop, although the church was owned by the cathedral. The third dimension of power was an economic one. All the churches (excepting Boconnoc and Bradoc) were appropriated benefices. This meant that the dean and chapter were technically the rector of each parish and enjoyed all the rights and revenues (the 'rectory') belonging to its church. The dean and chapter, of course, could not themselves do the clergyman's duties, so they appointed a vicar (a term meaning 'deputy') to serve the parish, his rights and revenues being known as the 'vicarage'. Broadly speaking, the cathedral took as the rector's perquisite the 'great tithes' or 'tithes of sheaves' from the parish: every tenth sheaf of grain that was grown, whether of wheat, barley, or rye. The vicar received the 'lesser tithes' of other produce (chiefly hay, legumes, animals, and fish) and the offerings and dues owed by parishioners that were known as the 'altarage' (*altilagium*).

The information of 1281 is generally fuller than that of 1331. It begins in each parish with an inventory of the church's possessions. This includes the fabric of the chancel, because according to canon (Church) law, the duty of maintaining the chancel belonged to the rector, in this case the cathedral. In fact, the cathedral often devolved this duty wholly or in part to the vicar and the parishioners, but the chancel was the most important part of the church where services took place, and the cathedral was evidently anxious that chancels be kept in good order even if others were responsible for them. The visitors did not usually pay attention to the nave, transepts, or side-chapels of the church beyond the chancel. Canon law required these areas to be maintained by the parishioners, although one feels that the cathedral should have exercised oversight of them in the case of Perranzabuloe and St Winnow, since it was replacing the role of the archdeacon. Nor were the visitors interested in the fittings in the church because these were also the concern of the parishioners, except that in some places orders were made that fonts should have locked covers and in one case (Veryan) that desks (seats for the priest and parish clerk) should be placed in the chancel. In consequence, we hear nothing about rood screens or church seating. This is a pity, because it would be helpful to know the dates at which these familiar features of churches made their appearance. The likelihood is that they were both in existence by the late thirteenth century. The word 'chancel', which came into usage by the early part of the century, is derived from the Latin word for an enclosure (*cancellus*), and implies that screens of some kind go back to at least about 1200, long before the earliest surviving examples. The same may be true of seats. They were to be found in some churches by 1287, when Bishop Quinil of Exeter convened a diocesan synod at which detailed regulations were issued about all aspects of church life. One of these was prompted by disputes that had arisen about seats, even leading to blows. Accordingly, the synod ordered that no one should claim a seat in a church except for church patrons or people of noble rank, but that those who first entered the church to pray should choose where they sat.[5]

By at least the early thirteenth century, the Church authorities tried to ensure that parish churches were properly supplied with materials for worship. An incomplete account of legislation issued by a synod organized by Bishop Brewer in Exeter diocese between 1225 and 1237 states that each church should possess a silver chalice for use at mass, other decent vessels, suitable linen and ornaments, appropriate service books, at least two sets of vestments, and a stone font.[6] Bishop Quinil's synod of 1287 went into much greater detail in this respect, but in doing so it was evidently only adjusting rules that had developed since Brewer's time rather than taking a wholly new initiative, because most of its stipulations are to be found in the visitation of 1281. Quinil's requirements encompassed about forty-five categories of equipment.[7] Beginning with the building, they ordered that the chancel and nave should both be lit with glazed windows. No reference was made to the provision of a high altar, which was evidently taken for granted, but mention was made of the possible existence of other altars. The high altar was to be dignified and protected by a canopy above it, and to display a pyx of silver or ivory with a lock. This was a small box, suspended below the canopy and containing a consecrated wafer, hence the lock for its protection. Each altar was to possess a frontal: a decorative cloth hanging down in front of it. Statues were to be placed at each end of the high altar: the patron saint at the north end and the Virgin Mary at the south. At the west end of the church, there was to be a stone font with a locked cover, because it always contained holy water to be ready for baptisms, held in this era on the day of a baby's birth.

For the celebration of services, the church was to have a chalice of silver or gilt for the wine of the mass and a paten to hold the wafer of bread. A cup of silver or tin was prescribed for use in the giving of communion to the sick, together with two corporals (linen cloths on which the bread and wine of the communion were placed during the service), and four towels for the high altar and for each other altar, of which two had to be blessed and one to have decorative apparel. Articles of dress for the clergy included two surplices (linen garments with wide sleeves, for the priest), a rochet (similar to a surplice but with close-fitting sleeves, for the parish clerk), and two sets of vestments (embroidered garments): one set for ordinary days and one for festivals. These would have comprised a close-fitting linen alb, a linen amice (or hood), and a chasuble, stole, and maniple to wear over them. Finally in the category of fabrics there had to be two veils: a small nuptial veil to be made available for brides at weddings, and a large Lenten veil for hanging in the chancel during Lent.

Parish clergy read their services from books, unlike monks who learnt them by heart. The synod of 1287 required each church to have a missal (containing the material for mass), and various books for the eight services that every clergyman (like monks) had to say every day of the year. These books did not include the breviary which contained the basic material for the eight services, because the priest was expected to provide his own copy. However, they had to comprise various supplementary texts, some of which were likely to be written within the same volume as others. Such texts consisted of a psalter (incorporating the psalms, sung through every week), an antiphonal (texts sung before and after psalms), a venitary (the psalm *Venite* sung at matins), a gradual (texts sung after the first lesson at matins), a troper (other texts sung at mass or matins), a hymnal (hymns sung at matins and other services), a collectar (collects or prayers for the day, said at mass and in the daily services), and a legend (longer passages from the Bible and from the Lives of the Saints, read at matins each day). The legend was in two parts and often two volumes: the legend of time, which was arranged according to the calendar of the Church year beginning in Advent, and the legend of saints with the readings for saints' days. Finally, there had to be an ordinal: a guide to the material to be used on any particular day of the year.

Despite this detail, the synod did not specifically mention two texts that appear in the visitation records and must also have been necessary. One was the capitulary, containing 'chapters' or short Bible passages read at services other than matins, and the other was the processional providing texts to be said or sung during processions. Nor did the synod prescribe the 'use' that the liturgical texts should follow. Service books at this date were not uniform as they became under the Church of England in 1549, and there were variations of detail in different parts of England and between parish churches and religious houses. The visitation of 1281 makes three references to books of the 'Use of Sarum' at Gwennap, St Issey, and Perranzabuloe. This was the format of services as they were observed at Salisbury Cathedral: a format that coming into general use throughout the province of Canterbury (southern and midland England) at this time. Quinil's synod forbade the use of monastic service books in parish churches. That this was a real issue is shown by the fact that, in 1281, St Erth owned a text following the usage of an unnamed religious order, and Gwennap an old antiphonal of the use of 'Merton', meaning Merton Priory, an Augustinian house in Surrey. This priory had a small dependent house at Tregony, which would explain how one of its service books came to be found in Cornwall.

The synod specified other kinds of equipment. The chrismatory was a box or vessel containing holy oil for baptisms and the anointing of the sick; this was to be of tin and to be locked. The pax was a disc painted with a picture of Christ and mounted on a rod; this was kissed by the priest after the consecration of the bread and wine at mass, and taken by the parish clerk around the church to be kissed by the congregation. Three cruets were required (for containing water, wine, and oil) along with a vessel for holding incense, a thurible for burning it, a vessel for holy water, a large candlestick and candle for the Easter season, two crosses—one fixed and one portable, and two processional candles. Sets of small bells were stipulated for ringing at mass, taking communion to the sick, and bringing the bodies of the dead to church. Two lamps or lanterns were required, with slightly different Latin names (*lucerna* and *boeta*); one may have been a lantern for the priest to take at night when visiting the houses of the sick or dying. Further items included a bier on which to carry the dead, a pall or cloth to cover their bodies, and a hearse (at this time a frame to hold candles, placed around the bier while the bodies lay in church). Finally, there had to be an immovable stone tabernacle (apparently a cupboard at this period, for housing the consecrated wafers used for giving communion to the sick, the chrismatory, and perhaps other ornaments), a box for offerings of money, and a chest for storing the books and vestments. All the items mentioned above had to be provided by the parishioners, except for the books needed for matins, the canopy over the high altar, and the chancel windows. These were the responsibility of the clergyman of the parish: the rector or vicar.

The findings of the visitation of 1281 can be divided into those that relate to chancels and to the church equipment. In four of the churches, the chancels were satisfactory in terms of their roofing and windows. These were Gwennap, St Issey, Veryan, and St Winnow. At St Breward, the roof was sound but the chancel was dark, presumably because windows were partly boarded up through lack of glass. Altarnun was less well roofed and St Erth badly so, as well as lacking whitewash inside and glass in one of the windows, while Perranzabuloe was also less well roofed and fenestrated. The parishioners of churches had to raise money each year through fund raising or donations to finance their own responsibilities of church maintenance. This money was known as the church 'store', and in Exeter diocese parishioners were expected to pay a tithe of it each year to the rector or vicar.[8] The tithe was apparently meant as a contribution to chancel repairs, but some communities refused or neglected to pay it: Altarnun, St Breward, and Perranzabuloe in both 1281 and 1331. The visitors therefore took the view that such communities should make a separate contribution to chancel maintenance. As for the equipment, the visitors found small defects at every church. Some items were worn or missing, but in no case was there a serious deficiency of what was needed for services. The impression given is that most churches were able to function at least minimally and often better: needing to be monitored in terms of their books and ornaments rather than subjected to serious remedial measures.

The 1281 visitation is illuminating about the revenues in each parish that belonged to the rectory (taken by the cathedral) and to the vicarage. The chief resource of the rectory, as already mentioned, was the tithes of grain to which were usually added two or three acres of the glebe, or 'sanctuary' as it was often known in Cornwall and is called in the visitation. The glebe was the group of fields belonging to the clergyman in each parish, most of which were assigned to the vicar. The acres reserved to the rector may once have been intended to support a local man who could deputize for the cathedral in collecting and storing the tithes of grain, but in practice these acres were often rented for money. Occasionally the cathedral also took a proportion of the income of the vicar when this was considered to be too large: 10s. at St Erth, £1 6s. 8d. at Gwennap, and £4 at Perranzabuloe. The economic management of the rectories involved a practice then known as 'farming', which we would call 'leasing'. Each of the cathedral canons had the right to be appointed as 'farmer' of one or more of the cathedral's rectories, with responsibility for administering the rectory revenues. He collected the tithes, rents, and other dues, and sold the tithes, unless he employed someone else to do these tasks on his behalf. From what he collected, he paid the cathedral an agreed amount every year, so that it had an assured and predictable income, and he usually had the duty of maintaining the property of the rectory: the church chancel, the clergyman's house, and buildings such as barns. The surplus after these outgoings belonged to the canon, who thus expected to make a profit from his 'farm'.

The most valuable of the cathedral's rectories in Cornwall was Perranzabuloe, a large parish including St Agnes and valued in 1281 at £43 plus odd shillings and pence. In descending order the others were St Issey (£28), St Erth (£27),

Veryan (£26), Altarnun (£24), St Breward (£20), St Winnow (£13), and Gwennap (£12). The parish vicars received much less; indeed they were rather poorly remunerated. The best paid was the vicar of St Breward with £10. His counterpart at Veryan had once received the same, but there part of the earnings came from fish tithes which had fallen because of a dearth of catches, so the total was somewhere between £5 and £10. The vicars of Gwennap and Perranzabuloe received £9, but the latter had to pay two parish chaplains which would have left him with very little. The income at St Erth and St Issey was £6, and at Altarnun and St Winnow £5. These sums were not far above the basic salary of a hired chaplain which Quinil's synod was to set at £3.[9] It is interesting to compare these figures, which are probably accurate, with those reported a few years later in 1291 when the whole Church in England was assessed for taxation purposes by the pope—an assessment subsequently used also by the English king for raising money from the clergy. This assessment, known as 'the Taxation of Pope Nicholas', was made by panels of clergy who erred on the side of leniency, so that the rectory of Veryan was valued at £10, Altarnun £8, St Breward, Perranzabuloe, and Gwennap £7, St Issey £6, St Erth £5, and St Winnow £2. In the case of the vicarages, Altarnun, St Issey, Perranzabuloe, and Veryan were assessed at £2 plus odd shillings and pence, and St Breward, St Erth, Gwennap, and St Winnow at £1 or a little more.[10] The figures of 1291 were used for taxing the clergy up to 1535, but the visitation made ten years earlier shows that that the figures were very inadequate. Still, this helped the vicars, since the tax was levied at ten per cent, meaning that they paid only 2s. or 4s. from their incomes.

Most of the information about the Cornish churches is what one might expect to find about any parish in England. There are, however, three references to local saints. Veryan possessed 'one little bell of St Symphorian', its patron saint. He was a Roman martyr, but one wonders if the bell was of a later 'Celtic' kind like that of St Piran, mentioned below. Altarnun had 'the Life of St Nonn [*Nonnite*] [and of] St David' appended to the 'ordinal' or guide to services. Nonn was the patron saint of the church and, in Welsh hagiography, the mother of David. No Life of her survives, other than mentions of her in those of David, and the loss in this case is regrettable because it might have contained legends about both saints that were current in Cornwall.[11] The biggest array of information about a Cornish saint relates to Piran at Perranzabuloe. Here there were several relics associated with him: his head, kept in a locked reliquary; his body, preserved in a shrine; his silver bowl; his pastoral staff worked with silver, gold, and precious stones; and his little copper bell. At certain times, although it is not known on which days, the relics of Piran were carried around the parish and apparently into neighbouring areas, perhaps to promote healing and certainly to gather donations.[12] The vicar of the parish received the donations from these tours, whereas the parishioners had a share of the offerings made in the offertory box in the church, a share estimated to be worth 30*s*. or 40*s*. per annum.

The visitation of 1281 concluded with an inspection of the manor of Methleigh in Breage. This was the only piece of land in Cornwall owned by the cathedral, apart from the glebes of its parish churches. It seems to have belonged to the bishops of Exeter in about 1100, but they apparently lost possession of it until it was regained by Bishop Robert II in about the 1150s. He conveyed it to the cathedral in or after 1158, with the remark that his predecessors had not owned it 'for the past forty years and more'.[13] The manor was in a pastoral landscape where sheep farming was important, and most of its fourteen tenants paid a fee known as *scyphild*, apparently meaning 'sheep hold', as a due levied on the rearing of sheep or in return for allowing them to graze on the manor pastures. Some of them also rendered sheep as a payment. There was a mill on the manor, which was let for 24*s*. per annum. The estate was leased to a farmer, probably a canon as with the churches, and was said to be worth over £11 per annum. However, because of its remoteness from Exeter or the complexity of its tenancies and management, the cathedral canons decided soon after 1281 to dispose of it. In 1284, they conveyed it to a local knight, Serlo de Lanhadron (or Nansladron), in exchange for the church of Constantine.[14]

The visitation of 1331 differs in some respects from its predecessor. It gives a full account of churches only in the cases of Perranzabuloe and St Winnow, the two churches within the cathedral's peculiar jurisdiction. Even here, the record lacks the detailed account of glebes and revenues given in 1281. Apart from the condition of the churches and their contents, the visitor at St Winnow noted the ruinous state of the house of the rector of Bradoc and the fact that the vicar of St Winnow was receiving ludicrously small tithes from the five mills in his parish, apparently through his laxness or timidity. At Perranzabuloe there was another example of a dispute over the maintenance of the chancel, because the parishioners did not pay tithe on their church store. They were willing to pay the tithe if the cathedral and vicar would take full responsibility for the chancel, or as an alternative, would allow them to fix collecting boxes in the church to finance chancel maintenance. The visitor added as a comment, 'Hitherto, the parishioners have carried the relics of St Piran inordinately to various and remote places, as previously'.

Apart from these issues, the visitation of 1331 discovered the usual kinds of defects in chancels, church ornaments, and service books. However, it did not make thorough inventories of them as was done in 1281. This time, there is a stronger sense of the archdeacon's duty to correct what was amiss, and sometimes shortcomings are simply described in general as something for him to sort out. At Altarnun, the visitor commented that 'it belongs to the archdeacon of the place to visit and make correction concerning these [chancel repairs] and other defects'. At Constantine, 'there are many defects in the church, which are to be repaired by the visitation of the archdeacon'. At Sancreed, 'there are there some defects to be corrected by the visitation of the archdeacon'. Churches whose failings were specified included Altarnun, where the chancel east windows lacked glass; St Erth, the victim of burglars who had entered the church, 'taking away a chalice, books, wax, and other things'; Gwennap, with poor roofing and inadequate windows; St Issey, where the chancel was dilapidated; and Veryan, with another dark chancel. At Mullion, the visitor noticed the poverty of the vicar's endowment, to which his attention was apparently drawn by local people. A problem with this endowment had been noted in 1310, when it was defined by Bishop Stapledon. As usual he assigned the vicar most of the glebe, small tithes, and offerings, but ordered this to be supplemented by a payment of £1 6s. 8d. per annum from the cathedral exchequer. Evidently this extra money was not sufficient.[15]

The state of the churches of Cornwall, as recorded in 1281 and 1331, is very much what one would expect. The Church authorities had laid down requirements for the maintenance of buildings and the provision of materials for holding services. Most of the necessary items were in place, but they were not always in good condition and some were lacking. The responsibility for this lay variously with the cathedral canons as rectors of the churches, the particular canons who farmed the church revenues, the vicars, or the parishioners. There were also some examples of good practice. In 1281 the manor of Methleigh was in a better state than the canon-farmer had received it. He had built a good house there, partly roofed with stone. At Veryan in 1331 a former farmer, Bartholomew of St Laurence, had built a new clergy house with a hall, chamber, garderobe, cellar, and kitchen. In the same year at Gwinear, everything was 'in a good state'. One hears mentions of discontent and illegalities. In 1281 a local knight was accused of taking away tithe corn from St Winnow that belonged to the cathedral. In the same year, a man at Gwennap who had given property to support masses at the chapel of St Day, had withdrawn his gift because the masses were not being said. In 1331 there were the report of the burglary at St Erth and complaints at Perranzabuloe about a piece of land, presumably glebe, from which local people were no longer allowed to take turf or furze for fuel. In three parishes already mentioned the community was refusing to pay tithe from the church store, and the visitors were pressing them to make contributions to the upkeep of chancels. We are reminded of how cellular the Church has always been: differing from parish to parish. The authorities tried to monitor the parishes and succeeded to an extent, but they were never able to ensure that every parish was well administered in all respects at every time.

1. VISITATIONS MADE IN 1281

(Translated from the Latin text in Exeter Cathedral Archives, D&C 3672A)

[f. 1r] Visitation of the manors [and churches] belonging to the church of the Blessed Peter of Exeter made by Sirs Richard de Brendesworth and Gilbert de Tytyngs in the year of grace 1281.[16]

[f. 7v] **Survey [*extenta*] and visitation made at Veryan [*Elerky*]**

There is there one silver chalice wholly gilt, of the weight of 20s.[17] Three adequate [*sufficientia*] sets of corporals. Twenty towels blessed and two not blessed. One frontal of one cloth of raines [*reyns*].[18] Three adequate surplices and two rochets. Also one pyx of ivory for the eucharist with a lock. A tin chrismatory without a lock. A good and suitable tabernacle. Four adequate tin cruets. An adequate font with a lock. Also one very suitable [*competens*] processional cross of metal and another old one of metal. One adequate banner. One old and unbecoming vessel for holy water. Two candlesticks of tin. Two adequate thuribles. Also one capitulary for the office of the dead. Also two adequate bells. Also a little bell of St Symphorian. Also one small ring with bells. Two small bells. Also one adequate missal with a gradual not notated.[19] One gradual adequate in itself and another old and inadequate. Two adequate tropers with one processional. One manual with an adequate collectary. One ordinal adequate for mass. One good antiphonal with a collectar, capitulary, hymnal, venitary, and psalter in one volume. One legend of the saints inadequate in itself. A legend of time, of no value. One old and less adequate psalter. One good locked chest for storing the ornaments of the church. A good chancel well fenestrated [f. 8r] and well plastered and well roofed. One iron box for making offerings.

An inquisition [was] made there through Thomas de Trempole, Roger de Tredenyl, Paul de Treuylry, William Lippe, Philip the clerk of Veryan [*Elerky*], and William le Marescal, who say that the vicarage consists of all the altarage and has all the sanctuary [*sanctuarium*] except for three English acres which belong to the rectory [*personatum*], which sanctuary contains by estimation one half of a Cornish acre,[20] and the whole vicarage with the sanctuary except for the tithe of fishes is worth 100s. [£5].[21] The tithe of fishes was wont to be valued at 100s. per annum at one time, and because there is a deficiency of fish they do not know how to estimate it now. Also to the rectory belong three acres as has been said and one house with a curtilage which return 3s. annually. Also the tithe of sheaves is worth 40 marks [£26 13s. 4d.] per annum. Total £26 16s. 4d.

Survey and visitation made at St Winnow [*Sanctum Wynnocum*]

There is there one silver chalice gilt inside and all black outside of the weight of 16*s*. Two sets [*paria*] of corporals. Two adequate sets of vestments. Four towels blessed and two not blessed. One surplice, no rochet. One pyx of ivory bound with silver for the eucharist without a lock. A wooden chrismatory suitable enough, with a lock. A small tabernacle. Three tin cruets. An adequate font with a lock. Also one wooden processional cross, less well adequate, and no cross of metal. No banner. One Lenten veil. One inadequate thurible. No candlestick. One earthenware vessel for holy water. Also one adequate missal. One adequate gradual with a troper. Also one adequate troper. One manual. Also another manual, less adequate. No ordinal in itself. One good legend in two volumes. One good antiphonal with a capitulary, collectar, hymnal, and psalter. One psalter with a hymnal. Also two bells. Two small bells. Also a suitable small ring with bells. Also a chancel well fenestrated and roofed. One iron box for making offerings. One chest for storing ornaments.

An inquisition [was] made there through Philip de Trewynno, Robert de Polstoc, Roger the smith [*fabrum*], Alexander de Penmelen, Henry of the same, and Roger de la Cumb, [and] Reginald de Bodon, jurors, who say that there are nine acres in the sanctuary with the premises of the court[22] in the hands of the farmer, price per acre 6*d*., and all the buildings of the court are badly roofed and the solar is almost ruinous. Also at the chapel of St Nectan [*sancti Nectani*] is one ferling[23] of land from which the vicar is allowed two English acres and the rest is let for rent for 6*s*. 8*d*. which the farmer receives. Also the tithes of sheaves of the church of St Winnow with the two chapels[24] are commonly worth 20 marks [£13 6*s*. 8*d*.]. Also the vicarage consists of all the altarage and the two English acres of land aforesaid, which is estimated in value at 6 marks [£4] annually. And let it be remembered that the church of Bradoc [*Broc*] was accustomed to render 16*s*. 8*d*. annually to the church of St Winnow which the vicar says the Lord Walter [Bronescombe], formerly bishop of Exeter, assigned to the vicar. Also the church of Boconnoc [*Boskennoc*] was accustomed to render 16*s*. 8*d*. in the same manner as the church of Bradoc and this was assigned in the same manner, but for the procurations which belong to the chapter of Exeter, that is to say 40*d*. from each church; this is in arrears.[25]

Inquisition made at the chapel of St Nectan. There is one old inadequate missal. One silver gilt chalice weighing half a mark. One set of complete vestments. One set of corporals. Two towels blessed and one not blessed. One cruet. A suitable font. One good bell. Also they say that Martin le Wal, reeve of Boconnoc, and Roger de Torhbi, villein of Sir Thomas de Ken[26] and now reeve, came in the autumn of the year 1279 to the parish of St Nectan [*Nyctani*] within the boundaries of the parish [of St Winnow] and despoiled and carried away the tithes of the sheaves of the chapter of Exeter, that is to say about fifteen bushels of rye and half a quarter of oats. And in the following year servants and men of the aforesaid Thomas came and carried away the tithes of one acre of rye and four acres of oats in the aforesaid place within the boundaries of the aforesaid church.

[f. 9r] Visitation and survey made at Altarnun

There is there one silver chalice partly gilt of the weight of 16*s*. Also another worn chalice partly gilt of the weight of 10*s*. Also two adequate sets of vestments. One cope of silk. Also four adequate towels blessed. Two towels not blessed. Two sets of corporals. Also one pyx of metal for the eucharist with a lock. An adequate tin chrismatory with a lock. Three adequate surplices. One rochet. Also one processional cross of metal. Two adequate banners. An adequate tabernacle. An adequate font. Also three tin cruets. Two tin candlesticks. One hanging bowl with chains. Also one brass bowl for holy water. Also two bells. Also one small ring with bells. Also three bells for carrying before the bodies of the dead. Also one old missal of no order or value. Also an adequate gradual with a troper. Also one adequate gradual without a troper. Also one troper of no value. Also one good adequate legend in two volumes. Also one adequate antiphonal with a psalter, collectar, [and] capitulary with a psalter. Also one good psalter in one volume by itself. Also a good and adequate ordinal with the life of St Nonn [*Nonnite*] [and of] St David. Also a good processional by itself. Also a good hymnal in one volume by itself. Also one worn and inadequate manual. Also another adequate antiphonal. Also a good and adequate thurible. Also one chest to store the ornaments of the church. Also a chancel less well roofed, and the parishioners ought to roof it and maintain it because they give no tithe from the store of the church.

Inquisition made through Edward the taylor [*cissorem*], Geoffrey de Alternon, David le Marreys, tenants of the sanctuary, [and] Drew [*Drogo*] de Carnisue, who say that there are in demesne[27] two Cornish acres of land of which half an acre is assigned to the vicar. Also there are there five tenants and the vicar who hold at will one and a half Cornish acres and return annually to the farmer 20*s*. 2*d*., and each of them is bound to reap once in the autumn with one man with food, and the service of each of them is worth one penny. Also Richard le Churl holds one Cornish acre by homage, rendering from it one halfpenny annually, and if he dies the heir shall give 12*s*. 6*d*. for a relief.[28] All the house is well maintained and roofed. Also the jurors say that the tithes of sheaves are worth 28 marks [£18 13*s*. 4*d*.]. Also they say that the vicarage is worth 15 marks [£10] from which it returns 100*s*. [£5] to the chapter of Exeter.[29] The sum of everything belonging to the rectory [is] £19 13*s*. 1½*d*.

apart from the 100s. which the vicar pays to the exchequer of Exeter and not to the farmer.

Visitation and survey made at St Breward [*sancti Bruererd'*]

There is there one silver chalice partly gilt of the weight of 18s. Four adequate sets of corporals. Also three complete adequate sets of vestments. Also eight adequate towels blessed. Also one suitable frontal. Also one pyx of metal for the eucharist, not hanging, with a lock. An adequate wooden chrismatory with a lock. A good and adequate tabernacle. Also one processional cross. Two adequate banners. Also two surplices. An adequate rochet. Two tin cruets. [f. 9v] Two tin candlesticks. One tin vessel for holy water. Two bells. Also two small bells. Also one old inadequate missal, wherefore [there is] none. Two adequate graduals and two adequate tropers. One good antiphonal with a capitulary, collectar, and hymnal, and another psalter less good with an antiphonal. One inadequate legend of time, wherefore [there is] none, and another adequate legend of the saints. One less good psalter. One processional and one adequate ordinal. One worn and inadequate manual. One good and adequate thurible. Also a good cupboard [*almarium*] for storing the ornaments of the church, with a lock. Also a good and well roofed chancel but very dark and badly fenestrated. And the parishioners give no tithe from the store of the church, nor do they maintain anything of that chancel in the judgment of the [cathedral] chapter.

The rectory consists of the common tithe of sheaves except for the tithe of Lower Lank [*de Minori Longk*] which is assigned to the vicar and is estimated at 40s. And the vicar has the whole residue [of dues] belonging to the church. And the tithe of sheaves that belongs to the rectory is estimated at 30 marks [£20]. Also there are two English acres of land which belong to the rectory and they are assigned to the vicar for an annual rent of 12d. at will unless anyone wishes to give more.[30] Memorandum that the archdeacon takes annually sometimes 2s. or 3s., sometimes 5s., when he makes his visitation for amending the defects of the church, and nothing is amended of the defects. The names of those through whom the inquisition was made [were] Roger Longk, William de Ros, Henry de Capella, Joel de Pencoyt, Stephen Hethia, James the fuller [*fullonem*], jurors, who say that the vicarage is worth 15 marks [£10]. Also that the tithe of sheaves which belongs to the rectory is worth 30 marks [£20] as is estimated above. The sum of all that belongs to the rectory, £20 12d.

Survey and visitation made at St Issey [*Egloscruc*]

There is there one good gilt chalice of the weight of 20s. Two festal sets of vestments with a tunicle[?][31] and dalmatic, and two other good enough sets of vestments. Five adequate sets of corporals. Nine towels blessed. One pyx of copper for the eucharist without a lock. Two tin cruets. One processional[32] cross of metals and another wooden. One adequate locked chrismatory of wood. Three banners. A fair and good tabernacle. Three adequate surplices. One rochet. An adequate font. One tin vessel for holy water. Two tin candlesticks. Also one adequate missal. Two adequate graduals and two tropers. One legend in two volumes. One adequate breviary without a psalter. No antiphonal in itself. Two adequate psalters. One adequate ordinal of the Use of Sarum. Also an adequate manual. Two great bells. Three small hand bells. Also one good frontal. One adequate thurible. A good chancel honourably fenestrated and well roofed. Also one small ring with sixteen small bells for a day of solemnity. One good and adequate processional in the volume of the other troper.

Inquisition made through John the clerk, Robert de Tredour, Miles de Burgo, [and] William de [f. 10r] Trenantros, jurors, who say on their oath that the tithes of sheaves which belong to the rectory are worth £28 5s. And the vicarage consists of all the altarage and the whole sanctuary except for three English acres and it is estimated at 9 marks [£6].[33] And the other three acres aforesaid are let to Sir Walter the vicar,[34] to render thence 2s. annually if the chapter shall consent, and he ought to have an indenture made for this if the chapter shall consent.

Survey and visitation made at Perranzabuloe [*Sanctum Pyeranum*] on the day of St Barnabas the Apostle [11 June]

There is there one silver chalice partly gilt of the weight of 20s. Two small silver chalices of the weight of 10s. Two adequate sets of vestments and one inadequate and old set of vestments. Two adequate sets of corporals. Eight towels blessed and ten not blessed. One silver pyx for the eucharist with a lock. Five tin cruets. One good processional cross. Five banners which are not worth a halfpenny. Also one chrismatory of no colour and without a lock. A good and adequate tabernacle. Two adequate surplices. One rochet. One suitable enough frontal. Also one reliquary [*capsis*] in which is the head of St Piran [*sancti Pyerani*] with other relics, bound with iron and locked. Also another reliquary in which is the silver bowl [*scutella*] of St Piran. Also one pastoral staff of St Piran fabricated with silver, gold, and precious stones. Also one tooth of St Brendan and one tooth of St Martin which are placed in a certain silver box. Also one silver cross in which are placed small relics of St Piran. Also one shrine [*feretrum*] in which is placed the body of St Piran [*Pyrani*]. Also one cross of St Piran made of bone and one little bell of St Piran of copper. Also one inadequate thurible. No candlestick. Also one new empty shrine, finely painted. One tin vessel for holy water. Also two bells. One locked chest for placing the ornaments of the church. Also one adequate

Lenten veil. Also one woven cloth covered with gold and silver. Also a suitable locked font. Also there is there one good missal, badly bound, with a troper and a well notated gradual. One old and inadequate gradual. One adequate troper. One good adequate legend of time with [that of] the saints in four volumes with two psalters. Also an old antiphonal of no value. One inadequate breviary. One psalter adequate in itself. Two manuals. One adequate ordinal of the Use of Sarum. Also a chancel less well roofed and less well fenestrated.

Inquisition made through John le Rus, Roger le Rus, Andrew son of Andrew, John son of Hugh de Ton, Richard Busseuole, and Walter de Trenan, jurors, who say that there are 43*s*. 2½*d*. of fixed rent and 10*s*. of the demesne, because it [the demesne] is damaged beyond [its customary] manner by the sand. Also it is presented that Sir John le Lambron, knight, sold one quarter of barley at Pentecost which was worth 5*s*. 4*d*. at market at that time. He conveyed [it] reciprocally up to the feast of St Michael for 8*s*. Also the parishioners give no tithe from the store of the church and they have a portion of the offerings that come to the offertory box [*truncum*], which portion is estimated to be worth 30*s*. or 40*s*. per annum. Also the tithe of the sheaves of the church of St Piran without the chapel [of St Agnes] was sold last year for £12 18*s*. 4*d*. Also the tithe of the chapel of St Agnes, £13 11*s*. 8*d*. Also the vicar bears [as a charge] to the farmer, £4 annually. Also the vicarage consists of all the altarage, which he receives wholly except for the tithe of sheaves [f. 10v] and the fixed rent, [and] which is worth and estimated at 20 marks [£13 6*s*. 8*d*.] and from this he renders £4 to the chapter as aforesaid [*sic*], and he is bound to maintain two chaplains besides himself.[35] The total sum belonging to the rectory, £43 3*s*. 2½*d*.

Survey and visitation at Gwennap [*sanctam Weneppam*]

There is there one silver chalice of the weight of 10*s*. Two complete sets of vestments and furthermore one chasuble of silk. One tunicle [?][36] and one dalmatic. Two adequate sets of corporals. Six towels blessed. One surplice and one rochet [both] adequate and two inadequate surplices. Also one pyx of ivory for the eucharist with a lock. An inadequate tin chrismatory without a lock. An adequate tabernacle. Three adequate tin cruets. Also two adequate processional candlesticks of tin. One inadequate banner. Also one inadequate small processional cross of metal. Also one tin vessel for holy water. Two bells. Two small bells to carry before the bodies of the dead. Memorandum that Master Osbert, spokesman of Master Henry de Bollet, carried away one small bell to Penryn of the weight of about eight pounds which used to be rung at the sacrament.[37] Also an adequate font. An adequate Lenten veil. One adequate frontal of silk. One thurible of no value. Also one adequate missal with a notated gradual. One gradual adequate in itself. Two tropers adequate in themselves. One adequate manual. One ordinal, capitulary, [and] collectar in one volume of the Use of Sarum. One complete legend [but] incorrect and inadequate. One good antiphonal with a psalter, capitulary, collectar, and hymnal in one volume. One worn antiphonal of the order of Merton. One psalter adequate in itself and another worn. One adequate locked chest for storing the ornaments of the church. An adequate chancel. One iron box made for offerings.

Inquisition made through Robert de Tresyns, John de Treuart, [and] Oliver of the same township, jurors, who say that there is there one carucate[38] of land of the sanctuary which the vicar has in demesne which is estimated to be worth 20s. per annum. Also they say that the vicarage consists of all the residue [of church income] except for the sheaves and three acres of land that belong to the rectory, which [vicarage revenues] are worth about 15 marks [£10] in ordinary years.[39] Also they say that the three acres of land which belong to the rectory are worth 2s. annually. Also the sheaf is estimated at 16 marks [£10 13s. 4d.] and it was sold last year for 22 marks 3s. [£14 16s. 4d.], and in the year immediately before for 30 marks [£20]. And furthermore there are four acres of land of the sanctuary at the chapel of the Holy Trinity[40] which were given to the chapel that lie waste because the giver of them distrains [them] day by day until it should be possible to deliver two masses each week in the aforesaid chapel which he claims ought to be delivered by an agreement. And the same giver sold a border strip [limbam] of the aforesaid three [sic] acres, and other profits are taken which are produced from them. Also the vicar is charged with [a payment of] 2 marks [£1 6s. 8d.] to Master Henry de Bollet, who is the farmer. Memorandum that the archdeacon of Cornwall has jurisdiction over this church and has and takes his procuration. Memorandum, let it be known and enquired why the chapter of Exeter does not have procurations in its jurisdiction like the archdeacon. The sum total belonging to the rectory, £12 2s.

Survey and visitation made at St Erth [Lannudno] on the Saturday [7 June] next before the feast of St Barnabas the apostle, in the year of the Lord 1281

There is there one silver chalice of the weight of 16s., the inside gilt. Also one small silver chalice not gilt of the weight of 6s. Also three suitable enough complete sets of vestments. Also one alb and one amice apart from the three sets aforesaid. Also ten towels blessed. Also three not blessed. Also three adequate sets of corporals. Also one suitable enough frontal. [f. 11r] One silver pyx for the eucharist with a lock. One tin chrismatory without a lock. A good and adequate tabernacle. Four suitable enough cruets of tin. Four adequate tin candlesticks. Also one old and worn processional cross of metal. No banner. Also one tin vessel for holy water. One basin for the same. Two suitable enough bells and two small bells to carry before the bodies of the dead. Also an adequate Lenten veil. An old and inadequate thurible. One cloth of raines [*reyns*] to cover the bodies of the dead. A beautiful and adequate font but without a lock. Two adequate surplices and one adequate enough rochet. Also one tolerable missal of time with a notated gradual. Two adequate graduals. Two adequate tropers. One inadequate manual. No ordinal. Also two adequate enough antiphonals, namely one of time and the other of the saints with a capitulary and collectar, hymnal, and psalter, of a [religious?] order. One old breviary in small letters and no other legend. One psalter. One processional and hymnal in one volume. One chest and two suitable enough coffers to store the ornaments of the church. Also a chancel badly roofed and not whitewashed, adequately fenestrated but the glass is deficient in part of one window.

Inquisition made through Richard Trelowyt, Philip de Polkellomp, Stephen de Trewinnat, and Martin de Lanwdno, who say that there is one carucate of land in the sanctuary[41] which is assigned to the vicar and it is estimated to be worth 2 marks [£1 6s. 8d.] per annum, and he has the whole of the sanctuary except for three English acres of land and he has all the altarage, which is estimated with the aforesaid sanctuary at about 10 marks [£6 13s. 4d.], and he renders 10s. from that to the farmer annually and he bears the ordinary ecclesiastical burdens.[42] It is estimated [that there are] three acres belonging to the rectory as aforesaid and one house, and they return annually half a mark [6s. 8d.]. Also they say that the tithe of sheaves was sold last year for 40 marks [£26 13s. 4d.] and for more in the preceding year. The sum total of everything belonging to the rectory, £27 10s. Memorandum that Richard de Trelowyt seeks 6s. 10d. which he spent in the removal of the high altar and the not making of the same by the lord archdeacon of Cornwall.

Survey and visitation made at Methleigh [*Methele*] on the Sunday [15 June] next after the feast of St Barnabas the apostle in the year of the Lord 1281

Inquisition made through William Tyrel, Awred de Methele, Richard Betto, Roger de Fentenwen, and Richard Chantecler, John Corbyn, attorney of Sir John Petyt, [and] Richard de Treleyn, jurors, who say on their oath that Sir Odo le Archedekene, knight, holds one Cornish acre and a half of land and renders 3s. at the feast of St Michael,[43] and he makes suit of court and is bound to be one of the twelve jurors. Also Sir John de Reskymer holds one Cornish acre rendering from it 2s. 6d. annually and the same service as the aforesaid Sir Odo. Also the same Sir John renders annually 2½d. by *scyphild*.[44] Also Sir John le Petyt, knight, holds one acre in *Kenegky* and three ferlings elsewhere rendering from them 4s. 4½d. annually. Also the same renders 2½d. for *scyphild*. Also the same one mother sheep and one lamb. Also the same 2d. for half a hoggaster [*hogastre*].[45] Also the same 6d. for aid and the same common service as Odo. Also Mauger de Belligren holds one Cornish acre rendering 2s. 3d. and the same service as Odo. Also Richard Prespinic holds two Cornish acres rendering 5s. and he is bound to carry two sheep and one lamb to pasture [*herbagium*]. Also the same 5d. for *scyphild*. Also the same 6d. for aid, and the same service as Odo. Also Michael de Lanner holds one Cornish acre of land and renders 2s. 6d. Also one mother sheep with one lamb. Also the same 2½d. for *scyphild*. Also the same 6d. for aid and the same service as Odo. Also Henry the young [*iuvenis*] holds one Cornish acre and a half. He renders 3s. 9d. Also the same one mother sheep with one lamb, and he owes 2½d. for *scyphild*. Also 6d. for aid and the same service as Odo. Also Richard Treleghen holds one acre and three ferlings rendering 4s. 1½d. Also the same one sheep with one lamb. Also 2d. for half a hoggaster. Also 2½d. for *scyphild*. Also 6d. for aid, and the same service as Odo. Also John de Penros holds three Cornish acres rendering 8s. 1½d. Also the same for *scyphild*, 7½d. and the same service as Odo. Also William Tyrel holds two acres rendering 6s. Also the same for *scyphild* 5d. and the same service as Odo. Also Philip Curtehuse holds one acre rendering 2s. 6d. Also the same owes for *scyphild* 1¼d. and the same service as Odo. Also Master Peter de Antrovon[46] holds one croft and renders 6d. annually for all service. The total rents and services aforesaid, 49s. 0¾d. Also six mother sheep and six lambs.

Also Agnes de St Elvan [*sancto Ylvano*] holds half an acre at will. She renders 10s. and suit of court. Also Richard Chanterel holds one ferling of land rendering 4s. and suit of court. Total 14s.

Also they say that there are there two carucates of land in demesne and the whole was transferred on the feast of the apostles Philip and James [1 May] in the year of the Lord 1281. The conventionary tenants [*conuencionarii*][47] render the sum of £7 annually and suit of court for all service. Also there is there one mill which is let to farm for 24s. and the lord is bound to maintain the mill. Total 24s. The total of the totals, £11 7s. 0¾d. besides seven [*sic*] sheep and seven lambs which are worth 7s.

Also they say that the manor is in a better state than the farmer received it. And he has erected a good hall with a chamber and a garderobe in the other part, roofed with stone. The remaining parts of the house, badly roofed with straw, are now roofed.

2. VISITATIONS MADE IN 1331

(Translated from the Latin text in Exeter Cathedral Archives, D&C 2851)

View of the defects of churches and places in Cornwall belonging to the reverend men, the dean and chapter of Exeter, by Sir Richard de Brayleghe, co-brother of the same lords the dean and chapter and special representative [*nuncium*] deputed for the purpose, after the feast of Easter [9 March] in the year of the Lord 1331.[48]

Altarnun [*Alternon*]

The windows at the head of the chancel there, ruinous and the glass broken. Other defects both in the roof and in the walls, the repair of which belongs to the parishioners and also of all the other ornaments and matins books, since the parishioners do not pay tithes of the [church] store. And they are similarly bound to construct and repair the chancel if it should be necessary, as appears from actions and an agreement made on these matters. It belongs to the archdeacon of the place to visit and make correction concerning these and other defects.

Boconnoc [*Bodkonok*]

Is within the peculiar jurisdiction of the dean and chapter of Exeter at St Winnow. The [communion] cup for the sick is wanting [*deficit*]. There are there two corporals, without suitable burses [*repositoriis*]. One set of vestments is wanting. The embroidery [*parura*] of the towels of the high altar is want-ing. One surplice is wanting. One rochet is wanting. The Lenten veil and the nuptial [veil] are wanting. The pall of the dead is wanting, and the [altar] frontal. An inadequate missal. There is there a worn troper. The ordinal is wanting. The lock and fastenings of the pyx are wanting. A worn chrismatory and without a lock. An inadequate board for the pax. Worn cruets. The vessel for the incense is lacking, and the paschal candlestick. A worn portable cross. The font without a lock. The canopy above the high altar is wanting.

Bradoc [*Brothake*]

All things here are virtually [*quasi*] defective for the celebration of divine service. The cemetery badly enclosed and the house of the rector ruinous.

Respryn [*Reprina*]

In the chapel of Respryn all things are virtually defective for the celebration of divine service. There is, however, a perpetual chantry,[49] and certain parishioners there receive all the sacraments, except only for burial.

St Winnow [*apud Sanctum Wynnocum*]

There are there three corporals without burses, but one [is] worn. A rochet is wanting. A Lenten veil and a nuptial [veil] and a pall of the dead are wanting. An improper banner. There is a gradual, badly bound. The pyx for the eucharist worn and without a lock. The board for the pax badly painted. A vessel for the incense is wanting, and a paschal candlestick. A canopy above the high altar is wanting. Small bells for the dead and infirm and a small bell for the elevation of the Body of Christ are wanting. A lock on the font is wanting. A small window of one light in the chancel inadequate and without glass. There are certain people of the parish who are called the parishioners of St Nectan, where by agreement they will have twelve masses per annum at certain times, who at other times withdraw themselves and do not frequent the mother church nor, as they are bound, do they contribute to the repair of the mother church, except for a few [*paucis*].[50] In the said chapel of St Nectan necessary things are wanting for the celebration of divine service.

It is disclosed that a certain part of the east park of Boconnoc, and part of the south park of the same, is in the parish of St Nectan. Also it is disclosed by the parishioners of St Winnow that the vicar of St Winnow does not receive the tithes due from the mills existing in the parish, that is to say from the mill of St Winnow, which is worth 30*s.* per annum, he receives only 6*d.*; from the mill of *Sepwasche*, which is worth 11*s.* per annum, he receives 6*d.* for tithes; from the mill of Polscoe [*Polscoth*], which is worth 8*s.* per annum, he receives 6*d.* for tithes; for the two mills of *Dounans*, that is to say from one water-mill and one fulling-mill, which are worth 16*s.* per annum, he receives 6*d.* for tithes. It was said to the vicar that he should act and exact just and due tithes.

Veryan [*Elercus*]

There is here a barn [*grangea*], the walls of which are of earth and can be repaired for a modest amount. It contains five poles[51] and there are four good pairs of crucks; beams and wattles are wanting and it is almost unroofed. There is there a new hall, chamber, and garderobe, cellar, and kitchen of the construction of Master Bartholomew de Sancto Laurencio.[52] The court[53] is badly enclosed. Three English acres of land belong to the farmer; the rest of the sanctuary, which is long and wide, belongs to the vicar. The chancel is dark; on another occasion it was ordained that windows should be made in the chancel and desks [*desci*],[54] to the repair of which and of the other defects the vicar is liable. And Sir John Cook, now vicar, received from the executors of his predecessor nine marks of silver [£6] and a large quantity of timber for the repair of the defects.[55]

Gwennap [*Weneppa*]

The chancel is badly roofed throughout; the glass windows dark. The legend badly bound and not covered. And although in another previous visitation it was set down that the defects of the chancel, the books, and the ornaments ought to be repaired at the common expense of the dean and chapter of Exeter and the vicar, the vicar says that he is liable for nothing except only for the episcopal and archidiaconal obligations and for the chantry of the chapel of the Holy Trinity, according to the ordinance of his vicarage.[56] There is there one barn badly roofed, and one door removed and the other dilapidated [*debile*]. The said barn requires repair or it will soon fall into ruin.

Constantine [*Constantinus*]

There is there a worn and badly bound legend. The repair of defects belonging to the rectory belongs to the vicar. The vicar says that he has no ordinance.[57] The house that the vicar inhabits belongs to the rectory, as some say. There are many defects in the church, which are to be repaired by the visitation of the archdeacon. The vicar this year received tithes of sheaves from two crofts.[58] And the parishioners say that there were wont to be orchards in these crofts in part, and in part peas and beans to be cultivated, from which the vicar was accustomed to receive tithes.[59] As for other crops of grain cultivated there, they do not know who ought to receive tithes. The vicar says that he has stored them safely until it is known whether they belong to the rectory or the vicarage.

Mullion [*Melanus*]

There is there a suitable legend, badly covered and without buckles. An ordinal with a venitary, badly bound. Until now almost all the previous defects remain to be corrected, except for the chancel, well constructed anew by the executors of the lord Thomas [Bitton], bishop of Exeter.[60] The matins books are wanting and are defective, to the repair of which the said executors are liable, as it appears in the previous visitation. The vicarage is very poor [*exilis*], on account of which there is a common complaint in those parts, and the court of the vicar [is] badly enclosed.[61]

Sancreed [*Sancredus*]

There are there some defects to be corrected by the visitation of the arch-deacon. Also, at the visitation it was enjoined to the vicar that a certain small house should be repaired at his expense and he should render to the farmer for the same 18*d*. At present that house is not built, and the vicar says that he is not bound to repair it.[62]

St Erth [*Ercus*]

There is there one barn badly roofed and the doors of the same are dilapidated. The vicar is bound to maintain the chancel and the matins books and the other ordinary obligations at his own expense, unless the chancel collapses by chance without blame to the vicar.[63] Then the rebuilding of the same will belong to the dean [and] chapter and to the vicar proportionately. This year thieves entered through the windows of the chancel and robbed the church, taking away a chalice, books, wax, and other things. Whence the parishioners petition that the dean and chapter, or the vicar, repair the damage caused to them in this respect.

Gwinear [*Wynierus*]

The vicar is bound to maintain the chancel, the matins books, and to bear all the ordinary obligations. At present, so it seems, all things are in a good state there.[64]

The Chapel of St Agnes [*Capella Sancte Agnetis*]

The clasps for the missal are wanting. The gradual, antiphonal, and brev-iary inadequate and without clasps. The pyx for the eucharist is wanting. The chrismatory wooden, inadequate, and without a lock. A vessel for incense is wanting. A nuptial veil is lacking. Small bells for the sick and for the elevation of the Body of Christ[65] are wanting. A bier for the dead, a hearse, and a pall are wanting. A lock for the font is wanting. An inadequate thurible. And the vest-ments are worn, and [there are] other defects in the chancel, both in the walls and in the roof. The parishioners of the said chapel are bound to maintain the said chapel and to find all things necessary there for celebrating divine service.

Perranzabuloe [*Pieranus*]

There is one adequate chalice there. Six sets of corporals with burses, of which some are worn. Three worn surplices. A nuptial veil is wanting. A worn pall of the dead. An inadequate and badly bound missal. Two graduals, of which one [is] adequate and the other badly bound. A troper gnawn and badly bound. Two legends of time and two of the saints, of which one of time is badly bound and without boards. An inadequate antiphonal. A worn ordinal. An inadequate capitulary and a collectar. An ivory pyx without a lock. A chrismatory without a lock. A board for the pax without a picture. A worn paschal candlestick. A lantern[*lanterna*] and lamp [*boeta*] are wanting.[66] Small bells for the sick are wanting. A font without a lock. A choir cape is wanting, and a reliquary. The glass windows in the nave of the church are wanting.

The parishioners of St Piran are bound to maintain the chancel and to find the matins books, in that hitherto they have taken the tithe of the store of the said church and have undertaken the aforesaid obligations. Now, however, it is said that through their carelessness the store is wanting for the most part. And they say that they are prepared to make good the tithe of the store provided that the dean, the chapter, and the vicar undertake the burden of remaking the chancel and finding the matins books and the other things belonging to the rectory or the vicarage. Alternatively, that they may be allowed to fix a box in the church, and to receive all the offerings there along with the offerings of each of the altars of the said church to maintain the aforesaid obligations, except for the offerings of the parishioners at the statutory times.[67] Hitherto, the parishioners have carried the relics of St Piran inordinately to various and remote places, as previously.

The tenants of St Piran complain in that they were wont to have peat and furze at Carnkief (*Kerkyf*) and they are now prevented and impleaded about this in the king's court by a certain [*blank*], to whom Sir William de Milleborne,[68] having the said land of Carnkief at farm, has demised the same for the term conceded to him by the dean and chapter.

St Issey [*Egloscruk*]

There is there a dilapidated chancel, badly roofed and ruinous. An antiphonal with a legend, worn, obscure, and badly bound, and two quires are wanting in the first part. A suitable legend of saints, except at the beginning which is corrupt. Two breviaries, worn and badly bound. A worn ordinal. Three worn psalters of which one is adequate. A worn canopy in the chancel. The chancel dilapidated and the wall ruinous. There is there a certain small area belonging to the rectory, containing half of an English acre and badly enclosed.[69]

St Breward [*Brueredus*]

There is there one suitable breviary and legends of time and of the saints in one volume. An old and worn antiphonal. A good missal. Two adequate graduals. A suitable ordinal, and the rest of the books for mass [are] suitable. A canopy above the high altar is wanting. The vicar, according to the ordinance of the vicarage, is bound to acknowledge all ordinary obligations.[70] But in the time of Sir Robert,[71] the last vicar there, a composition was made between him and the parishioners that the said parishioners should receive the tithe of all the store of the church and maintain the chancel, and if it were appropriate to remake it anew. And they should provide matins books and other things belonging to the rectory or the vicarage in the aforesaid church.

Notes and references

1. The records are reviewed in Nicholas Orme, *Victoria County History of Cornwall*, Vol. ii (London, 2010), under the headings of the monasteries concerned.

2. Exeter Cathedral Archives, Dean and Chapter (hereafter D&C) 3672A, 2851. The latter is printed in *The Register of John de Grandisson, Bishop of Exeter*, ed. F.C. Hingeston-Randolph, 3 vols (London and Exeter, 1894–99), ii, pp. 605–11.

3. Below, p. 00.

4. G.G. Coulton, 'A Visitation of the Archdeaconry of Totnes in 1342', *English Historical Review* 26 (1911), pp. 108–24.

5. *Councils and Synods II: A.D. 1205-1313*, ed. F.M. Powicke and C.R. Cheney, 2 vols (Oxford, 1964), ii, pp. 1007-8.

6. Ibid., i, pp. 232–33.

7. Ibid., ii, pp. 1005–6.

8. Ibid., ii, p. 1053.

9. Ibid., ii, p. 1026.

10. *The Registers of Walter Bronescombe and Peter Quivil, Bishops of Exeter*, ed. F.C. Hingeston-Randolph (London and Exeter, 1889), pp. 465–72.

11. On Nonn and David, see Nicholas Orme, *The Saints of Cornwall* (Oxford, 2000), pp. 205–7, 102–3.

12. Nicholas Orme, 'Parish Processions in Medieval and Tudor Cornwall', *Journal of the Royal Institution of Cornwall* (2011), pp. 73–82 (pp. 78–79).

13. *English Episcopal Acta, XI: Exeter 1046–1184*, ed. Frank Barlow (London, 1996), p. 52.

14. D&C 1388–90; *Calendar of Patent Rolls 1281–92* (London, Public Record Office, 1893), p. 171.

15. *The Register of Walter de Stapeldon, Bishop of Exeter*, ed. F.C. Hingeston-Randolph (London and Exeter, 1892), 341–42.

16. Richard de Brendesworth, canon of Exeter Cathedral from 1275 until at least 1282; Gilbert de Tyting[s], canon from 1280 until at least 1289 (J. Le Neve, *Fasti Ecclesiae Anglicanae 1066–1300*, Vol. x: *Exeter*, ed. Dianne Greenway (London, 2005), pp. 45, 65).

17. The weights mentioned in the visitation were equivalent to those of coins of the day, so the weight was also the value.

18. raines: fine linen cloth from Rennes, Brittany.

19. i.e. without musical notation.

20. In 1680 the glebe was estimated at 45 (English) acres (*A Calendar of Cornish Glebe Terriers 1673–1735*, ed. R. Potts, Devon and Cornwall Record Society, new series, 19 (1974), p. 168).

21. On the vicarage endowment, see D&C 3625, ff. 95v, 96r-v.

22. court: the house of the clergyman.

23. ferling: the fourth part of a hide, perhaps thirty acres or a little more if rented at 6*d.* an acre.

24. Presumably the chapels of Respryn and St Nectan.

25. procurations: small annual fees paid by churches. The ordinance for the vicarage made by Bishop Bronescombe in 1269 awarded the vicar the altarage and the two payments from Boconnoc and Bradoc that are stated here (D&C 3625, ff. 90v-91r; printed in *Reg. Bronescombe*, ed. Hingeston-Randolph, p. 256).

26. Sir Thomas de Kent (de Cantia) was lord of Boconnoc (*Reg. Bronescombe*, ed. Hingeston-Randolph, pp. 115, 242; *The Register of Walter Bronescombe Bishop of Exeter 1258–1280*, ed. O.F. Robinson, 3 vols, Canterbury & York Society, 82, 87, 94 (1995–2003), ii, p. 81).

27. demesne: the land owned by the church in the parish.

28. relief: payment by the tenant's heir to the lord of the property, i.e. the cathedral.

29. The ordinance for the vicarage made in 1261 gave the vicar the altarage and the benefice house with the obligation of paying £5 per annum to the dean and chapter (D&C 3625, ff. 92v-94r, partially printed in *Reg. Bronescombe*, ed. Hingeston-Randolph, p. 106).

30. In 1278, Bishop Bronescombe awarded the vicar the altarage, the sanctuary excepting two English acres, and the tithes of Lower Lank, as stated here, as well as the whole tithe of hay (*Reg. Bronescombe*, ed. Hingeston-Randolph, pp. 243–44; *Reg. Bronescombe*, ed. Robinson, ii, 122; D&C 3625, ff. 94v-95r).

31. MS almatica, sometimes a form of dalmatica, but that word immediately follows.

32. MS cessional', probably for processionalis.

33. An undated award gave the vicar the altarage and sanctuary, plus three English acres and a payment of 5*s.* from five acres at *Trecruc*: slightly differing from what is said here (D&C 3625, f. 91r-v, printed in *Reg. Bronescombe*, ed. Hingeston-Randolph, p. 250).

34. Probably Walter Prior, instituted in 1266 (*Reg. Bronescombe*, ed. Hingeston-Randolph, p. 173; *Reg. Bronescombe*, ed. Robinson, ii, p. 15).

35. In 1269, Bishop Bronescombe awarded the vicar all the altarage of the parish church and the chapel of St Agnes with the offerings made when the relics of St Piran were taken on journeys, in return for a payment of £4 per annum to the dean and chapter (*Reg. Bronescombe*, ed. Hingeston-Randolph, p. 177; *Reg. Bronescombe*, ed. Robinson, ii, p. 33; D&C 3625 f. 95r-v).

36. MS almatica.

37. Henry de Bollegh(e), provost of Glasney *c.*1272–6; archdeacon of Totnes 1275–84; canon of Exeter Cathedral from 1278; archdeacon of Cornwall from 1284; died 1289–96 (Le Neve, *Fasti 1066–1300*, x, pp. 29, 35, 47. As mentioned below, he was farmer of the rectory.

38. carucate: an area of land varying from 80 to 144 acres, but the value (supposing 6*d.* an acre) suggests that this piece was in the region of 40 acres, and in 1727 the glebe was said to be only about 48 Cornish and 58 English acres (*Cornish Glebe Terriers*, ed. Potts, p. 48).

39. An undated award gave the vicar the altarage and the sanctuary except for three English acres, as stated here, but not the obligation to pay £1 6s. 8d. (D&C 3625, f. 90v, printed in *Reg. Bronescombe*, ed. Hingeston-Randolph, p. 249).

40. At St Day, a chapel containing a famous image of the Trinity frequented by pilgrims (Orme, *The Saints of Cornwall*, p. 246).

41. In 1679 the glebe was estimated at about 68 acres (*Cornish Glebe Terriers*, ed. Potts, p. 35).

42. An undated award gave the vicar all the altarage and sanctuary except for a barn and three English acres, with the obligation to pay 10s. per annum to the cathedral and to maintain the chancel and other church costs, as stated here (D&C 3625, f. 92v, printed in *Reg. Bronescombe*, ed. Hingeston-Randolph, p. 246).

43. Michaelmas, 29 September.

44. *scyphild* (variously spelt: *scyp(h)il(l)d(d)(e)*), probably meaning 'sheep-hold' and hence a due levied on sheep flocks or for the right to graze one's sheep on the manor pastures.

45. hoggaster: a young sheep. The payment was perhaps in lieu of rendering the sheep itself.

46. If a misspelling of Antrenon, perhaps a clerical member of the local family of that name who took it from Antron in Sithney parish.

47. Tenants holding land by defined agreement rather than custom (*Oxford English Dictionary*, s.n. 'conventionary'; Richard Carew, *The Survey of Cornwall*, ed. J. Chynoweth, N. Orme, and A. Walsham, Devon and Cornwall Record Society, new series, 47 (2004), f. 38v).

48. Richard Braylegh, canon of Exeter Cathedral from 1318, subdean 1318–35, dean from 1335, died 1352 (J. Le Neve, *Fasti Ecclesiae Anglicanae 1300–1541*, Vol. ix: *Exeter Diocese*, ed. Joyce M. Horn (London, 1964), pp. 4, 6, 25).

49. i.e. an endowment for a priest to say daily services in the chapel including the celebration of mass for the dead.

50. A few people, or alternatively 'except for a little', i.e. in amount.

51. i.e. measurements of length.

52. Bartholomew of St Laurence: canon of Exeter Cathedral by 1296; archdeacon of Exeter, occurs 1296–c.1310; dean of Exeter Cathedral, 1310 till death in 1326 (Le Neve, *Fasti Ecclesiae Anglicanae 1300–1541*, ix, pp. 4, 12, 22). He was presumably a previous farmer of the benefice.

53. court: house precinct.

54. desks: seats for the clergyman and parish clerk.

55. John Cook was instituted as vicar in 1329 (*Reg. Grandisson*, iii, p. 1273); his predecessor may have been William de Ywefforde (*Reg. Stapeldon*, p. 258).

56. Correctly so, according to the ordinance of the vicarage (D&C 3625, f. 90v, printed in *Reg. Bronescombe*, ed. Hingeston-Randolph, p. 249).

57. i.e. the bishop's ruling on his rights and duties. None seems to exist. In 1321, after a dispute, it was simply agreed that the vicar was responsible for all burdens except those acknowledged by the dean and chapter (D&C 3625, ff. 94v-95r).

58. MS croftis, i.e. enclosed pieces of land.

59. He could lawfully take tithes from orchards, peas, and beans, but not from sheaves of grain.

60. Mullion church was purchased by the executors of Bishop Thomas Bitton between 1307 and 1310, for the cathedral to use as an endowment for the hospital of Clyst

Gabriel, east of Exeter (*Accounts of the Executors of Richard Bishop of London and . . . Thomas Bishop of Exeter*, ed. W.H. Hale and H.T. Ellacombe, Camden Society, new series, 10 (1874), 44).

61. For the endowment of the vicarage, see *Reg. Stapeldon*, pp. 341–42.

62. The vicar was correct: the ordinance of the vicarage, dated 1300, specifically excludes a small house with three English acres attached (D&C 3625, f. 91v, printed in *Reg. Bronescombe*, ed. Hingeston-Randolph, p. 431).

63. The account of the vicar's obligations is correct (above, p. 00 and note 00).

64. This is correct, according to the ordinance of the vicarage in 1319 (*Reg. Stapeldon*, pp. 332–33). The well-organized vicar was probably Andrew de Tregiliou, instituted in 1314 (ibid., p. 252); the next known vicar was instituted in 1335 (*Reg. Grandisson*, iii, p. 1309).

65. Small bells were rung when the priest consecrated and held aloft the bread and wine at mass.

66. A *lanterna* presumably had an enclosed flame and was suitable for carrying out of doors, e.g. in taking communion to the sick. A *boeta* appears to have been used in church and had a flame accessible in order to light other lamps (G. Oliver, *Monasticon Dioecesis Exoniensis* (Exeter and London, 1846), p. 273).

67. Parishioners were required to make offerings to the church four times a year.

68. Rector of Ruan Lanihorne, occurs 1308–20; canon of Glasney from 1320; rector of Creed from 1322, gone from there by 1344 (*Reg. Stapeldon*, pp. 219, 250, 257, 289–90; *Reg. Grandisson*, iii, p. 1341).

69. This area is mentioned in similar terms in the undated ordinance of the vicarage (D&C 3625, f. 91r, printed in *Reg. Bronescombe*, ed. Hingeston-Randolph, p. 250).

70. Correctly so, according to the ordinance of the vicarage of 1278 (*Reg. Bronescombe*, ed. Hingeston-Randolph, 243–44; ed. Robinson, ii, p. 122).

71. Robert de Gosham, dead by 1329 (*Reg. Grandisson*, i, p. 470).

5

The Duchy of Cornwall and the Wars of the Roses

Patronage, Politics, and Power, 1453–1502

R.E. Stansfield

Introduction

Edward III's foundation of the Duchy of Cornwall on 17 March 1337 for his seven-year-old eldest son, Edward, created an enduring and eternal institution for the purpose of providing the heir apparent with an income in perpetuity, and also formed one of the most important privileged territorial jurisdictions— or liberties—in the medieval British Isles.[1] The founding charter and successive concessions endowed the Duchy with seventeen 'accessionable' manors and a number of boroughs and towns in Cornwall, as well as properties in Lincolnshire, Hertfordshire, Yorkshire, Oxfordshire, Middlesex, Surrey, and Norfolk, and also established the principle that its landed assets were never to be scattered, separated, or alienated.[2] However, the Duchy was never merely a landed estate; it also derived its income and influence from several other prerogatives and regalities. The Duke possessed the advowsons of all churches and monastic houses connected with his properties, and was entitled to claim all wardships and escheats in his lands as well as *bona vacantia*.[3] The Duchy also held the privilege of nominating the sheriff of Cornwall (or undersheriff when the duke was *ex officio* sheriff), and was entitled to the profits of the county courts and those of eight and one-third of the nine hundred courts.[4] The Duke's rights encompassed various territorial and terrene prerogatives, such as those of treasure-trove and other rights relating to his lands. He enjoyed the profits of the eight tin-mining districts—Stannaries— of Cornwall and Devon, and the annual revenues from the weighing, valuing, and stamping—the coinage—of the tin.[5] He also claimed marine regalities, such as the customs and profits of ports in Cornwall, and those of Plymouth, Devon, as well as various other rights, such as the custody of certain estuarine fisheries and rights to wreck of the sea.[6] Such a commanding catalogue of the Duchy of Cornwall's regalities calls for comparison with the rights of other liberties: there are similarities yet there are also singularities.

Acclaimed by some historians as a 'little government all of its own' yet described by others as 'more an aristocratic estate', the Duchy of Cornwall enjoyed—and still retains—a distinctive constitutional and political status in the English polity.[7] Although the Duchy possessed some of the prerogatives associated with a palatinate, its singular status has been more appropriately defined as 'quasi-palatine' in nature.[8] Certain difficulties arise from heralding the Duchy as a 'miniature government' because it was not the sovereign power in *all* Cornish affairs: the Duchy-designated sheriff or under-sheriff presented his shire accounts at Westminster; Cornwall's commissions of the peace and of array (as well as those of *oyer et terminer*) were appointed by the monarch not by the Duke; Cornwall was included in the circuits of the royal justices (in contrast to the county palatines of Cheshire, Lancashire, and Durham); and Cornwall returned knights of the shire, and its boroughs elected burgesses, to Parliament (in contrast to Cheshire, Lancashire, and Durham).[9] The Duchy certainly retained an 'aura of semi-independence', and the hybridity of its status was as much the legacy of its tenth-century-kingdom and Norman-earldom antecedents as it was the creation of its charter of foundation.[10]

The remnants of the regalities and regnal solidarity of the tenth-century Cornish kingdom may be traced in the post-Conquest earldoms of Cornwall, created for William I's half-brother, Robert of Mortain (d.1090); for Henry I's natural son, Reynold de Dunstanville (d.1175); for Richard I's brother, later king, John; for John's second son, Richard (1209–72); for Edward II's favourite, Piers Gaveston (d.1312); and for Edward III's brother, John (d.1336). These successive recreations ensured a degree of continuity from kingdom to Duchy—i.e. an ancestry—and therefore presented a central focus for Cornish identity.[11] The heritage and history of a liberty, such as the Duchy of Cornwall, performed a fundamental role not only in its endurance and continuance but also in contributing to the development of local appreciations of loyalty and community. Alongside its lineage, the beneficence of a liberty's governing structures and judicial organization may also be considered essential elements in nurturing the emergence of allegiant and societal sentiments; however, perhaps the most important factor concerns a liberty's ability to offer opportunities for involvement and advancement in its institutions, administration, and structures of governance.[12] In studying liberties and identities, therefore, it is necessary to examine both the liberty's principal administrative apparatus and its participants.

In 1927, Mary Coate evaluated that 'there can be few institutions which have so successfully eluded the serious historian as the duchy of Cornwall'.[13] Even though significant advances in our understanding have been made since then, this statement still retains some degree of accuracy. Our knowledge of the Duchy's role in local society and in the local and regional economy during its first centuries has been the subject of some notable research; yet otherwise the Duchy's officers have received little detailed attention and have remained largely unexplored.[14] Few lists of Duchy office-holders have been published: R.R. Pennington provided a listing of lords warden and vice-wardens of the Stannaries from earliest times to the nineteenth century;[15] S.M. Campbell compiled a register of haveners and controllers of the havenary from 1337 to 1485, which has been supplemented by Maryanne Kowaleski's recent research on the haveners between 1287 and 1356;[16] and Graham Haslam's unpublished lists of lords warden, receivers-general, auditors, attorneys-general, haveners, feodaries, and controllers of the coinage cover the era from 1485 to 1650.[17] In an attempt to correlate each of these—sometimes conflicting—lists, this analysis and its accompanying appendix concentrates on the Duchy's principal offices and office-holders—its administrative elite —whilst also, in some small way, attempting to illuminate aspects of the governance of the Duchy of Cornwall during the later Middle Ages. This survey is by no means comprehensive and its conclusions should be regarded as provisional since further research may require their revision or reassessment (see Appendix). Nevertheless, the prosopography of the Duchy's officers is fundamental to any examination of political elites in Cornwall, as well as Devon and south-west England, and is also essential in the amelioration of our understanding of governance, and of the importance of liberties in the late-medieval polity.

The centrality of the Duchy in Cornish society is indisputable, but did the potency of its authority in Cornwall inhibit the emergence of an influential local gentry thus spurring ambitious local men to pursue their careers and to seek their chances elsewhere, as Julian Cornwall has suggested?[18] The Duchy of Cornwall was certainly an abundant arsenal of patronage, with numerous offices, advowsons, leases of lands, mills, and mines, as well as hunting, fishing, and mineral rights, and other regalities at its disposal. These rewards, conferred on loyal local gentry and other individuals could both secure allegiance and bestow local authority and status. As a consequence of the Duchy's particular political and constitutional status (as well as its close connection with the heir apparent and the monarchy), Duchy patronage may also have assumed a national relevance: was Duchy office-holding dominated by the appointment of courtiers, royal-household servants, and outsiders (non-native to Cornwall)? If prime Duchy offices were principally populated by figures of national stature and significance did this necessarily denote that the Duchy had ceased to operate as an arena of participation and avenue of advancement for local society? Moreover, what implications might this have for the cultivation of identities?

Clearly, any survey of the Duchy's structures of governance must both outline the principal offices which had evolved around the administration of its regalities, and explore involvement in Duchy positions by examining the officers themselves. Whilst the Duchy of Cornwall's estates extended across the kingdom from Byflete to Berkhamsted and from Launceston to Lincolnshire, the primary emphasis of this survey is on the Duchy's estates and regalities in Cornwall and in Devon. Accordingly, the first part of the ensuing analysis explores the Duchy's organization sequentially in terms of its estates, Stannaries, ports and customs, and administration of revenues and accounts. Duchy office-holding cannot be viewed in isolation from local, regional, and national events: the Duchy enjoyed considerable influence in Cornwall, Devon, and south-west England, and was—after all—the apanage of the heir to the English crown. During the later fifteenth century, the four dukes of Cornwall—none of whom reached their majority—were: Henry VI's son Edward, from 1453 to 1461 (and 1470 to 1471); Edward IV's heir Edward, from 1471 to 1483; Richard III's son Edward, from 1483 to 1484; and Henry VII's son Arthur from 1489; hence this survey begins with Prince Edward's birth in 1453 and concludes with Prince Arthur's death in 1502. In the intervening era, the country bore witness to civil strife which had important implications for politics, governance, and for the crown itself. Consequently, in the second part of the ensuing analysis, it is necessary to explore the Duchy's relationship with the crown and its pertinence to core-periphery relations during the later-fifteenth century.

Prerogatives, Patronage, and Personnel

Some of the Duchy's more consequential Cornish estates (annexed to the Duchy in its founding charter) were Launceston, Lostwithiel, Restormel, Tintagel, and Trematon, each of which—with its castle—was a sentinel of Duchy authority. It was only these castles and certain deer parks which remained after Richard II had dispersed almost all the other Duchy estates through his lavish awards to his relatives and adherents. Most of the alienated properties were recovered by Henry V who also expanded the Duchy's land-holding and influence in south-west England by appending several 'foreign manors' (namely ten manors and lands in Somerset and Dorset, as well as others in Berkshire, Kent, and Wales) in compensation for alienating the manor of Isleworth, Middlesex.[19] These ten Somerset manors were later alienated by Act of Parliament in 1483: William Herbert, Earl of Pembroke (d.1492), was persuaded to resign his earldom and Welsh lands (subsequently granted to Edward, Prince of Wales) receiving the earldom of Huntingdon and alienated Duchy lands in recompense. Thus some of the Duchy's supposedly inalienable estates were sacrificed to Edward IV's preoccupation with consolidating and expanding the influence of his eldest son in Wales as one facet of his policy of regional governance (which will be discussed later). These estates were eventually restored to the Duchy in 1495.[20] Apart from this brief episode, the Duchy's landholdings remained constant during the later fifteenth century: the administration of the castles, estates, and parks was entrusted to, and undertaken by, a series of local stewards, keepers, and bailiffs whilst the Duchy's local and legal rights were protected by a feodary and an attorney-general.

Estate Administration: Properties, Castles, and Parks

Since the Duchy possessed the rights to feudal incidents (principally those of escheat and wardship) relating to its Cornish estates, an officer was selected to protect these privileges: the feodary (or escheator) investigated the forfeited or escheated lands accruing to the Duchy, and retained quasi-legal powers in this regard (see Appendix I.3). The feodary probably utilized the facilities of the Duchy buildings at Lostwithiel, and normally employed deputies (with responsibility for specific localities) to serve and support him in his work. The office of feodary would have also required cooperation with the county administrations of Cornwall and Devon since the jurisdiction of the annually-elected shire officer, the escheator, encompassed both Cornwall and Devon.[21] During the later fifteenth century, several feodaries were members of the royal household: the clerk of Queen Margaret's jewels, Edward Ellesmere;[22] the king's yeoman of the crown, Avery Cornburgh (d.1487) of London and Bere Ferrers, Devon;[23] the knight of the body, Sir Richard Edgcumbe (d.1489) of Cotehele, Cornwall;[24] and his son, the knight of the body, Sir Piers Edgcumbe (d.1539);[25] and others were Queen Elizabeth Woodville's cousins, Sir John Fogge of Ashford, Kent, and his son, John (d.1525).[26] In order to preserve and perpetuate its prerogatives, the Duchy employed an attorney-general, who was responsible for pleading cases and advising the prince and his officers on legal matters (see Appendix I.4). Usually this appointment included responsibility not only for the Duchy's legal affairs but also for those of Wales and the earldom of Chester; thus this post, principally attached to the prince's household, was remunerated from Duchy revenues.[27] Two attorneys-general were speakers of the House of Commons: Sir William Allington (d.1479) of Bottisham, Cambridgeshire (who also later became the Duchy's chancellor);[28] and John Mordaunt (d.1504) of Turvey, Bedfordshire.[29] Others included Thomas Throckmorton (d.1472) Coughton,

Warwickshire, and Throckmorton, Worcestershire;[30] and John Twynho (d.1485) of Cirencester.[31]

One of the most infamous episodes of the Wars of the Roses is that of the rivalry between Sir William Bonville (d.1461) and Thomas, Earl of Devon (d.1458), which was edged into private warfare as a result of appointments to conflicting Duchy of Cornwall offices.[32] It is an example of one of the local feuds that escalated, demonstrating Henry VI's inadequacies and contributing to the realm's political turbulence. In 1437, Sir William Bonville had been granted stewardship of the Duchy's lands in Cornwall.[33] This action alone was sufficient to enrage the Earl of Devon but incredibly, in 1441, the earl was granted the same office.[34] The stewardship was used as an expedient excuse by the earl to attack Bonville and his associates, and the earl's position as steward was eventually upheld.[35] This contention was a symptom of a much greater problem arising from Devon's frustrated ambitions, and his desire for the restoration of his family's honour; but this occurrence is illustrative not only of local rivalries or of difficulties arising from administrative errors, but of the crucial importance of the office of steward.

Whereas a steward might usually be accorded the supervision of one or a number of properties within a locality (such the Honour of Wallingford in Berkshire), the preponderance of the Duchy's estates in Cornwall and Devon dictated that it was more efficient and effective to assign one steward as supervisor of all the Duchy's lands within one county. For example, the Duchy's steward in Cornwall was particularly influential in county affairs since the office awarded him responsibility for maintaining tenants' rights, and for presiding over the manorial courts (which duties he might delegate to others). He would also select the stewards and bailiffs of eight of the nine Cornish hundreds thereby extending Duchy authority to the hundred courts. More generally, the steward's most important duties related to ensuring the efficiency of estate management and administration, visitation of estates, and superintendence of the range of bailiffs and foresters who maintained individual properties.[36]

As a consequence of the nature of the Duchy's prerogative rights, the steward was also accountable for supervising the Stannary districts within his jurisdiction; for instance, the royal servant John Trevelyan was designated as 'steward of all castles, lordships, manors, lands and other possessions of the duchy of Cornwall within Devon, and of warden of the stannaries in the same' on 30 October 1442.[37] So, it appears that—even though it is rarely explicit in many appointments and accounts—the offices of steward and lord warden were conjoined: the steward of Cornwall was invariably lord warden of the Cornish Stannaries (Appendix I.5) likewise the steward of Devon was usually also lord warden of the Stannaries of that shire (Appendix I.6). If a Devon steward failed to be chosen then ultimate responsibility for his duties may have been assumed by the Cornwall steward; hence the steward of Cornwall appears to have been the more senior officer. However, at various times, a lord (or chief) steward bore responsibility for all duchy estates throughout the realm (Appendix I.1): for example, the first lord steward seems to have been Thomas Tickhill who was nominated chief steward and surveyor of all castles, lordships, manors, and other properties pertaining to the Duchy of Cornwall, the Principality of Wales, and the earldom of Chester in October 1413.[38] Therefore, it appears likely that there was a degree of correspondence between the offices as well as a degree of collaboration and cooperation between the officers.

The predominance of Sir William Bonville, now Lord Bonville, in the affairs and politics of Devon and Cornwall dictated that he should regain his former position as steward of duchy lands and lord warden of the Stannaries in Cornwall, and master forester of Dartmoor in March 1452; whilst the esquire of the body John Trevelyan of Nettlecombe, Somerset, and Restormel, Cornwall, continued as steward and lord warden in Devon.[39] In July 1454, the king's cousin, Richard, Duke of York (d.1460) was granted the keeping of the king's Devon and Cornwall mines and this was confirmed, in 1456, when he was granted custody of *all* mines of gold, silver, and other metals, which may have accorded him some influence within Cornwall and Devon.[40] In January 1457, the chamberlain of England and chief steward of Queen Margaret's estates, John, Viscount Beaumont (d.1460), was appointed chief steward and surveyor of all lands of the prince, which clearly extended his jurisdiction to include Devon and Cornwall.[41]

After the Yorkist victory in 1461, Roger Dinham (d.1490) became steward and lord warden of the Stannaries in Devon;[42] whilst the royal servant Thomas Clemens (d.1473) of Liskeard, Cornwall, became steward in Cornwall.[43] In June 1461, Clemens was replaced by Edward IV's leading courtier, Humphrey Stafford (d.1469) of Hooke (Dorset) and Southwick (Wiltshire).[44] He was later ennobled as Lord Stafford of Southwick in 1464, and was endowed with estates and crown offices across the south-west region: in March 1465, Lord Stafford was selected to be steward and lord warden in Devon, which—combined with his stewardship in Cornwall—meant that he became lord steward of the Duchy and lord warden in both counties (the implications of which will be discussed later).[45]

During the Earl of Warwick's rebellion in 1469, Lord Stafford (recently elevated to the earldom of Devon) had been executed, and the Devon magnate John, Lord Dinham (d.1501) became steward and lord warden in Devon in October 1469.[46] One month later, Sir John Stafford (d.1473) was chosen as steward and lord warden in Cornwall and all lands of the Duchy.[47] It is unclear whether existing Duchy officers continued in office or were removed during the Readeption, but Sir John Stafford (now earl of Wiltshire) was reappointed steward and lord warden in Cornwall in December 1471.[48] In March 1473, the queen's brother, Anthony, Earl Rivers (d.1483) was nominated as 'chief steward' (having become receiver-general in February).[49] By 1476–7, the knight of the body, Sir Thomas Bourchier (d.1491) had become steward and lord warden in Cornwall (whilst Earl Rivers remained lord steward);[50] and in April 1477, Bourchier was replaced by the queen's son by her first marriage, Thomas Grey, Marquess of Dorset (d.1502).[51] Earl Rivers remained lord steward even after the creation of the new post of chancellor in around 1476, which was conferred on the Duchy attorney-general, Sir William Allington (d.1479).[52] The chancellor's duties probably entailed the keeping of the prince's great seal but could have also extended to include broader responsibilities since the lord steward, Earl Rivers, may have been preoccupied with other concerns as both the Prince of Wales's 'governor' or tutor as well as adviser to Prince Richard, Duke of York and Norfolk and his council in East Anglia.[53] The creation of this post at this time may also be indicative of administrative alterations within the Duchy reflecting wider developments in the management of the crown estates which were intended to encourage efficiency and increase revenues during this period (see Appendix I.2).[54] If Rivers and Dorset were still lord steward and steward in Cornwall in 1483, they were removed—along with other Woodville associates—by Richard III: in May 1483, Lord Dinham was chosen as lord steward of the Duchy.[55] However, by August 1484, Richard's master of the henchmen, Sir James Tyrell (d.1502) of Gipping, Suffolk, had become steward and lord warden in Cornwall, thereby removing Cornwall from Lord Dinham's direct jurisdiction.[56]

Henry VII's victory brought the appointment of Sir Robert Willoughby (d.1502) of Broke (Wiltshire), later Lord Willoughby de Broke and steward of the king's household, as steward and lord warden in Cornwall and Devon (as well as 'receiver').[57] However, days later, Sir Walter Courtenay (d.1504) of Exeter became Devon's steward and lord warden;[58] and, in October 1486, Willoughby was replaced as Cornwall's steward by Sir John Halliwell (d.1500) of Trenode, Cornwall, and Bigbury, Devon, who later became a knight of the king's body.[59] Under Prince Arthur, the Dean of Exeter, John Arundell (d.1504), was chosen as 'chancellor and keeper of the great seal', in February 1490;[60] and had been replaced by the prince's almoner, Robert Frost, by 1502.[61] In December 1502, Robert, second Lord Willoughby de Broke (d.1521)— the son of the steward and receiver-general—was selected as steward and lord warden in Cornwall, steward and lord warden in Devon (therefore lord steward), and master forester of Dartmoor; from henceforth, each of Lord Willoughby's successors has been granted this combination of offices.[62]

Whilst the Duchy's stewards enjoyed some powers of patronage and bore responsibility for nominations to lesser posts (such as reeve or bailiff), there were numerous other offices—including constables of castles, stewards of manors, and rangers and parkers of parks in Cornwall and Devon—which provided the monarch or duke with valuable patronage with which to reward loyal service. In addition, other offices were also created at various times: in July 1461, the royal retainer Thomas Clemens was given charge of the maintenance of duchy buildings as 'controller of the works of the king's castles and manors in the duchy of Cornwall'.[63] Briefly, during the 1430s and 1440s, there seems to have been an attempt to create the post of 'surveyor of all the game', with responsibility for the supervision of all parks.[64] In October 1434, Sir Philip Courtenay (d.1463) of Powderham (Devon) had been appointed master of the king's venison within Cornwall including supervision of the king's parks there;[65] and in May 1443, the king's esquire Thomas Whalesburgh (d.1481) of Whalesburgh (Cornwall) was designated 'master of the game of the king's deer in Cornwall', for life.[66]

The Duchy possessed a series of major landed assets, namely a number of important parks in Cornwall as well as the forest and chase of Dartmoor in Devon. Carrybullock Park was three leagues in circumference and had contained around 150 deer in 1337.[67] The keeping of the park also included custody of the woods of Heregard, Northwood, and Grendescombe, and warrens relating to the manors of Carrybullock, Calstock, and Rillaton (Appendix V.1). Its keepers included Thomas Grayson (d.1495) of Dartmouth and Kennford, Devon, who was later a member of the royal household;[68] the royal retainer Avery Cornburgh;[69] and the royal servant Sir Richard Edgcumbe.[70] The custody of the parks of Helsbury and Lanteglos—located in Helston-in-Trigg manor, north of Carrybullock Park—was often jointly awarded to a single recipient, who would also enjoy supervision of a large number of deer (some 180 in 1337).[71] William Bradley surrendered his office of 'parker and *equestri*' (ranger) to the king's esquire John Arundell (d.1473) of Lanherne, Cornwall, in September 1445 (Appendix V.2).[72] Other keepers included the king's guard and escheator of Cornwall/Devon, Henry Ley of Bere Ferrers, Devon;[73] and Edmund Arundell (d.1503/4) of Tremodret, Cornwall.[74] Liskeard Park's keepers were also responsible for the care of a large deer population (some 200 deer in 1337);[75] in 1447, John Lematon surrendered his custody of the park to Thomas Bodulgate (d.1471) of Trencreek, Cornwall, and the yeoman of the crown John Trevelyan (Appendix V.3).[76] By 1461, another household servant Thomas Clemens had become keeper;[77] and in August 1477, the park was entrusted to Edward IV's chamberlain, William, Lord Hastings (d.1483).[78]

The royal forest and chase of Dartmoor was assigned its own officer whose title was subject to slight fluctuations, but mostly was described as the master forester or *equestri* (ranger or rider), (Appendix V.4, VI.6). By virtue of his office, the master forester was constable of Lydford Castle and keeper of the Stannary gaol there, as well as custodian of the manor and borough of Lydford and steward of South Teigne, but these duties were only infrequently explicit in individuals' appointments. The master foresters were William, Lord Bonville;[79] and Sir John, later Lord, Dinham.[80] Humphrey, Lord Stafford of Southwick was assigned the stewardship of Dartmoor in November 1464, which presumably meant that Dinham remained as master forester but that Stafford gained the overall supervision of the forest.[81] John, Lord Dinham became 'keeper of Dartmoor' in October 1469, and was appointed as 'rider or master forester' in June 1483.[82] Sir Walter Courtenay (d.1504) became keeper from September 1485;[83] and, in December 1502, Robert, Lord Willoughby de Broke (d.1521) was nominated 'rider or master forester', and thereafter this office was always bestowed on the single lord steward and lord warden of the Stannaries.[84]

The supervision of the Duchy's other major landed assets—its historic castles—was often accompanied by the oversight of parks and other related appurtenances. The custody of Lostwithiel Castle (Palace)—the Stannary gaol for Cornish tinners—had been, by tradition, entrusted to the Duchy's Havener (who will be discussed later), (Appendix VI.2). The constables of Launceston Castle were also keepers of the park there, which contained a small deer herd (amounting to fifteen in 1337), (Appendix VI.1).[85] The constables and keepers included some royal-household servants, such as the clerk of the queen's jewels, Edward Ellesmere;[86] and the yeoman of the crown, Avery Cornburgh.[87] Queen Elizabeth Woodville's relatives Sir John Fogge and his son, John Fogge;[88] and Richard III's northern supporter Halnath Mauleverer (d.1502) of Ashwater, Devon, and Allerton Mauleverer, Yorkshire, also enjoyed this castle's keeping.[89] In September 1485, the royal servant Sir Richard Edgcumbe became keeper; after his death in 1489, his son, the esquire of the body, Piers Edgcumbe, succeeded him in this role.[90] Restormel Castle's custody was entrusted to a constable who was also keeper of the adjacent park which was capable of sustaining a large deer population (some 300 in 1337), (Appendix VI.3).[91] In addition, the keeping of the waters of the River Fowey was attached to the Honour of Restormel: the royal retainers John Trevelyan and Avery Cornburgh both enjoyed custody of the fishery when they were the castle's constable.[92] Under Henry VII, the keeper was the Devon magnate, Edward Courtenay, Earl of Devon (d.1509).[93] Trematon Castle's constables were also responsible not only for supervision of the castle's park (which had maintained around 42 deer in 1337) but also for the manor of Calstock and the borough Ash as well as the waters of the River Tamar (Appendix VI.5).[94] The custodians included Thomas Bodulgate, and royal servants: the yeoman of the crown John Trevelyan;[95] the king's 'chief cook', John Hemyngburgh (d.1466);[96] and the groom of the king's chamber, Hugh Moresby (d.1480).[97] Lastly, the custody of Tintagel Castle was entrusted to Thomas Bodulgate and a succession of royal-household servants: John Trevelyan;[98] Thomas

Clemens;[99] and Richard III's master of the henchmen, Sir James Tyrell (Appendix VI.4).[100] It is evident that offices relating to the maintenance and supervision of the duchy's castles, parks, and property rights provided a wealth of patronage but the administration of the Duchy's other terrene prerogatives also presented further opportunities.

Stannary Administration: Coinage, Courts, and Convocations

The origins of metalliferous mining in Cornwall and Devon may be traced to the Bronze Age; accordingly, local mining or Stannary customary laws—pre-dating the English tenth-century subjugation of Cornwall—assimilated not only ancient Cornish but also Anglo-Saxon as well as Norman influences during its evolution. Hence the structures mediating the supervision of the Stannaries in Cornwall and Devon (absorbed into the Duchy's administration in 1337) owed their origins to developments in earlier centuries.[101] By the twelfth century, old customary laws had largely become embodied in Assize of Mine regulations which guided the systems of mining, smelting, and coining of tin. Metal and mineral prospecting—or bounding—was generally unrestricted by landowners' claims or rights (though the Duchy and other landlords could levy Toll Tin as a royalty for mining on their lands) but it was necessary for the boundaries (or bounds) of every individuals' prospecting plot to be recorded and registered. During the Middle Ages, tin extraction was mostly limited to the 'streaming' of alluvial deposits and to the pursuit of bountiful strata and seams through shallow shafts, pits, or trenches.[102] Once extracted, a series of smeltings—in local blowing houses—was required in order to remove impurities, refine the tin, and forge ingots before the bars could be weighed and assayed, coined (stamped with the duchy emblem), and subjected to a ducal duty (which during the later fifteenth century amounted to 40*s.* per thousand-weight) enabling it to be legally sold and removed from the Stannary. For these purposes, each Stannary district had its allocated coinage hall in which these processes of valuation and verification would be undertaken by Stannary officials: in Cornwall, the semi-annual tin coinages were held at Bodmin, Helston, Liskeard, Lostwithiel, and Truro (from 1305) and, in Devon, at Ashburton, Tavistock, and Chagford (from 1305), and Plympton (from 1328).[103] In 1495, new ordinances concerning smelting houses and the annual review and renewal of bounds were introduced but these soon proved unpopular with Cornish tinners: the miners' disregard for these regulations forced Henry VII to suspend their privileges. Understandably, this provoked a hostile reaction and may have inspired many Cornishmen to participate in the June and September Uprisings of 1497. Their objections did not remain unacknowledged and Henry later set his seal on Stannary administration with his granting of the Charter of 1508, whereby he provided pardons for miners and endorsed the Stannaries' convocations.[104]

The origins of the Stannaries' administrative machinery can be traced to 1198 when Richard I convened miners' juries to announce and affirm the laws and practices relating to tin mining; also appointing a lord warden to oversee these juries. Thereafter, tinners met in general assembly every seven or eight years until 1305 and thereafter at the discretion of the lords warden: the Cornish tinners' convocation which assembled at Hingston Down near Callington, comprised a total of 24 jurates or stannators nominated by the mayors and burgesses of the four Stannary towns of Launceston, Lostwithiel, Helston, and Truro; whereas the Devonian tinners' 'Great Court', which assembled at Crockern Tor, Dartmoor, was composed of a total of 96 stannators elected by tinners at sessions of the Stannary courts. Both convocations possessed legislative powers with regard to mining, smelting, and trading in tin.[105]

It was John's charter of 1201 which emancipated miners from serfdom, and made them subject to the jurisdiction of the lord warden. Consequently, there arose—during the course of the thirteenth century—a system of Stannary courts administering the law of the common law courts at Westminster except as varied by stannary customs or the acts of the Stannary convocations. Edward I's two charters of 1305 established tinners' exemption from certain local and national taxes, and their exemption from the jurisdiction of the ordinary courts (except for serious offences concerning life, land, or limb) ensuring that in all other instances they were subject to the jurisdiction of the Stannary courts. The chief courts of the Stannaries later became settled at Truro in Cornwall and at Lydford in Devon, whilst district courts were held regularly in each of the Stannary towns in Cornwall and Devon. These courts—composed of a jury of tinners under the presidency of a steward—were invested with magisterial and judicial functions in the prevention of offences and the trial of both civil and criminal cases, and also dealt with issues such as the registration of bounds, the verification of weights and measures, and the efficiency of Stannary administration. Those tin-miners judged guilty of a crime could receive a custodial sentence to be served in the Stannary gaols at Lydford Castle (for Devonian tinners) or at Lostwithiel Castle (Palace) (for Cornish tinners). Naturally, a path of appeal against the judgements of the stewards' courts emerged which led to the development of the equitable jurisdiction of the lords warden.[106]

The custody and supervision of the Stannaries in Cornwall and Devon appears to have been contiguous with the stewardships of the Duchy's estates (Appendix I, 5, 6), and the lords warden also enjoyed the right to muster the tinners in both Cornwall and Devon (as discussed earlier). With overall responsibility for both estate administration and stannary administration, it is understandable that each lord warden would delegate some of his multiplicity of duties to various deputies.[107] Enjoying quasi-legal powers as the Stannaries' chief judicial officers, the lords warden supervised the apparatus of Stannary courts and nominated stewards—as their representatives—to preside over each court. Accountable for overseeing the Stannary structures, the lords warden appointed bailiffs for each of the four districts in Cornwall (Blackmore, Fowey Moor, Penwith-in-Kerrier, and Tywarnail) and each of the four districts in Devon (Ashburton, Chagford, Plympton, and Tavistock).[108] This system of bailiffs and stewards was supervised by the bailiff-itinerant (or bailiff-errant) who also assisted in the collection of monies from a range of Duchy taxes (Appendix II.2).[109] The bailiffs-itinerant included Richard Lannargh from 1466;[110] the royal retainer John Trevelyan;[111] and Edward IV's steward of the household, Thomas, Lord Stanley (d.1504).[112]

In order to people and police the tin-coinage apparatus, a multitude of agents was essential: each Stannary's administration required receivers of coinage, controllers, collectors, weighers and assay masters, as well as numerous porters and peasers. However, it was the deputy of the lord warden, the controller of the coinage (or assay master) who was chiefly responsible for safeguarding standards and supervising the process of assaying, assessing, and stamping tin. Consequently, the post would have required some metallurgical knowledge, and awareness and understanding of the practices and processes of tin-extraction and mining operations. Furthermore, it was a role of some import since the controller also kept the counter-roll or duplicate accounts thereby ensuring that the lord warden followed proper process (Appendix II.1).[113] The controllers included the Cornishman William Treffry (d.1504) of Fowey, Cornwall;[114] the Devonian John Wykes (d.1489) of Bindon-in-Axmouth, Devon;[115] as well as several royal servants: the treasurer of the king's chamber and keeper of the king's jewels, John Merston;[116] the royal retainer Avery Cornburgh;[117] the knight of the body Thomas Vaughan (d.1483);[118] and the esquire and later knight of the body Sir John Sapcotes (d.1501) of Bampton, Devon, and Elton, Hampshire.[119] Similarly to the Duchy's rights concerning the Stannaries and their organization, the regalities regarding the administration and profits of ports, customs, and other marine perquisites had been attached to the earlier earldoms, and the supervision of these rights offered numerous prospects for service.[120]

Havenary Administration: Ports, Customs, and Fisheries

With its extensive coastlines and fruitful fisheries, the Duchy of Cornwall provided numerous opportunities for generating income from its maritime prerogatives. The right of wreck of the sea entitled the Duchy to claim half the value of any goods washed ashore along the Cornish coast. The prerogative of royal fish meant that any whales, grampuses, sturgeon, or porpoises washed ashore or caught in Cornish waters were the duke's perquisite. Likewise, the right of waif—privilege to claim goods abandoned or forfeited by their owners —was also a Duchy regality. Furthermore, the Duchy owned all Cornish ports as well as the port of Plymouth, and therefore levied annual rents, as well as a series of customs and tolls, from these fishing and trading havens. Ships and seafarers were governed by maritime law therefore, because of its prerogatives, the Duchy arbitrated disputes arising at sea or between mariners or merchants in its maritime courts whose judgements could, for example, impose fines on merchants or on individuals for concealment of merchandise from wreck. All profits from such maritime courts accrued to the Duchy. With such an array of marine and maritime privileges to administer in Cornwall and Devon, the management of the ports and collection of revenues was the jurisdiction of the Havenary: its chief officers were the havener and his deputy, the controller of the Havenary.[121]

Bearing responsibility for shipping, petty customs, and for collecting revenues, the havener's work was complex and multifaceted (Appendix III.1): expertise in finance and commerce (for understanding of freightage and commodity prices), and familiarity with merchants, mariners, and ship-owners were essential requirements. Besides the annual rents from Cornwall's seventeen fishing ports, the havener also received revenues from various tolls, customs, and dues ranging from the operation of ferries across the River Tamar, the use of sand from the seashore in construction and agriculture, the anchorage and moorage of ships, and the storage of cargoes, to fishing fines, and the levying of the toll paid by dealers in fish (Trantery). However, the more important of the customs were levied on hides and wools exported by denizens and alien merchants (Cocket); on all merchandise sold by alien merchants (Maltot); and on wine imported by foreign merchants (prisage of wine). The prisage of wines was the most significant custom since the duke was entitled to take a portion of each wine cargo: from smaller ships (one tun of wine) and from larger ships holding more than twenty tuns (two tuns, paying 40s.). The havener was accountable not only for the collection, storage, and conveyance of these wines, but also for wine sales (with profits accruing to the Duchy), for replenishing the duke's wine cellar at Lostwithiel, and for the dispatch of supplies to the duke's household.[122]

The office of havener incorporated duties as 'pesager' (peaser or weigher) of tin, and as keeper of the tinners' gaol at Lostwithiel, hence successive haveners were also linked with the custody of Lostwithiel Castle from 1361 onwards. The havener possessed quasi-legal powers and presided over the administration of the courts maritime, which were held at several locations (such as Plymouth, Portlooe, and Mounts Bay). The havener's stewards presided at each court, and his other deputies supervised the ports, collected customs, and collected Trantery and fishing fines; in short, the Havenary required a multitude of deputies, reeves, and bailiffs in order to collect the Duchy's dues and to preserve its entitlements.[123] During the later fifteenth century, the haveners included Thomas Treffry of Fowey, Cornwall;[124] John Delabere;[125] William Richmond;[126] Thomas Bodulgate;[127] and the London citizen and horner, Geoffrey Kidwelly (d.1484) of Little Whittenham, Berkshire. In addition, some royal-household retainers were also employed as havener, such as Thomas Clemens and Richard Edgcumbe;[128] Thomas Vaughan;[129] and Sir James Tyrell.[130]

The lucrative nature of the earnings that could be accrued from sea wrecks as well as many of the other maritime dues proved a temptation not only for local inhabitants but also for some Duchy officials. Hence, the havener's deputy – the controller of the Havenary – acted as a check on any possible malpractices by ensuring that the havener and his officials had followed appropriate procedures; the controller kept the counter-roll or duplicate accounts, and compiled his annual accounts or *compoti* (Appendix III.2). The controllers of the Havenary included the Cornishman, Peter Beville;[131] the Londoner, Thomas Oxeney (stepson of the royal-household retainer and Duchy officer, Avery Cornburgh);[132] and Henry VII's yeoman of the guard, Robert Walsh.[133]

Whilst the havener and his administration was accountable for supervising those ports in Cornwall pertaining to the Duchy, they were not directly responsible for collecting revenues from ports such as Tintagel, Fowey, or Sutton Water, whose rights were derived from the duke's tenure of particular properties. Even though the manor of Fowey was owned by the Priory of Tywardraeth, jurisdiction over the River Fowey was a right attached to the Duchy's Honour of Restormel. Despite the fact that Fowey was the heart of the havener's administration (as the location where all wines of prise were collected, as the nearest tin-trading port to the coinage centre at Lostwithiel, and as the chief port for exporting hides and fish), the custody of the river waters and its estuarine fishery (extending from Polruan to Respryn in Lanhydrock) was entrusted to a bailiff (Appendix III.3).[134] The maintenance of the Fowey and the rights of fishery, quayage, and various other perquisites was the responsibility of the keepers who included the royal servants John Trevelyan;[135] and Avery Cornburgh.[136] Similarly, authority over the estuarine waters of the River Tamar and Sutton Water was derived from the Duchy's Honour of Trematon. Sutton Water (Plymouth) was the most profitable of the Duchy's ports: it handled the largest amount of trade, with significant numbers of its harbouring vessels being involved in the wine trade. Hence the bailiff was an important figure, with responsibility as supervisor of the saltwater marine fisheries, as steward of the maritime court, and as collector of the presage of wines (Appendix III.4).[137] One of the keepers was the king's household retainer, Avery Cornburgh.[138] Whilst these bailiffs, and other of the havener's officials, aided in the collection of monies and revenues, ultimate responsibility for the administration of financial resources was in the charge of other officers.

Financial Administration: Revenue, Audit, and Account

In the management of a great landed estate, such as the Duchy of Cornwall, the receiver and the auditor were pivotal figures in the administrative hierarchy because of the importance of amassing and maintaining income from the estates and the superintendence of the Stannaries and ports. The role of auditor was a crucial one since it required expertise in accounting, legal affairs, and estate administration (Appendix IV.2) and this role was also the means through which the Exchequer could supervise the Duchy's finances. On their annual visits, the auditors reviewed all ministers' accounts and manorial court accounts, determining rents and incidents owed by tenants, and thereby providing an important link between tenantry, local receivers and ministers, and central administration.[139]

The receiver was a central administrative position bearing responsibility for the collection of all monies owed from a variety of sources, such as landed rents, and revenues from Stannaries, boroughs, county and hundred courts, the Havenary, and the feodary. The receiver would account for money due during the financial year and for arrears from previous years and, in this task, he would be assisted by various local reeves, bailiffs, and subordinate receivers collecting revenues from particular estates. During the fourteenth and early-fifteenth centuries, several receivers had been accountable for collecting revenues from particular Duchy estates or within specific shires, such as the Receiver for Cornwall; but, on 2 April 1413, John Willecotes was nominated as 'receiver-general of the duchy in Cornwall and Devon' and 'in all counties of the realm'.[140] This appointment established the receiver-general's overall authority to oversee the work of all deputies in Cornwall, Devon and the rest of England, and the work of subordinate receivers; henceforth, this officer became ultimately responsible for all the financial business of the Duchy, and for matters arising from the collection of revenues, for the payment of fees and salaries, and for the maintenance of the duchy's castles, parks, and other properties (Appendix IV.1).[141] Understandably, given its importance, the office was dominated by a succession of royal servants: in 1444, the clerk of controlment of the royal household, John Brecknock (d.1476) of Horsenden, Buckinghamshire, became receiver-general.[142] His successor was the usher of the king's chamber and husband of one of Queen Margaret's ladies, Robert Whittingham.[143] From 1461, Edward IV's chamberlain, Lord Hastings, fulfilled this role;[144] he was succeeded by Queen Elizabeth Woodville's brother, Earl Rivers.[145] Richard III nominated the household retainer Sir John Sapcotes to this post from May 1483.[146] Henry VII appointed Sir Robert, later Lord, Willoughby de Broke (d.1502);[147] who was succeeded by the knight of the body, Sir Richard Nanfan (d.1507) of Birtsmorton (Worcestershire) and Trethewell (Cornwall).[148]

Evidently, a series of administrative structures had evolved around the particular regalities that the duchy enjoyed and exploited—the revenues requiring collection, and the rights requiring preservation. At the apex of each of these structures presided its primary officer: the lord steward or other stewards (as applicable) superintending landed assets, terrene rights, and stannary structures; the havener supervising ports and marine perquisites; and the receiver-general surveying financial affairs. These officers—along with the attorney-general and perhaps certain others—comprised the Duchy's chief officers. During times when there was a duke of Cornwall, each of these individuals would have been ultimately accountable to the duke himself; so would these officers have formed a supreme policy-making body, a council?

Princes, Councils, and Councillors

Reporting to their duke, just such a council could have directed, controlled, and co-ordinated the regional and local administration of the Duchy's estates, ports, and other rights, and could have utilized its network of stewards and receivers to implement in the localities those decisions enacted at the centre. The Black Prince had instituted a council to administer his affairs in 1346 and—although this was intended to function only during his absence from the realm—it seems likely that this could have continued in operation as an advisory body during his lifetime.[149] In the absence of any further records of such a council, its existence during the fifteenth century remains pure conjecture, and any such body would have ceased to operate when the Duchy reverted to being subject to crown estate administration. However, even so, Duchy administration might be considered and evaluated within the broader context of the evolution of structures surrounding successive Princes of Wales during the later fifteenth century.

Throughout the medieval period, provision was made for the keeping of the prince's council chamber within the Palace of Westminster, which was utilized as an exchequer as well as a depository for the Duchy's records.[150] Even if this chamber became so encumbered with archives that a formal or informal meeting could not assemble there, a council could have been convened at another duchy residence, such as Kennington Palace or the Prince's Palace, in Old Jewry, London, where the 'prince's wardrobe' was located.[151] The nomination of a succession of keepers of the great wardrobe indicates the likely financial arrangements within the prince's household during this period, but the existence of a separate household for the Duke of Cornwall as well as the creation of a Council of the Prince of Wales at various times during the later fifteenth century may also obscure and cloud understanding of Duchy governance.[152] In 1457, Henry VI's son and heir, Edward, Prince of Wales (d.1471), was granted a council, which was intended to govern Wales and the marches, Cheshire, and Cornwall.[153] The eleven individuals described as the prince's 'councillors' were clearly members of this council, but how did this body interact with the Duchy's administrative structures? The only south-western landowner chosen as a councillor was James Butler, Earl of Ormonde and Wiltshire (d.1461) who later enjoyed Queen Margaret's favour and became, in effect, a regional magnate in south-west England.[154] Thus it was John, Viscount Beaumont, as chief steward of all the prince's lands (including the Duchy), who personified the only prime link between duke and Duchy amongst the prince's councillors.

Similarly, in July 1471, Edward IV's eldest son, Edward, Prince of Wales (d.1483), was granted a council for the supervision of Wales and the marches, Cheshire, and Cornwall.[155] Petitions to this council during the 1470s indicate that this body enjoyed jurisdiction over Cornwall and the Duchy; thus such matters were incorporated into the council's business.[156] Yet, of its fifteen councillors, none were Duchy officers—those such as the receiver-general or havener appear not to have been members of the Council of Wales. When the prince's council was reinstituted in February 1473, only one of the twenty-five councillors was a Duchy officer. Just as Viscount Beaumont had provided a link between Cornwall and council by virtue of his roles as councillor and lord steward of the Duchy, the prince's uncle, Earl Rivers came to represent a similar connection from 1473 as a result of his appointment as both the Duchy's lord steward and receiver-general. Earl Rivers also re-placed Richard Fiennes, Lord Dacre as lord steward of the prince's household by November 1476;[157] therefore, descriptions of the earl as the prince's 'lord steward' would have been doubly accurate. But similar such references may lead to misunderstanding since Sir William Stanley (d.1495) of Holt, Cheshire, had replaced Rivers as lord steward of the prince's household (but not lord steward of the Duchy) by February 1481.[158] Similarly, references to the prince's 'chancellor' clearly refer to the Abbot of Westminster and later Bishop of Hereford, Thomas Milling (d.1492), who was chancellor of the prince's household by February 1475;[159] and also to the prince's teacher John Alcock (d.1500), Bishop of Rochester, who had replaced Milling by February 1483.[160] Yet this post was unrelated to the office of chancellor of the Duchy of Cornwall held by Sir William Allington (as mentioned earlier).[161]

Such a council appears not to have been recreated for Richard III's son,

Edward, Prince of Wales (d.1484): the ten-year-old prince and his advisers were mostly preoccupied not with the Council of Wales but with northern England and with what was later to become the Council of the North.[162] The endowment of Henry Stafford, Duke of Buckingham (d.1483) with almost vice-regal authority in Wales may have ensured that the duke had some involvement in Duchy affairs before his disaffection.[163] After the October Rebellion of 1483, it was Richard's supporter William, Earl of Huntingdon— as a consequence of being restored to his lands, earldom of Pembroke, and awarded offices in Wales –who presumably became most influential in Duchy matters.[164] The council of Arthur, Prince of Wales (d.1502) seems to have been formed in around 1489, and the organization of his council and household appears to have borne some similarities with those of his predecessors.[165] By Michaelmas 1489, the Dean of Exeter, John Arundell, had been nominated as the prince's chancellor, and was also designated as the Duchy's chancellor in February 1490.[166] However, on account of the prince's youth, the overall supervision of this council was entrusted to the prince's grand-uncle, Jasper Tudor, Duke of Bedford (d.1495) who had been awarded several Welsh offices but gradually retired from public life after 1492.[167]

Evidently, it appears that the Duchy of Cornwall may have been represented at successive princes' councils by a small number of individuals, such as the lord steward and chancellor. If only one or two officers were answerable and accountable for Duchy administration to the prince and his council then this suggests that this officer, the lord steward or another, must have been fully acquainted with the entirety of the Duchy's affairs. Yet, in order to be so acquainted, it would have been necessary for the lord steward to consult and confer with the Duchy's other chief officers which, again, suggests the existence of a separate, albeit informal, Duchy council. The membership of such a body remains unclear since it is difficult simply to equate its members with the princes' councillors but it seems likely that, primarily, it would have comprised the Duchy's chief officers (perhaps with additions from amongst the prince's councillors or other pertinent personalities). Whilst the operation of a Duchy council remains mere supposition, irrespective of its existence it is evident that the Duchy's administration cannot be viewed in isolation—the prince's Duchy, the prince's council, and the prince's household structures were intricately interwoven.

Just as each of these structures was entwined, so was the relationship between the princes and their provinces: the princes' power derived from their territories whilst, simultaneously, the very validity and continuity of their provinces' autonomy or 'semi-autonomy' derived from their prince. Hence it has been suggested that the prince's government provided an 'institutional corset' within which local loyalties and identities developed.[168] As the core of royal authority in Cornwall and south-west England and—in combination with the prince's other territories—as one of the central facets of royal authority in the realm as a whole, the Duchy of Cornwall was clearly a resource of paramount importance in late-medieval governance. Naturally, then, the Duchy's significance—alongside its singular constitutional status—dictated that its personnel would incorporate figures of national relevance; but did this affect the Duchy's ability to offer opportunities for members of local society to contribute and participate as well as to provide prospects for promotion and progress? Moreover, what was the pertinence and position of the Duchy within a broader perspective of governance and core-periphery relations?

Polity, Power, and Periphery

During the later fifteenth century, significant national figures were chosen as Duchy of Cornwall officers, including courtiers such as Lord Stafford, Lord Hastings, Earl Rivers, and Sir James Tyrell. How much significance should be attached to such courtiers' nominations? Were these appointments merely sinecures? If these were absentee office-holders, should consideration of their influence be discarded in favour of considering that of their designated deputies? On the contrary, in the world of government and politics where—as a Wildean epigram might espouse 'appearance is everything'—perception, image, and symbolism were important considerations: even honorific appointments held meaning and provided their recipients with some status. Selection to fulfil Duchy office was indicative of a courtier's status, standing, and influence in the king's company, and this was itself an immense source of power which might then be wielded at a local or regional level. Irrespective of whether the courtier was industrious or indolent in discharging the demands of his office in person, such nominations were accompanied by the condition that should he fail to fulfil the requisite duties then he was required to ensure sufficient alternative provision; thus, even in the absence of the courtier, his deputy represented him, his lordship, his patronage, and his power at a local level—akin to the way in which a courtier represented his sovereign in a locality. Hence rather than discarding consideration of courtiers' appointments, it is necessary to give apposite attention to the impact and influence of these individuals' selection.

Crown, Cores, and Courtiers

The monarch's patronage was a key instrument of political management: judicious, restrained, and balanced distribution of patronage was one measure of good governance. Royal favour conferred status and authority therefore it constituted real political power for the recipient and indirect local influence for the king. Those 'closely and positively connected with authority . . . possess a vital relationship to the center [*sic*]': thus by awarding a particular magnate with estates, his local power could be legitimized, endorsed, and expanded thereby altering and augmenting his region of lordship and sphere of influence.[169] By awarding local or regional offices, a magnate's lordship could be further strengthened, giving him even greater influence as a result of his jurisdiction over others' men in the king's name.[170] Greater influence for a royal favourite therefore translated—in the language of government—into even greater local influence for the monarch himself. If a magnate represented a 'vital relationship' with the centre then a magnate endowed with a significant concentration of estates within a region might be described as a subsidiary core of power: bringing royal authority more strongly into the locality thereby becoming the region's locus as well as the centre's regional representative. Yet the excessive fragmentation—or the extreme fusion—of power was liable to promote and provoke instability.

If an individual could become the focus of a region of lordship, an institution could also exert a powerful force in local affairs through its region of influence: its direct relationship with the crown ensured that the Duchy of Cornwall radiated royal authority throughout Cornwall, Devon, and south-west England, and was a significant supplement to the other agencies of royal power in the localities. If the Duchy with its political hinterland—as a subsidiary core—symbolized sovereign power, then its principal office-holders were also representatives of the crown. Should the authority of Duchy office be awarded to a recipient who already commanded considerable sway in local or regional affairs, the supplement of Duchy power would enhance his region of lordship whilst, simultaneously, his personal authority would expand the Duchy's sphere of influence.

At a time of enfeebled monarchy, Henry VI's lack of leadership may have meant that local gentry and Duchy officers sought immediate security and benefaction from alternative sources. Lord Bonville's prominence in Devon affairs—combined with his Duchy office—therefore may have led Cornish gentry to seek his patronage thereby expanding and reinforcing his provincial leadership and causing Cornwall to be further entangled in the wider theatre of south-western politics. In order to remedy Henry VI's inadequate kingship, it seems that Queen Margaret's direction of government from 1457—with her exploitation of the power of the crown estates and creation of regional hegemonies for her favourites—was designed to reassert royal authority.[171] In the same way, Edward IV's 'regional policy' of governance with magnates representing the realm's regions in the North, the Midlands, Wales, East Anglia, and Cornwall and the south-west—also appears to have pursued the aim of restoring the status of the crown.[172] Exhibiting a close relationship with their sovereign, such regional 'governors'—as ancillary centres of royal authority—could represent and reassert royal authority more effectively at a local level; however, more importantly, a governor in possession of Duchy office could become an especially prominent local representative of monarchical power. Lord Stafford's landed estates made him a significant figure in Somerset and Dorset but his rewards with forfeited Lancastrian lands, the earldom of Devon, and a number of Duchy offices meant that he assumed a vicegerential role in the south-west during the 1460s, with a region of influence extending from Cornwall to Wiltshire.

All magnates were expected to uphold justice and preserve the stability of local society, offer access to royal patronage and opportunities for service, assistance, and support: ideally, a regional magnate would have a greater capacity to provide all these aspects. However, should the potentate's lordship prove to be unjust or unacceptable the king might prove unwilling to intervene since such action would undermine his chosen magnate's authority. Disillusioned clients or rivals would therefore have a limited ability to seek redress of their grievances thereby provoking tensions within local society. Simultaneously, a regional governor would be closely tied into royal authority by 'enmeshing' between 'prominent members of his retinue' and members of the king's affinity thereby forming a 'network of royal governance and control';[173] but such quasi-regal status meant that he occupied an immensely powerful position. Possessing the ability to array the king's men and with enormous resources at his disposal, a regional governor held the potential to fortify or fragment—to defend or destroy—the crown's authority. Moreover, identification of such a figure as representing royal authority entailed identification of his actions as sanctioned and supported by the crown itself: hence, potentially, any abuses would taint royal authority with a perception of partiality thereby enervating the status of the crown.[174] It may have been the combination of these consequences of regional governance which led to Lord Stafford's execution and to Henry VI's Readeption.

During Edward IV's second reign, the awarding of Duchy office to Thomas, Marquess of Dorset would have consolidated his influence in the region, which was based on his marriages to two south-western heiresses (though the extent to which he was able to establish his position before 1483 remains uncertain).[175] The nature of Edward's gubernatorial system— the reservation of royal favour within a select circle of courtiers—may have compromised his impartiality thereby provoking calls of exclusivity and inciting antipathy; simultaneously, his dependence on the concord and cooperation of his governors vitiated the status of the crown itself. Thus Edward's over-endowment of his brother Richard, Duke of Gloucester, with power in northern England may be blamed for the events of 1483 and the deposition of the uncrowned Edward V. Duchy office appears to have been utilized by Richard III in order to win the support of Lord Dinham and to extend Sir James Tyrell's local influence; however, by bestowing almost vice-regal authority in Wales on his chief supporter Buckingham, Richard was fated to face the same negative consequences of regional governance in the form of the October Rebellion of 1483.[176] In contrast, Henry VII's more equitable and more extensive distribution of Duchy patronage appears to indicate that he recognized the constraints and consequences of vast concentrations of power: he utilized Duchy offices in order to expand the local standing of individuals only on a very much smaller scale, as represented in the example of the steward of his household, Lord Willoughby.[177] The invocation of Duchy authority to amplify the influence of a succession of regional magnates during the later fifteenth century clearly had profound implications: it may have adjusted the dynamics of local and regional politics and power and intensified instability with its concomitant consequences for the crown. However, the invocation of Duchy authority in this manner also demonstrates the prime importance of the Duchy of Cornwall in the governance of south-west England, and the realm as a whole.

Polity, Locality, and Affinity

Courtiers were not the only embodiments of a connection between core and country, polity and periphery—numerous members of the royal household enjoyed Duchy office (whether active or absentee), such as John Merston and John Trevelyan during Henry VI's reign; Avery Cornburgh and Thomas Grayson under Edward IV; Halnath Mauleverer and Sir John Sapcotes during Richard III's reign; and Richard and Piers Edgcumbe under the first Tudor king. In addition to these household retainers, during Edward IV's second reign a number of Woodville associates had been granted Duchy offices, such as the queen's cousin Sir John Fogge and his son, John (joint-feodary, and joint-constable of Launceston Castle), the prince's chamberlain, Thomas Vaughan (havener and controller of the Stannaries), and the prince's attorney-general, Sir William Allington (chancellor). Whilst the replacement of some Duchy officers by Woodville protégés may have played some part in spurring some to support Richard III's usurpation, such appointments were hardly unique to the Duchy (being echoed throughout the households of the king, the queen, and the princes) and it may have been the close-knit nature of these royal households which also provoked complaints against the exclusivity of Edward's governance.[178] With such a preponderance of royal servants in the Duchy's administration, would their awards have limited and inhibited the involvement of local gentry?

Whilst, the honour of Duchy office may have been given and granted to various royal retainers, several notable officers were members of local society, such as the Cornishmen, Edmund Arundell of Tremodret, Thomas Bodulgate of Trencreek, and William Treffry of Fowey, and the Devon landowner Walter Courtenay of Exeter. Moreover, there were also a multiplicity of opportunities for remunerative participation in the Duchy's structures: as seen, members of local society could contribute as porters, peasers, weighers or receivers in the Stannaries' coinage administrations, as bailiffs of the Stannaries, as stewards or jurors of the Stannary courts, as jurates or stannators of the Stannaries' convocations, as bailiffs and stewards in manorial and hundred courts, as customs officers, port officials, as stewards in maritime courts, and in various other roles as reeves, bailiffs, and other officials who were required to ensure the fluent operation of the Duchy's machinery of governance. Clearly, then, the incidence of royal retainers appears to be of slighter significance when evaluated within the overall perspective of the entirety of the Duchy's administrative structures.

The multitude of means by which members of local society could become involved in Duchy structures may have provided residents of Cornwall and Devon with an advantage in comparison to their contemporaries from elsewhere. Whilst we cannot say definitively that anterior Duchy service facilitated entry into royal service, there appears to have been some correlation and coincidence between them: for some individuals, a successful Duchy career may have been a mile-mark along a path of progression destined for royal-household service. If the Duchy's administrative opportunities enabled many members of local society to aspire to—and to achieve—positions at court then would it not be natural to find Duchy offices populated by courtiers and royal servants? Indeed, many of the courtiers granted Duchy offices had risen to national prominence from Cornwall, Devon, or the wider south-west: Lord Dinham, was a Devon landowner; Lord Stafford, was a native of Dorset with wider south-western interests; and Lord Willoughby, possessed lands in Cornwall and Devon. Moreover, many royal-household servants originated from the region: the Devonians Thomas Grayson of Dartmouth, Henry Ley of Bere Ferrers, and Sir John Sapcotes of Bampton; and the Cornishmen Thomas Clemens of Liskeard, Thomas Whalesburgh of Whalesburgh and his son-in-law, John Trevelyan, John Arundell of Lanherne, Sir Richard Nanfan, and the Edgcumbes of Cotehele. Even Richard III's henchman, Sir James Tyrell, claimed a Cornish connection on account of his marriage to a daughter of John Arundell of Lanherne.

Whilst it may be appealing to attempt to categorize Duchy officers as figures of local, regional, or national stature, such discernment and classification is problematic because the distinction between such county, region, and court personalities is an indefinite one. The intertwining between Duchy and royal retainers would entail the strengthening and supplementing of Duchy influence in the localities, and the presence of courtiers and royal retainers as Duchy officers again indicates the central importance of the Duchy to the monarchy. With each household retainer embodying a personal link between Cornwall and the court, the royal connection with the Duchy would become further fortified thereby aiding and assisting in the development of sentiments of difference and distinctiveness.

Conclusions

Politically and constitutionally, the Duchy ensured that Cornwall remained distinctly different from England and Wales yet reflected the realm as a whole: it was a microcosm of national politics and government, with numerous courtiers, members of the king's council, and royal retainers peopling its elite. The Duchy's officers exhibit the advance and atrophy—the rise and retreat—of fortunes in local, regional, and national politics and governance whilst also indicating broader dynamics and developments in governance: in the Duchy's patronage we can delineate the consequences of Henry VI's inadequacy, the contours of Edward IV's regional governance, and the nature of Henry VII's patronage. Just as many magnates suffered because of their partiality during the Wars of the Roses and many gentry survived because of their impartiality, in the Duchy's administration most senior officers (mainly peers) were relatively evanescent whilst more junior officers (largely gentry) were more enduring—with many enjoying continuity in office.

Interpretation of Duchy administration as either a medium by which Cornishmen ascended to royal service at court, or as a medium abused by courtier-officers presents an impression of simplicity; reality presents an image of complexity. Ranging from the local gentry who prospered in royal-household service to the courtiers who preserved Cornish connections and estates, many recipients of Duchy offices foil and defy definitive categorization as figures of exclusively local, regional, or national significance. Whilst concentrating on examination of the Duchy's principal officers, this survey has highlighted some of the numerous opportunities which the Duchy offered to miners, mariners, merchants, tenants, and landowners. Since admittance to the Duchy's elite was secured not only by landed status but also by personal associations and expertise, the administration provided an agency for advancement, careerism, and social mobility thereby contributing to the fortuity and fortunes of various families and individuals in terms of their power, position, and opulence. Trading and tin-mining were interests embraced by a cross-section of society, from women, yeomen, and tradesmen, to landowners, gentry, and religious guilds. Likewise, marine activities such as fishing and trading also encompassed a wide range of participants from mariners and merchants to landowners and gentry. Thus the Duchy's range of tolls and fines, Stannary and maritime jurisdictions, and officers and officials also embraced a broad social spectrum of society meaning that the Duchy's influence pervaded and permeated almost every aspect of local life. As a consequence, Duchy office would have featured strongly in the aspirations of many, from tenantry to gentry; therefore it is also likely that the Duchy's singular structures of governance would have acted as a cohesive focus for local loyalties and a prominent force in the modelling and moulding of local identities.

The Duchy's singular structures encouraged participation whilst also feeding and fuelling senses of solidarity and separation: if the tenth-century kingdom was a spring, the earlier Norman earldoms were rivulets—tributaries to the Duchy—which, like a river, coloured and cultivated the landscape of Cornish identity. Whereas in many English counties, gentry identities may have coalesced predominantly around shire institutions, the concurrence and conjunction of region, county, and Duchy may have meant that the Duchy braced and buttressed county structures whilst also presenting an alternative arena of royal service.[179] This coincidence and combination of aspirations and affections for the Duchy may have engendered a vivid and vehement attachment to the crown in Cornwall, as exemplified during the Wars of the Roses and in later Royalist support during the seventeenth century's British Civil Wars.[180]

Yet, always, such loyalties remained symbiotic: Cornish appreciation of the Duchy depended on the Duchy's appreciation of the Cornish, their customs, and their liberties. It was a relationship reliant on reciprocation; hence, when the crown was believed to have reneged on its responsibilities (such as in 1497 and 1549), the Cornish rose to restore their rights and to remedy this relationship's perceived inequity. If some liberties' capacity to inspire loyalty, command allegiance, and encourage bonds of community might be queried, it appears that such a challenge is posed with some difficulty with regard to the Duchy.[181] Far from detracting from the monarch's sovereign power, the Duchy of Cornwall appears to have been one of the foremost factors in the development of local loyalty and identity in Cornwall, constituting a crucial component in the governance of a peripheral province as represented in its patronage, politics, and power during the Wars of the Roses.

Appendix

The Principal Officers of the Duchy of Cornwall, 1453–1502

The primary aim of this appendix is to offer a list of the principal office-holders of the Duchy of Cornwall between 1453 and 1502. By no means all Duchy offices are recorded in the following lists, but the principal positions and the more important of the posts relating to Cornwall and Devon—such as those relating to castles and parks—have been included (whilst details of individuals' salaries, annuities, and other aspects have been omitted). The nature of the extant archives may mean that a complete picture of Duchy administration can never be reconstructed: this list—and the conclusions drawn from it—must be regarded as merely provisional in nature, being subject to amendment and correction as a result of further research. This appendix has been arranged to reflect the structure of the preceding analysis, being divided into sections relating to the Duchy's regalities: estates (I); Stannaries (II); ports, customs, and fisheries (III); revenues and accounts (IV); and sections detailing the officers of the duchy's parks, forests, and chases (V) and castles (VI) in Cornwall and Devon. Cross-referencing (indicating where individuals held multiple offices) has been kept to a minimum, and has been undertaken primarily with regard to the offices of lord steward and lord warden, steward and lord warden in Cornwall, and steward and lord warden in Devon, in order to illustrate the correlation between these posts.

I. Estates in Cornwall and Devon

1. Lords Steward and Lords Warden of the Stannaries in Cornwall and Devon

1457	Jan 20	John Beaumont, Viscount Beaumont
1465		Humphrey Stafford, Lord Stafford of Southwick (later Earl of Devon)
		See Stewards in Cornwall (1461); Stewards in Devon (1465)
1469	Nov 7	Sir John Stafford (later Earl of Wiltshire)
1473	Mar 15	Anthony Woodville, Earl Rivers
1483	May 20	John Dinham, Lord Dinham
		See Stewards in Cornwall (1483); Stewards in Devon (1483)
1485	Sep 17	Sir Robert Willoughby (later Lord Willoughby de Broke)
1502	Dec 9	Robert Willoughby, Lord Willoughby de Broke

2. Chancellors and Keepers of the Great Seal

1476		Sir William Allington
1490	Feb 20	John Arundell, Bishop of Coventry and Lichfield
1502		Robert Frost

3. Feodaries (or Escheators) in Cornwall and Devon

1451	Jun 28	Edward Ellesmere
1460	Oct 16	Avery Cornburgh
1473	Feb 14	Sir John Fogge and John Fogge
1484	Feb 17	Thomas Sapcotes
1485	Sep 20	Sir Richard Edgcumbe
1489	Nov 15	Peter Edgcumbe
1502	Dec 9	Sir Peter Edgcumbe and Roger Holland

4. Attorneys-General

1457	Feb 20	Thomas Throckmorton
1472	Jun 22	Sir William Allington
1477		John Twynho
1490	Feb 5	John Mordaunt

5. Cornwall: Stewards of Estates and Lords Warden of the Stannaries

1452	Mar 8	William Bonville, Lord Bonville
1457		John Beaumont, Viscount Beaumont
		See Lords Steward (1457)
1461	May 1	Thomas Clemens
1461	Jun 15	Sir Humphrey Stafford (later Lord Stafford of Southwick and Earl of Devon)
		See Lords Steward (1465)
1469	Nov 7	Sir John Stafford (later Earl of Wiltshire)
		See Lords Steward (1469)
1473		Anthony Woodville, Earl Rivers
		See Lords Steward (1473)
1476		Sir Thomas Bourchier
1477	Apr	Thomas Grey, Marquess of Dorset
1483		John Dinham, Lord Dinham
		See Lords Steward (1483)

1484	Aug 9	Sir James Tyrell
1485		Sir Robert Willoughby (later Lord Willoughby de Broke) *See Lords Steward (1485)*
1486	Oct 12	Sir John Halliwell
1502		Robert Willoughby, Lord Willoughby de Broke *See Lords Steward (1502)*

6. Devon: Stewards of Estates and Lords Warden of the Stannaries

1442	Oct 20	John Trevelyan
1457		John Beaumont, Viscount Beaumont *See Lords Steward (1457)*
1461	Jul 18	Roger Dinham
1465	Mar 27	Humphrey Stafford, Lord Stafford of Southwick (later Earl of Devon) See Lords Steward (1465)
1469	Oct 17	John Dinham, Lord Dinham
1469	Nov 7	Sir John Stafford (later Earl of Wiltshire) *See Lords Steward (1469)*
1473		Anthony Woodville, Earl Rivers *See Lords Steward (1473)*
1483	Jun 24	John Dinham, Lord Dinham *See Stewards in Cornwall (1483)*
1485		Sir Robert Willoughby (later Lord Willoughby de Broke) *See Lords Steward (1485)*
1485	Sep 20	Sir Walter Courtenay
1502		Robert Willoughby, Lord Willoughby de Broke *See Lords Steward (1502)*

II. Stannaries in Cornwall and Devon

1. Controllers of the Stannaries (Deputy Lords Warden), Controllers of the Coinage, and Masters of Assay

1432	Jul 22	John Merston
1455	Mar 23	Avery Cornburgh
1461	Jul 20	John Wykes
1471		Sir Thomas Vaughan
1483	May 19	Avery Cornburgh
1485		Thomas Hourde

1485		William Treffry
		See Constables of Lostwithiel Castle (1486)
1490		John Sapcotes

2. Bailiffs-Itinerant

1441	Oct 4	John Trevelyan
1466		Richard Lannargh
1472	Apr 4	Thomas Stanley, Lord Stanley (later Earl of Derby)
1486	Oct 4	John Rode

III. Ports, Customs, and Fisheries in Cornwall and Devon

1. Haveners (Keepers of the Havenary) in Cornwall and the Port of Plymouth in Devon (and Bailiff of the Stannary of Blackmore)

1431	Nov 8	Thomas Treffry
1454		John Delabere
1455	May 5	Thomas Bodulgate and Geoffrey Kidwelly
1461	Aug 1	Thomas Clemens, Richard Edgcumbe, and Geoffrey Kidwelly
1461	Dec 11	Nicholas Loure
1471		Sir Thomas Vaughan
1472		William Richmond
1477		Richard Holton
1483		Sir James Tyrell
1485		Robert Walsh
1486		John Monkeley
1502		Thomas Elyot

2. Controllers of the Havenary (Deputy Haveners) in Cornwall and Devon

1462	Mar 2	Thomas Oxeney
1486	Sep 20	Robert Walsh
1502		Peter Beville

3. Cornwall: Keepers of the Waters of the River Fowey in the Honour of Restormel

1443	Nov 12	John Trevelyan
1466	Jan 20	Avery Cornburgh

4. Cornwall/Devon: Bailiffs of the Waters of Sutton Water (Plymouth) in the Honour of Trematon

1460	Oct 16	Avery Cornburgh
1502		William Robyns

IV. Revenues and Accounts

1. Receivers-General

1444	Sep 23/4	John Brecknock
1456	Sep 26	Robert Whittingham
1461	May 8	William Hastings, lord Hastings
1473	Feb 14	Anthony Woodville, Earl Rivers
1483	May 21	Sir John Sapcotes
1485	Sep 24	Sir Robert Willoughby (later Lord Willoughby de Broke)
1503		Sir Richard Nanfan

2. Auditors

1445	Sep 21	Richard Flint and Richard Bedford
1452	Jun 9	Thomas Pygge and Richard Bedford
1454	Jul 8	John Eltonhede and Richard Bedford
1455	Jul 28	Robert Burton
1461	Jul 23	Thomas Aleyn
1461	Sep 9	John Broke
1477		Robert Coort
1484	Aug 20	Thomas Aleyn
1485	Sep 21	Robert Coort
1485	Sep 23	Thomas Aleyn
1493		Thomas Hobson

V. Parks, Forests, and Chases in Cornwall and Devon

1. Cornwall: Keepers of Carrybullock Park (and keepers of the woods of Heregard, Northwood, and Grendescombe, and the warrens of Carrybullock, Calstock, and Rillaton)

1448	Nov 20	John Nayler
1461	Jun 29	Thomas Grayson
1461	Dec 9	Avery Cornburgh and Thomas Grayson

1468		Avery Cornburgh
1485	Sep 20	John Parker
1486	Jun 7	Sir Richard Edgcumbe
1490	Mar 8	William Treffry

2. Cornwall: Keepers of Helsbury and Lanteglos Parks

1445	Sep 12	John Arundell
1461	Dec 6	Thomas Melley
1465	Mar 1	John Penfoun
1471	Jul 19	John Robyns
1485	Sep 24	Henry Ley
1501		Edmund Arundell

3. Cornwall: Keepers of Liskeard Park

1447	Apr 28	Thomas Bodulgate and John Trevelyan
1461	Mar 6	Thomas Clemens
1477	Aug 18	William Hastings, Lord Hastings
1485	Sep 24	William Frost

4. Devon: Master Forester or Ranger of the Forest and Chase of Dartmoor

1446	Dec 1	Sir Philip Courtenay and Edmund Hungerford
1452	Sep 8	William Bonville, Lord Bonville
1461	Jul 22	John Dinham (later Lord Dinham)
1464	Nov 11	*Steward:* Humphrey Stafford, Lord Stafford of Southwick (later Earl of Devon)
1469	Oct 17	John Dinham, Lord Dinham
1485	Sep 20	Sir Walter Courtenay
1502	Dec 9	Robert Willoughby, Lord Willoughby de Broke *See Lords Steward (1502)*

VI. Castles in Cornwall and Devon

1. Cornwall: Constables of Launceston Castle (and keepers of the park)

1451	Jun 28	Edward Ellesmere
1460	Oct 16	Avery Cornburgh
1473	Feb 14	Sir John Fogge and John Fogge

1483		Halnath Mauleverer
1485	Sep 20	Sir Richard Edgcumbe
1489	Nov 15	Peter Edgcumbe
1502	Dec 9	Sir Peter Edgcumbe and Roger Holland

2. Cornwall: Constables of Lostwithiel Castle (and keepers of the Stannary gaol)

1444	Feb 1	Thomas Bodulgate and John Trevelyan
		See Havener (1455)
1486	Oct 17	William Treffry

3. Cornwall: Constables of Restormel Castle (and keepers of the park)

1448	Nov 14	John Trevelyan
1461	May 13	William Sayer
1466	Jan 20	Avery Cornburgh
1486	Feb 8	Edward Courtenay, Earl of Devon

4. Cornwall: Constables of Tintagel Castle

1444	Feb 1	Thomas Bodulgate and John Trevelyan
1452	Sep 3	Thomas Bodulgate and Thomas Clemens
1461	Jul 28	Thomas Clemens
c.1484		Sir James Tyrell
1486		John Upcott
1490	Oct 10	Henry Wynselowe

5. Cornwall: Constables of Trematon Castle (and keepers of the park, and of the manor of Calstock and the borough of Ash)

1448	Nov 14	John Trevelyan
1461	Jul 27	John Hemyngburgh
1466	Aug 9	Hugh Moresby
1486	Sep 20	Robert Walsh

6. Devon: Constables of Lydford Castle (keepers of the stannary gaol, keepers of the manor and borough of Lydford, and stewards of South Teigne)

See Master Foresters of Dartmoor

Notes and references

1. I am grateful to Professor M.J. Hatcher and the external reader for their comments on an earlier version of this paper. All manuscript references refer to those held at The National Archives, Public Record Office, Kew, unless otherwise stated, and references with the prefix DCO concern documents held at the Duchy of Cornwall Office, London.

2. The accessionable manors included Trematon, Saltash, Tintagel (Bossiney), Grampound, Helston, Camelford, Lostwithiel, Launceston, and Liskeard (Cornwall). The Duchy's other estates included the castle, manor, and park of Mere (Wiltshire); Castle Rising (Norfolk); the Honour of Wallingford and St Valery (Berkshire); the Honour of Berkhamsted (Oxfordshire); the manors of Byflete and Kennington (Surrey), Cheylesmore (Warwickshire), Newport (Essex), Shoreham (Sussex), Rockingham (Northamptonshire); and the Soke-in-Kirton in Lindsay (Lincolnshire): *Calendar of the Patent Rolls, 1334–8* (London, 1895–1963), p. 447 (hereafter *CPR*); M.J. Hatcher, *Rural Economy and Society in the Duchy of Cornwall, 1300–1500* (Cambridge, 1970), pp. 3, 5–6; G. Haslam, 'Evolution' in C. Gill (ed.), *The Duchy of Cornwall* (Newton Abbot, 1987), pp. 24–26, 29.

3. *The Caption of Seisin of the Duchy of Cornwall (1337)*, ed. P.L. Hull, Devon and Cornwall Record Society, new ser., 17 (1971), pp. 140–1; cf. J.R. Dickinson, *The Lordship of Man under the Stanleys: Government and Economy in the Isle of Man, 1580–1704*, Chetham Society, new ser., 41 (1996), p. 22.

4. The eight hundreds were East Wivel, West Wivel, Stratton, Lesnewth, Kerrier, Pydar, Powder, Trigg, and a one-third moiety of Penwith: *Caption of Seisin*, ed. Hull, pp. 133–34.

5. Hatcher, *Rural Economy*, pp. 5–6; Haslam, 'Evolution', pp. 27–28.

6. *The Haveners' Accounts of the Earldom and Duchy of Cornwall, 1287–1346*, ed. M. Kowaleski, Devon and Cornwall Record Society, new ser., 44 (2001), pp. 1–78; Campbell, 'Haveners', pp. 113–44.

7. A.L. Rowse, *Tudor Cornwall: Portrait of a Society* (London, 1941), pp. 9, 82; J. Cornwall, *Revolt of the Peasantry, 1549* (London, 1977), p. 42; cf. J.P.D. Cooper, *Propaganda and the Tudor State: Political Culture in the West Country* (Oxford, 2003), pp. 172–73.

8. B. Deacon, *Cornwall: A Concise History* (Cardiff, 2007), p. 37.

9. R. Lomas, *North-East England in the Middle Ages* (Edinburgh, 1992), pp. 77–80; T. Thornton, 'Fifteenth-Century Durham and the Problem of Provincial Liberties in England and the wider Territories of the English Crown', *Transactions of the Royal Historical Society*, 6th ser., 11 (2001), pp. 83–100; M.L. Holford, 'Office-Holders and political society in the liberty of Durham, 1241–1345 (Part I)', *Archaeologia Aeliana*, 5th ser., 36 (2007), pp. 97–99; D.J. Clayton, *The Administration of the County Palatine of Chester*, Chetham Society, 3rd ser., 35 (1990); T. Thornton, *Cheshire and the Tudor State* (London, 2000).

10. P.J. Payton, *The Making of Modern Cornwall: Historical Experience and the Persistence of 'Difference'* (Redruth, 1992), p. 48.

11. *CP*, iii, pp. 427–34. For the relevance of regnal solidarities in the formation of identities: R.R. Davies, 'The Peoples of Britain and Ireland, 1100–1400: II. Names, Boundaries, and Regnal Solidarities', *Transactions of the Royal Historical Society*, 6th ser., 5 (1995), pp. 9–10, 12–13, 25–26.

12. K.J. Stringer, 'Tynedale: Power, Society, and Identities, *c*.1200–1296' in M.L. Holford and K.J. Stringer (eds), *Border Liberties and Loyalties: North-East England, c.1200–c.1400* (Edinburgh, 2010), pp. 231–90; K.J. Stringer, 'Tynedale: A Community in Transition, 1296–*c*.1400' in Holford and Stringer (eds), *Border Liberties and Loyalties*, pp. 291–358; K.J. Stringer, 'Redesdale' in Holford and Stringer (eds), *Border Liberties and Loyalties*, pp. 359–412.

13. M. Coate, 'The Duchy of Cornwall: Its History and Administration 1640 to 1660', *Transactions of the Royal Historical Society*, 4th ser., 10 (1927), p. 135.

14. One study of the Duchy's history from 1337 is Gill (ed.), *Duchy of Cornwall*. Studies of the medieval duchy include: Hatcher, *Rural Economy*; *Caption of Seisin*, ed. Hull. Studies of the Tudor and Stewart Duchy are M. Coate, *Cornwall in the Great Civil War and Interregnum, 1642–60: A Social and Political Study* (Oxford, 1933; 2nd edn, Truro, 1963); Rowse, *Tudor Cornwall*; G. Haslam, 'The Duchy and Parliamentary Representation in Cornwall, 1547–1640', *Journal of the Royal Institution of Cornwall*, new ser., 8 (1980), pp. 224–42; G. Haslam, 'The Elizabethan Duchy of Cornwall: An estate in stasis', and 'Jacobean Phoenix: The Duchy of Cornwall in the principates of Henry Frederick and Charles' in R.W. Hoyle (ed.), *The Estates of the English Crown, 1558–1640* (Cambridge, 1992), pp. 88–111, 263–96.

15. R.R. Pennington, *Stannary Laws: A History of Mining Law of Cornwall and Devon* (Newton Abbot, 1973), pp. 223–26.

16. S.M. Campbell, 'The Haveners of the Medieval Dukes of Cornwall and the Organisation of the Duchy Ports', *Journal of the Royal Institution of Cornwall*, new ser., 4 (1962), pp. 113–44; *Haveners' Accounts, 1287–1346*, ed. Kowaleski, pp. 11–17, 315–21.

17. G. Haslam, 'An Administrative Study of the Duchy of Cornwall, 1500–1650', unpublished PhD thesis, Louisiana State University, 1980, pp. 303–5.

18. Cornwall, *Revolt of the Peasantry*, pp. 42–43; cf. Cooper, *Propaganda and the Tudor State*, p. 179.

19. Hatcher, *Rural Economy*, pp. 137–38, 159–60, 198; Haslam, 'Evolution', pp. 24–26.

20. *The Parliament Rolls of Medieval England, 1275–1504* (hereafter *PR*), ed. C.J. Given-Wilson (Woodbridge, 2005), xiv, pp. 422–24; xv, pp. 233–39; xvi, pp. 144ff; *CPR 1467–77*, pp. 275, 289, 566; *CP*, x, pp. 402–3; 'Herbert, William, first earl of Pembroke' (R.A. Griffiths), *ODNB*.

21. Haslam, 'Administrative Study', pp. 19–20; R.E. Stansfield, *Political Elites in South-West England, 1450–1500: Politics, Governance, and the Wars of the Roses* (Lewiston, NY, Queenston, and Lampeter 2009), p. 88.

22. SC 6/816/2, m. 2; SC 6/816/3, m. 2; SC 6/816/4, mm. 3, 10; *CPR 1446–52*, p. 456; *CPR 1452–61*, p. 541; A.R. Myers, 'The Household of Queen Margaret of Anjou, 1452–3' in A.R. Myers, *Crown, Household, and Parliament in Fifteenth-Century England*, ed. C.H. Clough (London, 1985), pp. 205–6.

23. C 81/779/10918; C 81/782/19; SC 6/816/6, m. 1; SC 6/816/6, m. 9; SC 6/816/7, mm. 2, 10; SC 6/816/8, mm. 2, 7; DCO 207, mm. 2, 5; DCO 208, m. 2; *CPR 1452–61*, p. 630; *CPR 1461–7*, pp. 19, 64. Cornburgh was a yeoman of the crown and became an esquire of the body (1475), and keeper of the great wardrobe (1486–7); he served as sheriff of Cornwall (1464–5, 1468–9), as well as a commissioner of the peace and of array in Cornwall: R.E. Stansfield, 'A Duchy Officer and a Gentleman: The Career and Connections of Avery Cornburgh (d.1487)' in

P.J. Payton (ed.), *Cornish Studies: Nineteen* (Exeter, 2011), pp. 9–34; Stansfield, *Political Elites in South-West England*, pp. 217, 253–55, 263, 291. Given the present lack of a revised and updated *History of Parliament* for the period from 1422 to 1504, references to the existing biographies have been included, despite their inaccuracies, wherever relevant: J.C. Wedgwood, *History of Parliament: Biographies of the Members of the Commons House, 1439–1509* (London, 1936), pp. 223–4 (hereafter *HPB*).

24. DCO 212, m. 8; *CPR 1485–94*, p. 7; Edgcumbe was exempt from the Act of Resumption of 1485: *PR*, xv, p. 295. Edgcumbe served as escheator of Cornwall/Devon (1467–8), was sheriff of Devon (1486–7), and was a commissioner of array in Cornwall, and a JP in Cornwall (1474–5, 1485–92): *CPR 1467–77*, pp. 609–10; *CPR 1485–94*, pp. 279–80, 483; *HPB*, pp. 291–92; 'Edgcumbe, Richard' (J.L. Kirby), *The Oxford Dictionary of National Biography* (Oxford, 2004), (hereafter *ODNB*); Stansfield, *Political Elites in South-West England*, pp. 292–93, 304–5, 323–29, 331–37, 342.

25. DCO 213, m. 1; DCO 213, m. 4; DCO 214, mm. 1, 4; DCO 211, m. 4; *CPR 1485–94*, p. 293; *CPR 1494–1509*, p. 300. Edgcumbe was elected sheriff of Devon (1494–5, 1497–8), elected under-sheriff of Cornwall (1498–9) and sheriff (1505–6), and also served as JP for Cornwall (1498–1509) and Devon (1501–9): *CPR 1494–1509*, pp. 633–36; *HPB*, pp. 291–92; 'Edgcumbe, Richard', *ODNB*; Stansfield, *Political Elites in South-West England*, pp. 331–37, 342.

26. DCO 209, mm. 2, 5; DCO 210, m.2; *HPB*, p. 342; P.W. Fleming, 'The Hautes and their "Circle": Culture and the English Gentry' in D. Williams (ed.), *England in the Fifteenth Century: Proceedings of the 1986 Harlaxton Symposium* (Woodbridge, 1987), pp. 85–102.

27. Haslam, 'Administrative Study', pp. 16–17; Stansfield, *Political Elites in South-West England*, p. 90; cf. the Lord of Man's council also included an attorney: Dickinson, *Lordship of Man*, p. 34.

28. DCO 209, m. 5; SC 6/1208/1, m. 2. Allington was also elected as burgess-in-parliament to represent Plympton, Devon (1467–8): *HPB*, p. 9; J.S. Roskell, 'William Allington of Bottisham, Speaker in the Parliaments of 1472–5 and 1478', *Proceedings of the Cambridge Antiquarian Society* 52 (1958), pp. 43–55.

29. DCO 213, m. 3; DCO 214, m. 4. Mordaunt was speaker of the Commons in the Parliament of 1487, and also served on the bench in Cornwall (1494–5, 1497–1502), Devon (1501–2), and in other shires. He was appointed to commissions of gaol delivery at Launceston and elsewhere on the Western Circuit (1494–9): *CPR 1476–85*, pp. 553–80; *CPR 1485–94*, pp. 479, 481–508; *CPR 1494–1509*, pp. 117, 147, 149, 160, 179, 629–69; *HPB*, pp. 607–8; 'Mordaunt, John' (H. Summerson), *ODNB*.

30. *CPR 1452–61*, p. 335. Throckmorton was involved in local government in Warwickshire and Worcestershire and served on numerous commissions of peace, array, and *oyer et terminer* relating to those and adjacent shires: *CPR 1446–52*, pp. 140, 285, 299, 384; *CPR 1452–61*, pp. 409, 558, 565; *CPR 1461–7*, pp. 489, 491; *CPR 1467–77*, pp. 29, 218; *HPB*, pp. 852–53.

31. DCO 210, m. 8. Twynho was recorder of Bristol, and served as a commissioner of the peace, array, and *oyer et terminer* in Gloucestershire and other shires: *CPR 1476–85*, pp. 109, 111, 130, 319, 322, 345, 355, 398, 490; *HPB*, pp. 886–87.

32. For the Bonville-Courtenay rivalry see R.L. Storey, *The End of the House of*

Lancaster (London, 1966), pp. 85–92, 165–74; R.A. Griffiths, *The Reign of King Henry VI: The Exercise of Royal Authority, 1422–61* (London, 1981), pp. 475–76; M. Cherry, 'The Crown and the Political Community in Devonshire, 1377–1461', PhD thesis, University of Wales, 1981, pp. 223–24, 237–38; M. Cherry, 'The Courtenay Earls of Devon: The Formation and Disintegration of a Late-Medieval Aristocratic Affinity', *Southern History*, 1 (1979), pp. 95–7; M. Cherry, 'The Struggle for Power in Mid-Fifteenth-Century Devonshire' in R.A. Griffiths (ed.), *Patronage, the Crown, and the Provinces in Later-Medieval England* (Gloucester, 1981), pp. 124–29; Stansfield, *Political Elites in South-West England*, pp. 151–89.

33. *CPR 1436–41*, p. 133; *Calendar of the Close Rolls, 1435–41* (London, 1891–1963), pp. 195–96 (hereafter *CCR*); SC 6/815/11, m. 4; SC 6/815/13, m. 5; *The Complete Peerage of England, Scotland, Ireland, and the United Kingdom* (hereafter *CP*), ed. G.E. Cockayne, et al. (London, 1910–59), ii, pp. 218–19; 'Bonville, William, Baron Bonville' (M. Cherry), *ODNB*.

34. SC 6/815/15, m. 5; *CPR 1436–41*, p. 532; *CP*, iv, pp. 326–27; 'Courtenay, Thomas, Earl of Devon' (M. Cherry), *ODNB*.

35. *CPR 1441–6*, pp. 54, 410.

36. Hatcher, *Rural Economy*, pp. 37, 43–45.

37. DCO 205, m. 11; SC 6/815/15, m. 5; SC 6/816/1, m. 8; SC 6/816/2, m. 10; SC 6/816/3, m. 10; SC 6/816/4, m. 8; *CPR 1441–6*, p. 134; *CPR 1452–61*, p. 50; see n. 39; Stansfield, *Political Elites in South-West England*, pp. 179–82.

38. *CPR 1413–16*, p. 107.

39. SC6/816/3, m. 9; *CPR 1446–52*, p. 526. Trevelyan was a yeoman of the crown (1441), groom of the chamber, then esquire of the body (1448). He became keeper of the armoury of the Tower of London (1446–60), and keeper of the council chamber (1447–50). He was elected escheator of Cornwall/Devon (1442–3), under-sheriff of Cornwall (1459–60), and also served on the Cornish bench (1455–9), and as a commissioner of array and *oyer and terminer*: *CPR 1452–61*, pp. 402, 489–90, 495, 518, 557–59, 562, 613, 662–63; *HPB*, pp. 873–74.

40. *CPR 1452–61*, pp. 158, 291; *CP*, xii(2), pp. 905–9; 'Richard of York, Third Duke of York' (J.L. Watts), *ODNB*; G.R. Lewis, *The Stannaries: A Study of the English Tin Miner* (London, 1924), pp. 75–77.

41. *CPR 1452–61*, p. 338; *CP*, ii, p. 62.

42. SC 6/816/6, m. 6; *CPR 1461–7*, p. 19; *CCR 1461–8*, p. 31. Roger Dinham was the brother of John, Lord Dinham, and served as a commissioner of array in Devon (1472): *CPR 1467–77*, pp. 350–51.

43. C81/782/57; SC6/816/6, m. 7. Clemens was a commissioner of the peace (1460–72), of array, and of *oyer et terminer* in Cornwall and also served briefly as JP for Devon (1461): *CPR 1452–61*, pp. 662–63; *CPR 1461–7*, pp. 40, 488, 529, 561–63, 571; *CPR 1467–77*, pp. 102, 246, 628–29; *HPB*, p. 188; Stansfield, *Political Elites in South-West England*, pp. 217–18.

44. SC 6/816/8, m. 6; DCO 207, m. 5; *CPR 1461–7*, p. 120; his offices were exempt from the Acts of Resumption of 1463 and 1467: *PR*, xiii, pp. 129–30, 257–8; *CP*, iv, pp. 327–28; *HPB*, pp. 793–94; 'Stafford, Humphrey, Earl of Devon' (M.A. Hicks), *ODNB*.

45. SC 6/816/7, m. 9; DC O207, m. 5; *CPR 1461–7*, p. 439; for the context of Lord

Stafford's regional influence: Stansfield, *Political Elites in South-West England*, pp. 191–225.

46. *CPR 1467–77*, p. 173; *CP*, iv, pp. 378–82; 'Dinham Family' (K. Jankulak), *ODNB*; 'Dinham, John, Baron Dinham' (M.A. Hicks), *ODNB*.

47. *CPR 1467–77*, p. 175; *CP*, xii(2), pp. 724–26.

48. DCO 208, mm. 3–4; Stansfield, *Political Elites in South-West England*, pp. 218–19, 228, 245, 252–53.

49. DCO 209, m. 4; DC O210, m. 4; *CP*, xi, pp. 22–4; 'Woodville, Anthony, first Earl Rivers' (M.A. Hicks), *ODNB*. The Act of Resumption of 1473 allowed duchy officers to be re-appointed by the Prince of Wales's letters patent: *PR*, xiv, pp. 172–73.

50. DCO 209, m. 5. Bourchier was one of the sons of Henry, Earl of Essex (d.1483), and husband of Isabel, widow of Humphrey, Lord Stafford of Southwick: *HPB*, p. 96; Stansfield, *Political Elites in South-West England*, p. 259.

51. DCO 210, m. 8; *CP*, iv, pp. 418–19; 'Grey, Thomas, first Marquess of Dorset' (T.B. Pugh), *ODNB*; Stansfield, *Political Elites in South-West England*, pp. 236–37, 250–51, 259–60, 262–64.

52. DCO 210, m. 8; SC 6/1208/1, m. 2; *HPB*, p. 9; Stansfield, *Political Elites in South-West England*, pp. 253–54.

53. N.I. Orme, 'The Education of Edward V', *Bulletin of the Institute of Historical Research*, 57 (1984), pp. 119–30. Rivers's designation as constable of the duchy citadel of Castle Rising, Norfolk, in August 1472, may have proved important in consolidating his own and the Duke of York's power base in that region: DCO 209, m. 4; DCO 210, mm. 4–5.

54. For example: 'Ordinances for the Duchy of Lancaster', ed. R. Somerville, in *Camden Miscellany XXVI*, Camden Society, 4th ser., xiv (1975), pp. 1–29; R. Somerville, *History of the Duchy of Lancaster* (London, 1953), pp. 243–55; B.P. Wolffe, *The Crown Lands, 1461 to 1536: An Aspect of Yorkist and Early Tudor Government* (London, 1970), pp. 51–65.

55. Lord Dinham was selected as 'chief steward' in 1483: *British Library Harleian Manuscript 433* (hereafter *HM*), ed. P.W. Hammond and R.E. Horrox (Gloucester, 1979–83), i, pp. 130, 265; and as 'steward of Cornwall' in May 1483: *HM*, i, p. 20; his stewardship of Cornwall was confirmed in February 1484: C 81/888/109; *CPR 1476–85*, p. 430. In June 1483, Dinham became 'steward of Cornwall' and 'steward of the borough and manor of Bradninch and lands in Devon of the duchy, and the keeping of all tin pits': C 81/892/350B; *HM*, i, p. 161; *CPR 1476–85*, p. 386. In March 1484 his nomination as 'steward of Bradninch and Devon, and warden of the stannaries' was confirmed: *CPR 1476–85*, p. 386. Lord Dinham was exempt from the Act of Resumption of 1485: *PR*, xv, p. 324; Stansfield, *Political Elites in South-West England*, pp. 268, 285–92, 295–96, 300–1.

56. Tyrell was chosen as 'steward of the duchy' in 1484: *HM*, i, p. 125; and became 'steward of the duchy of Cornwall in Cornwall' in August 1484: *CPR 1476–85*, p. 474. Tyrell was also a knight of the body, chamberlain of the Exchequer, and captain of Guines. He also served as sheriff of Cornwall (1483–4), and as a JP and commissioner of array in Cornwall: *CPR 1476–85*, pp. 397–8, 556; *HPB*, pp. 889–90; 'Tyrell, James' (R.E. Horrox), *ODNB*; Stansfield, *Political Elites in South-West England*, pp. 268, 282, 289, 294–97, 301.

57. Willoughby was designated as 'steward of the duchy' on 17 September 1485: DCO 212, m. 1; and on 24 September became 'steward of all the king's mines in Cornwall and Devonshire in which there is any gold or silver': *CPR 1485–94*, p. 13; *CP*, xii(2), pp. 683–6; 'Willoughby, Robert, Baron Willoughby de Broke' (D.A. Luckett), *ODNB*; D.A. Luckett, 'The rise and fall of a noble dynasty: Henry VII and the Lords Willoughby de Broke', *Historical Research*, 69 (1996), pp. 254–65; Stansfield, *Political Elites in South-West England*, pp. 304–5, 310–11, 318–19, 322–27, 330–45.

58. *CPR 1485–94*, p. 21. Courtenay was the fourth son of Sir Philip Courtenay (d.1463) of Powderham, Devon, and served as escheator of Cornwall/Devon (1472–3), as a commissioner of *oyer et terminer* in Devon, and as JP in Cornwall (1502–4) and Devon (1502–4): *CPR 1494–1509*, pp. 145, 633–6; *HPB*, p. 231.

59. DCO 212, m. 8; DCO 213, m. 3; *CPR 1485–94*, p. 35. Halliwell served as escheator of Cornwall/Devon (1473–4), and as sheriff of Devon (1485–6, 1489–90); he was JP for Cornwall (1486–8, 1492–1502) and for Devon (1471–4, 1480–3, 1487–1501) as well as a commissioner of array and of *oyer et terminer* in Devon: *CPR 1467–77*, pp. 246, 350–1, 611–12; *CPR 1476–85*, pp. 557–58; *CPR 1485–94*, pp. 279–80, 322, 348, 483, 485; *CPR 1494–1509*, pp. 633–36; *HPB*, pp. 406–7; R.H. Geare, 'Admiral of the Fleet Sir John Halliwell', *Devon and Cornwall Notes and Queries*, xxv(7), (1953), pp. 195–201.

60. DCO 213, m. 3; DCO 214, m. 3; 'Arundell, John' (N.I. Orme), *ODNB*.

61. DCO 211, m. 3; SC 6/HENVII/1594; J. Beverley Smith, 'Crown and Community in the Principality of North Wales in the Reign of Henry Tudor', *Welsh History Review* 3 (1966–67), p. 164.

62. DCO 211, m. 3; DCO 211, m. 4; *CPR 1494–1509*, p. 311; *CP*, xii(2), pp. 683–86; for the lords steward and lords warden from 1502 to 1650: Haslam, 'Administrative Study', pp. 4–5.

63. E 101/461/20ff.; *CPR 1461–7*, p. 40; Hatcher, *Rural Economy*, p. 46; see n. 43.

64. Hatcher, *Rural Economy*, p. 46; *Caption of Seisin*, ed. Hull, p. 141; for deer parks during the later Middle Ages: J.R. Birrell, 'Deer and deer-farming in late-medieval England', *Agricultural History Review* 40 (1992), pp. 112–26.

65. *CPR 1429–36*, p. 428; *HPB*, pp. 229–30.

66. *CPR 1441–6*, p. 170.

67. Hatcher, *Rural Economy*, pp. 178–84; *Caption of Seisin*, ed. Hull, p. 141.

68. *CPR 1461–7*, p. 16. Grayson was a groom of the chamber by 1476 and had become a yeoman of the chamber by 1478. He was a customer in Exeter and Dartmouth from 1479, represented Dartmouth in parliament (1478), and was mayor of Plymouth (1483–84, 1486–87, 1489–90): *CPR 1467–77*, pp. 595, 525; *HPB*, pp. 389–90; Stansfield, 'Duchy officer', pp. 14, 28, 34.

69. Cornburgh and Grayson were nominated as joint keepers (1461): SC 6/816/7, mm. 12–13; SC 6/816/8, m. 7; *CPR 1461–7*, p. 7. By 1468, Cornburgh was sole keeper: DCO 207, m. 7. This appointment was renewed *c.*1483: *HM*, i, p. 204; see n. 23; Stansfield, 'Duchy officer', pp. 14, 22.

70. *CPR 1485–94*, p. 93; see n. 24.

71. Hatcher, *Rural Economy*, pp. 178–84; *Caption of Seisin*, ed. Hull, pp. 24, 141.

72. DCO 205, m. 12; SC 6/815/15, m. 6; SC 6/816/1, m. 10; SC 6/816/2, m. 12; SC 6/816/3, m. 12; SC 6/816/4, m. 9; SC 6/816/6, m. 11; *CPR 1441–6*, p. 373; *CPR*

1446–52, p. 558. Arundell was reappointed in 1461: *CPR 1461–7*, p. 123. Arundell served as under-sheriff of Cornwall (1457–58) and sheriff (1469–70), as well as sheriff of Devon (1464–65); he was also a commissioner of the peace in Cornwall (1445–62, 1463–63) and in Devon (1472–73), and was involved with commissions of array and *oyer et terminer* relating to Cornwall: *CPR 1441–46*, p. 468; *CPR 1446–52*, p. 587; *CPR 1452–61*, pp. 171, 308–9, 402, 489–90, 495, 518, 557–59, 562, 613, 662–63; *CPR 1461–67*, pp. 488, 529, 561–63, 571; *CPR 1467–77*, pp. 102, 219, 220, 246, 609–12; 'Arundell Family' (P.Y. Stanton), *ODNB*; Stansfield, *Political Elites in South-West England*, pp. 175–78, 183–84.

73. DCO 212, m. 8; DCO 213, m. 3; DCO 214, m. 3; *CPR 1485–94*, p. 30; Ley's office was exempt from the Acts of Resumption of 1485 and 1495: *PR*, xv, pp. 233–39; xvi, p. 144. Ley also served as escheator of Cornwall/Devon (1487–88).

74. DCO 211, m. 3. Arundell was under-sheriff of Cornwall (1495–96), a commissioner of *oyer et terminer* in Devon (1497), and JP for Cornwall (1498–1504): *CPR 1494–1509*, pp. 145, 633–34; 'Arundell Family', *ODNB*.

75. Hatcher, *Rural Economy*, pp. 179–84; *Caption of Seisin*, ed. Hull, p. 141; R.A. Brown, H.M. Colvin, and A.J. Taylor, *The History of the King's Works* (London, 1963), p. 980.

76. SC 6/815/15, m. 6; SC 6/816/1, m. 10; SC 6/816/2, m. 12; SC 6/816/3, m. 11; SC 6/816/4, m. 9; *CPR 1446–52*, p. 87; *Trevelyan Papers Prior to 1558*, ed. Payne Collier, pp. 29–30; see n.39. Bodulgate was chosen to sit on the county bench in Cornwall (1441–59), and was also a commissioner of array and *oyer et terminer* in Cornwall: *CPR 1441–46*, p. 468; *CPR 1446–52*, pp. 531, 587; *CPR 1452–61*, pp. 402, 489–90, 495, 557–59, 562, 613, 662–63; *HPB*, pp. 87–88.

77. SC 6/816/6, m. 11; SC 6/816/7, mm. 11–12; SC 6/816/8, m. 8; DCO 207, m. 6; *CPR 1461–67*, p. 11; see n. 43.

78. DCO 210, m. 7; *CP*, vi, pp. 370–74; 'Hastings, William, Baron Hastings' (R.E. Horrox), *ODNB*.

79. SC 6/816/3, m. 2; SC 6/816/4, m. 2; *CP*, ii, pp. 218–19; *The History of Parliament: Members of the House of Commons, 1386–1421*, ed. J.S. Roskell, C. Rawcliffe, and L.S. Clark (London, 1992), ii, pp. 284–88; 'Bonville, William, Baron Bonville' (M. Cherry), *ODNB*.

80. SC 6/816/6, m. 11; SC 6/816/7, m. 11; SC 6/816/8, m. 8; DCO 207, m. 6; *CPR 1461–67*, p. 126; *CCR 1461–68*, pp. 111, 286–87; *CP*, iv, pp. 378–82; 'Dinham Family' (K. Jankulak), *ODNB*; 'Dinham, John, Baron Dinham' (M.A. Hicks), *ODNB*.

81. SC 6/816/7, m. 2; SC 6/816/8, m. 1.

82. *CPR 1467–77*, p. 173. This appointment was confirmed in 1470, 1483, and 1484: PSO 1/34/1773; C 81/892/343; *HM*, i, p. 161; *CPR 1476–85*, p. 386. Lord Dinham was exempted from the Act of Resumption of 1485: *PR*, xv, p. 324.

83. *CPR 1485–94*, p. 21; *HPB*, p. 231; *Calendar of Inquisitions Post Mortem, Henry VII* (London, 1898–1955), iii, no. 97; see n. 58.

84. DCO 211, m. 4; *CPR 1494–1509*, p. 311; *CP*, xii(2), pp. 683–6; 'Willoughby, Robert', *ODNB*; Luckett, 'Lords Willoughby de Broke', pp. 254–65.

85. Hatcher, *Rural Economy*, pp. 178–84; *Caption of Seisin*, ed. Hull, pp. 1–2, 141–42; Brown, Colvin, and Taylor, *King's Works*, pp. 693–94.

86. *CPR 1441–6*, p. 373; *CPR 1446–52*, p. 456.

87. C 81/779/10918; C 81/782/19; SC 6/816/6, m. 9; SC 6/816/7, m. 10; SC 6/816/8, m. 7; DCO 207, m. 5; *CPR 1452–61*, p. 630; *CPR 1461–7*, pp. 19, 64; *CCR 1461–8*, p. 123; see n. 23; Stansfield, 'Duchy officer', pp. 13–14, 19–20.

88. DCO 209, m. 5; DCO 210, m. 5; Stansfield, *Political Elites in South-West England*, pp. 253, 291–92, 296.

89. *HM*, i, p. 245. Mauleverer was sheriff of Cornwall (1470–71), sheriff of Devon (1479–80, 1483–84), a commissioner of the peace in Devon (1470–71) and in Cornwall (1483–85), and was involved with commissions of *oyer et terminer* and array in both shires: *CPR 1467–77*, pp. 246, 611–12; *CPR 1476–85*, pp. 397–98, 488–90, 556.

90. DCO 212, m. 8; *CPR 1485–94*, p. 7; Edgcumbe was exempt from the Act of Resumption of 1485: *PR*, xv, p. 295; see n. 24. Piers Edgcumbe was nominated in 1489: DCO 213, m. 4; DCO 214, m. 4; *CPR 1485–94*, p. 293; he was reappointed as joint keeper with Roger Holland in 1502: DCO 211, m. 4; and reappointed sole keeper in 1504: *CPR 1494–1509*, p. 354; see n. 25.

91. Hatcher, *Rural Economy*, pp. 178–84; *Caption of Seisin*, ed. Hull, pp. 40–41, 141–42; Brown, Colvin, and Taylor, *King's Works*, pp. 804–5.

92. Trevelyan: *CPR 1441–6*, p. 238; *CPR 1446–52*, p. 251; *CCR 1447–54*, p. 84; *CPR 1452–61*, p. 50; see n. 39. Cornburgh: *CPR 1461–67*, p. 447; this office was confirmed or restored in 1473: DCO 210, m. 8; and reappointed in around May 1483: *HM*, i, p. 204; see n. 23; Stansfield, 'Duchy officer', pp. 14, 22, 28.

93. DCO 213, m. 3; DCO 214, m. 4; DCO 211, m. 3; *CPR 1485–94*, p. 81; *CP*, iv, pp. 328–30; 'Courtenay, Edward, Earl of Devon' (S.J. Gunn), *ODNB*; Stansfield, *Political Elites in South-West England*, pp. 312–13, 318–19, 323–26, 328–33, 336, 339.

94. Hatcher, *Rural Economy*, pp. 178–84; *Caption of Seisin*, ed. Hull, pp. xxii, 121–22, 141–42; Brown, Colvin, and Taylor, *History of the King's Works*, p. 847.

95. SC 6/815/15, m. 1; DCO 205, m. 2; SC6/816/2, m. 1; SC 6/816/3, m. 1; SC 6/816/4, mm. 1–2; DCO 206, m. 2; *CPR 1441–6*, p. 238; *CPR 1446–52*, p. 251; *CPR 1452–61*, p. 50; *Trevelyan Papers Prior to 1558*, ed. J. Payne Collier, Camden Society, lxvii (1857), pp. 35–37; see n. 39.

96. SC 6/816/6, m. 11; *CCR 1461–68*, p. 113; *CPR 1461–67*, pp. 48, 80, 126.

97. SC 6/816/7, m. 15; SC 6/816/8, m. 10; DCO 207, m. 7; DCO 208, m. 4; DCO 209, m. 6; DCO 210, m. 6; *CPR 1461–67*, p. 532; *CCR 1461–68*, p. 420; *CPR 1476–85*, pp. 153, 189.

98. DCO 205, m. 2; SC 6/815/15, m. 1; SC 6/816/1, m. 1; *CPR 1446–52*, p. 80; see n. 39, 76. For Tintagel Castle: *Caption of Seisin*, ed. Hull, pp. 27–28, 142; Brown, Colvin, and Taylor, *King's Works*, pp. 845–46.

99. Bodulgate and Clemens were chosen as joint-constable in 1452: *CPR 1452–61*, p. 18. Clemens was sole constable in 1461: *CPR 1461–67*, p. 40; see n. 43, 76.

100. *HM*, i, p. 286.

101. For the antecedents of stannary administration: W.R. Powell, 'The Administration of the Navy and the Stannaries, 1189–1216', *English Historical Review* 71 (1956), pp. 177–88; Lewis, *Stannaries*, pp. 33–34, 59, 65–84; Pennington, *Stannary Laws*, pp. 14–19, 35–42. For the tin industry: Hatcher, *Rural Economy and Society*, pp. 288–90; M.J. Hatcher, *English Tin Production and Trade before 1550* (Oxford, 1973).

102. Lewis, *Stannaries*, pp. 1–32, 43–45, 96, 157–70; Pennington, *Stannary Laws*, p. 7, 71–101; Hatcher, *Rural Economy and Society*, pp. 188–91.

103. Lewis, *Stannaries*, pp. 44–45, 132–35, 150–55, 208–26; Pennington, *Stannary Laws*, pp. 19, 127–46; Cooper, *Propaganda and the Tudor State*, pp. 204–5.

104. Lewis, *Stannaries*, pp. 125–26; Pennington, *Stannary Laws*, pp. 17, 19–21, 80–90; I. Arthurson, 'The Rising of 1497: A Revolt of the Peasantry?' in C.F. Richmond and J.T. Rosenthal (eds), *People, Politics, and Community in the Later Middle Ages* (Gloucester, 1987), pp. 1–18; P.J. Payton, '"A . . . concealed envy against the English": A Note on the Aftermath of the 1497 Rebellions in Cornwall' in P.J. Payton (ed.), *Cornish Studies: One* (Exeter, 1993), pp. 4–5, 8, 12; Cooper, *Propaganda and the Tudor State*, pp. 55, 192–94, 258.

105. *CPR 1494–1509*, pp. 578–79; Lewis, *Stannaries*, pp. 35–40, 85–86, 125–27; Pennington, *Stannary Laws*, pp. 11–29; J.A. Buckley, *Medieval Cornish Stannary Charters* (Pool Camborne, 2001).

106. Lewis, *Stannaries*, pp. 38–39; Pennington, *Stannary Laws*, pp. 29–35; Haslam, 'Administrative Study', p. 5.

107. Lewis, *Stannaries*, pp. 38–41, 86–92, 104–9, 116–18, 134–35, 151; *Caption of Seisin*, ed. Hull, pp. lv–lvi, 133–34; Haslam, 'Administrative Study', pp. 5–7.

108. Lewis, *Stannaries*, pp. 86–90, 108–9, 135–36; also see H.P.R. Finberg, 'Bounds of the Devon Stannaries', *Devon and Cornwall Notes and Queries*, 22(4), (1942), pp. 121–23; P. Hambling, *The Dartmoor Stannaries: Tin-Mining on Dartmoor in the Middle Ages, 1100–1600* (Newton Abbot, 1995).

109. Lewis, *Stannaries*, pp. 131–50; *Register of Edward, the Black Prince* (London, 1933), i, p. 11; ii, pp. 4, 8, 171; Hatcher, *Rural Economy*, p. 45.

110. SC 6/816/7, m. 13; SC 6/816/8, m. 7; DCO 207, m. 7.

111. Trevelyan was designated 'bailiff-itinerant in Cornwall' (1441): DCO 205, m. 12; SC 6/815/15, m. 6; SC 6/816/1, m. 10; *CPR 1441–6*, p. 21; and reappointed in 1452: *CPR 1452–61*, p. 50; see n. 39.

112. DCO 208, m. 4; DCO 209, m. 6; DCO 210, m. 6; *CP*, iv, pp. 205–7; 'Stanley, Thomas, Earl of Derby' (M.J. Bennett), *ODNB*.

113. Lewis, *Stannaries*, pp. 35–36, 150–51; Pennington, *Stannary Laws*, pp. 15–16, 29–33; Haslam, 'Administrative Study', p. 17; Stansfield, *Political Elites in South-West England*, pp. 88–9.

114. Treffry was exempt from the Act of Resumption of 1485: *PR*, xv, pp. 233–39. He was reappointed in 1486: DCO 212, m. 8; DCO 213, m. 3; DCO 214, m. 3; DCO 211, m. 3; *CPR 1485–94*, p. 36. Treffry also served as under-sheriff of Cornwall (1500–2).

115. *CCR 1461–8*, pp. 7, 15; SC 6/816/6, m. 8; SC 6/816/7, m. 10; SC 6/816/8, mm. 7, 10; DCO 207, m. 5. Wykes was exempt from the Act of Resumption of 1467: *PR*, xiii, pp. 257–58. Wykes was the customer of Poole, Dorset (1454–71), and was selected to sit on the county bench in Gloucestershire (1474–83) and Dorset (1485–91): *CPR 1467–77*, pp. 607–38; *CPR 1476–85*, pp. 553–80; *CPR 1485–94*, p. 485; *HPB*, p. 926.

116. *CPR 1429–36*, pp. 203, 214, 225; SC 6/815/10, m. 1; SC 6/815/11, m. 5; DCO 205, m. 11; SC 6/815/11, m. 2; SC 6/815/13, m. 5; SC 6/815/15, m. 5; SC 6/816/1, m. 9; SC 6/816/2, m. 10; SC 6/816/3, m. 10; SC 6/816/4, m. 8; *CPR 1436–41*, p. 48; *CPR 1452–61*, p. 293; Griffiths, *Henry VI*, pp. 316–19.

117. *CPR 1452–61*, p. 217. Cornburgh was again nominated in May 1483: *HM*, i, pp. 41–42, 76; *CPR 1476–85*, p. 465; see n. 23; Stansfield, 'Duchy officer', p. 11–12, 22.

118. DCO 208, m. 4; DCO 209, m. 5; DCO 210, m. 5; *HPB*, pp. 902–3.

119. Pennington, *Stannary Laws*, pp. 223–26. Sapcotes was married to Elizabeth (d.1516), sister of John, Lord Dinham (d.1501), and was an esquire of the king's body from 1472, becoming a knight of the body in 1488; he was sheriff of Devon (1477–8), and a commissioner of the peace (1481–83, 1483–1501), of array, and of *oyer et terminer*: *CPR 1476–85*, pp. 397–98, 488–90, 557–58; *CPR 1485–94*, pp. 279–80, 322, 348, 485; *CPR 1494–1509*, pp. 145, 635–36; *HPB*, pp. 740–41; Stansfield, *Political Elites in South-West England*, pp. 249–50, 287–89, 292, 300, 321–22, 329, 333, 335.

120. Powell, 'Administration of Navy and Stannaries', pp. 177–88; *Haveners' Accounts, 1287–1356*, ed. Kowaleski, pp. 1–2, 4.

121. *Caption of Seisin*, ed. Hull, pp. xxii, l, lvi, 136–39; *Haveners' Accounts, 1287–1346*, ed. Kowaleski, pp. 1–78; Campbell, 'Haveners', pp. 113–44; H.S. Cobb, 'The Medieval Royal Customs and their Records', *Journal of the Society of Archivists* 6 (1979), pp. 227–29; cf. the office of water-bailiff in the Isle of Man: Dickinson, *Lordship of Man*, pp. 21, 33, 73–4, 109–26, 221–46.

122. *Caption of Seisin*, ed. Hull, pp. xxii, l, lvi, 136–9; *Haveners' Accounts, 1287–1356*, ed. Kowaleski, pp. 3–10, 11–60, 316–17; Campbell, 'Haveners', pp. 123, 129–30, 136–37, 139; Hatcher, *Rural Economy and Society*, pp. 191–92.

123. *Haveners' Accounts, 1287–1356*, ed. Kowaleski, pp. 41–3; Haslam, 'Administrative Study', pp. 19–20.

124. SC 6/815/10, m. 1; SC 6/815/11, m. 1; DCO 205, m. 4; SC 6/815/15, m. 2; SC 6/816/1, m. 3; SC 6/816/2, m. 2; SC 6/816/3, m. 2; SC 6/816/4, m. 3; Campbell, 'Haveners', pp. 119–20, 144. Treffry purchased the farm of the Havenary in 1431, and served as a commissioner of array, as well as a commissioner of the peace (1472–4): *CPR 1461–67*, p. 561; *CPR 1467–77*, pp. 350–51, 609–10.

125. In 1444, Delabere was appointed to the 'office of Havener in Cornwall and in the port of Plymouth' to be held from 1454 until 1470: *CPR 1441–46*, p. 274.

126. DCO 209, m. 2; Campbell, 'Haveners', pp. 119–20, 144.

127. Bodulgate was chosen jointly with Kidwelly in 1455: DCO 206, m. 2; *CPR 1452–61*, p. 228; Campbell, 'Haveners', pp. 119–20, 144; see n. 76.

128. Kidwelly, Clemens, and Edgcumbe were to serve jointly in this post: Campbell, 'Haveners', pp. 119–20, 144; see n. 24, 43.

129. DCO 208, m. 4; Campbell, 'Haveners', pp. 119–20, 144.

130. Campbell, 'Haveners', pp. 119–20, 144.

131. DCO 211, m. 4. Beville was a commissioner of array in Cornwall (1490), under-sheriff of Cornwall (1494–5), and JP for Cornwall on various occasions (1488–1509): *CPR 1485–94*, pp. 322, 483; *CPR 1494–1509*, pp. 633–4.

132. SC 6/816/7, m. 13; SC 6/816/8, m. 7; DCO 207, m. 7; DCO 209, m. 6; DCO 210, mm. 6–7; *CPR 1461–7*, p. 217; Campbell, 'Haveners', pp. 119–20, 144; see n. 23; Stansfield, 'Duchy officer', pp. 15, 29.

133. *CPR 1485–94*, p. 27.

134. *Haveners' Accounts, 1287–1356*, ed. Kowaleski, pp. 46–47, 52–55.

135. SC 6/815/15, m. 1; see n. 39.

136. *CPR 1461–67*, p. 447; see n. 23; Stansfield, 'Duchy officer', pp. 14, 22, 28.

137. *Caption of Seisin*, ed. Hull, p. 131; *Haveners' Accounts, 1287–1356*, ed. Kowaleski, pp. 43–55.

138. C 81/779/10918; C 81/782/19; *CPR 1452–61*, p. 630; *CPR 1461–67*, p. 16. He was reappointed in 1473: DCO 210, m. 8; and reappointed *c*.1483: *HM*, i, p. 204; see n. 23; Stansfield, 'Duchy officer', pp. 13–14.

139. Hatcher, *Rural Economy*, p. 46; Haslam, 'Administrative Study', pp. 12–13.

140. *CPR 1413–16*, p. 19; Hatcher, *Rural Economy*, pp. 42–43.

141. Hatcher, *Rural Economy*, pp. 45–47; Haslam, 'Administrative Study', p. 9.

142. DCO 205, mm. 1, 11; DCO 206, m. 1; SC 6/815/15, m. 5; SC 6/816/1, mm. 1, 9; SC 6/816/2, m. 10; SC 6/816/3, mm. 1, 10; SC 6/816/4, mm. 1, 8; *CPR 1441–46*, p. 295. Brecknock was treasurer of the household from 1457: *HPB*, pp. 106–7.

143. *CPR 1452–61*, p. 323; *CPR 1446–52*, p. 410; *HPB*, pp. 943–4. Whittingham became keeper of the queen's great wardrobe from 1458: *CPR 1452–61*, p. 429.

144. SC 6/816/6, m. 1; SC 6/816/6, m. 8; SC 6/816/7, m. 9; SC 6/816/8, mm. 1, 6; DCO 207, mm. 1, 5; DCO 208, mm. 1, 4; *CPR 1461–7*, pp. 9, 221. Lord Hastings was exempt from the Acts of Resumption of 1463 and 1467: *PR*, xiii, pp. 129–30, 257–8.

145. DCO 209, mm. 1, 4; DCO 210, m. 4.

146. Sapcotes was appointed in May 1483: *HM*, i, p. 18; *CPR 1476–85*, p. 348; and was confirmed in July 1483: PSO 1/56/4; *HM*, i, pp. 35, 74; *CPR 1476–85*, p. 364.

147. DCO 213, m. 1; *CPR 1485–94*, p. 20. Lord Willoughby was exempt from the Act of Resumption of 1485: *PR*, xv, p. 268; see n. 57.

148. DCO 211, mm. 1, 3. Nanfan was under-sheriff of Cornwall (1479–80), and sheriff (1488–89), as well as under-sheriff of Worcestershire (1485–88), and was a JP for Cornwall (1485–1504), Warwickshire (1485–1507), Worcestershire (1493–1504), Gloucestershire (1493–1502), Herefordshire (1493–96), and Shropshire (1493–96): *CPR 1485–94*, pp. 481–508; *CPR 1494–1509*, pp. 629–69; *HPB*, p. 623; 'Nanfan, Richard' (I. Arthurson), *ODNB*; Stansfield, *Political Elites in South-West England*, pp. 292–93, 338.

149. *Register of the Black Prince*, i, p. v; cf. the lord's council: Dickinson, *Lordship of Man*, p. 29.

150. Haslam, 'Administrative Study', pp. xv, 1–2; Hatcher, *Rural Economy*, pp. 37, 43. William Walker was keeper of the prince's council chamber from 1473: DCO 209, m. 6; DCO 210, m. 6. Thomas Stodor was keeper of the prince's council chamber from 1493: DCO 214, m. 5. The registrar (and keeper of the register) had charge of some duchy records and may have fulfilled these duties at Westminster and at the Prince's Palace. John Burton fulfilled these duties from 1473: DCO 209, mm. 5–6; DCO 210, mm. 5–6. John Penycokwas designated registrar in 1492: DCO 214, m. 4; DCO 211, m. 4.

151. Haslam, 'Administrative Study', p. 1. Robert Legh was keeper of Kennington Palace in 1452–53: SC 6/815/3, m. 15. Richard Willy was keeper of the Prince's Palace in 1460–61, and was reappointed in 1462 and 1470: SC 6/816/5, m. 8; SC 6/816/7, m. 11; PSO 1/34/1760. Giles St Loe became keeper of Prince Edward's great wardrobe in 1457: *CPR 1452–61*, p. 334. Even though there was no heir to the throne, Robert Savage was selected as custodian of the wardrobe in 1462: DCO 207, m. 6. Nicholas Green was its keeper from 1473: DCO 209, m. 6; DCO 210, m. 6. From 1483, John Kendale, was granted 'custody of the prince's wardrobe in the city of London': *HM*, i, p. 268; *CPR 1476–85*, p. 540. Roger Cotton was

8

custodian in 1493–4: DCO 213, m. 3; DCO 214, m. 4. Giles Dedes was keeper in 1502–3: DCO 211, m. 4.

152. For the Council of Wales in general: R.A. Griffiths, 'Wales and the Marches in the Fifteenth Century' in S.B. Chrimes, R.A. Griffiths and C.D. Ross (eds), *Fifteenth Century England, 1399–1509: Studies in Politics and Society* (Manchester 1972), pp. 145–72; R.A. Griffiths, *The Principality of Wales in the Later Middle Ages: The Structure and Personnel of Government, I: South Wales, 1277–1536* (Cardiff, 1972); S.J. Gunn, 'The regime of Charles, Duke of Suffolk in North Wales and the reform of Welsh government, 1509–25', *Welsh History Review* 12 (1985), pp. 461–94; W.R.B. Robinson, 'Princess Mary's itinerary in the marches of Wales, 1525–27: A Provisional Record', *Historical Research*, 71 (1998), pp. 233–52; P.H. Williams, *The Council in the March of Wales under Elizabeth I* (Cardiff, 1958); P.H. Williams, 'The Star Chamber and the Council in the Marches of Wales, 1558–1603', *Bulletin of the Board of Celtic Studies*, 16 (1956), pp. 287–97; P.H. Williams, 'The attack on the Council in the Marches, 1603–42', *Transactions of the Honourable Society of Cymmrodorion*, old ser., (1961), pp. 1–22; P.H. Williams, 'The activity of the Council in the Marches under the early Stuarts', *Welsh History Review* 1 (1961), pp. 133–66.

153. *CPR 1452-61*, pp. 338, 359; Griffiths, 'Wales and the Marches', pp. 145–72.

154. *CP*, x, pp. 126–29; 'Butler, James, first Earl of Wiltshire and fifth Earl of Ormond' (J.L. Watts), *ODNB*; R. Somerville, *History of the Duchy of Lancaster*, (London, 1953), i, pp. 428–29; Stansfield, *Political Elites in South-West England*, pp. 151, 159–61, 164–65, 172–73, 182, 187–88, 351.

155. D.E. Lowe, 'The council of the Prince of Wales and the decline of the Herbert family during the second reign of Edward IV (1471–83)', *Bulletin of the Board of Celtic Studies*, 27 (1977), pp. 278–97; D.E. Lowe, 'Patronage and Politics: Edward IV, the Wydevills, and the Council of the Prince of Wales, 1471–83', *Bulletin of the Board of Celtic Studies* 29 (1980–82), pp. 545–73; Williams, *Council in the March of Wales*, pp. 3–11; M.A. Hicks, *Edward V* (London, 2005), pp. 91–136.

156. For example, see SC 8/344/E1265–75, E1289; SC 8/345/E1319–21, E1326, E1335, E1338, E1340–7, E1349–59D.

157. *CPR 1467-77*, p. 283; Lowe, 'Patronage and Politics', pp. 555–56.

158. SC 6/782/4, m. 6; The British Library, London (hereafter BL), Sloane MS 3479, f. 53v.; M.K. Jones, 'Sir William Stanley of Holt: Politics and Family Allegiance in the Late Fifteenth Century', *Welsh History Review* 14 (1988), pp. 1–22.

159. E 163/8/36; Lowe, 'Council of Wales', p. 282.

160. BL, Sloane MS3479, f.53v; Lowe, 'Council of Wales', pp. 281–82. Alcock had been appointed to the council in 1473 and later became its president: *CPR 1467-77*, pp. 401, 417; 'Alcock, John', *ODNB*.

161. SC 6/1208/1, m. 2; DCO 210, m. 8.

162. For the Council of the North and its origins: R.R. Reid, *The King's Council in the North* (London, 1921); F.W. Brooks, *The Council of the North* (London, 1953); also A.J. Pollard, *North-Eastern England during the Wars of the Roses: Lay Society, War, and Politics, 1450–1500* (Oxford, 1990), pp. 353–61.

163. PSO 1/56/2, 7–12;*HM*, i, 9, 13–18, 23–32, 47, 70–2; iii, pp. 2, 193; *CPR 1476–85*, pp. 349–50, 356, 361; Griffiths, *Principality of Wales*, pp. 161, 187, 203, 221, 239.

164. *HM*, i, pp. 94, 139, 187; ii, pp. 105, 137; *CPR 1476–85*, pp. 431, 538.

165. Prince Arthur's councillors included John Arundell (later Bishop of Coventry

and Lichfield from 1496), Richard Pole, Robert Frost, Richard Croft, Thomas Englefield, William Udall, and Thomas Lynom: SC 6/HENVII/1484; SC 6/HENVII/1594–8; SC 6/HENVII/1672; Beverley Smith, 'Crown and Community', p. 161; W.R.B. Robinson, 'Prince Arthur in the Marches of Wales, 1493–1502', *Studia Celtica*, 36 (2002), pp. 89–97. For Prince Arthur's education: F. Hepburn, 'Arthur, Prince of Wales and his Training for Kingship', *The Historian* 55 (1997), pp. 4–9; S.J. Gunn, 'Prince Arthur's Preparation for Kingship' in S.J. Gunn and L. Monckton (eds), *Arthur Tudor, Prince of Wales* (Woodbridge, 2009), pp. 7–20.

166. DCO 213, m. 3; DCO 214, m. 3; SC 6/HENVII/1591; Beverley Smith, 'Crown and Community', p. 160.

167. *CPR 1485–94*, pp. 47, 64–5, 84, 252, 376; 'Tudor, Jasper, Duke of Bedford' (R.S. Thomas), *ODNB*.

168. T. Thornton, 'Dynasty and Territory in the Early-Modern Period: The Princes of Wales and Their Western British Inheritance', *Welsh History Review* 20 (2000), pp. 2, 24; M.J.D. Stoyle, 'English "Nationalism", Celtic Particularism and the English Civil War' (Review), *Historical Journal* 43, (2000), pp. 1121–22.

169. E. Shils, 'Center and Periphery' in E. Shils, *Center and Periphery: Essays in Macrosociology* (London, 1975), pp. 3–16.

170. G.L. Harriss, 'Introduction: The Exemplar of Kingship' in G.L. Harriss (ed.), *Henry V* (Oxford, 1985), p. 18; R.E. Horrox, 'Local and National Politics in Fifteenth-Century England', *Journal of Medieval History* 18 (1992), pp. 391–403.

171. H.E. Maurer, *Margaret of Anjou: Queenship and Power in Late Medieval England* (Woodbridge, 2003), pp. 127–202; Stansfield, *Political Elites in South-West England*, pp. 183–89.

172. D.A.L. Morgan, 'The King's Affinity in the Polity of Yorkist England', *Transactions of the Royal Historical Society*, 5th ser., xxiii (1973), pp. 18–21; D.A.L. Morgan, 'The House of Policy: The Political Role of the Late Plantagenet Household, 1422–85' in D.R. Starkey, et al. (eds), *The English Court: From the Wars of the Roses to the Civil War* (London, 1987), pp. 64–66; M.A. Hicks, 'The Changing Role of the Wydevilles in Yorkist Politics to 1483' in C.D. Ross (ed.), *Patronage, Pedigree, and Power in Later Medieval England* (Gloucester, 1979), pp. 220–28; also see Stansfield, *Political Elites in South-West England*, pp. 1–12.

173. K.J. Stringer, 'Periphery and Core in Thirteenth-Century Scotland: Alan son of Roland, Lord of Galloway and Constable of Scotland' in A. Grant and K.J. Stringer (eds), *Medieval Scotland: Crown, Lordship, and Community: Essays presented to G.W.S. Barrow* (Edinburgh, 1993), pp. 82–113.

174. Stansfield, *Political Elites in South-West England*, pp. 8–12, 19, 73–79, 351–54.

175. *CP*, iv, pp. 412–19; v, pp. 212–15; *CPR 1467–77*, pp. 449, 456, 514; *CPR 1476–85*, p. 36; for the wider context of Dorset's position: Stansfield, *Political Elites in South-West England*, pp. 260–65.

176. For an overview of south-western politics during Richard III's reign: Stansfield, *Political Elites in South-West England*, pp. 298–305.

177. For Henry VII's settlement in the region: Stansfield, *Political Elites in South-West England*, pp. 339–45.

178. D. Mancini, *The Usurpation of Richard III*, ed. C.A.J. Armstrong (Gloucester, 1989), p. 65.

179. P. Coss, *The Origins of the English Gentry* (Cambridge, 2003).

180. For the sense of difference in later centuries: M.J.D. Stoyle, 'Pagans or Paragons? Images of the Cornish during the English Civil War', *English Historical Review* 111 (1996), pp. 299–323; M.J.D. Stoyle, 'The Dissidence of Despair: Rebellion and Identity in Early-Modern Cornwall', *Journal of British Studies* 38 (1999), pp. 423–44; M.J.D. Stoyle, *West Britons: Cornish Identities and the Early Modern British State* (Exeter, 2002); P.J. Payton, '"A Duchy in Every Respect Un-English": Discourses of Identity in Late-Modern Cornwall' in B. Lancaster, D.R. Newton, and N. Vall (eds), *An Agenda for Regional History* (Newcastle, 2007), pp. 317–31.

181. Holford, 'Office-Holders and Political Society', p. 105; also see M.L. Holford and K.J. Stringer, 'Introduction' in Holford and Stringer (eds), *Border Liberties and Loyalties*, pp. 1–14; K.J. Stringer, 'States, Liberties, and Communities in Medieval Britain and Ireland, c.1100–1400' in M.C. Prestwich (ed.), *Liberties and Identities in Medieval Britain and Ireland* (Woodbridge, 2008), pp. 5–36.

6

Justifying Imperialism
English representations of Ireland and Cornwall before and during the Civil War

James Harris

Introduction

Tudor ascendancy to the English throne brought with it the rise of an English Empire, primarily interested in imperial control of the neighbouring Celtic nations.[1] Early English imperialism was often brutal; combining cultural, economic and administrative dominance with military conquest and colonization. Consistently derogatory representations of the Celts were used to justify and facilitate English imperial control, based on preconceived notions of the Celtic peoples, their religion and their behaviour. This was hardly objective but motivated instead by the politics of expansion. Essentially, the English imagined a dichotomy between themselves and their Celtic neighbours, where the English were seen as civilized, logical and rational, and the Celts as backward, barbarous, and poor.

Ireland and Cornwall's differing experiences of English imperialism led to differing representations of each. Yet these representations were used consistently to justify and facilitate imperial control. But what *were* the similarities and differences between English representations of Ireland and Cornwall before and during the English Civil War? How consistent were English representations of Ireland and Cornwall? How subtle were these representations? What was the relative importance of religion in forming English representations of Ireland and Cornwall? What role did the local gentry play? What impact did the Civil War have on English representations?

Differences between representations of Ireland and Cornwall hinged on their different experiences of English imperialism and the Civil War. Cornwall experienced gradual dominance from 800 and yet, despite imposed Norman rule after 1066, preserved an ethnic difference which (many argue) persists to this day.[2] As Alan M. Kent has suggested, imperial control was maintained by convincing Cornwall of its 'deficiencies' and incorporating the region within the English polity as a 'junior partner'.[3] To maintain loyalty and unity, Cornish ethnic difference was tolerated but considered inferior. Late fifteenth-century Ireland, by contrast, was ruled largely by Gaelic lords, and only a minority of the population could speak English.[4] Compared to the Cornish experience, English imperialism intruded much later in Ireland, after 1540, with especially aggressive methods, including major plantations of settlers. The Reformation was part of this intrusion, with English Protestantism pitted against 'papist' Cornwall and Ireland. Religious hostility, fuelled by Irish and Cornish rebellion, added religious overtones to English representations that persisted into the Civil War and beyond.

English state expansion in the early modern period can be viewed through the prism of today's theories of imperialism. Edward Said provides most useful definition of imperialism, describing it as 'the practice, the theory and the attitudes of a dominating metropolitan centre ruling a distant territory'.[5] His inclusion of attitudes is particularly important in the context of English representations of the Celts. Said also defines colonialism as the 'establishment of settlements in a distant territory, usually but not always as a result of imperialist expansion'.[6] By focusing on English representations of Ireland and Cornwall before and during the Civil War, this study is in effect exploring the imperialist attitudes of the early modern English state. By emphasizing the differences between the English and Celts, England could 'understand' its superiority over the Celts and subdue them appropriately. This was in-extricably linked to economic, political and administrative dominance, and therefore to imperialism and colonialism as defined by Said. And by deploying Foucauldian themes of knowledge and power, it can be shown how English production of 'knowledge' about the Celts was used to exercise power over them. Foucault argues that the goals of power and the goals of knowledge are the same; 'in knowing we control and in controlling we know'.[7] Yet as much as this knowledge helped the English understand the Celts, it simultaneously helped define 'otherness' and by extension notions of incivility. Moreover, Foucault highlights how 'knowledge linked to power, not only assumes the authority of "the truth" but has the power to make itself true'.[8] Hence, English knowledge of the Celts, however flawed it may be, was considered accurate.

Parallels can be drawn to Said's theories proposed in his study *Orientalism*.[9] There is a number of definitions of 'Orientalism' proposed by Said, but the most appropriate in this instance describes Orientalism as 'a western style for dominating, restructuring and having authority over the Orient' which 'promoted the difference between the familiar and the strange'.[10] There are elements of this Orientalist perspective that can be applied to English imperialism towards the Irish and Cornish in the early modern period. There was a consistent sense of contention between England and the Celtic territories, which was partly inherited from the past, and deeply imbedded by the Civil War. Subtle but persistent and false assumptions underlay English attitudes towards both Ireland and Cornwall, attitudes that were bent on self-affirmation.

Said highlights a 'textual attitude' whereby the West would rely on representations from other sources when forming their perceptions of the Orient.[11] Although Ireland and Cornwall are not on the other side of the world, they would have been remote to the English in the 1500s and such a textual attitude did exist. Few English people would travel to Ireland or Cornwall but the information they sent back would have formed the perceptions of those who had not. Increasingly, subjective perceptions of the Celts were taken as fact. Again in *Orientalism*, Said has demonstrated that there is an 'assumption that fields of learning are constrained and acted upon by society'.[12] When applied to England, this suggests that once English superiority over Ireland and Cornwall became 'known', it was inevitable that they would be possessed through imperialism. As Said writes, 'knowledge gives power, more power requires more knowledge, and so on in an increasingly profitable dialectic of information and control'.[13] Eventually an unequal relationship develops, known as imperialism.

Referring to 'English' representations is perhaps problematic, as it suggests a homogenous English state, which was not always the case as internal conflict and factionalism were rife. However, shared English representations of the Irish and Cornish did exist. Yet sources are often problematic in terms of class and gender. Literary and theatrical representations of the Irish and Cornish were undoubtedly the most far-reaching in the early modern period. Written accounts would be read by a comparatively small yet influential section of society. It is perhaps inevitable that these readers and authors would be predominately upper-class males. It was a male-orientated world where only the rich could afford to publish or purchase literature and a minority of the population could read. But the influence of literary representations on the upper classes can be seen in letters between nobility, administrators and royalty as well as in deeds and contemporary essays.

It is harder to gauge the extent to which negative perceptions of the Irish and Cornish permeated through English society. Although there was a cultural gulf between the gentry and the masses, there is also evidence that the general populace believed the images fed to them from the upper classes. Negative representations of Ireland and Cornwall feature in popular plays of the early modern period. William Shakespeare's *1 Henry IV*, *2 Henry IV* and *Henry V* all have veiled references to English imperialism in Ireland and emphasize the might of the English state.[14] The pre-eminence of Shakespeare, combined with numerous other playwrights and poets of the early modern period, provides an excellent source-base for analysing the extent to which representations of the Irish and Cornish were filtered down to the lower orders of society.

For the Civil War, the most useful literary representations of the Irish and Cornish, from both Parliamentary and Royalist accounts, can be found in George Thomason's Tracts—a collection of pamphlets, books and news-sheets (1640–1661).[15] Being propaganda, there are countless exaggerated representations of the Irish and Cornish, which would have been widely read compared to other literature of the period. While female authors are scarce, there are numerous references to women within the Tracts. As we shall see, Celtic women were represented in the same terms as their male counterparts, and English women, it would appear, had broadly similar perceptions of Celts as English men. Overall, sources vary between stating very openly negative images of the Celts and alluding more subtly to their inferiority. Generally, representations of Ireland would be more open and images of Cornwall more unconscious, largely because of Cornwall's 'junior partner' status.

Some Historiography

This comparative study of English representations of Ireland and Cornwall is the first of its kind. However, it does utilize numerous fields of study including imperialist histories of Britain, the Civil War, and studies on English representations of Ireland and Cornwall. Not all accounts of English imperialism in the Celtic nations examine English representations of the Celts. Likewise, not all studies of English representations of the Celts view this within an imperialist framework.

Recent scholarly work suggests that the early modern period should be studied as part of a wider British historiography. The new British historiography takes a holistic, *British* perspective of British history rather than focusing on the separate roles of the territories that make up the British Isles. For Brendan Bradshaw and Peter Roberts, it is 'a political history of the Atlantic Archipelago as a coherent entity, not just as the sum of its national constituents'.[16] Yet where does this leave a study focused on English representations of Ireland and Cornwall? It remains, arguably, an Anglo-centric approach. English representations had unique and varying consequences for each of the Celtic nations. It is easy to lose regional identities and experiences in a holistic approach. As Peter Gaunt argues, it would be misleading to 'deny the separate histories of each of the component kingdoms and to tell only an archipelagic account'.[17]

Analysing the history of the British Isles using an imperial model has become increasing popular amongst historians. Michael Hechter's *Internal Colonialism: The Celtic Fringe in British National Development, 1536–1966* viewed Britain in terms of a 'core' and 'peripheries', while Hugh Kearney wrote of an 'English Empire', even if somewhat neglecting Cornwall.[18] Ireland has frequently been put forward as an example of early English imperialism.[19] Nicholas Canny's *Making Ireland British* is pre-eminent, showing how the English used settler plantations as their preferred counter to the 'Irish problem'.[20] While this is by no means a comprehensive historiography of imperialist studies of early modern Britain, Kearney and Canny are essential to any study of English imperialism in Ireland.

Histories of the Civil War do not generally focus on English representations of the Celts or the imperialist nature of the English state. The majority also neglect Cornwall, instead referring to the four nations of England, Scotland, Ireland and Wales. However, Mark Stoyle has unquestionably established the Cornish as one of the peoples of Britain. In *West Britons: Cornish Identities and the Early Modern British State* and *Soldiers and Strangers: An Ethnic History of the English Civil War*, Stoyle highlights an ethnic difference which permeated through Cornish society in this period.[21] Philip Payton's and Bernard Deacon's works are also vital in this respect.[22]

There is very limited research on English representations of the Cornish in the early modern period. Stoyle's chapter entitled '"Pagans or Paragons?": Images of the Cornish during the English Civil War' is one of the few.[23] Additionally, Kent's article, '"Art Thou of Cornish Crew?": Shakespeare, *Henry V* and Cornish Identity', studies representations of Cornwall in the work of Shakespeare.[24] However, studies on English perceptions of Ireland are far more common.[25] Two of the most influential authors of the early modern period, Shakespeare and Spenser, are the focus of Christopher Highley's *Shakespeare, Spenser and the Crisis in Ireland* (1997).[26] Between them, Shakespeare and Spenser had influence over almost every facet of English society.

Rebellion and Reformation: 1497–1594

Cornwall was considered a 'land apart', its inhabitants 'rough, hard-bred and brawny'.[27] In 1506 the Venetian Ambassador claimed: 'we are in a very wild place which no human being ever visits, in the midst of a most barbarous race, so different in language and custom from Londoners'.[28] Quick to classify 'otherness' as 'barbarity', the Ambassador had recognized a distinct Celtic ethnic identity. As historians have noted, the Duchy of Cornwall and Stannary Parliament gave Cornwall an 'aura of territorial semi-independence'.[29] The Stannaries in particular protected the ethno-occupational identity of

Cornwall's mining communities. Yet Cornwall's status as a Celtic nation and its ethnic distinctiveness also meant the English felt they needed to emphasize their perceived superiority over the 'backward' Cornish.

Likewise, Bernard of Clairvaux's assessment of the Irish described them as 'shameless in their customs, uncivilized in their ways, godless in religion'.[30] Underlying derogatory representations overarched English dealings with Ireland and Cornwall in the Tudor period. Yet Raphael Holinshed's influential *Chronicles of England, Scotland, and Ireland* (1577) only mentioned Ireland, not Cornwall.[31] The collection included a translation of Gerald of Wales's 'Expugnatio Hibernica' which portrayed the Irish as barbaric savages.[32] A further contribution from John Hooker viewed the Irish as 'wicked, effrenated, barbarous, and unfaithful' and argued that 'only coercion, not kindness, can control this', clearly demonstrating how negative representations could justify increased English imperial control.[33] As an unparalleled sixteenth-century account of Ireland, Highley highlights the importance of Holinshed's *Chronicles* in informing contemporaries, including Spenser and Shakespeare.[34] A 'textual attitude' clearly existed; the twisted representations in *Chronicles* were disseminated through English society.

Cornwall was not included in the title of Holinshed's *Chronicles* as it was considered a part of England, albeit a subordinate partner, and English representations of Cornwall differed vastly from those of Ireland. While negative representations exist throughout the period, the English also looked to accommodate Cornish ethnic difference, not least through the Duchy and Stannaries. This served to incorporate Cornwall into the English state as a loyal, junior partner. This was particularly significant as Anglo-Spanish relations deteriorated and Cornwall became strategically important. The Cornish gentry was increasingly Anglicized and aligned itself with English interests. This was mirrored in Cornwall's parliamentary representation; the number of Cornish MPs increased from fourteen to forty-four in the Tudor period, another feature of Cornwall's accommodation by the English state.[35]

The ambiguous relationship between Cornwall and England was further demonstrated by the Duchy of Cornwall. In reality it was a far less 'Cornish' institution than at first appears. Lancaster, Durham and Chester also had 'unique' courts.[36] The English state allowed Cornwall this separate institution because it was a means of binding Cornwall closely to the Crown while affording a measure of constitutional distinctiveness. In the 1540s the Duchy of Cornwall accounted for five per cent of the Crown's income and, importantly, was a mechanism for boosting and rewarding the loyalty of the Cornish gentry.[37] However, as Payton notes, a cultural gulf existed between the lower classes and gentry, which meant that England's attempts to pacify and annex the Cornish were less successful with the general populace.[38]

Popular uprisings were their preferred method of demonstrating frustration with Tudor centralization in Cornwall, leading in turn to English representations of Cornish 'rebelliousness'. The 1497 rebellion was sparked by high taxation and the suspension of the Stannaries in 1496. With the majority of Cornwall's gentry supporting the Crown, the uprising was defeated outside London. The ring-leaders, Audley, Angove and Flamank, were executed but, remarkably, the remainder of the rebels pardoned. Polydore Vergil, royal historian, claimed that this was 'out of consideration of their rustic simplicity'.[39] Vergil's comment illustrates the paradoxical nature of English representations of the Cornish. He is derogatory yet the Crown's leniency suggests a desire to foster Cornish loyalty. However, within two months another Cornish rebellion—Perkin Warbeck's abortive claim to the throne—began. After defeating the rebels, Henry II again sanctioned minimal executions, instead favouring financial punishment.[40] Payton has challenged the effectiveness of the penalty in cowing the Cornish into relative submission, arguing that the lower Cornish classes were far from pacified and ready to cement English representations of their 'rebelliousness'.[41]

Ireland differed vastly from Cornwall in the sixteenth century; the country was decentralized with over sixty distinct regions. Unable to utilize the local gentry as they did in Cornwall, the Crown installed loyal 'Old English' administrators. Significantly, they assisted the English in forming and disseminating negative representations of the native Irish. George Carew commented that 'until of late the old English race . . . despised the mere Irish, accounting them to be a barbarous people, void of civility and religion'.[42] The consistency of the representations fed from England's constant need to justify imperial control. Being a relatively minor issue compared to continental policy, the rule of Ireland was left to Old English. Yet in 1534 Henry VIII overthrew and executed the most powerful Old English family, the Kildares, and established a Lord Deputy and parliament in Ireland. The 'Act for th'Englishe Order' (1537) hinted at his justification for doing this: 'There is nothing which does more contain and keep many of [the King's] subjects of this saide lande in a certaine savage and wilde kind and manner of living, than the diversity between them in tongue, language, order and habit'.[43]

This powerful representation of the Irish attacks almost every facet of Gaelic culture in a way that was hardly necessary for the Cornish. It argues that 'diversity' is the fundamental problem, implying that centralization and imperialism would be an effective solution. Furthermore, the passing of the Act highlights London's concerns with the Old English. Increasingly assimilating Gaelic culture and resisting the Reformation had undermined their 'Englishness'.[44] To use a phrase from a later period of English imperialism, the Old English had 'gone native'. Although Catholicism was not explicitly mentioned, it was central to negative English representations after the Reformation. Canny claims that due to 'the peculiar nature of Catholicism in

Gaelic Ireland', English Protestants 'branded the native Irish as pagans'.[45] The Catholicism of the Old English was seen as an extension of this. Although they remained politically loyal, the stage was set for a new wave of Protestant English administrators. Clearly, Henry VIII sought to gain the sort of control he enjoyed in Cornwall.

For in the same period Cornwall outwardly appeared placated, with no major rebellion for almost half a century. Nonetheless, as in Ireland, the Reformation created negative English representations; in Cornwall's case, that of 'rebelliousness'. The 1549 *Book of Common Prayer*, which prohibited religious diversity and insisted on the use of the English language, sparked the Prayer Book Rebellion in Cornwall and Devon. The uprising resurrected and confirmed English fears of Cornish 'otherness' after a period of relative calm. This was not England's loyal partner but an underlying rebelliousness emanating from the lower classes. English representations emphasized this rebelliousness, justifying the devastating Cornish casualties in the subsequent conflict; ten per cent of the adult male population were killed.[46] Yet there was also a begrudging sense of admiration for Cornish fighting ability, which would become significant after the outbreak of Civil War in 1642.

Even these brutal measures were eclipsed by the methods employed in Ireland after 1570, and English representations of Ireland were correspondingly more disparaging than those of Cornwall. The new methods included early plantations, the policy of surrender and regrant, and the establishment of lord presidencies in Munster and Connacht; all aimed at suppressing the Gaelic world. Negative English representations highlighted the necessity of this action. Sir Henry Sidney, Lord Deputy of Ireland from 1565, wrote that 'there was never people of worse minds'.[47] Likewise, Sidney's secretary wrote that they 'commit whoredom, hold no wedlock, ravish, steal and commit all abomination without scruple of conscience'.[48] His reference to holding 'no wedlock' was an attack on Gaelic marriage traditions. English production of knowledge had twisted this to emphasize the differences between Irish customs and the perceived sanctity of marriage in English culture, implying cultural superiority.

As in Cornwall, the native Irish used rebellions to resist Tudor imperialism. With the support of the Gaelic Lords, Irish rebellions were arguably more effective. Yet the effectiveness of the Desmond Rebellions (1570s/1580s) in Munster, for example, merely provoked and justified increased imperial control. While England reasserted its dominance from Gerald Fitzgerald, Ireland experienced the most brutal loss of property and life in its story up to that point.[49] Naturally, the English legitimized this by highlighting the 'barbarity' of the rebels. During the aftermath England embarked on a major process of plantation in Munster. Robertum Legge summarized the justification for this to Queen Elizabeth in 1585, explaining that the policy was 'to have the said province . . . repeopled and inhabitated with civill loyall and dutifull subjects . . . according to the trewe and synceare religion of God'.[50]

Literary Representations

Certain literary representations of Ireland and Cornwall were particularly influential in this period. Richard Carew, a Cornishman but also a member of the Anglicized gentry, emphasized his admiration of the English language, declaring: 'our English language . . . is matchable, if not preferable before any other in use at this day'.[51] Carew's *Survey of Cornwall*, published in 1602, is an important text which serves to highlight the Anglicization of the Cornish gentry, and influenced the formation of English representations of the Cornish. Rather than overtly criticizing the Cornish, Carew reinforces Cornwall's status as England's subordinate partner, in the process apologizing for Cornwall's earlier 'commotions' or rebellions. In contrast, Edmund Spenser's writings on Ireland highlight the barbarity of the Irish and thus England's right to rule. A poet and member of the Old English community, Spenser produced two important works on Ireland; *The Faerie Queene* and *A View of the Present State of Ireland*.[52] An often cryptic insight to Spenser's views on Ireland, *The Faerie Queene* (1590, 1595) makes references to English activity in 'savage nations' throughout. It was 'ultimately an exemplary glorification of violence when it is employed in a worthy cause', according to Canny's summary.[53] Spenser saw violent Tudor imperialism in Ireland as justified; it was civility overcoming barbarity.

Spenser's *A View of the Present State of Ireland* (1633), which was first circulated in 1598, depicts dialogue between two characters, Eudoxus and Irenius, who seek 'better government and civility' in the 'savage nation' of Ireland to take advantage of the country's resources.[54] Eudoxus and Irenius agree that imperialism was justified, stating '[England should] prescribe a diet with streight rules and orders to be dayly observed, for fear of relaps into the former disease'.[55] Spenser's works influenced many English administrators in Ireland, with Canny arguing that he 'set the agenda' for England's activity in Ireland.[56] Spenser's production of knowledge seeks to establish power over the Irish, and his representations were disseminated through English society. This was a far more devastatingly critical work than Carew's *Survey*, highlighting the importance of the scale of imperialism in influencing the nature and intensity of English representations of the Irish.

The works of Spenser and Carew would have been read by the upper classes, and it is difficult to gauge how far their representations of Ireland and Cornwall permeated through society. Popular plays, however, can give an indication. The Irish were commonly used in dramas; including a wild

Irishman in *The Misfortunes of Arthur* and an Irish murderer in *Sir John Oldcastle*.[57] The 'barbarous' Irish image was often mirrored in their dress, speech and mannerisms on stage.[58] Representations of Ireland featured in the popular plays of Shakespeare. As a charged political issue, Ireland was rarely referred to explicitly but Highley suggests that Shakespeare used 'strategies of temporal displacement and spatial transcoding' to disguise references to Ireland.[59] He argues that the conflict between English and Welsh forces of Owain Glyndŵr in *1 Henry IV* is a thinly disguised veil for the problems in Ireland during the 1580s.[60] Furthermore, Highley suggests that *2 Henry IV* stages a 'reversed conquest' in order to 'foment anti-Irish sentiment and . . . justify English aggression as necessary'.[61]

Alan M. Kent's analysis of Shakespeare's *Henry V* highlights subtle representations of Ireland and Cornwall. The English camp scene featuring English, Welsh, Scottish and Irish captains meeting as part of a unified English Army is viewed as representing the problems of 'internal colonization'. Kent states that 'in rank, in dramatic importance and in linguistic competence, [the Celts] are comical second-order citizens'.[62] Interestingly, representations of the Cornish are very different. When a disguised Henry V was asked for his name by Pistol, the King replied, 'Harry le Roy'; recognizing the foreignness of the name, Pistol mistakenly asks, 'Le Roy! A Cornish name: art thou of Cornish crew?' Kent argues that although the supposedly 'Cornish' name is represented as foreign, the use of 'crew' suggests a fondness which is not extended to the Irish.[63] However, a 1644 pamphleteer later described the Cornish as 'wicked crue', suggesting the term was perhaps less favourable than Kent imagined.[64] But again, this hints at Cornwall's status as the subordinate partner of England—not as bad as Ireland but not England's equal either.

Imperialism and Insurrection: 1594–1642

Hugh O'Neill was a Gaelic lord; Catholic, educated and ambitious. In reaction to Tudor attacks on his people and religion, O'Neill led a nine-year rebellion (1594–1603), fought mainly in Ulster, to restore Catholicism in Ireland.[65] The rebellion experienced initial success; in 1600 O'Neill controlled more of Ireland than England did, including the Munster Plantations, causing Queen Elizabeth to send 20,000 English soldiers against him.[66] However, O'Neill's defeat at Kinsale and the resulting Treaty of Mellifont brought the Nine Years War to an end. Despite Elizabeth's desire to finish 'the arch-traitor with her sword', O'Neill was treated with leniency.[67] The Queen would die shortly after and in 1607 O'Neill fled to the Continent.

The end of O'Neill's rebellion ushered in a period of upheaval in English high politics. James Stuart was declared King of England and Scotland and a year later declared himself 'king of Great Britain', suggesting unity within his English Empire. Yet the so-called barbarity and rebelliousness of the native Irish demonstrated during the war served to justify a period of unprecedented imperial control under the Stuarts. English common law spread across Ireland and many Gaelic cultural traditions were declared illegal.[68] For the first time, England was in a position to form an Irish parliament featuring representatives from all over the country.

However, the most significant response to the Nine Years War was the English plantation of Ulster. Thomas Wentworth, a Protestant Lord Deputy from 1632, believed that 'plantations must be the only means under God . . . to reform this subject as well in religion as in manners'.[69] Renewed representations of Irish backwardness allowed the Ulster plantations to be conceived on a far larger scale than Munster. The principles of the plantation were simple: '[The] plantation concerns the future peace and safety of [Ireland] . . . the goodness and morality of it, esteeming the settling of religion the introducing of civility, order and government, amongst a barbarous and unsubjected people'.[70] Echoing the sentiments and motives behind the Munster plantations, the plan was to attempt the eradication of Gaelic culture and Catholicism in Ulster. The planters themselves also reaped substantial financial rewards, with some making fortunes through the exploitation of resources. These gains had been achieved by emphasizing the barbarity of the native Irish to rationalize English (and Scottish) colonization in the province. As Christine Kinealy notes with wry understatement, 'the native Irish had much to be discontented about'.[71] They were granted the marginal, barren areas of the plantation for 'the better civilizing and planting the country'.[72] Ulster was only the beginning; as R. F. Foster writes, 'there was no county in Ireland where some Englishmen did not establish themselves as new, progressive landowners'.[73] This widespread colonization was presented to the English public as embedding civilization into a barbaric country. Significantly, this logic was widely accepted and supported by literature and theatre.

These intensely defamatory representations of Ireland were hardly necessary in Cornwall in the early Stuart period. Cornwall remained England's subordinate partner. There had been no major Cornish resistance to English imperialism since 1549; the Duchy of Cornwall was centralized, and significantly the Cornish language, a marker of ethnic difference, was in decline. Abandoned by the gentry, its retreat was hastened by the severing of ties with Brittany after the Reformation and, as Payton observes, by the suppression of Glasney College which 'robbed the language of both scholarship and status'.[74] Moreover, under the Stuarts the Duchy was transferred to the English exchequer; Deacon describes it in 1603 as an 'administrative backwater, surviving because it had in part been forgotten'.[75] However, had Cornish inferiority been accepted by the Cornish lower classes? By the outbreak of the

Civil War, Cornwall would be ready to rise up and resist English intrusion, bringing a renewed intensity to English representations of the Cornish.

Consistent resistance to English imperialism in Ireland, however, resulted in consistently negative representations of Ireland. Since the Reformation, English attacks on Catholicism increased and came to include the Old English. Wentworth stated that as long as they 'continued popish, they are not a people for the crown of England to appear confident of'.[76] Therefore Ireland underwent a transitional process whereby Protestant English settlers replaced Catholic Old English in positions of power. It was a paradoxical political situation as the Old English still possessed power and played an important role in advising the Crown, even blocking anti-Catholic legislation in 1613.[77] Yet despite being consistently loyal to the Crown, the Old English were becoming ever more disillusioned with the Stuart government.

Old English disillusionment increased after Wentworth attempted to play the Catholics and Protestants off against one another. Wentworth was a known admirer of Spenser and had an ability to alienate almost every facet of Irish society. In a letter to Charles I, he discouraged the king from appointing the Catholic Randall MacDonnell to raise troops as it 'would be displeasing to all the English on this side, his religion nor yet his discent sortse not well with it'.[78] Although Wentworth was eventually executed, English representations of Catholicism had already turned sections of the Old English community against the Crown. They presented a list of grievances—the 'Graces'—to the Crown in 1628.[79] In stark contrast to the anglicized Cornish gentry, the king's failure to grant concessions to the Old English would have serious consequences for Ireland.

The 1641 Insurrection was an attempt by the Catholic Irish, including some Old English, to overthrow Protestant administrators and force concessions for Catholics in Ireland. John Temple's *The Irish Rebellion* (1646) immediately sought to vilify the Catholic Irish by emphasizing the planning of the rebellion and the Pope's alleged endorsement.[80] This was quickly regarded as the 'official' interpretation and accepted by many English. Recently, scholars have challenged Temple's narrative, suggesting that the Insurrection was the result of short-term considerations.[81] The failure of the crown to fulfil its promises and ratify the Graces has led Canny to argue that 'some Catholic landowners were at the brink of rebellion at any given point'.[82] Undoubtedly the growing conflict between the king and Parliament in England at this time had given them reason to believe their uprising could be successful.

Early successes encouraged others to express their anger and drive out Protestants from Catholic communities. Treatment of the Protestant settlers was brutal but the figure of 200,000 victims which spread through England was grossly exaggerated.[83] The myth was furthered by reports from Protestant landowners. In the opening month Lord Clanricarde wrote from Ireland of the: 'Great outrages committed by the Irish . . . destroying all his Fathors from works and all the English plantations . . . I cannot but admire what strange madness doth possess them to destroy their neighbours'.[84] Reports of this kind fuelled English representations of Irish barbarity. By 1642 the Old English and Gaelic Irish had formed the 'Confederation', effectively an independent parliament which claimed to be supporting the king by resisting the treacherous Protestant English.[85] But this did not curb the malicious English representations of the Irish that followed.

English reactions to the 1641 Insurrection were close to mass hysteria. It would be remembered as the 'horrid rebellion and massacre of poor English Protestants'.[86] Stories of inhumane atrocities spread like wildfire; one story described the murder of a Protestant male: '[The Catholics] being blood-thirsty savages . . . not deserving the title of humanity without any more words beat out his brains, then laid hold on his wife big with child, and ravished her, then ripped open her womb'.[87] This seeks to dehumanize the rebels, using emotive images of rape. Representations of this kind were prevalent in London pamphlets; twenty-five per cent of the Thomason Tracts dated from November and December 1641 refer to the Insurrection.[88] *Bloody News from Ireland* is a typical title which hints at Irish incivility.[89] With this ammunition, it was easy for the pamphleteers to express their perceived superiority over the Irish.

Yet there were very real fears that the insurrection would spread to England. Sir John Coke believed that 'the Irish profess they will root out the English and commit diverse barbarous cruelties upon them'.[90] The 1641 Insurrection prompted brutal representations of the Irish as English control of the country seemed to be in jeopardy. England's decision to place James Butler, the Earl of Ormonde, in command of an Irish army and send another 2,000 soldiers to Ireland highlights how seriously the Stuart state took the rebellion.

But English attentions soon turned away from Ireland. In August 1642 an alleged 'Popish' plot by the king, bringing to a head a wide range of grievances and controversies (including the apparent crumbling control over the Celtic nations), precipitated the Civil War between Crown and Parliament. Geo-graphically, Ireland was on the periphery of the conflict. Cornwall, however, played an important role in the war, intensifying and sharpening English representations of the region. While some of the anglicized Cornish gentry, particularly in south-east Cornwall, sided with the Parliamentarians, the majority of Cornwall was Royalist.[91] Loyalty to the Crown, cultivated by the Duchy of Cornwall, was the predominant expression of Cornwall's junior partner role, and it was not about to be transferred to the Parliamentarian cause. Indeed, the Cornish in the Civil War demonstrated many of the attitudes and motives of 1497 and 1549, especially resistance to English (in this case, Parliamentarian) intrusion. As Stoyle has argued, the Royalists 'channelled a pre-existent set of popular attitudes—political, religious and social', which heightened a sense of 'Cornish cultural defensiveness'.[92] Cornwall certainly developed an enhanced 'Royalist image'. To maintain this loyalty, Royalist representations of the Cornish were particularly favourable and even emphasized—and exploited—their ethnic difference. The Cornish were often praised for their military prowess, an image that had developed during the Tudor rebellions.

Without popular support, Cornwall's few Parliamentarians fled to Plymouth. Cornwall's prominent role in the war prompted malicious Parliamentary representations, with the region now considered equal in backwardness to Ireland. The Cornish were barbarous and uncivilized; usually described merely as 'rebels' to play down the significance of Cornwall in the war.[93] Even Cornwall's ethno-occupational identity was attacked, with one Parliamentarian critic complaining that 'the men of Cornwall are very heathens, a corner of ignorants and atheists, drained from the mines'.[94] Stoyle has argued that during the Civil War, Cornwall was increasingly viewed—and behaved—as an independent nation.[95] Certainly, this can be seen in Parliamentary attacks on Cornish ethnic difference. With the majority of Cornwall's anglicized gentry in Plymouth, English imperial control had no foothold in Cornwall after 1642.

The Parliamentarians used their Civil War pamphlets to launch their most scathing attacks on the Cornish, and to disseminate these through English society. Utilizing a handy set of images and clichés, the pamphlets drew on pre-existing stereotypes of foreignness. Again, it is Stoyle who has studied representations of the Cornish in the Civil War tracts in detail. Summarizing the pamphleteer's representations, he writes that the Cornish were considered a 'race of poverty-stricken, popish ignorants, who . . . pillage and plunder'.[96] Particularly after the 1641 Irish Insurrection, representations of Cornwall and Ireland began to coincide, not least through attacks on Catholicism in which images of Cornwall as 'popishly affected' becoming increasingly common.[97] One pamphlet insisted that the Parliamentarians would give 'no quarter to any Irish or Cornish', emphasizing Cornwall's new unflattering equality with Ireland.[98] The Civil War pamphlets were published mainly in London, forming part of a textual attitude, and would have been read primarily by the upper and middle classes. However, they were a useful means for Parliament to spread negative representations of the Cornish, and indeed the Irish, through the higher echelons of English society, and with some expectation that they would percolate down through society—not least in moulding the popular prejudices of Parliamentarian soldiers in the field.

Confederates and Civil War: 1642–1651

Following the outbreak of Civil War, Ireland became a side issue in England. Like English representations of the Cornish, representations of the Irish differed between Royalists and Parliamentarians. However, unlike Cornwall, neither side went so far as to openly praise the native Irish. The Confederate War was still underway creating a tense, religiously-charged, political situation. The Royalist's main concern was to reach a quick ceasefire with the Confederates, through the Earl of Ormonde, so they could exploit their colony and utilize Irish soldiers in England. But representations which had been formed in the Tudor period to justify and facilitate English imperialism backfired, as Charles' use of Irish soldiers caused alarm and discontent in Royalist circles.

Although fewer than 2,000 native Irish arrived in England, fears grew of an 'Irish invasion', especially after the 1641 Insurrection. Parliamentary pamphlets exaggerated the number of Irish in Royalist armies.[99] Even some Royalists felt betrayed, with Sir Ralph Hopton describing his Irish soldiers as 'verie mutinous and shrewdly infected with the rebellious humour of England'.[100] However, Parliamentary representations of the Irish eclipsed this, with women also being targeted. Pamphlets suggested that there were 'none more bloody' than the Irish female camp-followers.[101] Furthermore, many Irish Royalists captured in England were instantly executed. The negative representations of the Irish which had been propagated by the English state for hundreds of years justified the countless atrocities committed against Irish soldiers.

Likewise, derogatory Parliamentary representations of the Cornish became increasingly scathing as Royalist victories in which Cornish soldiers had participated soared. These climaxed after the earl of Essex's failed march on Cornwall. Vandalizing the church of St Bartholomew and plundering the Duchy Place in Lostwithiel, Essex's army took the form of an invading imperialist force targeting sites of ethnic significance.[102] Certainly, the Cornish viewed this as an attack on their nation, and responded by rising en masse and dispelling the Parliamentary army. Colonel John Were recalled Lostwithiel Bridge where there were 'many barbarisms used, some killed, others flung into the water, most plundered'.[103] Forced into the hills between Lostwithiel and Fowey, the Parliamentary army was crushed and eventually lost one-sixth of its force.[104]

Immediately, a renewed Cornish hate campaign commenced in Parliamentary pamphlets. Along with accounts like the one above, pamphlets explained how English soldiers 'most barbariously were pillaged, and plundered . . . but the time may come, we shall be even with the wicked crue'.[105] Several links can be drawn here to English reactions to the Irish 1641 Insurrection.

As in Ireland, representations sought to dehumanize the Cornish. Also, by highlighting the perceived threat of the Cornish, the English could later justify almost any means of revenge. And a desire for revenge against the Cornish was common. Parliamentary forces expressed their 'hopes to fight with their Cornish enemyes, whose barbarisme will never be pardoned until some proporcionable requitall'.[106] Civil War representations of the Cornish by Parliament were as scathing as anything that had been levelled against the Irish in the previous century. Often expressed in pamphlets, they formed part of a textual attitude which informed many English of the essential 'truths' of Cornwall.

This link to representations of Ireland cannot be more evident than when Parliamentary representations of the Cornish adopted a religious under-current. Fletcher regards religious conservatism as a cornerstone of Cornish Royalism, and for Stoyle this was inextricably linked to Cornish ethnic difference.[107] Clearly religion was an important aspect of Cornwall's involvement in the Civil War. However, it was not Cornwall's adherence to a conservative form of the established church that Parliamentarians attacked, but an imagined Catholicism. Although small pockets of Catholicism did exist in Cornwall, Deacon has noted that 'the majority of Cornish outwardly conformed to the rapid changes in religious fashion'.[108] Therefore, when Cornwall was accused of being 'a corner of ignorants . . . a place full of superstitious and popishly affected persons', it was a myth.[109] Yet these representations of Cornish Catholicism were common and a useful tool for Parliament to imply cultural superiority over the Cornish. This was a form of discrimination that Ireland had experienced since the Reformation, and which was used to justify increased imperial control.

The Civil War swung decisively in Parliament's favour during 1645 after the formation of the professionally trained New Model Army under the leadership of Thomas Fairfax and Oliver Cromwell. Charles I's desperate position meant he needed a quick resolution to the Confederate War to allow Irish soldiers to fight in England. He sent the Catholic earl of Glamorgan to work behind Ormonde's back. The so-called 'Glamorgan Peace' he proposed would guarantee leniency towards Catholicism, in return for 3,000 Irish soldiers.[110] Although the agreement was secret, it found its way into the Parliamentary pamphlets and gave the impression that Charles was working with Catholics. Given English representations of the Catholics in the previous century, it was a public relations disaster for the Royalists; the peace was abandoned and Charles distanced himself from Glamorgan. Despite the Royalists' need of Irish troops, the idea of working with Catholics was anathema for many English. When Ormonde eventually agreed to a peace in July 1646, after Charles' imprisonment, the Confederates were able to secure their main priority; the protection of the Roman Catholic religion.[111] This demonstrates how far English imperial control of Ireland had weakened during the Civil War.

As in Ireland, there was a change in Royalist representations of the Cornish post-1645. With the Royalist war effort deteriorating, Cornish soldiers increasingly looked to protect their borders.[112] Royalists questioned whether arming the Cornish was a good idea, with some believing they 'will suffer neither his Majesty's nor his Excellency's forces to come among them'.[113] Representations of the Cornish from English commanders turned ever more derogatory as they seemingly lost control of their Cornish troops. Hopton described them as 'disorderlie and mutinous', while Lord Goring wrote of 'a universal deadness and backwardness'.[114] Charles I's final attempt to entice Cornish loyalty was to appoint the Cornishman Richard Grenville to command Cornish troops and to order the unpopular Goring to stay out of Cornwall.[115] But this backfired as Grenville consistently placed his Cornishness above his Royalism, ordering his soldiers to 'secure the county' against the advancing Parliamentary army.[116] Now considered a threat to the crown, Grenville was arrested. In the end, when the Royalists realized their imperial control over the Cornish had eroded, negative representations came to the fore in an attempt to reassert some authority over the region.

Sensing the disharmony between the Cornish and other Royalists, Parliamentarians took up the English tradition of softening their representations of Cornwall in an attempt to woo them—hoping to reinstate Cornwall as *their* subordinate partner. First, Cromwell and Fairfax made an offer of a de facto independence from either side in return for a complete withdrawal of Cornish support for the king.[117] Then the House of Lords organized a charitable collection for 'the poor Cornish'.[118] Parliament clearly felt that favourable representations of the Cornish would allow them to quickly reassert English control over Cornwall so that they could concentrate on other spheres of war.

Although the first Civil War ended in 1646, by 1648 Charles I was ready to renew the conflict. The Battle of Preston was the crucial Parliamentary victory which effectively marked the end of this second Civil War. Charles was arrested, tried for treason and beheaded on 30 January 1649. In the wake of Charles' arrest Cromwell moved to conquer Ireland. The brutality which ensued was worse than anything experienced by Cornwall, and, correspondingly, the representations he used as justification were worse than any which had come before. Cromwell loathed Catholicism and considered the Irish to be 'part of the anti-Christ'.[119] He cited the 1641 Insurrection for justification of his actions, considering the rebellion 'the most unheard-of and most barbarous massacre, without respect of sex or age, that ever the sun beheld'.[120] For Cromwell, his role in Ireland was to end Catholic barbarity and restore civility. To achieve this, the country would be 'replanted with many noble families of this nation, and of the Protestant religion'.[121]

Twenty thousand men, artillery and naval backing formed Cromwell's formidable army in Ireland. By 1648 the Old English, Gaelic Irish and Protestant Royalists had united against the Parliamentarians. Cromwell stated that his aim in Ireland was to 'break the power of a company of lawless rebels who, having cast off the authority of England, live as enemies to human society'.[122] Indeed, the sieges of Drogheda and Wexford are now infamous for the brutal methods employed by the English invaders. Almost 2,000 men were slain in Cromwell's conquest of Drogheda, including Catholic priests; a tactic pursued to instil terror.[123] But it was Cromwell's actions in Wexford, October 1649, which would demonstrate the brutality of his actions in Ireland. Before Parliament stormed the town, Cromwell promised that 'noe violence shall bee offered' if they surrendered.[124] Upon their refusal of his terms, the town was attacked. As in Drogheda, the siege resulted in 2,000 Irish deaths.[125]

Unlike Drogheda, however, unarmed civilians were killed in Wexford. Cromwell justified the deaths by emphasizing Irish barbarity. In a report to Parliament he wrote that he had not wanted the deaths but: 'God . . . by an unexpected providence in his righteous justice, brought a just judgement upon them, causing them to become a prey to the soldier, who in their pyracies had made preys of so many families, and made with their bloods to answer the cruelties which they had exercised upon the lives of divers of poor protestants'.[126] Cromwell makes a clear reference to the Protestants killed during the 1641 Insurrection. He went on to recommend colonization, which would become a prominent feature of Cromwell's conquest of Ireland. The 1642 Act of Adventurers—which rewarded soldiers and financial investors of Parliament—was fully implemented by Cromwell using Irish land. Canny has argued that his was a continuation of the policy forged by Spenser and other sixteenth-century reformers.[127] Using negative representations to justify brutal English imperialism and colonization was never necessary for Cornwall as it had been for Ireland.

In contrast to what was happening in Ireland, Cornwall remained unusually quiet during the second Civil War. But in May 1648 Cornwall experienced its last armed action of the Civil War, following rebellions in the Penwith and Lizard peninsulas in the far west. In the former, an uprising against Parliament of between 300 and 500 men began in Penzance but was soon quelled in a short but bloody confrontation with Parliamentarian forces.[128] Meanwhile, on the Lizard, insurrectionists from Mullion and St Keverne (the latter also a focus of rebellion in 1497 and 1549) were soon preparing to march on Helston. The rebels were eventually defeated at the ancient earthwork at Gear, near St Mawgan village, in an action known thereafter as 'the Gear Rout'.[129] Many of the rebels had Royalist connections, but Stoyle especially likens the 1648 rising to Cornwall's Tudor rebelliousness, with the familiar

Cornish resistance to centralization.[130] As in other acts of Celtic opposition to English imperialism, Parliament responded with renewed negative representations of the Cornish. John Moyle, a Member of Parliament's county committee in Cornwall, wrote contemptuously of Penwith and the Lizard as 'those westerne heathen partes'.[131] It was the final justification needed for Parliament to reassert English control of Cornwall after the Civil War.

Conclusion

Throughout the Tudor, early Stuart and Civil War periods, the English used derogatory representations of the Irish and Cornish to reinforce and justify their imperial dominance. By portraying them as inferior, the English emphasized the perceived differences between themselves and the Celts. Hence England was able to justify often brutal imperial control as the act bringing civilisation to Ireland and Cornwall. This mirrors Edward Said's theory of 'Orientalism', where later British imperialism in the Middle East was excused by the same means. Likewise, a 'textual attitude' developed in which negative literary English representations of the Irish and Cornish were disseminated through English society. As we have seen, the experiences of Ireland and Cornwall were by no means identical during this long period, and English representations of the Irish and Cornish varied accordingly. But, as this study has shown, whenever English imperial control was threatened in either Ireland or Cornwall, negative representations were deployed to justify both the restoration of control and the means of asserting it.

Plainly, there is still much to explore regarding English representations of Ireland and Cornwall. Furthermore, similar studies of English representations of Wales and Scotland would produce interesting results. There is a tendency, of which this study is perhaps guilty, to frame British history as 'England versus Celts'. Yet inter-Celtic relations were far from amiable. Indeed, a comparative study of the Celtic territories' attitudes towards one another, and the reasons for these, would prove insightful. The long-term effect of English representations of the Celts in the early modern period is also worthy of study. To what extent did brutal English representations of early-modern Ireland contribute to the Republic of Ireland's unique status today as the only independent Celtic nation? Cornwall, by contrast, is often considered as merely a county of England, much like any other. But how far did English representations, which often framed Cornwall as a subordinate loyal partner, contribute to Cornwall's ambiguous status today?

Notes and references

1. Anne Ross has highlighted that 'the terms "Celt" and "Celtic" have different connotations for different scholars'. While the Celts can be viewed as those belonging to the linguistic family who speak the Celtic languages—Cornish, Welsh, Breton, Irish, Scottish Gaelic and Manx—this tends to over-simplify questions of ethnicity. Authors such as Nick Merriman suggest notions of Celt and Celtic are simply romantic portrayals of 'otherness'. However this essay challenges both of these views, perceiving Celtic as an ethnonym for, in the words of Barry Cunliffe, 'the inhabitants of Europe in the pre-Roman period' and in Britain, 'it was against these people that the Roman armies moved in the first centuries BC and AD, leaving only a Celtic fringe'. See Anne Ross, *Pagan Celtic Britain* (London, 1974), p. 33; Philip Payton, *Cornwall: A History* (Fowey, 2004), pp. 35-40; Barry Cunliffe, *The Celtic World* (New York, 1979), p. 7. For Merriman's views; Nick Merriman, 'Value and Motivation in Prehistory: The Evidence for "Celtic Spirit"' in Ian Hodder (ed.), *The Archaeology of Contextual Meanings* (Cambridge, 1987).

2. Bernard Deacon, *Cornwall: A Concise History* (Cardiff, 2007), p. 26.

3. Alan M. Kent, '"Art Thou of Cornish Crew?": Shakespeare, *Henry V* and Cornish Identity' in Philip Payton (ed.), *Cornish Studies: Four* (Exeter, 1996), p. 9.

4. R.F. Foster, *The Oxford History of Ireland* (Oxford, 1989), p. 96.

5. Edward Said, *Culture and Imperialism* (New York, 1994), p. 8.

6. Valerie Kennedy, *Edward Said: A Critical Introduction* (Cambridge, 2000), p. 18.

7. 'Michel Foucault', *Stanford Encyclopedia of Philosophy*, http://plato.stanford.edu/entries/foucault/, accessed 16 February 2013.

8. Michel Foucault, *Discipline and Punishment: The Birth of the Prison*, translated by Alan Sheridan (New York, 1977), p. 27.

9. Edward Said, *Orientalism* (Reprint, London, 2003).

10. Kennedy, *Said*, p. 21; Said, *Orientalism*, p. 43.

11. Kennedy, *Said*, p. 17.

12. Said, *Orientalism*, p. 201

13. Ibid., p. 36.

14. William Shakespeare, *The History of Henry IV, Part One*, (eds.) Barbara A. Mowat and Paul Werstine (New York, 2009); William Shakespeare, *The Second Part of King Henry IV*, (ed.) Giorgio Melchiori (Cambridge, 1989); William Shakespeare, *Henry V*, (ed.) Stanley Wells (Oxford, 2010).

15. Thomason Tracts, British Library.

16. Brendan Bradshaw and Peter Roberts (eds.), *British Consciousness and Identity: The Making of Britain 1533–1707* (Cambridge, 1998), p, 1.

17. Peter Gaunt, *The British Wars 1637–1651* (London, 1997), p. 80.

18. Michael Hechter, *Internal Colonialism: The Celtic Fringe in British National Development, 1536–1966* (Berkeley, 1975); Hugh Kearney, *The British Isles: A History of Four Nations* (Cambridge, 1989).

19. Victor Treadwell, *Buckingham and Ireland, 1616–1628: A Study in Anglo-Irish Politics* (Dublin, 1998); Nicholas Canny, *Making Ireland British, 1580–1650* (Oxford, 2001).

20. Canny, *Making Ireland British*.

21. Mark Stoyle, *West Britons: Cornish Identities and the Early Modern British State*

(Exeter, 2002); Mark Stoyle, *Soldiers and Strangers: An Ethnic History of the English Civil War* (London, 2005).

22. Payton, *Cornwall*; Deacon, *Cornwall*.

23. Stoyle, *West Britons*, pp. 66–90.

24, Kent, 'Cornish Identity', pp. 7–25.

25. See, Brendan Bradshaw, Andrew Hadfield and Willy Maley (eds.), *Representing Ireland: Literature and the Origins of Conflict, 1534–1660* (Cambridge, 1993); John Gillingham, 'Images of Ireland, 1170–1600: The Origins of English Imperialism', *History Today*, Vol. 37:2 (February, 1987), pp. 16–22.

26. Christopher Highley, *Shakespeare, Spenser and the Crisis in Ireland* (Cambridge, 1997).

27. Stoyle, *Soldiers and Strangers*, p. 34; Stoyle, *West Britons*, p. 66.

28. Payton, *Cornwall*, p. 106.

29. Deacon, *Cornwall*, p. 62.

30. John Gillingham, *The English in the Twelfth Century: Imperialism, National Identity and Political Values* (Woodbridge, 2000), p. 146

31. Raphael Holinshed, *Chronicles of England, Scotland, and Ireland*, Six Volumes (Reprinted London, 1808).

32. Gerald of Wales, 'Expugnatio Hibernica' ('The Conquest of Ireland') in Holinshed, *Chronicles*.

33. John Hooker, 'The Supplie of this Irish Chronicle' in Holinshed, *Chronicles*.

34. Highley, *Crisis in Ireland*, p. 9.

35. Deacon, *Cornwall*, p. 63.

36. Gillian Brennan, 'Language and Nationality: The Role of Policy Towards Celtic Languages in the Consolidation of Tudor Power', *Nations and Nationalism*, 7(3) (2001), p. 320.

37. Deacon, *Cornwall*, p. 81.

38. Payton, *Cornwall*, p. 105.

39. Polydore Vergil, *Anglica Historia* in David C. Douglas (general ed.) and C.H. Williams (ed.), *English Historical Documents* (London, 1967).

40. John Chynoweth, *Tudor Cornwall* (Stroud, 2002), p. 211.

41. Philip Payton, '". . . A Concealed Envy Against the English": A Note on the Aftermath of the 1497 Rebellions in Cornwall', in Philip Payton (ed.), *Cornish Studies: One* (Exeter, 1993), pp. 241–48.

42. PRO MS 600, George Carew, 'A Discourse of Ireland' (1601), p. 194.

43. Brennan, 'Language and Nationality', p. 329.

44. Highley, *Crisis in Ireland*, p. 3.

45. Nicholas Canny, *The Elizabethan Conquest of Ireland* (Hassocks, 1976), p. 123.

46. Deacon, *Cornwall*, p. 76.

47. Newton Key and Robert Bucholz (eds.), *Sources and Debates in English History 1485–1714* (Oxford, 2009), p. 81.

48. David Campbell, *Writing Security, United States Foreign Policy and the Politics of Identity* (Minneapolis, 1992), p. 120.

49. Foster, *Ireland*, p. 110.

50. NLI Ms. 7861, 'Letter from Robertum Legge to Queen Elizabeth' (1586).

51. Richard Carew, 'The Excellency of the English Tongue' in Richard Carew, *Survey of Cornwall, 1602*, (ed.) F.E. Halliday (London, 1953).

52. Edmund Spenser, *The Faerie Queen*, (ed.) Albert Charles Hamilton (Oxford,

1977); Edmund Spenser, *A View of the Present State of Ireland*, (ed.) William Lindsay Renwick (Oxford, 1970).

53. Canny, *Making Ireland British*, p. 18.
54. Spenser, *View*, p. 1.
55. Ibid., p. 3.
56. Canny, *Making Ireland British*, pp. 1–59.
57. Thomas Hughes, *The Misfortunes of Arthur*, (ed.) J. Payne Collier (London, 1828); William Shakespeare, *Sir John Oldcastle*, (eds) Michael Drayton, Anthony Munday, Robert Wilson and Richard Hathway (Amersham, 1911).
58. Stephen O'Neill, *Staging Ireland: Representations in Shakespeare and Renaissance Drama* (Dublin, 2007).
59. Highley, *Crisis in Ireland*, p. 6.
60. Ibid., pp. 86–109; William Shakespeare, *The History of Henry IV, Part One*, (eds.) Barbara A. Mowat and Paul Werstine (New York, 2009).
61. Ibid., p. 50; William Shakespeare, *The Second Part of King Henry IV*, (ed.) Giorgio Melchiori (Cambridge, 1989).
62. Kent, 'Cornish Identity', p. 11.
63. Ibid.
64. E.12 [4], *The Kingdome's Weekly Intelligencer* (1–8 October 1644).
65. R.B. McDowell (ed.), 'Hugh O'Neill's War Aims', http://publish.ucc.ie/celt/docs/E590001-003?fragment=all&refnav=View, accessed 2 May 2012.
66. Christine Kinealy, *A New History of Ireland* (Gloucestershire, 2004), p. 79.
67. Canny, *Making Ireland British*, p. 166.
68. Foster, *Ireland*, p. 113; Kinealy, *Ireland*, pp. 82–83.
69. Thomas Wentworth, W. Knowler (eds), *The Earl of Strafford's Letters and Dispatches*, Vol. I (London, 1739), p. 450.
70. T.W. Moody, 'Ulster Plantation Papers', *Analecta Hibernica*, No. 8 (March, 1938), p. 278.
71. Kinealy, *Ireland*, p. 86.
72. PRO MS 629, 'An estimate report made by Sir Laurence Esmond, Sir Edward Fisher, Knights, and the King's Surveyor General and Escheator of Leinster, lately employed for surveying and accepting surrenders of certain lands in the county of Wexford, whereunto the King hath ancient title', (1611), p. 142.
73. Foster, *Ireland*, p. 116.
74. Payton, *Cornwall*, p. 126; Deacon, *Cornwall*, p. 75.
75. Deacon, *Cornwall*, p. 81.
76. Thomas Wentworth, W. Knowler (ed.), *The Earl of Strafford's Letters and Dispatches*, Vol. II (London, 1739), p. 93.
77. Kinealy, *Ireland*, p. 91; Foster, *Ireland*, p. 98.
78. NLI Ms. 46,757, 'Letter from Thomas Wentworth, first Earl of Strafford, addressed to Charles I advising the King on the military needs of Ireland' (19 August 1638).
79. Kearney, *British Isles*, p. 181.
80. John Temple, *The Irish Rebellion; or, The History of the Beginning and First Progress of the General Rebellion Raised within the Kingdom of Ireland upon the Three and Twentieth Day of October 1641* (London, 1646).
81. Canny, *Making Ireland British*.
82. Ibid., p. 535.

83. Trevor Royle, *Civil War: The Wars of the Three Kingdoms, 1638–1660* (London, 2004), p. 139; Kearney, *British Isles*, p. 182.

84. NLI Ms. 2658, 'Letter from Lord Clanricarde to the Lord Chamberlain of the King' (6 December 1641).

85. NLI, Genealogical Office: Ms. 16, 'Preamble to the oath of association of the Confederate Catholics of Kilkenny' (26 July 1641), p. 107; Royle, *Civil War*, p. 143.

86. Diane Purkiss, *The English Civil War: A People's History* (London, 2006), p. 109.

87. Ibid.

88. Anthony Fletcher, *The Outbreak of the English Civil War* (London, 1981), p. 136.

89. E.179 [9], *Bloudy newes from Ireland, or the barbarous crueltie by the papists used in that kingdome* (1 December 1641).

90. Fletcher, *Outbreak*, p. 137.

91. Mary Coate, *Cornwall in the Great Civil War and Interregnum, 1642–1660* (Truro, 1963), pp. 26–44.

92. Stoyle, *Soldiers and Strangers*, p. 41.

93. Deacon, *Cornwall*, p. 85.

94. Payton, *Cornwall*, p. 147.

95. Stoyle, *Soldiers and Strangers*, p. 174.

96. Stoyle, *West Britons*, p. 73.

97. E.86 [3], *Special Passages* (17–24 January 1643).

98. G. Chapman, *The Siege of Lyme Regis* (Lyme Regis, 1982), p. 32.

99. J. Barratt, *Cavaliers: The Royalist Army at War, 1642–46* (Stroud, 2000), p. 140; Stoyle, *Soldiers and Strangers*, p. 61.

100. Stoyle, *Soldiers and Strangers*, p. 62.

101. E.31 [10], *The True Informer* (27 January to 3 February 1643).

102. Payton, *Cornwall*, p. 142.

103. Arthur Fisher, 'The Apologie, Relation and Petition of Colonel John Were', *Devon and Cornwall Notes and Queries*, No. 4 (1906–7), p. 160.

104. Deacon, *Cornwall*, p. 86.

105. E.12 [4].

106. Stoyle, *West Britons*, pp. 77–78.

107. Fletcher, *Outbreak*, p. 311; Stoyle, *Soldiers and Strangers*, p. 36.

108. Deacon, *Cornwall*, p. 78.

109. Payton, *Cornwall*, p. 142.

110. James Scott Wheeler, *Cromwell in Ireland* (New York, 1999), p. 30.

111. NLI Ms. 9051, 'Articles of peace concluded between the Earl of Ormond, acting for the king, and the Confederate Catholics' (January 1649).

112. Stoyle, *Soldiers and Strangers*, p. 49.

113. Payton, *Cornwall*, p. 146.

114. Stoyle, *Soldiers and Strangers*, pp. 175, 179.

115. Coate, *Civil War*, p. 173; Stoyle, *Soldiers and Strangers*, p. 181.

116. CRO Tremaine, T/1618/1-2, 'Letter from Richard Grenville to Col. Lewis Tremaine' (1 December 1645); Payton, *Cornwall*, p. 145.

117. W. C. Abbott, *The Writings and Speeches of Oliver Cromwell: Volume I, 1599–1649* (Cambridge, 1937), pp. 372–73.

118. LJ, Vol. VII, 'Message to the H.C. to appoint a Committee to meet with them; with the Petition in Behalf of the poor Cornish', (1644–45), p. 623, www.british-history.ac.uk/report.aspx?compid=33412, accessed 2 May 2012.

119. Oliver Cromwell, *Oliver Cromwell's Letters and Speeches Elucidations*, Vol. II, (ed.) Thomas Carlyle (London, 1871), p. 213.

120. Ibid., p. 210.

121. Denis Murphy, *Cromwell in Ireland* (Dublin, 1883), p. 261.

122. Cromwell, *Letters and Speeches*, p. 138.

123. Royle, *Civil War*, pp. 528–30.

124. NLI Ms. 6491, 'Facsimile of a letter from Oliver Cromwell to the commander in chief of the town of Wexford demanding the immediate surrender of the garrison' (11 October 1649).

125. Kinealy, *Ireland*, p. 100.

126. NLI Ms. 9696, 'Letter from Oliver Cromwell to William Lenthall, speaker of Parliament of England' (4 October 1649).

127. Canny, *Making Ireland British*, p. 552.

128. Stoyle, *West Britons*, pp. 118, 121; Payton, *Cornwall*, p. 148.

129. Coate, *Civil War*, p. 240.

130. Stoyle, *West Britons*, p. 132.

131. Ibid., p. 132.

7

The Duchy of Cornwall and the Crown

Disputes and accommodation

John Kirkhope

Introduction

The Royal Institution of Cornwall recently announced it had acquired the papers relating to the famous 'Cornwall Foreshore Dispute'[1] ('the Foreshore Dispute') about which much has been written and upon which many claims regarding the relationship of Cornwall to England are based. The problem, as it is hoped will be demonstrated in this article, is that others have failed to understand the context within which the Foreshore Dispute arose. Firstly there are the issues surrounding the debate about how the Crown should be financed in the light of its changing role, which led to the development of the Civil List and the treatment of the Duchy's of Cornwall and Lancaster as part of those considerations. Secondly, the Foreshore Dispute was but one of a number of disagreements which arose in the nineteenth century, some of which remain unresolved, in which the Duchy advanced arguments similar to those in the Foreshore Dispute but which did not succeed. Simply, to use modern jargon, the Disputes 'were all about the money'.[2]

'A mode of descent unknown to common law'[3]

To have some understanding of the Duchy it is necessary to have an appreciation of the unique form of descent created by the Charter of 17 March 1337 ('the Charter') which established the Duchy of Cornwall. There is nothing like it in English Law and it has been the source of much confusion for centuries.

As Rowse said, the consequence is that: 'There may not be a Duke there is always a Duchy'.[4]

The Duke of Cornwall is the eldest living son of the monarch being heir to the throne.[5] An example will illustrate what that means. When George VI ascended the throne there was no Duke of Cornwall since his heir was female. Upon Elizabeth II becoming monarch, Prince Charles immediately became Duke of Cornwall. During the period of the minority of Prince Charles from 1952 until 1969, the Duchy was managed by the Crown. If Prince Charles had died before having children his brother Prince Andrew, who would then have been the eldest living son of the sovereign being heir to the throne, would have become Duke of Cornwall. If Prince Charles dies before becoming King his son Prince William would not be Duke of Cornwall since he is the grandson of the monarch and not the son. During periods when there is no Duke, the Duchy reverts to but remains distinct and is managed separately from other Crown property. The Sovereign is, in effect, a trustee until a Duke of Cornwall appears. For about half the period since the Duchy was created there has been no Duke of Cornwall. The titles of Prince of Wales and Earl of Chester are always new creations and are traditionally bestowed upon male heirs to the throne who may not be Dukes of Cornwall.

The Duchy of Cornwall and the Civil List

The first Civil List Act was passed in 1697, during the reign of William III, by which Parliament assumed responsibility for certain government spending while the King remained responsible for expenditures on the civil side of government (hence Civil List). The King, as part of the arrangement, surrendered the 'Hereditary Revenues'[6] of the Crown including the Duchies of Lancaster and Cornwall. The agreement continued during the reign of Queen Anne.

On the accession of George I to the throne in 1714 it was agreed that he would receive a Civil List of £700,000. The Hereditary Revenues were surrendered, *except the Royal Duchies of Lancaster and Cornwall*, in exchange for the Civil List. The then Prince of Wales, the future George II, was to receive £100,000 from that Civil List *plus* the income from the Duchy of Cornwall. This pattern continued. The son of George II, Frederick who died in 1751 before ascending to the throne, received £50,000 from the Civil List plus the income from the Duchy. A Civil List broadly similar in shape to that with which we are now familiar was agreed with the accession to the throne of George III in 1760. The most extravagant of all the Georgians was the Prince Regent, the future George IV, who was voted a Civil List annuity in excess of £120,000 per annum. He received the income from the Duchy as well as the Civil List. When George IV came to the throne he received a Civil List annuity, together with the income from the Duchy of Cornwall, because his heir was his brother, the future William IV, and thus there was no Duke of Cornwall. Similarly William IV, whose successor was Victoria, also retained the income from the Duchy. Like her two uncles, who preceded her, Victoria initially kept the income from the Duchy of Cornwall. Her Civil List was regarded as exceptionally generous—'the appropriation to the Crown of the largely increased revenues of the Duchies made it more than liberal'.[7]

Victoria's son Prince Albert Edward (later Edward VII) was born in 1841, when he became entitled to the income from the Duchy of Cornwall. The Duchy was managed largely by his father, Prince Albert, the Prince Consort, who had been appointed by his mother Victoria, until he reached the age of twenty-one. Prince Albert Edward received a Civil List Annuity of £40,000 when he attained his majority in 1862 in addition to the net Duchy income of £46,000[8]. His total income in the last year of Victoria's reign was £106,000 which included the income from the Duchy (over £9 million in 2012).

The Sovereign Grant Act 2010 changes the way the monarchy is to be financed in the future. One consequence of which is that the Duchy of Cornwall will now be used to finance the heir to the throne whoever that may be, whether a grandson of the Sovereign or the daughter or indeed granddaughter of the Sovereign. The Duchy of Cornwall insists it is a private estate[9] but it is a private estate which is responsible for meeting the cost of a state function, that of the heir to the throne, which, to say the least, is unusual.

To sum up, the founding document of the Duchy created a form of inheritance the legal consequences of which to this day are not fully explored. The oscillation of the Duchy between the heir to the throne and the Crown creates a convenient ambiguity, which some argue, the Duchy of Cornwall exploits. Furthermore, it must be understood that with the Hereditary Revenues of the Crown being surrendered, the degree to which the Duchy of Cornwall succeeded in its disputes it managed to claw back from the Treasury for the Royal Household income and property that the Crown had otherwise foregone. For example, if the Duchy managed to establish its right to the foreshores of Cornwall, which would otherwise 'belong' to the Crown, it 'recovered' assets that had been surrendered by the Crown to the State. So, as we shall shortly discover, although disputes nominally were between the Crown and the Duchy, in fact they were between the Duchy and the Treasury. When the Duchy succeeded, Government revenues were reduced.

The Accession of Queen Victoria

Having presented some background, this article will now explore various disputes that occurred between the Crown and the Duchy and the way in which they were resolved. This examination will demonstrate that many of the claims made by and on behalf of the Duchy in regard to its constitutional status and privileges are based not on statute or judicial decision but contradictory and often unsatisfactory decisions of 'arbitrators'.

Since Victoria had not succeeded to the private property of William IV nor to the revenue of Hanover,[10] the then Chancellor of the Exchequer, Mr Spring Rice, reasoned she should not be asked to surrender the Duchies of Lancaster or Cornwall[11]. However, he proposed and it was agreed, annual reports on the Duchies should be submitted to Parliament. Thus we see the passing of the Duchies of Lancaster and Cornwall (Accounts) Act 1838, subsequently amended by the Duchy of Cornwall Management Act 1982, by which accounts of the Duchies have to be presented to Parliament. In the past the Duchies had been preserved from examination on the grounds they were the 'sovereign's private property'. Once accounts had to be submitted, they could no longer be regarded as purely private. Haslam explains that the Act meant the Duchy was: 'Not exactly a private company, nor a government department, the Duchy became a publicly accountable private estate, a paradoxical solution not untypical of the British constitution'.[12] But Haslam is wrong: the Duchy is not a 'private estate', nor is it 'publicly accountable'.

It should be noted the Duchy paid taxes including property tax, land tax and 'other taxes' from 1842,[13] at the same time Queen Victoria agreed to pay income tax on her Civil List. When Prince Albert, husband of Victoria, was appointed Lord Warden of the Stannary in 1842, this was not an honorary title. In effect, he became responsible for managing the Duchy, a role he fulfilled until his death in 1861. It is the only official position that Albert ever occupied, which may explain why he took such an intense interest in Duchy matters. In 1838, before Prince Albert was appointed to the Prince's Council, the Duchy's gross income was £24,885 (approx. £1,251,000 in 2011), leaving £11,536 (approx. £580,000 in 2011) after all costs had been paid. By 1861 gross income had grown to £60,753 (approx. £2,989,000 in 2011), leaving £46,676 (approx. £2,290,000 in 2011) after costs. It was an impressive achievement[14]. Prince Albert 'had brought the Duchy back from the precipice, reinvigorated it by establishing a new management structure and provided it with a sense of purpose'.[15]

Prince Albert established the foundations upon which the Duchy still rests. The tone of his stewardship of the Duchy, and the assertiveness that he brought to the Duchy, is suggested in correspondence sent in 1843, at his direction, in connection with a dispute which arose over the Waters of the Tamar. The Duchy wrote:

> During the Reign of George IV a statement with reference to these rights was by His Majesty's command addressed to the Lords of the Treasury with a view to obtaining compensation for the possessor of the Duchy of Cornwall. And His Majesty was graciously pleased at that time to communicate to the Government and Officers of the Duchy that His Majesty was fully aware of the necessity of supporting the rights and privileges of the Duchy of Cornwall, and that on no occasion would *His Majesty be disposed to yield those rights in the Crown without an adequate compensation under the sanction of Parliament* [emphasis added].

Later in the same correspondence:

> In consequence of the magnitude and importance of these claims, the [Duchy] Council are desirous that the attention of the Lords of the Treasury should be called to the subject at as early a period as possible, in order that their Lordships may consider what steps ought to be taken with a view to compensate the Prince of Wales, and at the same time *to prevent the great public inconvenience which must necessarily arise from the conflicting interests of the Crown and Duchy of Cornwall* [16] [emphasis added].

This correspondence serves as a summary of themes to which we will return. That is the demand for compensation for rights and the desire to avoid litigation.

The Isles of Scilly

The accession of Victoria to the throne marked a change in the Duchy fortunes. However, before considering disputes which arose during and after the reign of Queen Victoria, it is instructive to consider a disagreement which occurred in 1832/34 during the reign of William IV, both because it is interesting in its own right and because it allows the identification of themes to which we shall return.

The current website of the Duchy asserts: 'The Isles of Scilly have been part of the Duchy of Cornwall since the 14th Century'. Not everyone would agree with that statement. There are those who maintain the Isles of Scilly came to the Duchy following the attainder of the Marquis of Exeter in

1538;[17] others claimed they came to the Duchy following the dissolution of the monasteries during the reign of Henry VIII.[18] In 1832/34, the Crown questioned the entitlement of the Duchy to the Isles of Scilly. The dispute was submitted to the Law Officers of the Crown who concluded: 'upon the whole the Scilly Isles are to be considered as part of the properties of the Duchy of Cornwall and they do not belong to the Crown'. They went on to say: 'it is to be regretted that in a matter of so much importance there should not be a regular series of authentic public documents by referring to which the questions between the Crown and the Duchy of Cornwall might be at once satisfactorily decided'.[19] The Duchy itself acknowledged that its entitlement to the Islands were implicit. It observed in 1855: 'Unquestionably property of a most important character both as regard extent and value was not specified but nevertheless passed e.g. the Isles of Scilly'.[20]

The problem is that the Charters upon which the Duchy is based are inconsistent. The Charter of 17 March 1337, in translation, states: 'lest it may be in anywise hereafter be doubted what or how much the same Duke . . . ought to have *all things in particular which we will pertain to the same Duchy we have commanded to be inserted in this our Charter'*.[21] The Crown has argued that with the death of John of Eltham, the last Earl of Cornwall, in 1336 the estates reverted to the Crown and the Duchy had no more than granted explicitly by the founding Charter. The problem with this is that the Charter of 9 July 1343 says: 'considering therefore how the Earldom of Cornwall, now called the Duchy of Cornwall, hath sustained for a length of time a great dismemberment of its rights and desiring to make integral the Said Duchy and recollect its rights thus disperse'.

The Duchy has claimed that many rights which were not explicitly listed, nonetheless passed to it from the Earldom implicitly.

This dispute allows two points to be illustrated. First, when it arose there was no Duke of Cornwall which demonstrates that although, during such periods, the Duchy 'reverts' to the Crown it does not become absorbed in the Crown; otherwise, in this case, the Crown would have be in dispute with itself which is clearly nonsense. Secondly, it highlights the fact there is room for argument about the benefits enjoyed by the Duchy, since it is not clearly established whether or not it inherited the rights of the Earldom of Cornwall.

The Waters of the Tamar

The dispute between the Duchy and the Crown regarding the Tamar was maintained for several years. (There is correspondence on the topic continuing until 1933.) It was important because the Admiralty wished to develop

Devonport Dockyard and the question arose of the extent of the Duchy interest in Plymouth Sound and, therefore, the compensation to be paid. The Duchy was jealous and persistent in its claims'.[22] In a procedure repeated many times, the question was submitted in 1861 for arbitration—in this case to Edward Smirke, who was Vice Warden of the Stannaries. His decision did not determine the matter. The Office of Woods (the predecessor of the Crown Estate) wrote to the Lords of Treasury it was anxious to resolve the problem because: 'At the same time my Lords are desirous to prevent in future the long and expensive litigation to which a further agitation of the rights of the Duchy would give rise'.[23] They went on to say, pointedly:

> My Lords wish to observe in conclusion that Her Majesty's Government has a strong interest in supporting the just rights of the Duchy of Cornwall, and that it will be the desire, and it is the duty of this Board to prevent, as far as possible, the incurrence of unnecessary expense in the settlement of adverse claims between the Duchy and the Crown, but they must remark that the interests of the public, and of individuals must often be involved in the settlement of undefined rights, and that, with every disposition to approach these questions in a conciliatory spirit *they are unable to accept the proposition to which the recent application of the [Princes] Council would seem to point, that claims, in respect of boundaries, adverse to them should be accepted without evidence or legal Arbitrament* [emphasis added].

The desire to avoid the uncertainty and cost of litigation was a powerful motivation to agree to arbitration to decide disputes. In the same file of correspondence, a letter was written by the Duchy on 6 May 1864 in which it referred to the enquiry undertaken by Mr Smirke. The letter said:

> The question arose from the Officers of the Crown claiming a considerable portion of Plymouth Sound . . . as not being within the limits of the water. The Officers of the Prince of Wales felt fully satisfied that there was no substantial ground for the claim but as it was pressed on the part of the Officers of the Crown it was arranged by mutual consent that the matter should be referred to the arbitration of Mr Smirke . . . The claim put forward by the Crown involved as must always be the case when a question is raised as to the ancient rights of the Duchy of Cornwall the nature and extent of which are generally very imperfectly understood, a very laborious enquiry and examination of ancient records and documents on the part of the Duchy extending over 500 years'.

The Duchy then continues by insisting that since an enquiry was:

> forced upon the Duchy after strong remonstrance and every endeavour
> . . . unfortunately unsuccessful to convince the Crown of the erroneous
> nature of the claims. *The Duchy feels strongly that the Revenues of His*
> *Royal Highness should not be charged with any portion of the payments to the*
> *arbitrator*[24] [emphasis added].

An interesting insight into the opinion of the Duchy of itself is revealed in still more correspondence regarding the Waters of the Tamar, this time in the 1890s. On 13 April 1894, in a letter to the Board of Trade, the Duchy wrote, 'with a view to assisting the Board of Trade *the Department* [emphasis added] will be prepared'. In a further letter dated 21 April 1894, the Duchy added: 'but it would be of considerable assistance *to this Department* [emphasis added]'. A 'private estate', which regards itself as a Department of State, is an interesting notion.

The issues which arise from the above correspondence exemplifies the attitude of the Duchy. First, is the Duchy's persistence in its assertion of its rights and its insistence on being compensated before surrendering them. Next, is the tension which arises from claiming to be part of the Crown and entitled to the privileges of the Crown while demanding rights in conflict with the Crown. There is also the 'need' to resolve differences in a way that avoids 'public inconvenience' which would otherwise arise.[25]

A striking feature of the disputes which arose was the Duchy's assumption that the position they put forward and the legal arguments they deployed were so obviously correct that no contrary position could possibly be sustained. Further examples will be provided shortly. With regard to the Waters of the Tamar, the Duchy resisted paying for the arbitrator since the cost had been forced on them because of the 'erroneous nature' of the claims of the Crown. The Crown had, it will be noted, refused to accept Duchy claims 'without evidence or legal Arbitrament'. It should be emphasized that the disputes are characterized as disagreements between the Duke of Cornwall and the Crown. In fact, the future Edward VII had been born in 1841 and the issues were in practice pursued by Prince Albert, as the person who controlled the Duchy, and the Treasury via the Office of Woods. It was in the interest of Queen Victoria, despite the fact she nominally resisted the claims of the Duchy, to lose since it would mean her husband had won and her son thus increased his income. It appeared like a family squabble, except in this case the interest of the Queen coincided with that of her husband and son.

'The consent of the Duchy of Cornwall signified'

The first time, as far as can be established with the help of the Parliamentary Archives, when the Duke of Cornwall's consent was signified to a Bill before Parliament was for 'The West of England and South Wales Drainage Company Incorporation Bill', 1 August 1848 to 10 August 1848.[26] His consent would have been given by his mother, Queen Victoria, on the Duke's behalf since he was only seven years old at the time. This is comparatively late in Parliamentary history and it has not been possible to establish, despite much effort, why the process began. The House of Common's Archive advised that it 'cannot find any items that may obviously explain . . . the Duchy consents'.[27] Of course, the *assent* of the Sovereign is always required to Acts of Parliament. However, the Sovereign's *consent* is specifically required with regard to Bills affecting the prerogative, being the 'Hereditary Revenues, personal property or interests of the Crown and the Duchy of Lancaster'. However, the giving of consent by the Duchy of Cornwall has become a matter of Parliamentary usage almost by default, without any investigation of the basis on which that consent is required. The House of Commons Information Office explained that Erskine May 23rd Edition stated:

Bills affecting the prerogative (being powers exercisable by the Sovereign for the performance of constitutional duties on the one hand, or hereditary revenues, personal property or interests of the Crown, the Duchy of Lancaster or the Duchy of Cornwall on the other); require the signification of the Queen's consent in both Houses before they are passed. When the Prince of Wales is of age his own consent as Duke is given'.[28]

It is possible that there are occasions earlier than 1848 when the Duke of Cornwall's consent was required; however, Hansard only became a full official report from 1909. From 1803, when it started, until 1909 it existed in an unofficial form. It was not a full report; it focussed on public bills and therefore private bills were not always covered. It is clear, however, that the consent of the Duchy was not signified to the Duchy of Cornwall Acts passed in 1844.

Great importance is attached to the requirement that the Duchy give consent to certain legislation by those arguing for the distinct legal status of Cornwall. For example, John Angarrack states that the requirement:

only touch[es] the surface of this secretive constitutional arrangement . . . [it is a] reflection of parliament's inability to freely legislate in respect of the Duchy of Cornwall . . . the governance and legal identity of Cornwall lie within the jurisdiction of the Duchy of Cornwall, which itself, for many purposes, remain extra-jurisdictional to the UK Parliament.[29]

The evidence does not support these claims. It is clear the need for the consent dates from the 1840s, when Prince Albert controlled the Duchy, and would appear to be based on his desire to protect the Duchy's economic interests. If the constitutional implications were as suggested, it would be reasonable to suppose evidence of the need for Duchy consent would date back much further than 1848.[30]

The Queen's Remembrancer's Fees

There were, at least two disputes which arose between the Crown and the Duchy of Cornwall during the 1850s. The first dates from 1855 and relates to the fees claimed by the Queen's Remembrancer[31] from the Duchy of Cornwall.[32] The fees amounted to £12 8s. 4d. (about £600 in today's money) and were in connection with a suit between the Duchy and the Bristol Water Works Company. They arose under the Exchequer Court Act 1842. The opinion of the Attorney General to the Duchy was obtained. He said: 'it will be proper to resist the payments of these fees . . . communication should be made to the Lords of the Treasury that they instruct the Queen's Remembrancer to abstain from demanding them'. The Surveyor to the Duchy wrote to the Treasury, enclosing a copy of the Attorney General to H.R.H. Prince of Wales opinion, which said the view of Prince Albert had been sought, who gave as his judgement the fees should not be paid. The letter then continues: 'It will probably occur to the Lords Commissioners that in proceedings of this nature which effect the landed property of the Duchy the Attorney General of His Royal Highness *represents the Interest of the Crown as well as the interests of the Prince*' [emphasis added]. The Queen's Remembrancer in his response stated: 'it has been thought necessary to demand these fees . . . in consequence of the Prince of Wales being a party to the suit as a *subject suing for his own benefit and not in any way to be considered as suing on the part of the Crown or the Public*' [emphasis added]. He continued:

> it would seem he (the Prince of Wales) stands in the same predicament as any other suitor not the Crown or a Public Department of Revenue . . . the Duke of Cornwall may come within the exemptions contained within the Act . . . the exemption being only intended to apply to the payment of fees of such Public Departments as would only pay them out of public monies. This could not be held to be the case in regard to fees payable by the Duchy of Cornwall as *private party in a cause; and I have therefore been of opinion that these fees were properly demanded* [emphasis added].

The only possible argument by which I can conceive a claim to exemption to be supported would be founded upon a contingent claim of the Crown to the Revenues of the Duchy of Cornwall in the event of the death of the Prince of Wales; but I should submit that even supposing the exemption to be maintainable on the occurrence of that contingency (which might be doubtful) that possibility could not affect the position of the actual Duke of Cornwall *suing as a subject and liable to the conditions affecting subjects in this court* [emphasis added].

The Attorney General to H.R.H. Prince of Wales responded to the Queen's Remembrancer by suggesting he was mistaken that the suit against the Bristol Water Works Company was for the benefit of the Prince of Wales 'solely and personally', whereas in fact they:

were to the benefit of the Lands of the Duchy and thereby to the inheritance of the Crown. The possessions of the Duchy were inseparable from the Crown save for the purpose of supporting the dignity of the Prince of Wales for which purpose they were vested in His Royal Highness as it were temporarily and the claim of the Crown to the Revenues of the Duchy is not merely contingent on the event of the death of the Prince of Wales but the interest of the Crown in those revenues is permanent subject to the contingent claim of His Royal Highness'.

As happened so often the matter was submitted to the Government's Attorney and Solicitor General, who gave his opinion:

It therefore appears to us incorrect to say that the interest of the Crown in the Revenues is permanent subject to the contingent claim of H R H whenever a Prince of Wales exists. *It appears to us that it is the interest of the Crown that is contingent on the failure of a Prince of Wales.* At all events H R H has a present and immediate interest in the Revenues of the Duchy. He does not sue in the name or on behalf of the Crown but in his own account. The fruits of the suit will enure[33] to his immediate benefit. True it is that the Crown even where there is a Prince has an indirect interest (independently of its Reversionary Interest in the maintenance of the Revenue of the Duchy as forming a provision for the Prince) . . . *We are of the opinion therefore that H R H stands in the same position as any other subject or suitor in this Court of Exchequer and is liable to pay the fees in question* [emphasis added].

This file illustrates the themes to which attention has already been drawn. The Duchy claimed that it should enjoy the same privileges as the Crown, particularly when, as in this case, some economic advantage might be gained. The issue, of course, is of an estate sometimes being in the Crown and, therefore, presumably enjoying the privileges which accompany that status, and at other times in the hands of the Prince of Wales, Duke of Cornwall, a subject of the Crown 'though he is the greatest of subjects'[34] or, as the Queen's Remembrancer explained, a 'private party'. Finally, the recourse was to arbitration rather than litigation. In this matter a robust view was taken, the Duchy claim was denied, and the fees paid. It is important to note, since great importance is attached to the issue, that during the course of the correspondence the Duchy of Cornwall did not claim Crown Immunity (the principle that the Crown was not subject to an Act of Parliament unless it was specifically mentioned or by necessary implication) and the Government Law Officers never suggested it was applicable.

The Cornwall Foreshore Dispute

This unquestionably is the most well known dispute that arose between the Duchy and the Crown. The full title given in the papers is: 'The Tidal Estuaries, Foreshores, and Under-Sea Minerals, within and around the coast of the County of Cornwall'.[35] The significant and wide-ranging claims made on behalf of the Duchy included, for example, that the Duke of Cornwall was 'quasi sovereign within his Duchy', that the Crown had 'entirely denuded itself of every remnant of Seignory and territorial dominion . . . within the County or Duchy of Cornwall', that 'the Duke did become entitled to the whole county of Cornwall', and that 'within Cornwall the Duke was quasi sovereign'. The Crown challenged the assertions made by the Duchy. However, the arbitrator, Sir John Patteson, decided in favour of the Duchy and, as a consequence, the Cornwall Submarine Mines Act 1858 was passed. The introduction to that Act is significant. It says: 'An Act to declare and define the respective Rights of Her Majesty and of His Royal Highness the Prince of *Wales* and Duke of *Cornwall* to the Mines and Minerals in or under Land lying below High-water Mark, within and adjacent to the County of *Cornwall*, and for other Purposes'.

The Duchy's claims were made to secure an economic benefit. The 'Mines and Minerals in or under the Land lying below High-Water Mark' at this time had considerable value, and it was this that the Duchy was anxious to secure. Once more, a dispute was submitted to arbitration with the arbitrator being asked to choose between the competing claims of the Crown and the Duchy. The latter maintained it was part of the Crown but at the same time claimed a right against the Crown. The distinction was more apparent than real. The Hereditary Revenues of the Crown had been surrendered in favour of the Civil List. The more that could be clawed back from that which had been surrendered, the greater the economic advantage to the Royal Household, whether to the Sovereign or to her eldest living son.

Bernard Deacon considers: 'In 1855–7 the duchy lawyers were presenting the best legal case they could in Cornwall . . . Sometimes the duchy lawyers were just plain wrong'.[36] He is correct; the Duchy lawyers were doing what lawyers do and presenting their client's case in the best possible light. Similarly, the Crown's advocates tried their hardest to rebut the Duchy's case. The arbitrator, Sir John Patteson, a distinguished jurist, decided in favour of the Duchy. It is important to see the case in context. It was one of a number of disputes that the Duchy pursued, in some of which they succeeded and sometimes, as we have already seen, they failed. It is important to note the right to the Foreshore of Cornwall was, as the Duchy succeeded in arguing, implicitly inherited from the Earldom of Cornwall: it was not explicitly granted by the Duchy Charters. In an interesting commentary Mr A. Smith, MP, speaking in the House of Commons on 19 July 1858, said:

> It was remarkable that they never heard anything about the rights of the Crown to the bed of a river, or to land between high and low water mark on the shore of the sea, when there was anything to pay, but only when there was something to be received. If improvements were required the public had to pay for them; but if advantages were to be had, the Crown claimed them'.[37]

Right of Wreck

This dispute continued for many years. The Duchy perceived that this right, which had not been asserted with any energy for some time, might generate some income. The Secretary to the Duchy, James Gardiner, declared in 1860: 'the prerogative right of the Crown to wreck of the Sea so far as regards the entire County of Cornwall inalienably settled by the Legislature in the reign of Edward the 3rd upon the Heir Apparent of the Crown'.[38] Therefore, he stated, the Merchant Shipping Act 1854 did not apply to Cornwall and the Board of Trade had no jurisdiction. Gardiner went on to say: 'they seem to have assumed that there is no distinction between the County of Cornwall and other parts of the Kingdom and have dealt or propose to deal with the subject as if no distinction existed'. It was also asserted by the Duchy that the: 'Grant of the whole interest of the Crown in Cornwall [is] not identical to grants to ordinary Lords of the Manor'.[39] The matter was submitted to the Government's Law Officers. In 1862 they decided the Merchant Shipping Act 1854 did apply to Cornwall. Despite that, a new committee was formed in 1868 to enquire into the rights to wreck[40] before the issue was finally resolved.

There is now no question of the Duchy not being subject to the Act by virtue of it enjoying Crown Immunity.

Right to Royal gold and silver mines in Cornwall

The decision of Sir John Patteson in the Cornwall Foreshore Dispute, the Duchy said, meant that it had prima facie the right to the Royal Mines of gold and silver in Cornwall. Thus, the *Onus probandi*[41] rested with the Crown. It was for the Crown to rebut the argument rather than for the Duchy to prove its case.[42] The Duchy went on to insist on 11 February 1860: 'The mature decision of Sir John Patteson should be treated as setting at rest questions of this nature between the Sovereign and the Duke of Cornwall and that the superior title of the latter to all territorial rights whether prerogative or otherwise within the precincts of his Duchy should not now be questioned'. The papers were forwarded to the Government Law Officers with a statement from the Officers of Land Revenue which said, amongst other things:

> It is conceived that the decision of Sir John Patteson ['the Foreshore Dispute'] has no bearing upon the question—the right of the Crown to Royal Mines is not a Territorial but a Sovereign or Prerogative right and a grant of all the King's Territory in a particular county would not without express words pass the Sovereign's right to Royal Mines.

The Government Law Officers went on to say 'it is submitted that the burden of proving title to them clearly rests upon the Duchy'. The Opinion, dated 29 May 1860, was as follows:

> We are not satisfied that the facts and matters relied on in support of the claim are in anywise sufficient to countervail the general principle of law *that Royal Mines are a Prerogative Right of so high a character as not to pass by any royal grant except by express words of which we find none* [emphasis added] in the Charters by which the Duchy of Cornwall was created and its possessions granted.

> *It is however not seemly or proper that a question of this kind between Her Majesty and the Prince should be subject of legal proceedings* [emphasis added] and in the course of our Conference with the Prince's Attorney General it appeared to us and which view as we understood met with his full concurrence that the question should be considered by some former Judge of the Highest position and eminence [emphasis added].

The issue seems to have rested until 1879 when the question was again raised of submitting the matter to arbitration.[43] In 1880, it was suggested Lord Penzance act as arbitrator.[44] In a letter to Lord Penzance it was stated:

It is considered both by the Queen's Government and by the Prince of Wales in Council to be highly desirable *to have this question set at rest without adverse litigation* [emphasis added] between Her Majesty and His Royal Highness and it is considered that the best mode of proceeding will be to follow, as nearly as circumstances will admit the course adopted some years since when similar questions between the Crown and the Duchy as to undersea Mines were referred to the late Sir John Patteson.

The dispute would again appear to have been placed in abeyance until 1882–83 when the question was once more discussed. The Office of Woods wrote that it was undesirable the resolution to the question should be postponed, but the Duchy did not feel able to sanction the expenditure of a large sum of money to secure a 'right so small as has been received from Royal Mines'.[45]

In a letter dated 26 June 1883, the Duchy, which was clearly not keen for the matter to go to arbitration, said:

The confident hope is entertained that upon the facts and considerations now brought forward many of which are probably new to the Officers of the Crown, the Lords Commissioners of the Treasury acting on their advice will feel no hesitation in admitting the proposition contended for on the part of the Duchy and thereby give effect to the *great constitutional settlement* [emphasis added] effected by King Edward the Third and His Parliament.

The Crown however persisted in its view that the Duchy claims were not sufficient to: 'countervail the principle of law that Royal Mines are a prerogative right of so high a character as not to pass by any royal grant except by express words which are not to be found in the Duchy Charters'.

The matter was left and remains outstanding today. The website of the Crown Estate once asserted: 'Today the prerogative rights to gold and silver are part of The Crown Estate. This is true for all of the UK, although in the past, in some limited areas in Scotland, this right has been transferred from the Crown by ancient charter'.[46] The Crown maintains its position, as does the Duchy. Once again, the Duchy laid claim to a right that it asserted had been granted implicitly but which the Crown denied, and in this case, the Crown's case was supported by the Law Officer's Opinion.

The Report of the Prince's Council 1862

In 1862 the Prince of Wales, on reaching the age of twenty-one, could take full control of the Duchy and became entitled to all its income and the accumulated surplus from the Duchy of Cornwall, which amounted to £570,000 (at least £41 million in 2012) and was: 'expended on the purchase of Sandringham, the building of stables at Marlborough House and the provision of plate'.[47] A report was produced by the Prince's Council, which summarized 'the features of the system of management . . . and the results that have been produced'.[48] The report stated: 'It has been the anxious desire of the Council to avoid involving His Royal Highness in legal proceedings, and they have in all cases where it appeared practicable to do so without material prejudice to Duchy interests made disputed questions the subject of compromise or other mode of settlement, rather than recourse to law'. Examples of the disputes which arose and which it was hoped would be settled by compromise had been: 'an inquiry into the rights of the Duchy in the Forest and adjacent Commons of Dartmoor . . . these right are now involved in much obscurity, and their enforcement by legal process would necessarily be attended with expense'. Reference was also made to questions surrounding the Waters of the Tamar, 'particularly the soil and mineral under that water'. The dispute regarding the 'minerals under the sea and other tidal waters around and within Cornwall' likewise came in for comment. The Council stated:

> the real question being whether His Royal Highness stood in the position of merely an ordinary proprietor of certain specified estate within the county, or whether he was in fact the Seigniorial Lord of the entire county, *holding the same position there, so far as regarded territorial rights, as the Sovereign does in other parts of the Kingdom* [emphasis added]. It was considered that it would be highly desirable . . . to have the question set at rest without adverse litigation, which, if it had been resorted to, must have *nominally* been between Your Majesty on the one part and His Royal Highness on the other'.

The matter, as we have seen, was put to arbitration and, according to the Duchy: 'This decision, which in effect established the right of His Royal Highness as *superior Lord of the soil of the entire County of Cornwall*, and as such, his title to the foreshores was submitted to and confirmed by Parliament in an Act [emphasis added]'. (Note that the Duchy claimed it was 'Lord of the soil of the entire County of Cornwall', an issue to which we shall return). It was then explained the legal costs had amounted to £2,000 (approx £98,400 in 2012) but the income generated as a result of the finding in the Duchy's favour amounted to £4,800 (approx £236,200 in 2012). In other words, an investment in legal fees had generated a substantial income source and an increase in the capital value of the Duchy. The loser, of course, was the Treasury.

It was also revealed in the report that in 1842 the Duchy had disputed that the accounts of the Sheriff for Cornwall should be submitted to the Treasury as opposed to the Auditor of the Duchy, 'some revenue being derived from this source'. Eventually in 1846 the Council had agreed that accounts should be submitted to the Treasury with the proviso such agreement: 'was not to be considered as prejudicing in any way the rights and privileges of His Royal Highness the Prince of Wales'. Yet another argument surrounded the right of wreck in Cornwall, considered already. The Council explained: 'For many years no income was derived from it . . . It was considered desirable to take advantage of certain measures before Parliament. *Some small revenue may now therefore be anticipated from this source without material expense to the Duchy* [emphasis added]'.

To summarize, the Report of 1862 confirmed the insistence of the Duchy on its 'constitutional rights', when the assertion of those rights would generate some financial advantage to the Duchy. It also demonstrated the reluctance of the Duchy to engage in litigation, which would have been unseemly, expensive and of uncertain outcome.

Treasure Trove—Luxulian Cornwall 1864

According to National Archive records, Treasure Trove, being silver and gold coins from the reigns of Queen Elizabeth, King James and King Charles I, were found in the churchyard of Luxulian (today Luxulyan) Parish. They had very little value.[49] The Duchy asserted its right to them, and the Solicitor to the Treasury asked for copy documents under which 'the claim of the Duchy was founded'. Copies of the Duchy Charters were sent. It was made clear by the Duchy that: 'These Charters will enable you to form an unsatisfactory opinion as to the extent and nature of the property and rights intended to be conferred upon the Dukes of Cornwall'. The Cornwall Foreshore Case was referred to and it was explained Sir John Patteson had found it necessary to consider:

the early history of Cornwall and its Earls as well as Records and facts subsequent to the Creation of the Duchy. In that case as *in the present the right was inferential* only there not having been any express Grant of the Foreshore which Sir John Patteson nevertheless decided to be part of the Territorial possessions of the Duchy [emphasis added].

The Duchy continued:

The result of the enquiry leads to the conclusion that at all events so far as the County of Cornwall is concerned all rights previously vested in the Crown other than that of Royal jurisdiction were vested *jure ducutus* (rights of the Duke) in the Royal personage whether the *Sovereign or the Duke of Cornwall (considered in law to be one and the same person—see observation of the late Mr Justice Bayley in Rowe v Brenton (1828)[50]) for the time being entitled under the limitation contained in the Charter to the possessions of the Duchy. A particular argument in favour of the Duke's right to Treasure Trove may be deduced from the fact that this description of <u>casual revenue</u> was by Act of Parliament expressly recoverable for the Crown by the Coroner and the 3rd Duchy Charter which (according to the decision in *Jewison v Dyson* (1842)[51]) gives the Duke the right of appointing that Officer within Cornwall (the Duchy has, in fact, never appointed the Coroner for Cornwall) expressly prohibits any such Minister of the Crown acting within Cornwall [emphasis added].

Once more the Government Attorney and Solicitor General was asked to advise, and his opinion was:

We think that it would be inconsistent with the terms of the Charters for the Crown to hold any Inquest of Treasure within the Duchy of Cornwall: and it seems to us to be a legitimate inference from the general tenor of the Charters, and especially from the clauses which exclude all Ministers of the Crown from entering any lands of the Duchy to make execution of any writs [illegible] that the Duke of Cornwall and not the Queen, is entitled to the Treasure Trove in question.

This dispute is especially important because it refers to the Earls of Cornwall and rights not expressly set out in Duchy Charters but those arising through 'legitimate inference'.

Seaward Limits between the Crown and the Duchy of Cornwall 1865–1870

Seaward Limits was another matter submitted to arbitration, in this case to Sir John Taylor Coleridge. The Duchy did not enjoy the same success as when arguing its right to the Foreshores of Cornwall, even though relying heavily on the material previous submitted to Sir John Patteson. The statements made by the Duchy in support of its claims are instructive.

In reply to the response of the Crown to the initial claim, the Duchy argued, really rather angrily:

> that the Crown being in point of law, as against an ordinary subject, *prima facie* entitled to, and deemed in possession of the bed of the sea and maritime territories within the Realm, which puts such *ordinary subject to proof of his title, before the Crown can be dispossessed; and gives the Crown, without the necessity of proof of its own title, the somewhat oppressive advantage of making its case out of the weakness or want of completeness of that of the claimant; the same rule should apply, when property of a similar nature is the subject of discussion between the Duchy and the Crown, for no better reason, as it would appear, than the particular character of the property. This proposition has been before frequently asserted, on the part of the Crown, but always contested on the part of the Duchy* [emphasis added]. It was alluded to at the preliminary meetings before the Arbitrator, in the present case, and then protested against, and the Officers of the Duchy must beg to be understood as again most distinctly declining their assent to it.

The Duchy continued:

> *In asserting such a proposition, the Officers of the Crown appear to be unmindful of the relative position of the High Personages represented, in any question between the Crown and the Duchy;* to lose sight altogether of the object of the Parliamentary Charters relating to the Duchy of Cornwall, already alluded to in the Duchy statement, and of the exceptional position in which the property passing under these Charters, with all its incident Regalities and territorial rights is placed by their peculiar limitation; which effect a setting apart of a portion of the Hereditary Possessions of the Crown for a specific purpose. Such possessions still remaining Royal Possessions, and unsevered from the Crown.

Later:

> but that as against the Crown, a liberal construction ought to be given to the language of this part of the Act, with a view to give full effect to, and carry out the original intention of the Royal Founder of the Duchy of Cornwall; and which, it is submitted; in erecting, with the consent of the Legislature, the former Earldom of Cornwall, *with its ancient possessions*, into a Duchy, as a fitting maintenance for all time, for the Heir apparent of the Throne of the Realm of England, and *as a means of training and qualification for the future government of the Kingdom* [emphasis added], could only have set apart for that purpose from the

hereditary possessions of the Crown every territorial right, as well maritime, as inland, at the date of the Charters, belonging to or capable of exercise or enjoyment by the Crown, in that portion or section of the Realm of England, represented by the territory usually called the County of Cornwall. In this view the Duchy Charters can never bear the limited construction, as against the Crown, which might perhaps be placed upon them, *if they were grants to an ordinary subject but a more ample rendering of their provisions must always be allowed in every respect, considering the nature of the grants, the Personages to whom made, and the plain intention of transferring every species of Royalty, consistent with the subordination of the King's authority* [emphasis added].

The Officers of the Crown showed some little frustration in the exchange of correspondence. They claimed the Duchy did not know the difference between 'territorial and sovereign rights' and that 'The Prince of Wales carried no sovereign or territorial rights'. They also became irritated with the: 'Reliance on antiquarian suggestions as to the ancient status of Cornwall'.[52]

To summarize matters arising from this dispute: a significant disagreement was resolved not by judicial process but by arbitration, albeit by a distinguished member of the judiciary. Once more, a private estate objects to being treated like a private estate. In effect it is saying that it is not like others: it has a special position and should be treated differently. Next, note the reference of the Duchy to the 'peculiar' limitation of the Charters, such that sometimes the Duchy is in the Crown and sometimes in the 'hands' of a subject of the Crown. Finally, there is the significant claim that, by inference, the Duchy inherited the rights of the Earls of Cornwall.

Despite relying on the same evidence as presented during the Foreshore Dispute, the Duchy did not succeed in its claim to the territorial waters around Cornwall. If it had prevailed, it would have obtained the right to the mines and minerals under the seabed as well as those under the Foreshore.

Duchy of Cornwall—Land Tax and Valuation 1913

In 1913 a matter of great importance occurred which has been insufficiently recognized. From 1849, the Duchy had paid income tax to which all landlords were liable. On his father, George V, becoming King in 1910, the future Edward VIII became Duke of Cornwall. He received no Civil List Annuity and was the first Duke of Cornwall to be wholly reliant for his income on the Duchy of Cornwall. In 1913, the Inland Revenue approached the Duchy about submitting valuations and paying a new landlord's tax on income from mineral royalties arising under the Finance (1909–1910) Act 1910.[53] The

Government Law Officers were asked to advise. The instructions issued to them are a masterful summary by the solicitor acting for the Board of the Inland Revenue of the issues.[54] To quote from those instructions:

> the duty to give particulars . . . is resisted by the Duchy upon the broad ground that the Prince of Wales possesses the same prerogatives as the King,[55] and that inasmuch as the King is not bound by the provisions of a statute unless expressly named, the Prince of Wales either absolutely, or at all events so far as the lands of the Duchy of Cornwall are concerned, is not bound by the provisions of Part I of the Finance Act 1910.

The instructions then explained that the particular prerogative with which the instructions were concerned, Crown Immunity was unlike any other differing in 'substance' from other prerogative rights such as the right to royal fish and foreshore. The instructions point out under the Bill of Rights 1688, the Sovereign could not prevent application of an Act of Parliament by exercise of his prerogative power. The precise wording of the Bill of Rights is: 'That the pretended Power of Suspending of Laws or the Execution of Laws by Regall Authority without consent of Parliament is illegal'.[56] The solicitor to the Board of the Inland Revenue maintained the Prince of Wales is a subject of the Crown albeit the 'first of His Majesty's subjects' and that the estate is a 'private estate'. In those circumstances, the King could not choose to suspend an Act of Parliament as it applied to that 'private estate'. The instructions further added:

> Search has been made for any authority directly laying down the proposition that the Duke of Cornwall qua his rights over Duchy lands, or that the Prince of Wales as such, is not bound by statute unless expressly named. No such authority has been found and [the Duchy] when pressed on the point was not able to point to any authority'.

The Duchy had argued, it was pointed out, that the 'prerogative rights of the Duchy are identical with those of the Crown' and 'That in fact Duchy lands are Crown lands and the same principles apply'. The Board of the Inland Revenue acknowledged, for reasons set out in the instructions, that the Duchy was 'entitled to press the argument . . . to the fullest extent, but it is submitted that even when so pressed that argument does not go very far'. Reference was also made in the instructions to *The Attorney General to H.R.H. the Prince of Wales v St. Aubyn*[57] and *Rowe v Brenton*.[58] In particular, attention was drawn to the description of the Duchy given by Lord Tenterden in the latter case, where he refers to the 'very peculiar nature of the Duchy' and the 'Crown's peculiar interest in [the Duchy] at all times'. The Duchy once again referred to the Foreshore Dispute papers, which the Inland Revenue regarded to a great extent as 'irrelevant'.

The instructions to counsel prepared by the Board of the Inland Revenue represented a great deal of research. They identified that there was no basis in statute or case law for the Duchy enjoying Crown Immunity. The recognized authorities on the Prerogatives of the Crown had made no mention of such a privilege. The difficulty created by the fact the Duchy oscillates between a Duke and the Crown was also considered. The reply received from the Law Officers does not tackle any of these issues. They simply asserted that:

> We are of the opinion that the same principles which render the provisions of any Act of Parliament inapplicable to the Crown unless the Crown is expressly named, apply also to the Prince of Wales in his capacity as Duke of Cornwall. This result arises from the peculiar title of the Prince of Wales to the Duchy of Cornwall. In other respects the Prince of Wales as being the first subject of the Crown is like other subjects bound by Statutory enactments.

The Law Officers opinion, which ignored the issues raised by the Inland Revenue and the authorities they present, stretched the definition of the Crown in an unexpected way. This opinion is the basis upon which the Duchy of Cornwall continues to claim Crown Immunity today and, amongst other things, its privileged tax position.

The Law Officers then went on to say: 'We would strongly deprecate the bringing to an issue of questions such as those here set out. It is obvious that if such a matter were litigated the Duchy of Cornwall might find *that even though they succeeded their success in the Courts did not conclude the matter* [emphasis added]'. In 1921, the Law Officers were again consulted.[59] The Prince of Wales had continued to pay tax 'as an act of grace' but it was now claimed that:

> the circumstances have so materially altered as to necessitate reconsideration of the question. The net revenue of the Duchy has diminished considerably since the war owing to the higher cost of repairs and similar outgoings; the burden of taxation has enormously increased; whilst on the other hand the Prince having come of age, is taking a much more active part in public affairs which involves increased expenditure.

The Law Officers responded that their opinion was unchanged. The Prince of Wales agreed to pay £20,000 (approx £657,000 in 2012) per annum as a voluntary contribution in lieu of tax. From 1921 until 1982, although the Duchy continued to present its accounts to Parliament, as it was obliged to do, it did not publish them. The accounts which were provided to Parliament, show the voluntary contribution under the heading 'taxes and parish rates',[60] which was clearly misleading. During the negotiations in connection with his Abdication, Edward VIII claimed poverty since he had not benefited under the will of his late father. It transpired he had managed to 'tuck away' £1,000,000 (£52,000,000 in 2012 values), largely from Duchy revenues, a fact about which he kept very quiet and was the cause of great resentment when it was discovered.[61]

In 1971–1972, there was a Select Committee on the Civil List, which stated:

> The income from the Duchy of Cornwall is exempt from all taxes. The exemption is based on an opinion given by the Law Officers of the Crown in 1913 and again in 1921. The tax exemption apparently arose from 'the peculiar title of the Prince of Wales to the Duchy of Cornwall'. *The judgement was very short and a little inscrutable. It did not say what was peculiar or special.* Nevertheless, the Inland Revenue accepted it without question. There has been no further explanation or elucidation [emphasis added].[62]

Mr Strudwick, Assistant Secretary Board of the Inland Revenue, when he appeared before the Committee said in reference to the 1913 Opinion: 'Their answer, I am afraid, which is all I have, does not really take us much further, because they simply said [that Crown Immunity applies] . . . also to the Prince of Wales in his capacity as Duke of Cornwall . . . That is all they said'.[63]

It is extraordinary that an institution that describes itself as a 'private estate', and is similarly described by Government, should enjoy Crown Immunity and, therefore, such a privileged tax status based on a 'short and inscrutable' opinion which has never been challenged or revisited. The fact remains that the Duchy's right to Crown Immunity is not of ancient origin. It was claimed only when some economic advantage could be obtained, and is based on a questionable legal opinion.

The Duchy of Cornwall and Cornwall

The precise relationship of the Duchy of Cornwall to Cornwall continues to be a matter of heated dispute. It is well known that the Duchy of Cornwall enjoys unique rights in relation to Cornwall. These include *bona vacantia*, the right to appoint the High Sherriff, the right of wreck, treasure trove, the foreshores and riverbeds and so on. We have also seen the Duchy claim that it was established as 'a means of training and qualification for the future government of the Kingdom' and was to give effect to 'the great constitutional settlement'.

It is noteworthy that in 1864, the Government Law Officers confirm that Ministers of the Crown were excluded from entering Duchy lands to make execution of writs.

There is one particular aspect of the relationship between the Duchy and Cornwall, which will be the focus of the next section of this article. A.L. Rowse, the celebrated Cornish historian, sought to correct what he regarded as a common misconception when he wrote: 'It is first necessary to clear out of the way the popular confusion between the Duchy and the County of Cornwall. They are, of course, two entirely separate entities, utterly different in character.[64]

Yet it has been explained by the Duchy itself, that 'the Duchy has a special relationship with the County [of Cornwall]'.[65] Likewise, the Law Commissioners, in relation to their report on Land Registration (which led to the Land Registration Act 2002) admitted a degree of uncertainty or ambiguity: 'Due to the complex and arcane nature of the law that governs the land holding of the Crown and the Royal Duchies of Cornwall and Lancaster; the preparation of the relevant provisions of the Bill proved to be particularly difficult'.[66]

The purpose in this section is to disperse some of the 'popular confusion'; to explain one important aspect, the special relationship between the Duchy and Cornwall; and to unravel some of the complex and arcane land law relating to the Duchy of Cornwall. It will be demonstrated that, in one respect at least, the 'Duchy *is* Cornwall'. To aid understanding it is essential that some of the legal theory is set out, and in that regard, we might usefully start with Joseph Chitty who explained: 'That the King is the universal lord and original proprietor of all lands in his kingdom; and that no man doth or can possess any part of it, but what has mediately or immediately been derived as a gift from him, to be held upon feudal services'.[67]

The reference by Chitty to feudal service is valuable because to understand the system of land law within England and Wales, we must reach back to a time, long past, when people acquired rights in land usually in exchange for services. It might be the provision of horses or salmon or the financing of men at arms in times of strife. Thus, land in England and Wales is held by the landowner for a 'legal estate' in fee simple. The first and important point is that the landowner *does not own the land, he or she owns an interest in the land* or as lawyers explain it, a 'legal estate'. The only exception is land held by the Crown in demesne, for 'no subject can hold lands allodially'.[68] (Allodial land describes land which is owned absolutely, rather than land held of a superior lord or sovereign). Demesne lands, in this context, are those held by the Crown as Sovereign or Lord Paramount. The ordinary meaning of 'demesne' is land belonging to a feudal lord, which he retains in his own possession rather than 'parcelling out to his feudal tenants'.[69] In simple terms, while the rest of us have an 'estate in land', only the Crown can actually own land. The Crown has the power to create interests in land out of its demesne land. Indeed, this is the only way it can create a freehold estate—it is called 'infuedation'. No other landowner has a right to 'subinfuedate', a result of the Statute *Quia Emptores 1290* which can still be found on the Statute Law Database. All landowners hold land in fee directly or indirectly from the Crown. In summary, land held in demesne by the Crown has the following characteristics:

> The Crown has dominion over that land as Lord Paramount; and
> The Crown has no estate in land.

Now to examine the position of the Duchy of Cornwall in this hierarchy: confusingly, the Duchy of Cornwall can also hold demesne land, as can any lord of a manor, in the sense it is a landowner and has retained its interest in that land without granting any of it to his tenants. The Duchy, in modern usage, has a 'mesne lordship', which is a landlord who has tenants while holding his land from a superior lord. This is referred to as a 'Tenure', which denotes the holding of land by a tenant under his lord and is only appropriate where the feudal relation of lord and tenant exists.[70] The Duchy holds the Duchy in fee as tenant in chief of the Sovereign. The Duke of Cornwall is thus 'a feudal tenant of the Queen like the rest of us'.[71] Thus as far as the freeholders in Cornwall are concerned, the Duke stands between them and the Sovereign.[72] It is one of the few cases in which the second step of the feudal pyramid survives. The Duchy of Cornwall is one of the very rare examples where 'mesne lordship' can be proved, and has any continuing relevance. When 'tenure' exists over a number of manors, as in the case of the Duchy, it is known as a 'land barony' or 'honour'.

In support of the above analysis, the Land Registry relies on the Charter of 17 March 1337 which says:

> '*habendum et tenendum eidem duci et isius et heredum suorum regum Anglie filis primogenitis et dicti ducibus in regno Anglie hereditary successuris . . . de nobi et heredibus nostris impperpetuum*'.

Which the Registry has translated as:

> 'To have and to hold to the same Duke and the eldest sons of him and Heirs Kings of England and the Dukes of the same place hereditarily to succeed in the Kingdom of England . . . of us and his heirs for ever'.

'To have and to hold . . . of us and our heirs for ever' are standard words of infuedation by which a feudal superior grants to his tenants; thus, the Land

Registry claims, it is clear that the possessions of the Duchy are held feudally as tenant in chief of the Crown[73].

There are those (including, arguably, the Duchy), who would challenge the above analysis. They claim that the Duchy holds the lands in Cornwall allodially. This point will be addressed shortly. In *Chasyn v Lord Sturton* (1553)[74] it was confirmed: 'the said county should be given to Edward the son as in the name of the Duchy; and that this county of Cornwall should always remain a duchy . . . without being otherwise disposed of'. Similarly, in the *Princes Case* (1606),[75] Lord Coke declared that 'the whole county of Cornwall should always remain as a Duchy to the eldest sons of the Kings of England'. Baron Adams in the *Sutton Pool Case*[76] stated: 'When the Prince of Wales takes he takes an estate in fee-simple'. Later in the same case, Chief Baron Parker, furnishing some indication of the complexities which arise when considering the Duchy, said: 'It is clear, that the Crown does not take an absolute fee, but only a qualified fee, till the birth of the King's eldest son, and when there is a King's eldest son he takes a fee but only a qualified fee till he comes to the Crown or till his own death'. In other words, any Duke holds until he becomes King, or if the Duchy has reverted to the Crown for want of a Duke, the Duchy does not become absorbed in the Crown's demesne but is held in 'fee' until a Duke is born. In *The Solicitor of the Duchy of Cornwall v the Next of Kin of Thomas Canning* (1880)[77] the assertion was made and accepted that: 'The charters of the duchy have always been treated both by the Courts of Judicature and the legislature as having vested in the Dukes of Cornwall the whole interest and dominion of the Crown in and over the whole county of Cornwall'.

Today, the Duchy acknowledges its 'special relationship with Cornwall'. It also points out only 13 per cent of the land it owns is within Cornwall, which represents just 2 per cent of the geographical area of 'the County'.[78] While the percentages are no doubt accurate, they do not reflect the full extent of the connection between the Duchy and Cornwall. Indeed, possibly they are intended to obscure that relationship.

Nowhere is the position of the Duchy so forcefully set out as in 'Foreshore Case',[79] which includes the statement:

> the Duchy Charters are sufficient to vest in the Dukes of Cornwall not only the government of Cornwall but the entire territorial dominion in and over the county which had previously been vested in the Crown and all such royal prerogatives which would naturally accompany . . . including most if not all of the rights and privileges enjoyed by the owner of a County Palatine.

Later in the same section is added: 'It cannot, therefore, reasonably be doubted that this *Royal Seignory consisted of the King's demesne lands* [emphasis added], reversion, feudal services, rights and emoluments, with the prerogatives above enumerated, did, in fact, comprehend the whole territorial interest and dominion of the Crown in and over the entire County'. In reply to a question from the Government Law Officers, the Duchy answered: 'It is contended, that the Duchy in its creation was co-extensive with the County, in the sense in which that term is used: *not that its possessor was entitled to every acre of land in the County,* [emphasis added] but to the great seigniorial rights throughout the County, which under the circumstances, would have been vested in the Crown'.

Eight years after the Foreshore Dispute was arbitrated, the Duchy remained quite insistent in its position regarding Cornwall. For example: 'in so far as the County of Cornwall is concerned all rights previously vested in the Crown other than that of Royal jurisdiction were vested *jure ducatus* in the Royal personage whether the Sovereign or the Duke of Cornwall'.[80] The most explicit claim made by the Duchy was set out in 1860 as follows:

It is well known that the ultimate fees of all lands in England are vested in the Crown by reason of its prerogative in tenure and *are incapable of being transferred to a subject. But without doubt the ultimate fees of all lands within the County of Cornwall are by the express language of this 3rd Charter vested in the Duke of Cornwall* [emphasis added] and not only so but clothed with all those prerogative rights which would attach to those Fees in the hands of the Sovereign as fully as the Sovereign could have enjoyed them if (to use the language of this Charter) the Sovereign had retained the same fees in his own hands and that *non obstante prerogative* ['notwithstanding the prerogative]. It seems difficult to support this or any other construction than that the Duke as regards these possessions was substituted for and holds them as the Representative of the Sovereign. It will be observed that these provisions are confined to the County of Cornwall.[81]

Shortly after, in 1862, the Trustees to the Duchy stated that the decision in the Cornwall Foreshore Case established: 'His Royal Highness as the superior Lord of the soil of the entire County of Cornwall'.[82]

There are those who claim that the Duchy holds the whole of Cornwall allodially.[83] For them this is significant and one of the issues which indicate Cornwall's unique relationship with the English state. The implication is that the Duke of Cornwall did not hold the land from the sovereign as a vassal but owned the land independently of feudal obligations. It would not be difficult to argue, from the quotes above, that the Duchy adopts a similar position. In an attempt to clarify the situation, particularly in light of the passing of the *Quia Emptores* in 1290, the Land Registry was asked to answer the following question:

'Assume the Duchy wished to purchase freehold property in Truro and since the Duchy holds Cornwall in fee simple would the Duchy be granting a freehold interest to itself?'

The reply was:

'I do not really know the answer as to whether it is possible to hold a freehold interest of oneself, or whether that is technically what the result would be. I think it is possible because if the Crown Estate acquires freehold land by purchase I do not think the existing freehold comes to an end . . . In modern conditions the question has no practical consequences . . . and probably has not since the Tenures Abolition Act 1660'.[84]

Thus there is no clear answer to whether or not the Duchy owns Cornwall allodially (that is, it is the absolute owner of the land), or whether the Duchy has a freehold, or interest in land, in the whole of Cornwall. If the Duchy does hold Cornwall in fee simple then it does seem to be practicing subinfeudation, which has not been permissible since 1290. Whatever view is taken, in one sense at least it is true that 'The Duchy *is* Cornwall' even if 'Cornwall is not the Duchy'. It is difficult to think of any comparable situation applying in a territory in which the Queen is Sovereign. One cannot imagine, for example, the freehold in Staffordshire being granted to a subject of the Crown.

Conclusion

First, we notice a long-standing policy of resolving disputes by reference to opinions of the Government Law Officers or arbitrators. The difficulty here is that the opinions have not been tested by the Courts and are inconsistent one with another. So, in the case of the Isles of Scilly and the Foreshore of Cornwall it was concluded, by implication, that the Duchy had inherited the rights of the Earls of Cornwall. However, in the case of the Seaward Extent of the Duchy of Cornwall and Royal Mines there was no such implication. The fact is, unless and until the various decisions are examined by the Courts, there can be no certainty as to what rights are enjoyed by the Duchy of Cornwall.

Secondly, the disputes that arose were either about the Duchy claiming a right that would generate some economic advantage, or allow it to avoid paying fees or taxes. When the Duchy succeeded in clawing back from the Royal Household Hereditary Revenues, otherwise surrendered by the Crown, it was the Exchequer (and thus the taxpayer) that suffered.

Those rights enjoyed by the Duchy to which importance is attached by some observers keen to establish the constitutional distinctiveness of Cornwall—the right to give consent to legislation and Crown Immunity—are actually of recent origin and were concerned with the Duchy either protecting its economic interests or gaining a tax benefit. Yet, as noted above, there *is* a sense in which 'The Duchy *is* Cornwall', and the relationship between the Duchy and Cornwall remains more intricate and intimate than the mere 2 per cent of land ownership might suggest.

Notes and references

1. The Tidal Estuaries, Foreshore and Under-Sea Minerals within and around The Coast of the County of Cornwall—Arbitration by Judge Sir John Patteson (London, 1855).
2. With apologies to Miss Jessie J who it is understood is a singer of popular songs.
3. *The Princes Case* (1606) (8 Coke Rep 1a).
4. A.L. Rowse, *West Country Stories* (London, 1945), p. 3.
5. *Duchy of Cornwall Case* (1613) (1 Ves Sen 292) and *Lomax v Holmden* (1749) (1 Ves Senior 290) p. 294.
6. Hereditary Revenues derived principally from Crown Lands, feudal rights, profits from post office licenses etc.
7. Spencer Walpole, *A History of England*, Vol. iii p. 402 quoted in TNA T 38/837—Civil List Notes (1897).
8. HC—Report from the Select Committee on Grants to Members of the Royal Family 1889 HC271 p. 4.
9. www.duchyofcornwall.org.
10. Victoria could not become Elector of Hanover because of the operation of Salic Law which prevented females inheriting thrones or fiefs.
11. W.M Kuhn, 'Queen Victoria's Civil List, *Historical Journal* 36:3 (1993), p. 652.
12. G. Haslam, 'Modernisation' in C. Gill (ed.), *The Duchy of Cornwall* (Newton Abbot, 1987), p. 52.
13. TNA T 38/837—Civil List Notes (1897).
14. Haslam, 'Modernisation' in Gill (ed.), *The Duchy of Cornwall* (1987), p. 55–56.
15. Ibid., p. 57.
16. TNA TS 45/5—Duchy of Cornwall Rights in water of River Tamar (1822–1880).
17. Mary Coate, 'The Duchy of Cornwall: Its History and Administration 1640 to 1660', *Transactions of the Royal Historical Society* (1927), p. 147.
18. Robert Heath, *The Isles of Scilly: A Natural and Historical Account of the Islands of Scilly)*, (London, 1750); Fortescue Hitchins and Samuel Drew, *The History of Cornwall* (Helston, 1824), Vol. II p. 687.

19. TNA CRES 58/742—Scilly Isles (1832–1892).
20. The Tidal Estuaries, Foreshores and Under-Sea Minerals within and around the Coast of the County of Cornwall. Arbitration by Sir John Patteson (1855) Resume of Duchy Case, p. 12.
21. Statute Law Database.
22. TNA CRES 37/990—Cornwall Water of the Tamar Arbitration relating to the title between the Crown and the Duchy of Cornwall (1914–1938).
23. TNA CRES 58/694—Water of Tamar: Arbitration between the Crown and the Duchy of Cornwall.
24. TNA MT 10/927—Board of Trade Harbour Dept. Correspondence (1904).
25. There is an agreement dating from 1620 to which the Duchy and the Crown still adhere which explicitly states matters of dispute will be referred for 'arbitration' rather than litigation.
26. Lord Journal lxxx p. 736 HL/PO/JO/10/8/1692.
27. E-mail to writer from House of Commons Archive, 24 February 2012.
28. E-mail to writer from House of Commons Information Office, 21 April 2011. Since that time Erskine May 24th Edition has a different formulation.
29. www.duchyofcornwall.eu/latest.
30. After the case of Cabinet Office v The Information Commissioner (2012) (EA/2012/0200) the Cabinet Office has now placed on its website a document entitled 'Queen's or Prince's Consent' which explains the current procedure.
31. The Queen's Remembrancer—An ancient judicial post, the older judicial appointment in continuous existence, first created in 1154, continued to sit in the Court of Exchequer until the Court was abolished in 1882. Now held by the Senior Master of the Queen's Bench Division. The purpose of the role was to keep records of taxes paid and unpaid.
32. TNA TS 25/829—Duchy of Cornwall: Payment of fees claimed by the Queen's Remembrancer from the Duchy of Cornwall (1855).
33. To take or have effect to serve to the use benefit or advantage of a person.
34. *The Attorney General v The Mayor and Commonalty of the Borough of Plymouth* (1754) (Wight 134) p. 160.
35. Tidal Estuaries, Foreshore and Under-Sea Minerals within and around the Coast of the County of Cornwall 1854–56 Arbitration by Sir John Patteson.
36. B. Deacon, *Cornwall A Concise History* (Cardiff, 2007), p. 37.
37. HC Debate 19 July 1858, Vol. 151, cc 1750–1754.
38. TNA BT 243/262—Duchy of Cornwall: Legislation relating to right to wrecks of the sea (1856–1985).
39. Ibid.
40. TNA MT 9/5982—Duchy of Cornwall Investigations into manorial rights and title to unclaimed wreck (1868–1949).
41. The onus of proof.
42. TNA TS 27/818—Treasure Trove—mining rights claim by Duchy of Cornwall (1907–1932).
43. TNA T 1/16350—Duchy of Cornwall: Arbitration on Crown's right to royal gold and silver mines in Cornwall (1879).
44. TNA T 1/12673—Duchy of Cornwall—Question of title to Royal Mines to be settled by arbitration (1880).

45. TNA T 1/14831—Duchy of Cornwall title to gold and silver mines (1883).
46. http://thecrownestate.co.uk/our_portfolio/rural/minerals.htm Since questions were raised with the Crown Estate the website has been changed and its claims are now less obvious than before.
47. TNA T 168/52—Treasury Papers of Sir George Hamilton and Sir Edward Hamilton (1901–1904).
48. Report to Her Majesty the Queen from the Council of H.R.H. The Prince of Wales 1862 p. 12.
49. TNA TS 25/1330—Treasure at Luxulian: Claim by Duchy of Cornwall (1864).
50. *Rowe v Brenton* (1828) (8 B & C 737) (3 Man & Ry KB 133) (108 E.R. 1217).
51. *Jewison v Dyson* (1842) (9 Meeson and Welsby 540) (152 E.R. 228).
52. TNA LRRO 11/15—Statements relating to the dispute between the Crown and the Duchy of Cornwall concerning the seaward extent of Cornwall (1865).
53. TNA LO 3/467—Duchy of Cornwall—Land Tax and Valuation (1913).
54. P. Hall, *Royal Fortune* (London, 1992), p. 54.
55. At this time the King was George VI and the Prince of Wales was the future Edward VIII, Duke of Windsor.
56. Bill of Rights 1688.
57. *Attorney General to H.R.H. Prince of Wales, Duke of Cornwall v Sir John St. Aubyn and others* (1811) (Wight 167).
58. *Rowe v Brenton* (1828) (8 B & C 737) (3 Man & Ry KB 133) (108 E.R. 1217).
59. TNA IR 40/16549—The Duchy of Cornwall Taxation (1921).
60. Hall, *Royal Fortune*, p. 57.
61. Ibid., p. 70
62. HC *Report from the Select Committee on the Civil List* 1971–1972 HC29 para. 48.
63. HC *Report from the Select Committee on the Civil List* 1971–1972 HC29 p .348.
64. Rowse, *West Country Stories*, p. 94.
65. www.duchyofcornwall.org/abouttheduchy_history.acquisition.htm.
66. Law Commission and HM Land Registry land Registration for 21st Century: A Conveyancing Revolution Com. 271 (2001), p. 243.
67. J. Chitty, *A Treatise on the Law of the Prerogatives of the Crown* (1820), p. 211
68. J. Burke, *Jowitts Dictionary of English Law* (2nd edn 1977), p. 89.
69. E-mail correspondence with Land Registry, 12 March 2009.
70. Halsbury's *Laws of England* 39:2 Para 75 Land and Interests in Land.
71. E-mail correspondence with the Land Registry, 12 March 2009.
72. Ibid., 14 January 2010.
73. Ibid., 27 March 2009.
74. *Chasyn v Lord Sturton* (1553) (1 Dyer 94a) p. 205.
75. *The Princes Case* (1606) (8 Rep 1a) (77 ER 481).
76. *The Attorney General v The Mayor and Commonalty of the Borough of Plymouth and others* (1754) (Wight 134) p. 1208.
77. *The Solicitor to the Duchy of Cornwall v Canning* (1880) (% P.D. 114 Probate).
78. www.duchyofcornwall.org/faqs.htm.
79. The Tidal Estuaries, Foreshores and Under-Sea Minerals within and around the Coast of the County of Cornwall. Arbitration by Sir John Patteson (1855) Duchy Preliminary Statement p. 9.
80. TNA TS 25/1330—Treasure Trove at Luxullian Cornwall (1864).

81. TNA TS 27/818—Treasure Trove (1907–1932).
82. Report to Her Majesty the Queen from the Council of H.R.H. The Prince of Wales 1862.
83. See, for example, J. Angarrack., *Our Future is History* (Bodmin, 2002). See also www.duchyofcornwall.eu/latest/
84. E-mail from Land Registry, 1 June 2010.

8

Bishop Benson's Vision For Truro Cathedral and Diocese

The Umbrella and the Duck

David Miller

Introduction

Edward White Benson became first Bishop of Truro in May 1877. The Bill establishing the Diocese of Truro was passed by Parliament in August 1876 and the final legal process completed by December 1876. Prior to these events of 1876/1877, the Archdeaconry of Cornwall (the area of the new diocese) was one part of the diocese of Exeter, a vast diocese extending to the Isles of Scilly in the west and comprising Devon as well as Cornwall. In 1859, the newly created Exeter Diocesan Kalendar records 693 benefices and about 900 serving clergy. In 1848 Bishop Henry Phillpotts of Exeter estimated about 800 clergy in the diocese: 'No Bishop could even attempt to remember the names of the parishes, let alone the personal details of clergy and churchwardens, ecclesiastical state and needs of so many and so diverse parochial units'.[1]

A gradual change in the role of bishops and their function took place after the Great Reform Bill of 1832, (after which the Houses of Parliament were no longer the preserve only of Anglicans). Until then, bishops could often be occasional or annual visitors to their dioceses—their natural habitat being the West End of London and the Universities. Lord Houghton regretted the passing of this age when a clergyman 'no more expected an autograph letter from . . . (the Bishop) than from the Lord-Lieutenant, or thought of interviewing him any more than the Prime Minister'.[2] Houghton regretted that when distinguished scholars became bishops they all but stopped their academic work for a life of hectic episcopal activity.

In an age when retirement of bishops was nearly impossible and illness a constant possibility, the desire to reduce the burden on bishops by reducing the size of the dioceses was widely felt. It was said at one point that there was not one healthy bishop between London and St Ives.[3] The development of diocesan and regional consciousness also contributed to the desire to increase the number of dioceses during the nineteenth and early twentieth century. The government did not want to increase the number of bishops sitting in the House of Lords—but the agitation in the Isle of Man not to be amalgamated with the diocese of Carlisle was a reminder that a Bishop need not sit in the House of Lords since the Isle of Man had its own Parliament. The refusal of the dioceses of St Asaph and Bangor to amalgamate led to Manchester diocese being formed without its bishop sitting in Parliament.[4] An increase in dioceses could therefore be contemplated without increasing Anglican representation in the House of Lords (which would have been uncongenial to many non-Anglicans elected after the passing of the Great Reform Act in 1832).

New dioceses proliferated in the later nineteenth and early twentieth century, though only Liverpool and Truro began new cathedral buildings as opposed to adapting a previously existing parish church, abbey or minster for cathedral use. In the case of Liverpool, cathedral building did not begin until twenty-three years after the diocese was formed because its first Bishop, J.C. Ryle had other priorities.[5] There is no doubt that Benson came to Cornwall with a vision, and at the heart of that vision was the determination to see a cathedral built. When Benson was teaching the sixth form at Rugby school (shortly after graduating from Trinity College, Cambridge), a fellow teacher described Benson as the only man in England who would be able to build a cathedral. It was to this man that Benson wrote when he knew that he was coming to Truro to tell him that his prediction had come true.[6]

Benson's Vision

Why did Benson want to build a cathedral, even though it was not possible simply to extend St Mary's Truro, (the church that existed on the site of the new cathedral) by elongating the nave?[7] Other larger parish churches had earlier been suggested, particularly at Bodmin and St Columb Major, as possible parish churches suitable to be adapted into a cathedral during the long period of campaigning for a new diocese for Cornwall. Since one major reason for a new diocese was to increase the pastoral effectiveness of the bishop, a new cathedral was not necessarily the most important requirement.[8] Benson himself was sensitive to this accusation of draining Cornwall of its money at a time when it could not afford it. Benson's answer to this accusation, that he did not drain Cornwall of its zeal,[9] may suggest that he saw a vision for a new cathedral building as essential for uniting the diocese round one central project, which could then be zealously pursued. There were at least two component parts to this vision.

Firstly, Benson wrote in his diary, the day after presiding at the opening of Truro Cathedral in 1887, that he hoped that God would bring back the 'Holy and Great Spirit' to Cornwall that had raised the great mediaeval cathedrals in the first place: 'I felt that the Cathedral represented a power that had been suffered to fade away'.[10] Benson was very impressed by, and apprehensive about, the power of secularism and pluralism, both of which continued to increase as the nineteenth century progressed. The year 1880, when the foundation stones for Truro Cathedral were laid, was also a year of agitation concerning the possibility that Bradlaugh, elected by the constituents of Northampton, might sit in Parliament without swearing an oath invoking God on the grounds that he was an atheist. The coexistence of the cathedral project and the development of atheistic thought was neatly encapsulated by the edition of the *Graphic* magazine of 29 May 1880. The magazine depicted a series of triumphal arches designed by the prominent Methodist, Sylvanus Trevail, which adorned the streets of Truro on 20 May, the day the future King Edward VII laid the foundation stones of the Cathedral. These included a Masonic arch and a Cornish arch (with fish, tin and copper depicted on it). The *Graphic* magazine commented on the occasion in some detail. 'Apart from the arches, the streets are extensively decorated, Mr Netherton having a novelty in an illuminated motto in old Cornish EHAZ HA SEWEN WHATH DHOGEN ARLUIDH HAG ARLUDHES which may be freely translated "health and prosperity to the Duke and Duchess of Cornwall".' In the same issue of the *Graphic* was an article on the spread of secular thinking. A leading article on 'Mr Bradlaugh and the Oath' argued that denying Bradlaugh the opportunity to affirm his allegiance (rather than swear his allegiance using religious language) made Bradlaugh a victim of religious intolerance, rather than his arrival in Parliament being treated as an insignificant affair.[11]

Benson was acutely aware of the challenge which secularism posed and that building a cathedral did not of itself provide an answer. When Benson spoke at the Truro Diocesan Conference on 28 October 1880, he referred to the inauguration of the Cathedral at Cologne in Germany on 15 October 1880: 'The eyes of Europe have now watched the finial set on the head of the earth's loftiest spire above her mightiest church. But how? By a secular ceremony, aTe Deum sung by an Opera troupe, the Archbishop in exile.'[12] Cathedral building had to be complemented by the return of the holy and great Spirit that had been suffered to fade away.

Secondly, Benson studied the history of cathedral statutes in order to discover how what he called the Medieval Cathedral system operated. In his book *The Cathedral: Its Necessary Place in the Life and Work of the Church*, (first printed as an essay in the *Quarterly Review* and reprinted in an enlarged edition in 1878, the year after he had come to Cornwall), Benson developed his thinking. He argued that the cathedral could be an agency for the revival of a divine spirit that had guided the middle ages. The cathedral was to be the hub around which everything moved. Whereas Pugin (the great gothic revivalist and designer of much of the interior of the Houses of Parliament) and some others saw monasticism as a central beneficial part of the mediaeval world order, Benson asserted 'that the Cathedral, as an institution universal throughout Europe, had distinct and progressive functions in relation to society . . . For many centuries the extension and augmentation of its system and resources were promoted by governments, by potentates, by landowners and by the Christian masses. It battled long with monasticism. Puritanism assailed it in vain as the stronghold of church order'. Though cathedrals resisted both, after the Reformation they still became 'sources of revenue to mercantile dignitaries, the children's children of the adherents of successive governments. Thus they forfeited all sympathy. They forgot their traditions, their origin and their design'.[13]

Benson identified five particular functions of the mediaeval cathedral:

i) There was then, first the School of Architecture . . . maintaining communications with the progressive architects of the continent, radiating adaptations through the diocese, and influencing far and wide the taste of the county in every department of art. ii) There was the School of Music, which, under the headship of the Precentor . . . had offshoots . . . in every parish of the diocese. iii) There was the still more important School of Grammar under the Chancellor. The Chancellor is responsible for all the grammar schools of the city and county, and all the appointments made to them, save only singing—schools, prebendal schools and [how modern an exception!] those schools that are maintained by local managers.

The fourth purpose, Benson thought, was for the cathedral to be the seat of the divinity school and the 'headquarters' of the archdeacons, though Benson failed to persuade either Archdeacon to take a canonry at the cathedral—the first Archdeacon of Bodmin stating that the cathedral was too far from his home at St Ive in East Cornwall. 'Lastly,' he added, 'we come to the Cathedral service; the sole function of the great institution which was limited to its own walls.'[14]

Benson and Education

No area of the cathedral's work was more important to Benson than education. Writing to George Cubitt, patron of the living of Dorking in Surrey which Cubitt had offered to Benson, the future Bishop said:

> I wish above all things, if I could choose, to have a canonry, and if offered, I should accept it without reference to its value, for I think that at this time, the Church of England is in such danger of losing her hold—if it is not lost—on higher education for her clergy—her university tenure being most precarious—we are bound to supplement it, and the cathedral system offers an ancient, recognised, calm and safe mode of education if only a few more people would give themselves to its development.[15]

Besides the changes in university education, the1870s were also a key decade in the development of school education in the country. Forster's Education Act of 1870, supplemented by another important Act ten years later, attempted to provide an education to every child in the country even if many of the schools were not governed by the church but by a school board independent of any church. Benson accepted this change with greater equanimity than the changes in higher education that took place during the same decade, which enabled married tutors to take up posts and abolished religious tests—meaning that students and tutors could learn and teach at a university irrespective of religious commitment or lack of it. 'Universities . . . have been made to surrender all special obligation to work for the Church of England.'[16]

In the four years before Benson came to Cornwall, he was Canon Chancellor at Lincoln Cathedral (1833–1877). Here he helped to establish a theological college, Lincoln Theological College, which continued in existence until the late twentieth century. At Truro, Benson attempted to establish something similar, though the training college only continued in existence until 1900. He attempted also to establish a secondary school for girls, so Truro High School for Girls came into being.[17] This was not directly under the auspices of Truro Cathedral but nevertheless had some of the hallmarks of a Benson-inspired school and his wife Mary Benson was the first chair of governors. The school motto, 'with the light as our teacher', reflected an emphasis on the importance of education to lead students into the light. The journey of the magi with its theme of the kings/wise men of the world following the light of the star to offer gifts to Jesus was very congenial to Benson and the name was reflected in the Community of the Epiphany founded under his successor as Bishop of Truro, G.H Wilkinson. Benson was a strong supporter of education for women and moved in circles which promoted it. His wife's brother, the eminent Cambridge philosopher Henry Sidgwick, was prominent in the foundation of Newnham

College Cambridge, and Elizabeth Wordsworth, daughter of the Bishop of Lincoln that Benson served under, was closely involved with the foundation of two Oxford colleges for women—St Hugh's and Lady Margaret Hall.

Benson saw education and mission as interconnected and appointed two young Cambridge academics—A. J. Mason to be Canon Missioner and G.H. Whitaker to teach. Benson reported to the Diocesan Conference of October 1878 that during that year the Archdeaconry of Bodmin was formed and its first Archdeacon appointed (Ven. Reginald Hobhouse); also an Act forming the Chapter of Truro Cathedral had been passed:

> and a very important gain obtained by it for Truro over the old founda-
> tion was that it gave power to annex diocesan duties to the stalls. By this
> provision they have been enabled to appoint a Canon Missioner and a
> principal for the Divinity School, whose title by courtesy is Chancellor,
> and had the Bishop known that the Archdeacon of Cornwall would not
> have been present, he might have used the word with impunity . . . Already
> (there were) seventeen young men preparing for holy orders under his
> care.[18]

Lay workers, also trained by Whitaker, were advocated as a necessary part of evangelization by the same Diocesan Conference of 1878. 'Here on the Cornish moor . . . single-handed they [the clergy] had no more chance than the shepherd without comrade, boy or dog to gather in his sheep from the sides of Rowtor (applause).' The situation at St Mewan was not untypical: 'There were not ten houses within sight of the church; but a mile or two off there were two or three rather large villages . . . He (the Vicar of St Mewan) found that it was very much better to preach in such places without a form . . . There was a great need for lay help in such mission chapels.' Benson's idea was for 'Mason to spread the fire, Whitaker to broaden loving knowledge'.[19]

Liturgy and Architecture

Of the hallmarks of the mediaeval cathedral, as identified by Benson, two in particular were revived. Liturgically, the early years of Truro Cathedral were famous for creating the celebrated Nine Lessons and Carols on Christmas Eve (at 11 p.m.), first used in 1880, in the wooden building that acted as a temporary Cathedral once most of the old church of St Mary's had been knocked down and before the new Cathedral was built. The format of the service was the 'hymn sandwich', where hymns were interspersed with bible readings and sometimes prayers. It was a form of service much favoured in Methodism. The Methodist scholar Stephen Dawes writes: 'It is fashionable in some circles to dismiss the traditional Methodist Sunday service as a hymn sandwich, but that is actually quite a good title for what can be, when it is designed properly, an excellent menu for a certain sort of service of worship; and traditional Methodists can usually tell whether or not the menu has been carefully prepared or merely thrown together.' *The Oxford History of Christian Worship* dates the rise of 'what is often termed the hymn sandwich' to the late nineteenth century. Benson adapted a Methodist form of service in a way that has endured. The first seven lessons he chose are very similar to what could be chosen now. The Dean of King's College Cambridge made two important changes shortly after the First World War—the opening prologue and the last lesson with St John unfolding the mystery of the incarnation. Nevertheless, the structure of the service and much of the content remains as Benson conceived it.[20]

In the matter of reviving mediaeval architectural forms, John Loughborough Pearson was chosen as architect of the new Cathedral—beating off his nearest challenger, G.F. Bodley who actually submitted (now seemingly non-extant) designs for the building, unlike Pearson who was able to rely on a portfolio of work already designed. Pearson was brought up in Durham, a city with a magnificent Norman cathedral. He was given the opportunity to design a small church near Hull in the East Riding of Yorkshire and gradually built up a business designing, repairing and remodelling churches often in the East Riding or North Lincolnshire, and most notably in the early days giving Stow Minster a new 'Norman' chancel complete with vault. Vaults and spires, (as at South Dalton in the East Riding) became a Pearson speciality and both were included in Pearson's design for Truro Cathedral, submitted on 9 June 1879. 'As I much prefer the especially English arrangement of a central tower and two western towers for a cathedral,' he wrote, 'I have adopted it in my design; and I have endeavoured in every respect to impart to the design the style and character of a cathedral. I have carefully avoided every feature which in any way had a character belonging to a parish church, feeling that it would be altogether out of place.'[21]

Unlike Bodley's usually highly ornate and painted style, Pearson rarely embellished the interior with painting or decorative designs (St Augustine's Kilburn in London is a notable exception): 'The committee will see that this design is simple in its character, the details almost everywhere being of a plain description; and when they are not so, the enrichment is confined to prominent features, such as the porches.' Some of the enrichment, including at high level, was in Bath stone, thus providing Truro cathedral with one of its most controversial features. It is true, as Caradoc Peters points out, that some of the prominent buildings in Truro were built in Bath stone (Bath being a favourite place to visit by Cornish gentry of the eighteenth century). It is also true that Pearson visited Bournemouth to inspect a church built partly in Bath stone to a design of his friend G.E. Street some ten years after it was built and declared that, despite the proximity to the sea, it had weathered well. Nevertheless, the external Bath stone at Truro Cathedral was chosen by Pearson, despite vocal Cornish opposition, because he felt that the stone was easier to work than granite (though much Cornish granite was also used, including contributions from Mabe and St Stephen). There would be less waste carving Bath stone, so Pearson reasoned, than carving granite. Benson made a connection between Cornwall and Somerset through the person of Aldhelm, a Saxon missionary linked with the area of Cornwall near the Camel estuary. 'I perceive that Aldhelm . . . died at Doulting whence we are getting much stone for our Cathedral.' Benson chose Cornish saints for most of the canon's stalls of the new cathedral. Aldhelm, with his Cornish connections, was one of the few non-Cornish saints named in the Cathedral stalls.[22]

Lady Rolle (née Trefusis) had endowed the Cornish diocese with the gift of £40,000 to provide an income of over £1,000 per annum, on condition that the diocese was formed in her lifetime. There was a certain amount of money inherited from St Mary's Truro but most of the money for the new Cathedral had to be raised from scratch. Money proved very difficult to raise in the City of London and in the New World Cornish diaspora (Cornish-born Australians preferred to support famine relief in Cornwall). Almost all the money had to be raised in Cornwall (and Devon) or from people with strong links to the area. Pearson's original estimate of 12 May 1879 was £35,000 for the cost of the choir with its aisles, the crypt and the connection to the south aisle of St Mary's which was retained from the old building. A year later on 20 May 1880 when the foundation stones were laid, the Cathedral fund stood at £38,948 (though the estimated cost of the first phase had risen to £45,000) of which £22,181 had actually been received, including some significant donations on the day itself. Some of the shortfall was made up with Masonic money, an idea that seems to have originated in two of the largest houses of Cornwall—St Michael's Mount and Port Eliot. A letter from St Michael's Mount dated 23 November 1879 stated: 'My belief is that if it (the ceremony) could be done Masonically it would be most popular—a great thing both for the cathedral funds and for church interests in the county. I think it could be so arranged as not in any way to offend the clergy.'[23]

The high dignity and formality of 20 May 1880 was followed on Sunday 23 May by spontaneity and passion: 'The staging was still standing and it was occupied by 4,000 people at least. They were, with few exceptions, poor people . . . When the hymn after the sermon was ended, they were not ready to go. I gave out another—and the people poured down into the area, surrounded the pillar and sang most vehemently . . . They would have gone on all night.'[24]

A Cathedral for Cornwall

The first phase of the Cathedral project was completed in 1887—to be followed by the central Victoria tower and nave in 1902 and finally the two Western towers in 1910. In 1887, Benson (now Archbishop of Canterbury) returned and declared that the building surpassed expectations. Two years later, the *Royal Cornwall Gazette* wrote in an article entitled 'Truro Cathedral and its Uses':

> We have heard and read that if Truro Cathedral and its potential influence were in the hands of the Wesleyans it would have been finished by this time . . . A place has not yet been found in Wesleyan methods for the Cathedral system, and a great many people besides Wesleyans were sceptical with regard to the utility of building and endowing a great central church at Truro. The wisdom of those who laid the lines of this Cathedral establishment is however being gradually justified before the public gaze. As one looked upon the great gathering of railwaymen which took place at Truro Cathedral last Sunday it was being demonstrated to be the mother church not of church people alone, but of many other baptised people.[25]

This was very much Benson's hope, that the Cathedral would be a church for all Cornish people. Though all Cornish people were able to use it on an occasional basis, it did not take many away from their Sunday-by-Sunday loyalty to the Methodist church. Archbishop Randall Davidson preaching at the benediction of the nave in 1902 stated that it was not opinions that built the Cathedral but convictions. Methodist convictions were every bit as strong as Anglican and if church building expressed the strength of conviction then Methodists expressed their convictions vigorously throughout the nineteenth century by Chapel building, including Mrs Chirgwin laying the foundation stones of the United Methodist Free Church in Truro just six days before the Cathedral ceremony of 20 May 1880.[26]

Architecturally, Benson had found an architect at the height of his powers to design on a scale he had not previously attempted. The year 1880, was the year in which Pearson received the RIBA gold-medal and also the year when St Augustine's Kilburn in north London was opened, one of Pearson's most acclaimed works and one which, along with Lincoln Cathedral and Coutances in Normandy, may have influenced the design of Truro Cathedral. Liturgically, Benson devised an Anglican version of the hymn sandwich, one that remains as popular at Christmas as ever. Educationally, Benson's passion for education and his decision to link it so closely with mission produced an eclectic range of educational and missionary opportunities from teaching missions in parishes and street preaching by Mason to training for a variety of ministries by Whitaker.

One further characteristic of the mediaeval cathedral identified by Benson has affected his posthumous reputation to a significant degree for better and for worse: 'We have arrived at the conclusion that, while other important functions are "accidental", the "essential" character of the institution is conciliar.'[27] Conciliar government, or government by council, was not as democratic as it sounds because the Bishop was the one who chaired the council and could thereby dominate it. Benson's autocratic style is a constant feature of the most recent biography of Mary Benson and alluded to even by writers most sympathetic to Bishop Benson, such as David Newsome. Newsome writes movingly of the profound lifelong effect which losing their eldest son, Martin White Benson, to meningitis at the age of seventeen had on his parents, and is sympathetic to the black moods of depression that dogged Bishop Benson throughout his adult life. Newsome nevertheless acknowledges that Benson's regime as headmaster of Wellington College from 1859–1873 was severe even by the standards of the day. A.C. Benson's two-volume biography of his father illustrates vividly how difficult Benson found it to defer to anyone else, though he expected others to defer to him. Benson therefore found it much easier to work with subordinates than to work with equals, which led to his interventions in the House of Lords being generally less effective than much of his work in Cornwall.[28] The Bishop in Council, listening to others but still dominating proceedings, was the way in which Benson worked with the Cathedral committee in Truro, and other important examples can be discovered from his time as Archbishop of Canterbury.

Two important examples of the Archbishop in Council are the Lincoln Judgement of 1890 and the Lambeth Conference of 1888. Throughout his adult life, Benson studied the third-century bishop and theologian St Cyprian—his book on St Cyprian was published shortly after his death in 1896. According to Mark Chapman, Cyprian 'provides, at least on Benson's account, the foundation for the organic unity claimed by the Anglican Communion . . . [and] formulated under Benson's leadership in 1888 . . . Thus he [Benson] wrote "what the Bishop was to his own diocese that the whole united body of bishops was to the whole church"'. Benson, by stressing the importance of the College of Bishops at the Lambeth Conference and elsewhere, also underlined the importance of the Archbishop who chaired their meetings, an importance that has only increased since the Lambeth Conference of 1888.[29]

Support for liberal causes

In 1890, surrounded by legal experts, Benson presided over the prosecution of Edward King, Bishop of Lincoln, (the most senior high churchman of his day) by the low-church Church Association. Basing his judgements on the rubric of the Book of Common Prayer and his own deep knowledge of church law and not on secular precedents, Benson found in favour of the Bishop of Lincoln on five counts and the Church Association on two, on the issue of how much Catholic ceremonial in the Eucharist was legal in the Church of England. Benson was widely applauded for his judgement, which confirmed much moderate high-church practice as legal.[30]

On two earlier occasions Bishop Benson had intervened forcefully in support of liberal causes. He supported the appointment of Frederick Temple as Bishop of Exeter in 1869 (the year after Temple had contributed to a liberal collection entitled *Essays and Reviews*) which was opposed by many clergy including members of the Cathedral chapter. He also later supported the Burial Laws Amendment Act in 1880, opposed by thousands of clergy, which opened funeral services in Anglican churchyards to ministers of any denomination or no denomination. Benson's letter to the clergy of Truro Cathedral was widely imitated, even copied, by other bishops when writing to their clergy.[31] Until 1880, even a Methodist or Baptist minister buried in the Anglican churchyard would be buried by an Anglican clergyman using an Anglican form of service.

By finding in favour of the Bishop of Lincoln on a majority of issues, Benson confirmed the legal validity of what is now taken for granted in the celebration of the Eucharist in many Anglican churches. Under Benson's leadership the Lambeth Conference of 1888 formulated the Chicago/ Lambeth Quadrilateral 'which for many years was as near as the Anglican Communion approached to a formal constitution'. According to Benson's researches, as understood by Chapman, 'For Cyprian, no particular Bishop had absolute authority. Instead, the bishops form a college, for the episcopate is a single entity, made up of all the participating bishops. Consequently, the bishops were equal and in mutual respect were entitled to their own views and to administer their dioceses as they felt fit.'[32] The tension between bishops administrating their dioceses 'as they felt fit' and the idea of the episcopate as 'a single entity' was to be brought out into the open in the future. At the very least, holding the two concepts together required a very dominant role for the chair of the college of bishops, a role which Benson was always willing to play.

Conclusion

In conclusion, the four issues highlighted above where Benson helped to win a measure of Anglican consensus around controversial matters are all very considerable achievements, and Benson generally succeeded by means of the arguments he put forward—whether it was the letter to *The Times* in support of Temple, the *ad clerum* to the clergy of Truro diocese in support of churchyard reform, the scholarly appraisal of liturgical texts in the Lincoln judgement, or the lifelong research into Cyprian which influenced the Chicago/Lambeth quadrilateral. It is also important to state what Benson did not achieve. He could not persuade the archdeacons of Cornwall and Bodmin to become canons of the Cathedral. He failed to persuade Methodists and other non-Anglicans to join the Anglican Church in significant numbers. Indeed, a Baptist minister writing four months before Benson arrived in Cornwall declared that 'looking around on this great Nonconformist county we did not need a Bishop any more than a duck needs an umbrella. My statement as a Nonconformist is this, and I do but echo the opinions of thousands in the county, we do not need a Bishop'.[33]

An image used by Benson was of stars in the heavens: 'The church is a system like the solar. The Cathedral in the centre must flame out light and heat. The parishes have their own self-repeating orbits . . . And crossing their paths in all directions and waking them all up there must be comets as well as planets. And the comets are the missioners.'[34] A cosmic image might imply that all would come into its orbit by force of gravity. Despite Benson's forceful personality, this did not happen. But because of an increasingly pluralistic culture, both Methodism and Anglicanism took their place within a multi-denominational society.

In comparison with his friend Frederick Temple, Benson's posthumous reputation has fared less well. Two modern sympathetic studies of Temple by Simon Green and Frank Field have drawn attention to Temple's modernity, particularly his commitment to a genuinely meritocratic society and a thoughtful, educated understanding of Christian truth, even if his commitment to these principles caused controversy, such as his contribution to *Essays and Reviews* achieved.[35] Benson's achievements were almost the exact opposite of Temple's. Benson was particularly good at dampening down controversy by reconciling Temple's views with those of his opponents. Instead of courting controversy by advocating a way forward, which Field and Green argue has been partially achieved in the twentieth century, Benson looked back to historical and mythical elements of the past. It was famously said by a Foreign Secretary of the early nineteenth century, George Canning, that he called into existence the new world in order to redress the balance of the old world. It could be said of Benson that he called into existence the old world in order to try and redress the balance of the new world.[36] So much of Benson's scholarship depended on his love of the past—mediaeval architecture and cathedral statute, the rubric of the Book of Common Prayer and a lifetime of research into Bishop Cyprian. It was Benson's misfortune to live in an age that increasingly looked to new ideas, not past precedents, to solve its problems.

On St Mark's Day 25 April 1877, Edward White Benson was presented by two bishops at St Paul's Cathedral in London to be ordained bishop by the Archbishop of Canterbury (before Benson travelled to Cornwall a week later). These two bishops were Frederick Temple of Exeter and Christopher Wordsworth of Lincoln. The Wordsworths had been formidable opponents of Temple becoming Bishop of Exeter. Elizabeth Wordsworth had written to Benson criticizing his public support for Temple.[37] Yet Benson remained friends with all three. Benson fared better than most of his contemporaries in reconciling different groups within the Church of England. Indeed, Benson's ability to do so and to win round seemingly implacable opposition may have made him a suitable candidate to be Archbishop in the first place.[38] However, Benson never came close to persuading non-Anglicans, not least in Cornwall, to shelter under the umbrella of the Church of England.

Notes and references

1. H. Miles Brown, *The Catholic Revival in Cornish Anglicanism: A Study of the Traditions of Cornwall 1833–1906* (St Winnow, 1980), p. 81.

2. R.A. Soloway, *Prelates and People: Ecclesiastical Social Thought in England 1783–1852* (London and Toronto, 1969), p. 301–2; G.F.A. Best, *Temporal Pillars: Queen Anne's Bounty, the Ecclesiastical Commissioners and the Church of England* (Cambridge, 1964), pp. 359–60.

3. R.A. Burns, *The Diocesan Revival in the Church of England c1800–1870* (Oxford, 1999), p. 204: 'by 1868 there was no fit Bishop between London and St Ives'.

4. P.S. Morrish, 'The Manchester Clause', *Church Quarterly* 1 (1968 –9) pp. 319–26; 'History, Celticism and Propaganda in the Formation of the Diocese of Truro', *Southern History* 5 (1983) p. 238ff. See also R.A. Burns (1999), p. 196.

5. Twelve dioceses as were created in the Church of England between 1876–1918 (St Albans, Truro, Liverpool, Newcastle, Wakefield, Bristol, Birmingham, Southwark, Chelmsford, St Edmundsbury and Ipswich, Sheffield and Coventry). See P. Toon and M. Smout, *John Charles Ryle: Evangelical Bishop* (London,1976), chapter 3 section D: The Cathedral project.

6. A.C. Benson, *The Life of Edward White Benson, Sometime Archbishop of Canterbury*, 2 vols (2nd edn, London, 1900) Vol. 1, pp. 448–9.

7. The website archiseek.com/tag/Truro conveniently shows the outline of the successful design and five of the unsuccessful designs. None sought simply to modify St Mary's. It just was not big enough.

8. Truro Cathedral Muniments (TCM) 117/14. Earl of Mount Edgcumbe to Benson 19/10/1877 sending apologies to the first diocesan conference of October 1877.

'When I was one-day arguing with the Bishop of Exeter against the division of the diocese . . . he said that he considered that the appointment of what (I think) he called a purely pastoral Bishop would be a most important experiment . . . this view of his influenced me a good deal in modifying my opposition to the scheme.' Edgcumbe became in time one of Benson's best supporters for a new cathedral in Truro.

9. H. Miles Brown, *A Century of Cornwall: the Diocese of Truro 1877–1977* (Truro, 1977), pp. 32–33.
10. A.C. Benson, *Life*, Vol. 2, p. 148.
11. TCM 166.
12. A.C. Benson, *Life*, Vol. 1, p. 457.
13. E.W. Benson, *The Cathedral: Its Necessary Place in the Life and Work of the Church* (London and Truro, 1878), pp. 1, 2, 5; see also E.W. Benson, 'Cathedral life and Cathedral work', *Quarterly Review* 130:259 (January 1871), pp. 22 –55.
14. E.W. Benson (1878) pp. 33, 117–18 (p. 106).
15. A.C. Benson, *Life*, Vol.1, p. 317.
16. E.W. Benson (1878) pp. 29 –30.
17. See A.K. Clarke, *The Story of Truro High School* (Truro,1979).
18. TCM 40/1/2 Quotation from *Western Morning News*, 25 October 1878, included in archive.
19. TCM report of debate from same issue of Western morning news, quoting successively Canon Thynne (Kilkhampton) and Rev G.L. Woolcombe (St Mewan).
20. Stephen Dawes, *Desert Island Hymns—Faith which Sings with Heart and Mind* (Southleigh, 1996), p. 2; G. Wainwright and K.B Westerfield Tucker (eds.) *Oxford History of Christian Worship* (Oxford, 2006), p. 567; TCM 37/1/3 The nine lessons chosen by Benson were in order Genesis 3. 8–16, Genesis 22. 15–19; Numbers 24. 15–18; Isaiah 9. 6–8; Micah 5. 2–5; Luke 2. 8–16, John 1. 1–15 (for which all were to stand); Galatians 4. 4–8; I John 1. 1–5. Carols included Good Christian Men Rejoice, Bethlehem of Noblest Cities, The First Nowell and O, Come all ye faithful. Also included was the Hallelujah chorus which Benson also managed to include on 20 May 1880 at the foundation stones ceremony, despite the disapproval of the Earl of Mount Edgcumbe (TCM157/10, 157/16 and especially157/19—a letter dated 5/5/1880 from Edgcumbe to Benson 'I thought we had quite settled not to have Hallelujah Chorus and I told the Prince so').
21. TCM 41/1/1.
22. TCM 147/66 Diary entry of 23 May 1882; A.C. Benson, *Life*, Vol. 1, p. 428 when Benson was seeking to choose the names of the canons' stalls he wrote to a friend 'you know the Cornish Saints, and I hope you will help me to glorify them. Bye and bye I must get them into the windows'.
23. TCM 157/1; TCM 41/1/1 (Pearson's report of 12 May 1879) TCM 250/6/2. Edgcumbe mentions Lady Rolle's 'magnificent donation' in a letter to *The Times* dated 15 July 1880. TCM 250/6/3 and TCM 100 reveal fundraising from abroad which more generously supported the fund (of 1879) for the relief of the distress existing in the County of Cornwall. Support for Cathedral building from abroad was less systematic than support for famine relief.
24. A.C. Benson, *Life*, Vol. 1, pp. 453–54.
25. *Royal Cornwall Gazette*, 15 August1889, p. 4 c2.
26. Royal Cornwall Museum, River Street, Truro. Exhibit—Silver presentation trowel

presented to Mrs Chirgwin of Truro on laying a memorial stone of the United Methodist Free Church Tuesday 14th of May 1880, just six days before the ceremony at the Cathedral.

27. E.W. Benson, (1878), p. 106.

28. TCM 51 'Canon Harvey again deprecated our acquiring power. Ep. (Benson) said he wanted a Council to do work not to gain power.' 'Canon Rogers still favours power of two to carry the matter to the whole Chapter. Ep. (Benson) pointed out the Bishop could still decide for himself: they were never going to bind the Bishop.' (meeting held 27 October 1880). On Benson lacking deference see e.g. A.C. Benson *Life*, Vol. 1, p. 217. A.W. Verrall, invited by the biographer to reflect on E.W. Benson's time as headmaster of Wellington where A.W. Verrall was a pupil wrote 'during my four years and a half (1865–1869) I must have seen him in contact with the greater part of what was then most exalted in England (at successive speech days because of the way Wellington College was set up by the great and the good under the direction of Prince Albert). Yet I never saw, either then or for that matter afterwards any personage (with one single exception) over whom . . . the Headmaster could not easily take the lead'. Lord Derby, the then Prime Minister, was the exception. See also A.C. Benson, *Life*, Vol.1, p. 586: 'in the House (of Lords) he was nervous: the atmosphere of chilly criticism appalled him: moreover, having all his life held positions of command, he found it difficult to debate a question from a footing of perfect equality'. David Newsome, late Fellow and Senior Tutor of Emmanuel College Cambridge, has written extensively on the Benson family. See, in particular, on the death of Martin White Benson, *Godliness and Good Learning: Four Studies on a Victorian Ideal* (London, 1961); on Benson as schoolmaster, *A History of Wellington College 1859–1959* (London, 1959); on A.C. Benson, *On the Edge o f Paradise: A.C. Benson the Diarist* (London, 1980). For a much less favourable picture of Bishop Benson see Rodney Bolt, *The Impossible Life of Mary Benson* (London, 2012). For Benson in parliament see Peter Marsh, *The Victorian Church in Decline: Archbishop Tait and the Church of England 1868–1882* (Pittsburgh, 1969) p. 288: 'Benson, the new Archbishop of Canterbury was out of his element in Parliament and came to be treated by some political leaders such as Balfour with contempt.'

29. Mark D. Chapman, *Bishops, Saints and Politics: Anglican Studies* (London, 2007), pp. 64–68.

30. For an appraisal of the Lincoln judgement see G.K.A. Bell, *Randall Davidson* (London, 1936), chapter VI, pp. 124–49; *Read and others v the Lord Bishop of Lincoln. Judgement November 21, 1890*; E.S. Roscoe, *The Bishop of Lincoln's case: a report of the proceedings in the court of the Archbishop of Canterbury* (London, 1891). On the impact of the Lincoln judgment see Nigel Yates, *Anglican Ritualism in Victorian Britain 1830*-1910 (Oxford, 2000), p. 274.

31. TCM 249/3/a (Bishop Benson's 'ad clerum'). For uses this letter was put by other bishops see, for instance, 249/8/2 and 249/10 (Peterborough): 'After careful thought I felt that I cannot (do) better than by adopting the admirable words (of) the Bishop of Truro'. (249/10).

32. M. Chapman, *Bishops, Saints and Politics*, p. 62.

33. RCG 5/1/1877 p. 6. The letter was written by Edward Fish, Baptist Minister.

34. TCM 147/ p. 27 Benson's diary entry of 25 April 1882.

35. Simon Green, '*Archbishop Frederick Temple on meritocracy, liberal education and

the idea of a clerisy' in Michael Bentley (ed.), *Public and Private Doctrine: Essays in British History presented to Maurice Cowling* (Cambridge, 1993), p. 149f; Frank Field, *Saints and Heroes: Inspiring Politics* (London, 2010), p. 15f.

36. George Canning's speech in House of Commons 12 December 1826 as Foreign Secretary: 'I resolved that if France had Spain it should not be Spain with the Indies I called the New World into existence to redress the balance of the old'.

37. A.C. Benson, *Life*, Vol. 1, p. 279f. esp. p.306–08.

38. Lambeth Palace Archive: Archbishop Tait 267, f 201 speaks of opposition probably from clergy against the Burial Laws Amendment Act as upwards of 15,000, who had signed a petition. On the powerful opposition by the cathedral chapter to Temple's appointment as Bishop of Exeter see Peter Hinchliff, *Frederick Temple Archbishop of Canterbury: A Life* (Oxford, 1998), p. 123.Opposition came from outside the chapter also from Lord Shaftesbury, a very prominent evangelical layman and Edward Pusey who wrote in response to Temple's appointment to the see of Exeter, that he 'must henceforth long, pray, and work, as I can, for the severance of Church and State'. The reference is from S.A. Skinner, *Tractarians and the 'Condition of England': the Social and Political Thought of the Oxford Movement* (Oxford, 2004), p. 92. On the principle of different groups in society contesting cultural authority see the writings of Frank M. Turner especially *The Greek Heritage in Victorian Britain* (Yale, 1981), and *Contesting Cultural Authority: Essays in Victorian Intellectual Life* (Cambridge, 1993).

Acknowledgements

This article is based on my PhD awarded by the University of Exeter in 2012 for a thesis entitled 'The Episcopate of Bishop Benson 1877–1883 and the Beginnings of Truro Diocese and Cathedral: The Umbrella and the Duck'. My grateful thanks to my tutors Philip Payton and Garry Tregidga, ably assisted by many other members of the faculty at Tremough Campus in Penryn and, among many others, to Michael Swift and David Thomas for very helpful conversations; to my examiners, John Beckett and Anna Green and also all who have helped with the administration of the thesis. I would like to thank in Helston, my secretary Janet Jones, Michael and Heather Thorn for proof-reading and Beccy, Thomas and George Miller for technical assistance and wonderful support. I would like to thank the staff, past and present, of the Cornwall Records Office, the Bishop Phillpotts Library and the Courtney Library in Truro, the Cornish Studies Library in Redruth, Trinity College Library in Cambridge and Lambeth Palace Library in London. The thesis could not have been undertaken without the generous financial help of the Caroline L. Kemp bursary, for which I am very grateful.

9

Against Taxonomy
The Fairy Families of Cornwall

Simon Young

Introduction and Hunt's Classification

In the nineteenth century, as folklorists gathered material in a systematic fashion, it was natural, indispensable even, that they classify that data. Part of this effort was made to break down the many supernatural beings that they found into macro categories—'demons', 'fairies', 'giants' . . .—and then subdivide these macro categories into smaller groups: e.g. 'white ladies', 'poltergeists' and the 'uneasy dead' for ghosts. There is no question that in doing this they were, in part, following local traditions. But, as folklorists have long realized, including those same nineteenth-century folklorists,[1] there is enormous blurring in lore and very often taxonomic categories misrepresented the beliefs of a given area. This is particularly true of fairies. In this short article we want to look at this question from a Cornish perspective. Cornwall has several advantages for such a study. It is (i) a relatively small and a relatively homogenous area. It has (ii) a rich nineteenth-century folklore corpus, as several talented men and women worked on the fairy lore of this region. And there are (iii) a series of memorates from Cornwall, which come through to us independently of the folklore collectors and that allow us, to some extent, to check the collector's material and their interpretations.

The first systematic attempt at fairy classification for Cornwall was made by Robert Hunt in 1865 in his *Popular Romances*, a book dedicated, in part, to fairies.[2] Hunt was not Cornish: he had been born in Devon. But he grew up in Penzance and he had taken notes on the folklore of the region from the 1820s, when still a young man.[3] He was systematic in outlook; he was a chemist, a statistician, a pioneering photographer and a mine engineer as well as a poet and a philanthropist.[4] And he was determined, in a very Victorian way, to reduce the confusing galaxy of traditional names to order. 'It should be understood that there are in Cornwall five varieties of the fairy family, clearly distinguishable: 1) The Small People; 2) The Spriggans; 3) Piskies, or Pigseys; 4) The Buccas, Bockles, or Knockers [and] 5) The Browneys'.[5] The reader would be well advised to remember that phrase 'clearly distinguishable' in what follows . . .

Hunt's is the list that all subsequent writers on Cornish folklore have been confronted with and against which very many have rebelled. William Bottrell who had inspired Hunt and who, in turn, was inspired and provoked by him dithered, in his three publications, over how to divide up the Cornish fairy folk: he ultimately, as we shall see, declined to follow Hunt in his pentarchy. Margaret Courtney, writing some twenty-five years later, did away with browneys and reduced the list to four.[6] The Rev. W.S. Lach-Szymra listed five fairy types, but differed in what these five were: fairies, piskies/pixies, small people, good people and brownies.[7] Henry Jenner, in two essays in the 1910s, reduced Hunt's list to three: he united the first three categories as 'piskies', divided knockers and buccas and provisionally rejected browneys.[8] Enys Tregarthen accepted knockers and spriggans ('bad Piskeys'), conflated piskeys and small people, revealed that they were also called 'dinkies' or the 'little invisibles', and that there was too a species named 'nightriders'.[9] Then, in 1975, Tony Deane and Tony Shaw, in the most influential modern work on Cornish folklore, settled on three categories, uniting small people, spriggans and piskies and keeping knockers *and* browneys.[10] Jeremy Harte, in what is perhaps the most important general study of fairies in the last generation, united the first three, ignored knockers, and rejected browneys out of hand.[11] And Amy Hale, in our most important Celtic encylcopedia, subdivided piskies into spriggans, knockers, buccas and browneys.[12]

It will be noted that not a single one of the authors on this list is in agreement![13] And if individuals of the calibre of Harte and Jenner or Courtney and Tregarthen disagree, what hope is there for a new study? Were we intending to write a 'definitive' list, then none at all. But our aim here is not to settle on one or other combination of names: this would be to repeat the errors begun by Hunt a century and a half ago. It is rather to show the ultimate futility of lists where fairies (and other supernatural creatures) are concerned, particularly when our evidence is incomplete. Note we say 'ultimate' because it is inevitable that folklorists and tradition-bearers *will* classify. But while classifying we must remember that we are not entomologists with nets, boxes and pins. Our 'lists' and 'categories' are no more than epistemological tools to better understand an amorphous, flowing and yet poorly documented reality: they must not be confused with the reality itself.

Piskeys, Little People and Spriggans

Any study of Cornish fairies has to begin with 'piskey' the Cornish spelling of the standard south-western fey. The piskey is 'pixy' in Devon—the canonical spelling thanks to Coleridge and Bray—and it is also spelt sometimes as pigsey.[14] The geographical limits of pixy belief in early modern times are difficult to establish. Certainly, the four south-western counties feature pixy tales. But there are hints that pixies were known as far east as Sussex and as far north as the Welsh Marches.[15] Early evidence is lacking, either because our sources are inadequate or because that evidence never existed. And this is compounded by the fact that no one has ever given a convincing etymology for the word 'piskey', a word that possibly had its origin in the Brittonic language of south-west Britain, from which modern Cornish is derived. We say 'possibly' but the earliest known occurrence of pixy appears in 1636 (or thereabouts) in Devon.[16]

Given the ubiquity of 'piskey' it is hardly surprising that Hunt includes them in his list. More curious though are the references to spriggans and the small people. Here Jeremy Harte has suggested that 'the only difference lay in the choice of Standard English, West Country Dialect or vestigial Cornish to describe them' for respectively small people, piskeys and spriggans.[17] Harte seems to be basing his thoughts here on Jenner's work of almost a century before. Jenner wrote: 'if there is any distinction it would seem that "small people" is a more general term, spriggans are a more elegant and refined sort, perhaps influenced by the fairies of cultivated literature, and piskies more uncouth and rustic'.[18] However, if Harte and Jenner are correct—and this is far from certain—it is important to remember that for Hunt there were differences not just of name but of function as well.

The small people are described by Hunt as 'the spirits of people who inhabited Cornwall many thousands of years ago'—though he admits that it is 'by no means clear that the tradition of their origin does not apply to the whole five branches of this ancient family'.[19] Hunt underlines the fact that they are not only small, but 'smaller and smaller': they are shrinking through time. He also points to their benevolence:

> These Small People are exceedingly playful amongst themselves, but they are usually demure when they know that any human eye sees them. They commonly aid those people to whom they take a fancy, and, frequently, they have been known to perform the most friendly acts towards men and women.[20]

The spriggans, on the other hand, are malicious, which might have to do with their guarding ancient treasures. As one of Hunt's correspondents— Bottrell?—had it:

This is known, that they were a remarkably mischievous and thievish tribe. If ever a house was robbed, a child stolen, cattle carried away, or a building demolished, it was the work of the Spriggans. Whatever commotion took place in earth, air, or water, it was all put down as the work of these spirits.[21]

The piskey, on the other hand, is more mischievous than wicked. He likes to pixy-lead travellers and he is famous for his laughter.[22] In crude Freudian terms, the spriggans are the *id*, the piskies are the *ego* and the small people the *super ego* of the Cornish fairy world. The division in names also then involved or was understood by Hunt to involve a division in function and character. But—returning to Harte and Jenner's point—had Hunt split up what was an organic whole in tradition?

We have too little evidence, unfortunately, but the writings of three authors: Bray, Couch and Bottrell suggest that Hunt was guilty of splitting. To take the work of Bray first, she certainly described other supernatural creatures in her writings on south-west Britain. However, among the fairies, she only recognized the pixy.[23] There were no small people, there was no spriggan: in fact, even a fairy in a mine is called a pixy rather than a knocker.[24] Does this represent the more 'primitive' folklore of Dartmoor? Was it perhaps Bray's desire to simplify for readers from elsewhere (or the desire of her informants to do the same)? Possibly. But it is striking that Bray describes the pixies being sent on their tasks by the Pixy King who lived on the moor. And pixies working below ground belonged to the same kingdom as those misleading travellers in the bogs.[25] She also has an expert correspondent who confuses issues still more by twice calling the mine pixies 'small men'![26]

Thomas Couch published in 1855 the earliest extensive writing on the Cornish as opposed to the Dartmoor pixy, basing his experience on the village of Polperro where he and his family lived.[27] Couch was, like Hunt afterwards, an interested outsider: and his writing on fairy types is important because, almost uniquely in Cornish folklore writing, he predates Hunt's authoritative statements. Couch, like Bray, does not mention spriggans or little people. However, in an earlier version of that paper, preserved in the *Transactions of the Penzance Natural History and Antiquarian Society*, we can see his confusion as to classification, something that does not appear in this form in later drafts of his work:

Our domestic spirit, who rewards the thrifty servant, and punishes the slattern, and who, in the old manor house at Killigarth, when the family was at church, was wont to watch the joint as it roasted on the spit, and to admonish the servant to remove it when sufficiently drest, agrees with the gobelin of Normandy, the kobold of Germany, the nisse of Norway, and the Tom te gubbe of Sweden, and the brownie of Scotland, and may be found distinct from our little pastoral fairy whose chief amusement is music and dancing, laughter and mischief, and whom makes those rings in our meadows 'of which the ewe not bites'.[28]

Couch makes here the division—the division preferred by most twentieth-century folklorists[29]—between the domestic solitary fairy and the host of fairies outside: a division that Hunt effectively avoids. Couch then goes on to speculate about the existence of knockers, though with self-confessed ignorance.

> In Cornwall we might expect to find the 'swart fairy of the mine' occupy-ing a prominent place in our mythology. It would, therefore be interest-ing to know whether this is the case from those who are acquainted with the folk-lore of our mining districts, especially as it has been a disputed point whether the Duergars or dwarf-tribe, dwelling in hills and caverns, and distinguished for their skill in metallurgy, formed really a portion of the old belief, or were, as Sir Walter Scott thought them, the diminutive natives of the Lappish and Finnish nations driven to the mountains by their invaders.[30]

Couch, then, at Polperro, had heard nothing of Spriggans and Small People. Indeed, he struggled with typology, but broke down the fairies he knew ac-cording to function, albeit more general functions than Hunt. In his later published draft he complains that all fairy types had been subsumed by the pisky.[31]

Bottrell and Hunt on Fairy Types

Most interesting, however, are the comments of Bottrell. Jenner, in a notable passage, claims that Bottrell had ignored Hunt's classification.[32] But this is not strictly true. In fact, in each of his three volumes Bottrell includes reflec-tions on the division of fairies into groups. In the first volume, he seems to differentiate between piskeys and fairies (whom he calls 'the small people').[33] In the second volume he has a short essay entitled 'The Small People' with which 'Spriggans' are associated.[34] Then in the third volume, in an essay called 'The Fairy Tribe', Bottrell moves closer to Hunt's position: he talks of small people, spriggans (treasure-keepers) and piskeys.[35] However, he is not emphatic and his use of these words suggests a flexibility that is not there in Hunt's classification. Consider these passages (italics are our own):

'I wish we could but catch *a spriggan, a piskey, or a knacker,*' says Capt. Mathy one night, 'ef one can but lay hands on any of the *small people* unawares before they vanish, or turn into muryans (ants), they may be made to tell where the goold es buried.'[36]

I ventured to wipe the water from my face with my apron, and to open my anointed eye, and oh! the Lord deliver me from what I see'd—the place was full of *sprites and spriggans*; in all the folds of the nets and sails, that were thrown over the keybeams, in the clews of ropes that hung from the rafters, troops of *small-people* were cutting all sorts of capers;[37]

In his glossary to the second volume Bottrell writes that small people are 'fairies', spriggans are a 'sprite, fairy' and piskeys are 'a mischievous fairy that delights to lead people astray'.[38] There is overlap then, not Hunt's 'clearly distinguishable' categories.

If, as Jenner believed, Bottrell was far more of an authority on fairies than Hunt then what should perhaps strike us here is vagueness and an evolving system that responded to Hunt's writing. It is commonly appreciated that Hunt had read Bottrell's notes before publishing.[39] It is forgotten though that Bottrell's writings take Hunt's work into account and that he responds to that work. As we have noted elsewhere, Bottrell is perhaps the closest we have in nineteenth-century Britain or Ireland to a tradition-bearer writing folklore.[40] In a sense, Bottrell is not just writing about drolls, he is still part of that tradition: 'the last of the drolls'. His very vagueness about classifying fairies is what is most important. The categories of Hunt interest him, but though he hums and whistles a little, he does not, in the end, take up the tune. It is as if that tune were too restricting.

More shocking though is Hunt's occasional confusion that is, in some senses, profounder than Bottrell's. The following tale is entitled 'the Fairy Fair in Germoe'. Here we have confusion both in terminology (piskies/small people) and in function (the good small people are 'wicked, spiteful devils', who steal children). Again italics are our own:

Bal Lane in Germoe was a notorious place for *piskies*. One night Daniel Champion and his comrade came to Godolphin Bridge, they were a little bit 'overtook' with liquor. They said that when they came to Bal Lane, they found it covered all over from end to end, and the *Small People* holding a fair there with all sorts of merchandise—the prettiest sight they ever met with. Champion was sure he saw his child there; for a few nights before, his child in the evening was as beautiful a one as could be seen anywhere, but in the morning was *changed for one as ugly and wizened as could be*; and he was sure the *Small People* had done it.

Next day, telling the story at Croft Gothal, his comrade was knocked backward, thrown into the bobpit, and just killed. Obliged to be carried to his home. Champion followed, and was telling of their adventure with the *Small People*, when one said, 'Don't speak about them; *they're wicked, spiteful devils.*' No sooner were the words uttered than the speaker was thrown clean over stairs and bruised dreadfully, a convincing proof to all present of the reality of the existence of the *Small Folks*.[41]

This passage, together with Bottrell's previous two, suggest that, as Jenner noted, 'small people' is simply a generic term.[42] We wonder if 'small people' has not been romanticized because of the reasonable hope that the words are a calque on a Cornish phrase, *pobel vean*.[43] Spriggans, on the other hand, cluster in references from the west of Penzance: perhaps we are dealing then with just a local *genus*?[44] Certainly, the ideal way to look at fairy classification would be to look at fairy names on a micro level, parish by parish: the problem is we never or rarely have enough information to do so. Enys Tregarthen's writings though are a warning as different categories and names of fairies apparently existed in the north of Cornwall: e.g. 'dinkies' and 'nightriders'.[45]

Buccas, Bockles and Knockers

If piskies/spriggans and small people provide us with 'lumping' problems then Hunt's 'the Buccas, Bockles, or Knockers' perhaps demand splitting:

These are the sprites of the mines, and correspond to the Kobals of the German mines, the Duergars, and the Trolls. They are said to be the souls of the Jews who formerly worked the tin-mines of Cornwall. They are not allowed to rest because of their wicked practices as tinners, and they share in the general curse which ignorant people believe still hangs on this race.[46]

About knockers (or 'knackers'), we have already seen that there is danger of confusion with piskies.[47] Bockles barely exist outside this page of Hunt.[48] But then Hunt reports that 'in some districts' the word Bucca is also employed for mine spirits.[49] Crucially, Bottrell too refers to 'knackers' as buccas, calling them also 'underground spriggans'[50] But this does not seem to be the first or even the second meaning of Bucca. Indeed, in a long note Bottrell gives the following senses: (i) 'a poor, half-witted person of a mischievous disposition'; (ii) 'a ghost'; (iii) 'a scarecrow'; (iv) 'Old Nick' [when Bucca-dhu, black spirit] and (v) 'a divinity'.[51]

On this last point:

> Within easy memory every boat in Newlyn always set aside a portion of
> the catch, and left it in a collected heap on the beach to propitiate 'Bucka',
> and every fisherman noted, with superstitious awe, the remarkable regu-
> larity with which 'Bucka' fetched away his offerings, after dark.[52]

This examination is a reminder of how complicated tradition can become and
how our terms, rather than being surgical tweezers become unwieldy pliers
that damage what they pick up. Here we have a word that has several different meanings, presumably, in part, because of geography ('in some districts',
'Newlyn'); in part, because of natural polarities in myth; and, in part, because
of the complexity of language. It is striking that Hunt, who had a life-long
interest in Cornish traditions, did not write about the bucca on the beach at
Newlyn. Instead, he deprived the bucca of life by lumping him together with
the knockers of the mines. Bucca though deserves, on this evidence, a separate
existence either as a fairy or something else: Bottrell's 'divinity' perhaps.[53]

The Elusive Browney

We have dealt so far with the problems of lumping and splitting. What
now though about accidental invention? In 1865 Robert Hunt gave his own
description of the most mysterious supernatural being from Cornwall:

> This spirit was purely of the household. Kindly and good, he devoted his
> every care to benefit the family with whom he had taken up his abode.
> The Browney has fled, owing to his being brought into very close contact
> with the schoolmaster, and he is only summoned now upon the occasion
> of the swarming of the bees. When this occurs, mistress or maid seizes
> a bell-metal, or a tin pan, and, beating it, she calls 'Browney, Browney!'
> as loud as she can until the good Browney compels the bees to settle.[54]

With the very strange exception of the bees, this description of browney is one
that a reader could easily find in nineteenth-century England, to the north of
the Humber, and in Scotland. Brownie (the normal spelling) was a solitary
fairy, typically semi-nude and hairy, who worked loyally in households. He
would insist on cleanliness and yet rebel when offered clothes, leaving the
service of any household that 'misused' him in this way.[55] In Cornwall there
are several stories of this type though all involve 'piskeys' . . .[56] Browney, on
the other hand, presents problems of geography. How can a fairy appear at two
different ends of Britain, but not in any intervening region?

In fact, this dual appearance would not be quite as difficult to credit if other evidence was good. Most modern attempts to explain the word 'brownie' have employed Gaelic.[57] But Brownie is associated, above all, with northern England and the Scottish Lowlands, an area that was, like Cornwall, Brittonic-speaking in early medieval times. If 'brownie' could be shown to derive from a Brittonic word, then the distance between the two 'brownie' regions would not be such an obstacle. However, no such word has been found and there is also the fact that 'brownie' (or an obvious cognate) is absent from Welsh and Breton, the other Brittonic-speaking regions. At this point the natural scepticism over Hunt's Cornish browney returns.

This scepticism grows when it is realized that prior to Hunt there is no other mention of brownies for Cornwall or Devon. There are fairies that act like brownies—they are solitary and run away on being given a new suit of clothes—but they are, as we noted above, called 'piskeys'. Nor are the references that come after Hunt copious or convincing. Bottrell connects fairies and bees but refuses to use the word 'browney': a pointed and very significant omission.[58] In 1881 after a lecture in Penzance, a Mr Cornish describes how a 'brownie' (his spelling?) regularly visited a house in that town.[59] It is interesting that this brownie was a solitary fairy and that he was associated with a home. But is 'brownie' here the traditional term or just a term for a 'solitary fairy' popularized by the fairy writers of the previous generation, not least Hunt himself? Then, in 1910, Henry Jenner opined that 'brownie' was a foreign term, perhaps taken from books. However, he admits that he had recently come across a case of a 'brownie' in Sennen in West Cornwall.[60]

The only specific Cornish trait that browney has is his peculiar association with bees. Ariel in *The Tempest* famously sucks where the bee sucks. But we have been able to find no association between fairies and bees in traditional lore with one slight but possibly significant exception. Anna Bray writing in her *Description* quotes a seventeenth-century Tavistock poet recording, in verse, the popular belief that 'that fairies and pixies steal honey from the hives of bees':

> For as I oft have heard the wood-nimphs say,
> The dancing fairies when they left to play,
> Then backe did pull them, and in holes of trees
> Stole the sweet honey from the painfull bees,
> Which in the flower to put they oft were seene,
> And for a banquet brought it to their queene.[61]

Of course, Hunt's browney and this poem have only a vague connection: in one browney settles the bees, in one pixies or fairies steal honey from hives.

But there is a curiosity that must at least be noted. The poet in question was

William *Browne*.[62] Is it possible that Browne was confused in the memory of one of the nineteenth-century, south-western fairy writers? Browne was little read in the 1800s. But Bray was the point of reference for all those interested in south-western fairy belief. One of Hunt's informants or Hunt himself may have got a name mixed up while recalling legends about honey and fairies, particularly given the existence of the northern brownie.[63] Hunt and Bottrell as well as Thomas Couch (one of Hunt's sources) all admitted to having read Bray: and brownies were becoming, in turn, well known through writers such as Keightley.[64]

Now, it is likely that the words browney/Browne associated with fairies and honey represent no more than a coincidence. But the very fact that we can offer this kind of hypothesis is a reminder of the fragility of the proof for the *genus*. Harte is perhaps too emphatic when he writes that 'a whole species of fairy has been created, not by the folk, but by the folklorist'.[65] But there is a very real danger that this is what has happened here. For us, Bottrell's omission of 'browney', while discussing the same episode is the most important nineteenth-century data point.

Conclusion

The weight of all the previous arguments is that Hunt's list cannot be sustained. The splitting of spriggans, small people and piskeys is almost certainly a mistaken response to Cornish tradition; a response that Bottrell seems to have accepted and resisted by turns. There are *lacunae*, with bucca given a miner's pick when he should also have been given a room (or beach) of his own. Browney may be a misunderstanding or an import. In fact, in the end the only real division seems to be between underground and overground fairies. But, as we hinted above, even that is too-simplistic. Bray describes the fairies in the mine as a piskey.[66] We also have a precious reference from near Bodmin where Jack o'Lanterns are associated with the discovery of a mine.[67]

So, what can be done? Is it best to surrender and simply talk of Cornish fairies, or better piskies, with no subdivisions? It would be, but even the boundaries between fairies and other supernatural beings are blurred. After all, we learn that 'the small people' (and perhaps all of the fairies) were the spirits of the dead: a theme made much of by Lewis Spence.[68] The spriggans were the shrunk, reduced remnants of the giants.[69] The piskey and will-o'-the-wisp double up frequently: Jack-the-lantern is sometimes even called a piskey as, thinking of Devon now, is Joan-the-Wad.[70] We read one report of mermaids taking changeling children: as typically fairies would do.[71] In another account, a fairy widower swims in the water among the small people.[72] One non-canonical Devon source even suggests that there may have been some overlapping between piskeys and yeff hounds.[73] In the Middle Ages it proved impossible to hold a line between demons and fairies and fairies and Christian figures (Mary, angels . . .).[74] In modern times there have been several studies noting similarities between UFO and fairies encounters.[75] It should really come as no surprise that in the nineteenth century, in Cornwall and the south-west, among believers there was no firmly held line between different supernatural categories.

If Hunt's list is a vain attempt to classify then what lessons, if any, can we take away from this exercise? For this author, at least, one striking point is the difference between Bottrell and Hunt's attitude towards classification. Hunt, as a scientist, *needed* classification. It was the foundation for his work on the fairies: he is a taxonomist. Bottrell, on the other hand, essentially a literate droll, plays with classification and blurs categories, floating among and with the fairies. And Bottrell is better matched to the material, for folklore is protean and shifts according to time, place and circumstance.

All this begs a question: must we, in any attempt to understand folklore, eschew classification? To answer this question we will take an analogy from the study of history. It is useful for scholars and students alike to split European civilization into 'ancient', 'medieval' and 'modern', with 'dark ages' (or some politically-correct equivalent) and 'renaissance' intervening as minor epochs. But this is only scaffolding that allows us to get close to the past, not the past itself. Anyone who studies history has to constantly remind themselves that those people living hundreds of years ago did not structure their experience as we do. There is no question that it is difficult for the taxonomic mindset to separate invented structures and real content. But should we want to get closer to the folk experience of Cornish fairies, then we need to be a little more like William Bottrell and a little less like Robert Hunt.

Notes and references

1. Wirt Sikes, *British Goblins: Welsh Folk-Lore, Fairy Mythology. Legends and Traditions* (London, 1880), p. 11, summed this up very well: 'Fairies being creatures of the imagination, it is not possible to classify them by fixed and immutable rules. In the exact sciences, there are laws which never vary, or if they vary, their very eccentricity is governed by precise rules. Even in the largest sense, comparative mythology must demean itself modestly in order to be tolerated in the severe company of the sciences.' See also G.L. Kittredge, 'The Friar's Lantern and Friar Rush', *Proceedings of the Modern Language Association* 15 (1900), pp. 415–41 (p. 430): 'Fairies, goblins, witches, gradongs, elves, cats, ghosts, dwarfs, will-o'-the-wisps, familiars, white ladies and so on, are found, on occasion, performing each other's duties with baffling self-complacency.'
2. Robert Hunt, *Popular Romances of the West of England* (London, 1881), p. 80. Note

that we use the third edition throughout this essay, though we have checked to make sure that all points are also in the original 1865 edition.

3. Robert Hunt, *Popular Romances*, pp. 21–22.

4. Alan Pearson, 'Robert Hunt', *Oxford Dictionary of National Biography* (London, 2004) [accessed online] and Alan Pearson, *Robert Hunt* (London ,1976).

5. Hunt, *Popular Romances*, p. 80.

6. M.A. Courtney, *Cornish Feasts and Folklore* (Penzance, 1890), p. 120: 'The fairies of Cornwall may be divided into four classes, the Small People, the Pixies (pronounced Piskies or or Pisgies), the Spriggans, and the Knockers.'

7. 'M. Sebillot's System as Applied to Cornish Folk-Lore', *Transactions of the Penzance Natural History and Antiquarian Society* 1 (1882), pp. 132–50 (p.136): note that it is not clear that these are types, the author refers to 'names'.

8. 'Introduction [to Cornish section]' in W.Y. Evans-Wentz, *The Fairy Faith In Celtic Countries* (Gerrard's Cross, 1977), pp. 163–70 and 'Piskies: a folk-lore study', *Annual Report of the Royal Cornwall Polytechnic Society* 83 (1916), pp. 130–51 (p. 132).

9. Enys Tregarthen, *Pixie Folklore and Legends* (London, 1996), p. 12: 'In Cornwall they are generally called Piskeys, but they have many other names too. Some call them the Small People; others the Dinky Men and Women or the Dinkies; some speak of them as the Little Invisibles. There are many kinds of Piskeys, such as the nightriders or the tiny people who ride horses and colts and even dogs by night; and the knockers or little miners who work and play down in the old mines. There are Spriggans, too, bad Piskeys with whom no one wants to have anything to do.' For 'night riders' see Hunt, *Popular Romances*, p. 87.

10. Tony Deane and Tony Shaw, *The Folklore of Cornwall* (London, 1975), p. 90: 'Writers in the nineteenth century placed Cornish fairies into five categories, but the traditional stories and various personal accounts contradict themselves so much that the field can be narrowed down to three types. The knockers of the mines . . . rare accounts of brownies and the Small People . . .'

11. Jeremy Harte, *Explore Fairy Traditions* (Loughborough, 2004), p. 4.

12. 'Pisky', *Celtic Culture: A Historical Encyclopedia*, 5 vols, John Koch (ed.), (Santa Barbara, 2005), IV, pp. 1449–50 (p. 1449).

13. In other regions there was interaction between the terminology of folklorists and tradition: the lack of consensus in Cornwall, though, meant that there was no interaction on this side of the Tamar.

14. Coleridge mentioned the pixies in two early poems, Jeanie Watson, *Risking Enchantment: Coleridge's Symbolic World of Faery* (London, 1990), pp. 72–75: Anna Eliza Bray, *A description of the part of Devonshire bordering on the Tamar and the Tavy: its natural history, manners, customs, superstitions, scenery, antiquities, biography of eminent persons, &c. &c. in a series of letters to Robert Southey, esq* (London, 1836), 3 vols, marks though the real beginning of modern interest in this supernatural creature: see particularly her tenth letter, I, pp. 167–92.

15. For a good introduction Katharine Briggs, *A Dictionary of Fairies*, (London, 1976), pp. 328–31.

16. Thomas Westcote, *A View of Devonshire in 1630 with a Pedigree of Most of its Gentry* (Exeter, 1845), p. 433: 'and, peradventure, I shall by some be thought to lead you in a pixy-path by telling an old tale'. This is the oldest reference recorded in the OED.

17. *Explore*, p. 4. Note 'respectively' is our deduction based on Jeremy Harte's text.

18. 'Piskies' p. 132.

19. Hunt, *Popular Romances*, p. 80.

20. Ibid., p. 81.

21. Ibid. According to the OED Hunt is the first author to use the word 'spriggan'.

22. Ibid., pp. 81–82.

23. An interesting question is whether Bray was serious about fairies and pixies being different, or whether this was just a 'stunt': Bray, *Description*, I, p. 172 and, most intriguingly, Bray, *A Peep at the Pixies or Legends of the West* (London, 1854), pp. 11–12: 'Some people say [the Pixies] are the souls of poor children who die unbaptised, and others think that they are a kind of fairies, but more frolicsome, and have more power to do either good or harm. They are, however, generally considered a distinct race; for if you could but see a Pixy, my young friends, you would see at once how different was such a creature from a Fairy. Indeed, it is matter of tradition, that the Fairies wished very much to establish themselves in Devonshire, but the Pixies would not hear of it; and a terrible war ensued. Oberon was, with his host, defeated; and his majesty received a wound in the leg which proved incurable; none of the herbs in his dominions have hitherto had the least beneficial effects, though his principal secretary and attendant, Puck, has been in search of one of a healing nature ever since.' A genuine tradition or fairy fodder for Bray's juvenile readers?

24. Bray, *Peep*, pp. 30–32. Note though Evans-Wentz, *Fairy Faith*, p. 182, William Shepherd from St Just states 'There are mine piskies which are not the "knockers".'

25. Bray, *Peep*, p. 13: 'It is under the cold light of [the moon], or amidst the silent shadows of the dark rocks, where that light never penetrates, that on the moor the elfin king of the Pixy race holds his high court of sovereignty and council. There each Pixy receives his especial charge.'

26. Bray, *Description*, III, p. 256: 'these noises [in the mine] the men believe to be occasioned by the working of the fairies, or pixies, whom they call small men'.

27. Thomas Q. Couch, 'The Folk Lore of a Cornish Village: Fairy Mythology', *Notes and Queries* 11 (1855), pp. 397–98, 457–59.

28. Thomas Q. Couch, 'The Popular Antiquities of Polperro and its neighbourhood', *Transactions of the Penzance Natural History and Antiquarian Society* 2 (1864), pp. 149–61 (pp. 160–61); confusingly the earlier draft was printed after the later one. See also 'Penzance Natural History and Antiquarian Society: Folklore', *The Cornishman*, 11 November 1853, pp. 6–7 (p. 6).

29. For the best definition known to us, Diane Purkiss, *Troublesome Things: A History of Fairies and Fairy Stories* (London, 2000), pp. 8–9: 'There are fairies with their own household—who might entertain you or take you as a servant—and fairies who live in yours, and who might act as your servant.'

30. 'The Popular Antiquities', p. 161.

31. Couch, 'Folklore', p. 397: 'This creed has received so many additions and modifications at one time, and has suffered so many abstractions at another, that it is impossible to make any arrangement of our fairies into classes. "The elves of hills, brooks, standing lakes and groves" are all now confounded under the generic name *pisky*.'

32. Jenner, 'Piskies', p. 132.

33. William Bottrell, *Traditions and Hearthside Stories of West Cornwall* (1870–1880), I–III (the last volume entitled *Stories and Folklore of West Cornwall*), I, p. 42.

34. Bottrell, *Traditions*, II, pp. 138–39.

35. Ibid., III, pp. 245–46.

36. Ibid., I, p. 74

37. Ibid., I, p. 210.

38. Ibid., II, p. 291–92.

39. Hunt, *Popular Romances*, p. 3: 'Mr Botterell [sic] has, with much labour, supplied me with gleanings from his store, and his stories have been incorporated, in most cases, as he told them.' This is taken as being a reference to Hunt reading Bottrell's notes. We do not know though if Bottrell had any notes: it could easily be a reference to oral communications.

40. 'Six Notes on Cornish Changelings' forthcoming in the *Journal of the Royal Institution of Cornwall*.

41. Hunt, *Popular Romances*, p. 97. Does this 'confusion' come about because Hunt loyally recorded the narratives his sources gave him. Hunt took great pride in his editorial seriousness. Hunt, *Popular Romances*, pp. 16 and 31.

42. Evans-Wentz, *Fairy Faith*, pp. 170–85 sees a similar use of small people, going back to the early nineteenth-century. Note also Davies Gilbert *The parochial history of Cornwall, founded on the manuscript histories of Mr. Hals and Mr. Tonkin; with additions and various appendices* (London, 1838), I, p. 18: 'Mr. Hals here [on Treonike] relates a story of some child being missed by his parents and afterwards found; imputing the temporary loss to supernatural agency, perhaps of fairies, usually denominated in Cornwall The Small People, or Piskies'. Note that we will examine this episode in more detail in 'Six Notes on Cornish Changelings' forthcoming in the *Journal of the Royal Institution of Cornwall*.

43. Jenner, 'Introduction', p. 165. A lot would depend on comparative forms in the other Celtic languages.

44. Craig Weatherhill and Paul Devereux, *Myths and Legends of Cornwall* (Wilmslow, 1998), pp. 23–26. To the best of our knowledge Weatherhill and Devereux were the first to make this point.

45. Tregarthen, *Folklore*, p. 12.

46. Hunt, *Popular Romances*, p. 82.

47. See above note 24.

48. Jenner 'Introduction', p. 165: 'Bockle, which personally I have never heard used, suggests the Scottish bogle, and both may be diminutives of bucca, bog, bogie, or bug . . .'.

49. Hunt, *Popular Lore*, p. 347.

50. Bottrell, *Traditions*, I, p. 76.

51. Ibid., p. 142

52. Ibid., p. 143.

53. Interesting in this respect are the comments of Henry Maddern in Evans-Wentz, *Fairy Faith*, pp. 174–75: 'In this region there are two kinds of pixies, one purely a land-dwelling pixy and the other a pixy which dwells on the sea-strand between high and low water mark. . . . There was a very prevalent belief, when I was a boy, that this sea-strand piy, called Bucca, had to be propitiated by a *cast* (three) of fish, to ensure the fishermen having a good *shot* (catch) of fish.'

54. Hunt, *Popular Lore*, p. 82. Note also Briggs, *Dictionary*, p. 45.

55. For a good introduction Briggs, *Dictionary*, pp. 45–49.

56. Hunt, *Popular Romance*, pp. 168–69. A rare and early exception is in Couch 'The Popular Antiquities', p. 160, namely the 'domestic spirit . . . in the old manor house at Killigarth [in Polperro]'.

57. Lewis Spence, *The Fairy Tradition in Britain* (London, 1948), p. 34.

58. Bottrell, *Traditions*, III, pp. 92–93.

59. Courtney, *Feasts*, p. 123: note a more detailed description with several novel folklore perspectives can be found in Anon, 'Natural History and Antiquarian Society' *The Cornishman*, 17 November 1881, p. 7. The lecture was Lach-Szyrma, 'M. Sebillot's System', who had claimed, p. 136, that 'Brownies were friendly, but no belief in them now', a paraphrase of Hunt?

60. 'Introduction', p. 165.

61. *A description*, III, p. 22

62. The lines appear in *Britannia's Pastoral*, an unfinished work: see further William Browne, *The Poems of William Browne of Tavistock* (London, 1894), 2 vols, I, p. 294. We wonder whether Bray is correct to interpret this as a reference to local fairylore. It seems as likely to be Restoration fairy 'bumph'.

63. How might this have worked? We know from Bottrell that there was a ritual of banging pans at swarming bees: Bottrell, *Traditions*, III, pp. 92–93. If this had been associated with fairies in some way, the fairy expert might have remembered a passage in Bray about fairies and bees and 'Browne' and this last would have 'clicked' with the fairy word 'brownie'.

64. Thomas Keightley, *The Fairy Mythology: Illustrative of the romance and superstition of various countries* (1828), pp. 274–76, *inter alia*.

65. Harte, *Explore*, p. 4.

66. See note 24.

67. S.J. Vincent 'Old Moorland Philosopher', *Western Morning News*, 8 September 1934, 'The little invisible people known as pixies were supposed to be the spirits of persons who inhabited the moorland thousands of years before and who "though too good to be condemned to eternal punishment, were not good enough for the joys of heaven." Fifty years ago there were many respected old folk living on the vast Moor, and there may some now who believe still in ghosts, fairies, also "Jack o' lanterns", hovering round about the mineral lodes Was it not said that copper ore was discovered in the Caradon hills by seeing the small dancing lights known by old miners as Jack o' Lanterns'?

68. Lewis Spence, *British Fairy Origins* (Wellinborough, 1981).

69. Hunt, *Popular Romances*, p. 81.

70. Brought out very clearly in Anon, 'Penzance Natural History and Antiquarian Society: Folklore', 11 November 1853, pp. 6–7 (p. 6).

71. Hunt, *Popular Romances*, pp. 157–58.

72. Hunt, *Popular Romances*, pp. 114–19 and 120–26 and Bottrell, *Traditions*, II, pp. 173–85.

73. Attested in the late nineteenth century in 'Gleaner', 'Holsworthy: A Dovetailed Narrative', *Western Times*, 3 February 1882, p. 7; compare Theo Brown, 'Some Examples of Post-Reformation Folklore in Devon', *Folklore* 72 (1961), pp. 388–99 (p. 397).

74. J.A. McCulloch, *Medieval Faith and Fable* (London, 1932) has numerous examples of this in his chapters on demons (pp. 58–74) and the Virgin (pp. 102–19).

75. Peter M. Rojcewicz, 'Between One Eye Blink and the Next: Fairies, UFOs and Problems of Knowledge', *The Good People: New Fairylore Essays*, (ed.), Peter Narváez. (Lexington, 1997), 479–514.

10

'Where there were two Cornishmen there was a "rastle"'

Cornish Wrestling in Latin and North America

Mike Tripp

Introduction

During the second half of the nineteenth century, Cornwall experienced a catastrophic downturn in its economy, leading to a period of de-industrialization, which was precipitated by the collapse of the mining industry. Copper mining declined in the 1860s, culminating in the crash of 1866. Competition from producers such as the USA, Chile, Cuba and South Australia contributed to this decline, and to the consequent movement of investment to mining operations overseas.[1] Tin mining, which provided some respite through a minor boom in the early 1870s, was in decline by 1874. The demise of Cornish copper and the decline of tin mining, was accompanied by the ebb of mining-related engineering (in particular beam engine manufacturing), and was exacerbated by periods of general depression in the economy, including the agricultural crisis of the 1870s and the international downturn in the 1880s. This collapse, according to Philip Payton, 'created a profile of economic marginalisation which served to mark Cornwall off in a most striking way from the experience elsewhere in the United Kingdom.'[2]

One solution, especially for those with specialized skills no longer in high demand, was to leave Cornwall, to follow in the footsteps of those Cornish who in the first half of the nineteenth century had already made their way to distant corners of the earth. It has been estimated that approximately 230,000 people left the Cornwall for overseas destinations during the nineteenth century, which represented at least a third of the Cornish population,[3] and according to one observer Cornwall was 'probably an emigration region comparable with any in Europe'.[4] Wherever in the world they went, the Cornish clustered together in distinct ethnic communities, maintaining a strong sense of identity based on industrial pride and prowess. According to Ron James, the Cornish 'chose to perpetuate their ethnic character as an economic strategy to secure preferential employment in the mines'.[5] He suggests that, with their reputation as skilled hard-rock miners, the Cornish could 'profit by encouraging others to regard them as the best in their field'.[6] To be recognized easily, the Cornish nurtured their distinctive ethnic markers. The most obvious ethnic characteristics were Methodist chapels and choirs, brass bands, self-help societies, folklore, the Cornish dialect and surnames, the distinctive foods of pasties and saffron cake, and vocabulary, especially mining terms, as well as a strong and frequently voiced sense of separate identity.[7] To this list should be added Cornish wrestling, which was practised almost everywhere the Cornish went, especially in communities large enough to form a critical mass of wrestlers. Wrestling became an important signifier of 'Cornishness' throughout the diaspora. It was reputedly the Cornishman's favourite sport, and according to one observer, 'where there was a copper mine there was a Cornishman, where there was one Cornishman there was a cockfight, and where there were two Cornishmen there was a "rastle".'[8]

Given this proclivity for Cornish wrestling, it is surprising that there have been very few serious attempts to systematically record the history of the sport in the diaspora.[9] This article attempts to offer an at least partial corrective, detailing Cornish wrestling in Latin and North America during its nineteenth-century hey-day, and also fills a small gap in the sporting history of that continent. In a recent text tracing the development of sports history of the United States, Dyreson accepts that those working in the field have made much progress over the last thirty years. But he suggests that gaps in our knowledge remain, and insists that 'while new paradigms promise new insights, the older paradigms are hardly exhausted'.[10] That is the context for this investigation.

Cornish wrestling

The origins of Cornish wrestling are unknown, but what is certain is that it has existed for centuries. It is a form unique to Cornwall and is its oldest and longest surviving sport. By the beginning of the eighteenth century, wrestling was a widespread 'traditional' activity, deeply rooted in the local culture, and although 'there are few records available . . . there are sufficient to show that wrestling was still Cornwall's most popular sport'.[11] It reached the height of its popularity during the first half of the nineteenth century, with hundreds of participants competing for lucrative prizes at numerous tournaments, organized in the summer months throughout Cornwall, watched by thousands of spectators and widely reported in local newspapers.[12] It was also popular in London, where sporting entrepreneurs, usually publicans, organized and promoted wrestling in the Cornish style from the mid-1820s to the 1850s, when the best wrestlers were lured to the capital to perform for large prizes, witnessed by large crowds, which often included members of the nobility.[13]

The most distinctive features of Cornish wrestling are the absence of grappling on the ground (a feature of other styles) and the use of a short, loose, coarse canvas jacket on which all grips must be taken.[14] Victory is achieved when one wrestler 'backs' his opponent, which occurs when a wrestler throws his opponent onto his back so that at least three out of four 'pins' (i.e. shoulders and hips) touch the ground simultaneously. Prior to 1923, bouts lasted until the first back, however long that took, but today if no back occurs within a fixed time limit, the winner is decided on points, which are awarded to the wrestler who succeeds in throwing an opponent on to a pin or pins; one point for each pin down. All contests in Cornish wrestling take place on any piece of flat grass and are controlled by three 'sticklers' or judges, who ensure fair play between the wrestlers and decide which throws merit points, when a back occurs, or a foul has been committed.[15]

There were three types of Cornish wrestling prevalent during the nineteenth century, each of which was transported to the diaspora: informal matches, tournaments and challenge matches. Informal matches were arguably the most common and needed less space, time or participants than more formally organized events, and 'did not have to wait for holidays to be staged'.[16] They might have involved a father teaching his son the rudiments of the sport, or the settling of a grudge, or youngsters mimicking their elders. Tournaments, by contrast, were formally organized at major holidays, usually by a small committee of local 'gentlemen', often publicans, who collected subscriptions for prizes, chose a venue, advertised the event in the local press or on posters, appointed 'sticklers' from respectable persons present, and appointed 'matchers' to pair wrestlers according to ability and to ensure fair wrestling. In order to establish a winner, tournaments were arranged into several rounds; the first round, or 'single play' ended with 'standards' (or standing men), who had beaten two opponents outright, or had beaten one and had shown 'good play' (i.e. displayed a genuine attempt to throw an opponent) against a second. Further rounds ('double play', 'triple play', 'quadruple play', and so on) were held until the number of standing men equalled the number of prizes; the final round involved the settling of the prizes, the winner being the one wrestler not thrown. Challenge matches involved leading wrestlers of the day (or their representatives), challenging other wrestlers for lucrative prizes usually through the medium of local newspapers, and by so doing establishing a pecking order; as there was no such thing as an official 'championship' in the modern sense, the wrestler who was able to beat most, if not all of his adversaries, could claim to be 'champion'.[17]

Cornish wrestling in Latin America

According to Sharron Schwartz, early emigration to Latin America 'represents the first significant overseas migration flow of skilled Cornish labour, setting the trend for what was to become a global phenomenon'.[18] Cornish miners were recruited during the early 1820s on three-year contracts to work in the silver mines of Pachuca and Real del Monte, in the Mexican state of Hidalgo. These mines were backed by British investment and staffed by Cornish mine 'captains' (managers), engineers and foremen, who gave Cornish miners preferential treatment. This led to the creation of a large Cornish community by the 1830s, many of whom came from the Central Mining District of Camborne-Redruth-Gwennap, and which remained intact until the early twentieth century.[19] Cornish miners also emigrated during the 1820s to the Gongo Soco gold mine, 250 miles north of Rio de Janeiro in Brazil, where by 1843 there were 100 Europeans, mainly Cornish, living in the area. In the 1830s the gold mine of Morro Velho, 200 miles north of Rio de Janeiro, recruited Cornish miners, whose descendents were still resident in the area in the 1920s. Similarly, in the 1830s Cornish miners went to work in the Cobre copper mine in Cuba, but most had left by 1869, when the mine was abandoned. The Cornish were also found in Bolivia, Ecuador, Peru, and, most especially, in Chile.[20]

Cornish emigrants travelled to Latin America by ship, usually chartered by mining companies for the purpose. On one notable occasion the *Cambria*, bound for Tampico, a major port on the east coast of Mexico, went to the assistance of the *Kent*, an East Indiaman, which was engulfed by fire.[21] James Warren, a noted Cornish wrestler from Redruth, one of a group of miners recruited by the Anglo-Mexican Mining Company, played a prominent part in the rescue of survivors, by lifting them from the *Kent* lifeboats on to the deck of the *Cambria*.[22] According to one contemporary account, Warren forced the sailors of the *Kent* to return to their ship to help 'those whom they had left behind, and whom they were disposed to abandon; for which purpose he stationed himself in the gang way of the brig, and threatened to knock those overboard who refused'. As a result of his efforts he was so injured that he had to remain behind when the *Cambria* returned with the survivors of the *Kent* to Falmouth, 'it not being likely he would ever recover his former strength'.[23] However, within a few months he had clearly regained his powers, as he obtained a prize of six sovereigns by coming second in a tournament held at the *Eagle Tavern*, City Road, London, beaten by the celebrated Abraham

Cann, who was widely recognized at that time as one of the best wrestlers in Britain.[24]

Schwartz suggests that Cornish wrestling was never as popular in Latin America as it was in the USA or in South Australia, perhaps because many Cornish communities never reached the critical mass necessary to sustain regular tournaments, supported by local businessmen and watched by several hundred spectators. However, she did note that the miners at Morro Velho in Brazil held an annual tea treat and festival on St John the Baptist's Day at Midsummer (24 June), and that there were Cornish wrestling competitions throughout the 1850s and 1860s. By the turn of the twentieth century, however, the British leisure pursuits of cricket, football and rugby had replaced wrestling in the Cornishmen's affections, at least in Latin America. At Pachuca the favourite sport among the Cornish appeared to be cricket. But they also had the distinction of starting the first football club in Mexico, the Pachuca Athletic Club, which at its foundation was comprised entirely of Cornish from the surrounding mines.[25]

The most notable Cornish wrestling match held in Latin America took place at the Invicito Theater, Mexico City, on the hot, sultry evening of the 13 June 1892, between 'Professor' Willie, a teacher of wrestling from San Francisco, and Richard 'Schiller' Williams of St Day, 'a well-known athlete, who has on several occasions figured prominently in the wrestling matches of his native county.'[26] Several months earlier, in Pachuca, a Frenchman named Pardo, who was travelling with an American circus, issued a challenge to wrestle all comers, which 'Schiller' Williams accepted. Williams beat Pardo with so much ease that it persuaded those Americans who had witnessed the match to entice 'Professor' Willie to Mexico City, with a prize of $250 and half the entrance fees. The winner would be the first to obtain three falls following two rounds in the Cornish style, two in Graeco-Roman and if all square after that there would be a toss of a coin to decide the style in a fifth round. Willie accepted the chance of a large purse 'seeing it as a chance to redeem the honour of his fellow Americans and establish himself as the undoubted champion of America, and now Mexico'.[27] Betting was firmly in favour of the American, partly due to his reputation, based on his recent defeats of a giant Japanese wrestler and Tom Cannon, the former champion of America, but also as he had a more athletic appearance, being six feet tall and weighing 176 pounds. Williams was under five feet six inches and only 144 pounds.[28] The match was witnessed by Americans, curious local Mexicans, and hundreds of Cornish immigrants, many of whom had travelled by train for a full day from all over Mexico and from mining camps in the USA, drawn by 'the first exposition of the "manly art" in Mexico'.[29] Williams won the first round in the Cornish style, Willie won the second in the Graeco-Roman style and Williams won the third and fourth rounds in the Cornish and Graeco-

Roman styles respectively; 'the Cornishman thus winning the match amidst intense excitement'.[30]

'Schiller' Williams' curious name was acquired some years earlier, when, returning to Cornwall from Pennsylvania, the ship in which he was travelling, the *S.S. Schiller*, out of New York and bound for Hamburg via Plymouth, was wrecked the rocks off the Scilly Isles at 10.00 p.m. on 7 May 1875. Williams was washed overboard in heavy seas and dense fog, and following two and half hours in the water was eventually rescued, one of only forty-three survivors from a total of 355 passengers and crew. His survival was attributed to his strength and athleticism, and from this point on, he carried the moniker of 'Schiller'. On his return to Chacewater, his home at the time, a local poet hawked the following composition around the village:

> How many Cornish were on board:
> Their names we cannot gather,
> But Richard Williams has been saved,
> And his home is at Chacewater.[31]

It appears that 'Schiller' Williams led a life full of incident. In 1882 he travelled from Swansea to Chile in the barquentine, *Leon Christabel*. After fifty-three days at sea, the cargo of coal ignited and, although the ship was eventually wrecked near the Falkland Islands, Williams was able to continue his voyage to Valparaiso in a German vessel that was in the vicinity. His eventual return to Cornwall took more than five months, and it was assumed by his relatives and friends that the vessel he was travelling in had sunk. In 1890 he went to the goldfields of South Africa and in 1892 was in Mexico.[32]

Cornish wrestling in the USA

The first movement of Cornish emigrants in large numbers to North America was from 1832, when many emigrated to the lead mines of Wisconsin and by 1850 there was a significant Cornish community of 9,000 people living in Mineral Point.[33] The Cornish also helped to develop the 'Lakes' region of upper Michigan, especially the Keweenaw peninsula, following a 'copper rush' between 1843 and 1844.[34] In 1849 the Californian 'gold rush' drew Cornish miners not only from Cornwall but also from Wisconsin and Michigan, and they soon formed significant communities at Grass Valley, California, where gold was discovered in 1850, and at nearby Nevada City.[35] During the 1850s emigration continued to expand, those miners who spread across the USA, following mineral discoveries from one state to the next. During the 1850s Cornish emigrants moved to North Carolina; in the 1860s they were found in Utah, Colorado, Montana and Nevada; in the 1870s it was New Mexico; and in the 1880s Arizona became a popular destination. Between 1830 and 1900 the USA was the favoured destination for Cornish emigrants, who were attracted by higher wages, many employment opportunities, and the fact it was an English-speaking country.[36] By 1900 the Cornish were found working in almost every American state where there was mining or quarrying activity,[37] and wherever they settled they stuck together 'behaving as a distinct ethnic group'.[38] By 1900 they were 55 per cent of the population of Wolverine, Michigan, over 60 per cent of the population of Grass Valley, and reputedly 98 per cent of the population of New Almaden, California.[39] The USA was so popular and familiar with the Cornish that it became known as 'the parish next door.'[40]

One of the earliest, and possibly most prominent, places to stage Cornish wrestling tournaments in the USA was Grass Valley. Tournaments were similar to those 'back home' in Cornwall in that they were organized formally by a small committee of local businessmen, and they followed a format similar to that described above. The facilities provided for the wrestling were quite elaborate. In 1859, for example, a tournament was held in the rear of Samuel Hodges' brewery, on the corner of Main and Church Streets, and was restricted to Cornishmen, although in later years the competition was opened up to anyone interested in wrestling, irrespective of their ethnicity. The ring was sixty feet square, and in the middle of the arena were wooden boards covered in straw in order to make a relatively soft landing for wrestlers when thrown. Soft green turf would have been preferable but there seemed to be a lack of it in mining towns, and most outdoor surfaces would have been made very hard by the dry and hot conditions. In later years the surface of the rings were strewn with sawdust, which was softer than straw. Around the ring on all sides, there were seats for over 800 spectators, who were protected from the hot, strong sunlight by a light canvas, similar to a tent, while they watched up to forty individual matches, which lasted all day and evening. The tournament was organized by a committee, and the bouts were controlled by three sticklers, who decided on fair back falls.[41]

It seems that by 1862 Cornish wrestling tournaments in Grass Valley were being hosted by William and Elizabeth Mitchell, who bought the Wisconsin Hotel in that year. The building was situated on Stewart Street near Main and stood there for about eighty years, and was described by John Rowe as probably the most Cornish spot in the USA.[42] The wrestling ring, which was capable of accommodating 600 spectators, was located just outside the rear door of the hotel and so convenient for the bar, where the owners no doubt recouped their expenses for hosting the tournament and made a profit. In 1873 'Mitchell, Dawes and Co.' are described as the 'proprietors of the arena,'[43] in 1879 it is 'Hammil, Oates and Co.,'[44] in the following year 'Jas Gluyas,

Richards, Hosking and Co.' appear to be in charge, and by 1882 'Mitchell, Dawes and Co.'[45] are again the proprietors. Presumably these names refer to the various committees that promoted the wrestling. The Mitchell family eventually sold the property to Standard Oil, and the building was demolished in 1931 to make way for a gas station.[46]

For the following four decades, Cornish wrestling tournaments at Grass Valley were a regular feature of the sporting calendar as part of the Fourth of July celebrations. The *Grass Valley Daily Union* commented that, 'we believe that Grass Valley is the only place in the State at which this wrestling is celebrated annually, and so much of an institution has it become that the quartz mills and mines shut down for a week to give the Cornish miners opportunity to attend'.[47] Consequently, large numbers of competitors were attracted to Grass Valley, not only from California but also from other states. For example, in 1870 forty-six men, 'mainly Cornish miners', entered the first round, or 'single play' wrestling for six prizes;[48] in 1876 forty-eight men entered the first round, with twenty-four qualifying as standards;[49] and in 1888 the tournament was still attracting forty-eight men.[50] In order to ensure enough time was allowed for all the bouts to be satisfactorily completed, given that they lasted until the first 'back' occurred with no time limits, tournaments were spread over three days, usually starting on the Fourth (unless that coincided with a Sunday) and continuing for the following two days.[51] Even then, wrestling often concluded late on the third day. For example, in 1882 the *Grass Valley Daily Union* reported that 'the wrestling was so generally well contested that the shades of night were falling before the matches were finally concluded and the award of prizes made'.[52] On one occasion in 1884, rain forced the organizers of the Cornish wrestling tournament in Grass Valley to postpone proceedings on the second day, a Saturday, and to reconvene on the following Monday in order to finish all the bouts. It was so well attended on the first two days that the organizers felt it necessary to announce that, 'an extra train will be run [on Monday] from Nevada City on that day, leaving at 1.30 p.m., for the accommodation of all who wish to attend the amusement'.[53]

An important feature of the tournaments at Grass Valley was that promoters insisted that the rules of Cornish wrestling should be strictly adhered to, which meant that the Devonshire style of wrestling, involving kicking and the wearing of a heavy shoe, was censured. For example, in a preview of a Cornish wrestling tournament in 1859, the *Sacramento Daily Union* announced that, 'all Boots and Shoes to be taken off, and no kicking above the knees.'[54] One of the major attractions of the Fourth of July Cornish wrestling tournaments at Grass Valley was the lucrative prizes on offer, which were inevitably paid in gold coin. During the period from 1860 to 1900, it was rare for the total prize money to be less than $200 or the first prize to be less than $100. For example, in 1868 the tournament began on the Fourth and continued on the sixth and seventh of July, with a total prize money of $300.[55] In 1874, the tournament was held on the fourth and seventh of July, which Richard Andrews won the first prize of $100, William Nankervis was second with $70 and Joseph Coombs was third with $50. Consolation prizes of $40, $25 and $10 were awarded to Charles Temby, William Henry Mitchell and Samuel Nankervis for their commendable play.[56] The tournament with the largest total of prize money was in 1863, when $440 was awarded, which included $175 for first place, $100 for second, $75 for third, $50 for fourth, $25 for fifth and $15 for sixth.[57] In order to recoup some of their expenses for staging tournaments, including raising money for prizes, promoters charged spectators entrance fees. For example, in 1865 spectators of the Grass Valley tournament were charged 50 cents admission to the arena.[58]

Towards the end of the nineteenth century, Labor Day, held on the first Monday in September, replaced the Fourth of July as the occasion for Cornish wrestling tournaments in Grass Valley. Labor Day had become a federal holiday in the mid-1890s, and was now celebrated by most Americans as the symbolic end of summer. For example, in September 1911, with all business premises and mines closed, the third annual Labor Day picnic was held at Glenbrook Park, under the auspices of the Surface Workers' Union of Grass Valley and the Nevada City Miners' Union, and the Cornish wrestling tournament 'provided one of the most exciting of the day's diversions'.[59] In September 1921 the Labor Day wrestling, staged in Olympia Park, 'held under the auspices of the Mine Workers' Protective League, drew a monster attendance and it is estimated that fully 2,000 people, men, women, and children, visited the grounds during the day and evening'.[60] In September 1925 the Labor Day picnic was again held in Olympia Park and '[a]s in previous years, the biggest event of the day was the Cornish and catch-as-catch-can wrestling'.[61] Mann suggested that the 'size and organization of these gatherings [Cornish picnic and games] signalled the importance of the Cornish group in the community'.[62]

Although Grass Valley was possibly the most prominent venue in the USA for Cornish wrestling tournaments during the second half of the nineteenth century, it was not the only location. At the neighbouring mining town of Nevada City, a wrestling tournament was held in 1861, and the first prize of the champion's belt of the State of California and $275 was won by Thomas Eudy, formerly of St Austell, Cornwall. The second prize of $75 was won by Thomas Michell of Gwinear, and the third of $50 by Richard Edwards of Redruth. A Cornish newspaper of the time observed that, '[t]hus Cornishmen uphold the fame of their native county for wrestling, when they emigrate to distant lands'.[63]

Tournaments were also held at Brownsville, Colorado where there 'took place on a memorable evening in August 1877 one of the longest wrestling bouts ever recorded, when George Wedge and John Hall fought each other over a distance of four hours and eleven minutes'.[64] In 1864 a tournament took place at Virginia City, Nevada, the site of the famous 'Comstock Lode' silver strike.[65] In 1881 Bodie, California, a short-lived mining boom town, was the venue.[66] In 1888 a group of six wrestlers representing the Grass Valley Athletic Club travelled to San Francisco to compete against the Olympic Club of the latter city in a Cornish wrestling tournament; the top three prizes of $50, $30 and $20 were eventually won by those from the former club.[67]

In his study of Salt Lake City, Utah, McCormick noted that although the primary sport in the area was baseball, there were also cricket, lacrosse, track and field athletics and special events including a 'Grand English and Cornish Wrestling Tournament' during the Fourth of July celebrations of 1884, held in Washington Square, which from the 1870s was the city's main sports grounds. The tournament was organized by John Bastian and was limited to forty-eight wrestlers, who fought for the lucrative first prize of $150.[68] The *Salt Lake Herald* announced that it was 'a new and novel entertainment for this place, and on which has never failed to bring liberal patronage and enthusiastic attendance, at other places where such tournaments have been held'.[69] However, the anticipated large crowds did not materialize, as the same paper later reported that there was only a 'medium-sized audience assembled to witness the wrestling' and opined that Mr Bastian deserved 'a better patronage for the expense he has been to'.[70]

The Montana newspapers also gave considerable coverage to wrestling matches, especially in Butte City. For example, in 1882 the 'Annual Wrestling Match in Cornish Style' took place over three days between the 24 and 26 May, with $200 in prizes.[71] The wrestling arena was covered in sawdust, the Miners' Union Band was in attendance, and there was an admission charge of $1 for the spectators. A journalist who was present reported that, '[n]o one who has attended the three days' sport on the grounds south of East Park Street can fail to be particularly impressed with at least one unusual feature, and that is the general good humour and fairness of the contestants'.[72] Another major holiday in Butte City that featured Cornish wrestling was the 13 June, or the Miners' Union Day, which was held continuously from 1878 to 1914 and then resumed in 1934. The ballad *One Miners' Union Day* by Joe Duffy describes the holiday held at Columbia Gardens, which includes the following fourth verse. What is remarkable here is the juxtaposition of typically Irish and Cornish (and Scandinavian) surnames, an indication perhaps of ethnic rivalry as well as the willingness of the Cornish to open wrestling competitions to other groups:

The Sullivans and Harringtons, the Murphys and Malones,
Richards, Williams, Thomases, Trevithick and Treglowns—
Take-a-hitch [wrestle] and Six-year-itch, Olson, Johnson and Thor
Were the names of some contestants when they had the tug-o'-war.[73]

In 1916 the *West Briton*, starved of wrestling news in Cornwall due to the cancellation of the sport during the First World War, reported a tournament held at the Lake Avoca Grounds, Butte City, for the championship of Montana. The wrestling was organized by the Butte Cornish Association before 3,000 people, and a 'remarkable feature of the tournament was that all the prizes went to Cornish china clay workers, natives of the same locality—Old Pound, Whitemoor and Foxhole'.[74]

Cornish wrestling tournaments were also held in Michigan. For example, in 1870, there was Cornish-style wrestling advertised for the 2 and 4 July at Portage Lake on the Keweenaw Peninsula, by Bastian and Company of the *Red Jacket*;[75] on the Fourth of July 1875 there was wrestling at Negaunee, northern Michigan, which attracted over sixty contestants, although limited to men from Marquette County, and witnessed by 500 spectators; and there were also over sixty wrestlers reported at the same place in June 1882.[76] The *Mining Journal* of Marquette carried the obituary of one John Rowe, who was brought to the USA by his parents when he was five, later becoming the Sheriff of Gogebic County, City Marshall of Bessemer, and in 1910 the undefeated 'world champion' of Cornish-style wrestling.[77] By the beginning of the twentieth century, the locus of Cornish wrestling tournaments in the USA appears to have shifted to Michigan. In fact, in 1902 an editorial in one newspaper, in anticipation of Cornish wrestling tournaments in the Upper Peninsula in the summer of that year, felt able to announce that the sport 'is peculiar to that part of Michigan and to Montana,' and that the 'Lake Superior copper district has turned out the best Cornish wrestlers in the world'.[78] Calumet and Houghton both became centres for tournaments in Michigan. For example, in 1903 a two day tournament at Houghton was billed as the 'biggest of its kind ever pulled off in this country,' with 'nearly one hundred jacket and mat artists being entered,' for $500 of prizes.[79]

The acknowledged skill of the Cornish hard-rock miners, their clannishness and the favouritism by shown Cornish mine 'captains' in allocating employment to their own kind, sometimes sparked resentment among their fellow workers. The antagonism between the Cornish and the Irish in particular, often expressed in violence, was a constant feature of life on the American mining frontier.[80] The Cornish and Irish often competed in wrestling tournaments against each other, as noted above, which not only '[gave] the event[s] a sense of international conflict,'[81] but also served to increase tension. For example, in 1866 Joseph Lawrence, who was reported as half Cornish and half Irish, won first prize at the annual Fourth of July wrestling tournament at Grass Valley, 'and this is said to have greatly exasperated the Cornish, who were chagrined that a half-Cornishman should be declared champion of their favourite game'.[82] Lawrence was later convicted of second-degree murder.[83]

There were also other ethnic groups that competed in Cornish wrestling tournaments; for example, Jaouen notes that a Breton wrestler named Guyader was champion in the Grass Valley tournament each year between 1893 and 1895.[84] Breton wrestling shared many features in common with its Cornish counterpart, and Guyader's performance at Grass Valley anticipated the later Breton-Cornish wrestling contacts of the twentieth century. Additionally, French-Canadian lumbermen living in upper Michigan learnt to wrestle from the Cornish with whom they worked. As one of them remarked: 'I was always fascinated in seeing those wrestling matches with the participants barefooted and using duck jackets; and if the wrestlers were paired off at equal size the Cornish always won'.[85]

Cornish miners at Butte City were often perceived as lazy because of their acknowledged skill they often avoided doing simple, menial tasks, a prejudice encapsulated in the following poem by Walt Holliday, entitled, *That's Different*:

> He can take an eighty penny spike
> And bend it in his hand—
> The strongest little Cousin Jack
> That ever struck the land.
>
> Though when it comes to loading rock,
> He will not do it—nay;
> He wouldn't load a car of ore
> Not in a twelve-hour day.
>
> In wrestling down upon the mat,
> This Cousin's the best bet;
> But the fellow who can make him work
> Has not seen daylight yet.[86]

Challenge matches were also a feature of wrestling in the USA, and were prevalent from the mid-nineteenth century, although they increased in number from the mid-1880s onwards at the expense of tournaments, which experienced a concomitant decline in popularity. Challenge matches were more appealing largely because they only lasted for part of a day and were therefore less time-consuming for spectators than a two or three day tournament. They were also more attractive to wrestlers as the winner received all the stakes, rather than a fraction of prize money on offer at tournaments.[87] There are many instances when wrestlers challenged each other in the Cornish style for substantial stakes; for example, at the conclusion of the annual Grass Valley Fourth of July tournament in 1867, the winner of the fourth prize, William Reynolds, challenged the winner of the first prize to wrestle the best of three fair back falls in the Cornish style, for a prize of $300 a side.[88] Six years later in 1873 many Cornish miners had moved from Grass Valley to work at the famous Comstock Lode, Nevada, among them William Reynolds. The *Grass Valley Daily Union* remarked that, 'the boys on the Comstock had better not tackle him in a Cornish wrestle.'[89] In 1876 Joe Williams from Grass Valley accepted the challenge from Alf Williams, a 'Comstocker' from Virginia City, who was described as the champion of the Gold Hill Camp in Nevada. The match was staged in the Alhambra Theater, Virginia City for a prize of $250 a side in the Cornish style and the best of three fair back falls. Joe Williams, who at the time was 50 years old, five feet four inches tall and weighed 133 pounds, easily beat his opponent, who was half his age at 25, five feet five inches tall and weighed 144 pounds. It appears Joe had a good record, having beaten the champion of England in the previous year and thrown only once in thirty-nine years,[90] which led Rowe to describe him as probably 'the greatest of the Cornish wrestlers in America'.[91] During the 1880s James Pascoe from Arizona became a successful wrestler in the Cornish style winning many challenge matches; for example, in January 1881, in Bodie, California, he defeated Rod McInnis, a Scot, for a prize of $250 a side 'and all the gate money'. Although Pascoe won, his opponent broke his collarbone in the last fall.[92] A few months later McInnis had sufficiently recovered to meet Pascoe in a return match, again in Bodie, but this time the match lasted for five hours with no falls and the referee decided to declare it a draw.[93]

Another feature of challenge matches was that it became common practice for wrestlers to demonstrate their skill by wrestling in a number of different styles, although Cornish wrestling was almost always included. For example, in 1883 James Pascoe fought Jes Farnsworth from Bodie in the San Francisco Union Hall in the best of three styles of wrestling—Cornish, catch-as-catch-can and Greco-Roman—for $500 a side and the entire gate receipts. The *Sacramento Daily Union* reported that the match finished acrimoniously with no clear winner.[94] In 1887 James Seymour fought Gage in Grass Valley in the best of three styles, collar-and-elbow, Cornish and side hold for a prize of $100. The *Sacramento Daily Union* noted that not only was Gage 35 pounds heavier and two inches taller than the other man, but also that 'all who were there were satisfied of the genuineness of the match'.[95] In 1902 the so-called 'Professor M.J. Dwyer' met Frank Gehle at Jacques' Auditorium, Waterbury, Connecticut in three styles, Cornish, Greco-Roman and catch-as-catch-can for 50 per cent of the gross receipts and a side bet of $100 each. In a preview of the match, the *Bridgeport Herald* commented that the Cornish style was new to the state of Connecticut, 'though in the west, where both Dwyer and Gehle have wrestled, it is a favourite style'. The editor also felt it necessary to provide a brief explanation of the rules of Cornish wrestling for his readers.[96]

One man in particular was renowned for challenge matches, the Cornish-American, Jack Carkeek. He was the son of Tom Carkeek (or Karkeet), originally from Redruth, Cornwall, who was himself a proficient wrestler being at one time the champion of Lake Superior, Michigan. Between 1877, when Jack Carkeek first made an appearance in a wrestling ring at the age of sixteen, and May 1887 he appeared in thirty-two matches and tournaments and was only defeated on two occasions; on 25 April 1885 against Tom Cannon at San Francisco, in a match of six styles; and on 2 January 1887 against G.P. Donner, at Hurly, Wisconsin. It appears that prior to 1882 Carkeek only wrestled in ordinary tournaments in Michigan, where he worked as a miner, and the western states of Wisconsin, Iowa and Montana, but after this date he seems to have concentrated on challenge matches for lucrative money prizes, in a variety of styles, although his reputation was based on his skill as a Cornish wrestler. For example, in December 1884 he defeated James Pascoe, the champion Cornish wrestler of the Pacific Coast, for $500 in Butte City; in February of the following year he defeated H.C. Bell of Darlington, Wisconsin for $500 a side in the Cornish style; in July 1886 he defeated the Japanese wrestler Sorakichi Matsuda in less than one hour at Dodgeville, Wisconsin, in both Graeco-Roman and catch-as-catch-can styles.[97]

During the late 1880s Carkeek wrestled in a series of challenge matches in Cornwall, which became mired in controversy amid claims of 'faggoting', the practice of wrestlers agreeing to share prize money with opponents. Prior to his match against John Pearce in July 1887 at Redruth, a letter appeared in a local newspaper claiming the result had been previously arranged by agreeing to two falls each and to share the gate money, which the writer felt should 'be strongly deprecated, but in such a match as this it would be a lasting disgrace to both men, and would assuredly give rise to much unpleasantness'. In the event the match ended 'in a most disgraceful and degrading manner' when, following a dispute, Pearce left the ring and refused to re-enter, leaving the referee no option but to declare it undecided, with the *West Briton* declaring that '[w]restling in Cornwall will for ever from this time be regarded with more than usual suspicion'.[98] There was also an unsatisfactory ending to Carkeek's match against Philip Hancock a month later, when after an equal number of falls, the latter left the ring claiming he had injured his shoulder, but refused to allow a doctor to examine him, thus arousing the suspicion of the spectators who thought it 'was a "sell", got up with no other object than that of making money and duping the public'.[99] In 1888 the *Daily Alta California* reported that Carkeek had been arrested in Chicago 'for having swindled a man out of several hundred dollars by means of a "fake" contest'.[100]

At the beginning of the twentieth century, Carkeek toured the British provincial and London music halls, giving wrestling exhibitions and challenging all-comers and was one of a handful of talented wrestlers who were responsible for starting the boom in music-hall wrestling before the First World War. In 1904 he was hired by Harry Rickards, a theatrical entrepreneur from Sydney, Australia, to repeat his performances in his theatres. Carkeek travelled to Australia with two 'stooges' and when he challenged all-comers he had men planted in the audiences, which led to charges of deception.[101]

'Faggoting' was the scourge of Cornish wrestling in Cornwall, and was one contributory factor in the decline of the sport towards the end of the nineteenth century.[102] It was also a problem in the USA and promoters found it necessary to warn competitors against the practice; for example, in 1874 the *Grass Valley Daily Union* announced that, 'the rules will be strictly enforced, and any two or more men agreeing to throw off a wrestle, or make any other agreement as regards a fall, will be barred from the ring'.[103] The vigilance of the promoters appears to have been effective as the same paper reported, in relation to a tournament in 1877, that the wrestling 'was the best that has ever been held here . . . every one who went into the contest went there to win; there was not a single match thrown off '.[104]

Decline of Cornish wrestling in the USA

After the First World War, Cornish wrestling struggled for survival, although there were challenge matches and tournaments in the 1920s. For example, in 1925 there was a tournament at Iron Mountain, in the Upper Peninsula region of Michigan, as part of the Sons of St George celebrations.[105] However, by the 1930s the sport had virtually disappeared from the USA, although there was an unsuccessful attempt to revive it. In August 1934, the committee of the third annual Cornish picnic at Electric Park, Houghton announced they had raised an estimated $100 towards cash prizes which they hoped would stimulate interest in a Cornish wrestling tournament for their 1935 event, but nothing came of it.[106] Cornish wrestling was still in evidence in Central City, Colorado in the 1950s, although by then it was dying as a spectacle.[107]

Cornish wrestling eventually disappeared from the USA for three main reasons. Firstly, there was a gradual decrease in the number of participants, which was clearly indicated by the gradual disappearance of competitors with recognizably Cornish names. Those who had chosen to permanently settle in the USA and who had been nurtured in the sport in Cornwall, had either grown too old to compete or had died. The next generation was less interested, as it became more fully assimilated into American culture, preferring home-grown sports such as baseball, basketball and bowling. Philip Payton has suggested that another possible factor was the emergence of drilling competitions, which were far more inclusive as they allowed all ethnic groups to compete on equal terms.[108] Secondly, the boom and bust nature of the mining industry led inevitably to the fragmentation of Cornish emigrant communities as hard-rock miners, the very men who entered tournaments or challenge matches, left to find work elsewhere, especially South Africa, which led to the gradual decline of Cornish emigration to the USA. Thirdly, Cornish wrestling became less popular with participants and spectators alike as other styles grew in popularity, especially catch-as-catch-can, which was faster, involved grappling on the ground and was perceived as more exciting. It later developed into freestyle which was, with Greco-Roman, one of two styles adopted for inclusion in the Olympic Games, and an important precursor in the development of professional wrestling.[109] Therefore, Cornish wrestling gradually became redundant as a style in the USA.

Revival of Cornish wrestling in the USA?

In July 2009, at the nineteenth annual Gathering of the California Cornish Cousins, which also hosted the North American Gathering of Cornish Cousins, there was a demonstration of Cornish wrestling by members of the Nevada Union High School wrestling team in Memorial Park, Grass Valley.[110] A decade earlier, in July 1999, at the tenth North American Gathering of Cornish Cousins, Arnie Weeks, a Cornish-Canadian from Ontario, organized a demonstration of Cornish wrestling in Weona Park, Pen Argyl, Pennsylvania by forty wrestlers from two local high schools.[111]

The 'emergence' of Cornish wrestling in the late twentieth and early twenty-first centuries in the USA exemplifies a resurgence of interest in Cornish identity, both inside and outside of Cornwall, which has been evident since the 1970s. Other manifestations of this resurgence includes such things as a renewed sense of Cornishness; a growth of interest in genealogy and family history; the formation of numerous Cornish Associations, such as the Cornish American Heritage Society founded in 1982; the holding of an annual Cornish Festival in Mineral Point, Wisconsin; and the annual celebration of St Piran's Day by the inhabitants of Grass Valley in recognition of the area's Cornish heritage. Although the demonstrations of Cornish wrestling aroused some interest, there is little evidence to show there is a real appetite in the USA for sustained participation in the sport. It is, therefore, likely to remain as one aspect of a 'revived' Cornish identity, brought out for demonstration purposes on special occasions, but unlikely to re-enter popular sporting culture.

Cornish wrestling in Canada

In a study of emigration to Canada in the first half of the nineteenth century, Margaret James-Korany estimated that between 1831 and 1860, at least 42,000 emigrants left Cornwall for Upper Canada, although it was not possible to be more precise as the Cornish were not listed in the 'Blue Books' as a separate ethnic group, nor could the numbers who used the route to slip into the USA be calculated.[112] Cornish emigration to Upper Canada in significant numbers started in the 1820s, but petered out in the late 1850s. However, by then the gold fields of British Columbia had become a popular destination for hard-rock miners, until the start of the twentieth century. In the 1840s Cornish miners had also migrated to the iron mines on the shores of Lake Huron.[113]

There is evidence of Cornish wrestling tournaments in British Columbia. For example, in December 1864, as part of the Christmas festivities a tournament was held, 'between Cornish, Devonshire and Lancashire men at the Royal Hotel tap on Johnson last evening . . . each fought according to own custom'. The *Daily British Colonist* also reported that Cornishmen won the first three prizes; Jessie Pierce, John Bryant and Manwell; Eli Quick from Lancashire was fourth.[114] In 1901 the local mines were closed for the Labor Day celebrations in Greenwood, British Columbia, which included Cornish wrestling and drilling contests and 'the miners furnished the life of the proceedings'.[115] In 1903, as part of the Christmas Sports at Roseland, a challenge match was held between John Tippett and Billy Dunstan, both miners from Cornwall, for £200 a side, with John Roberts, also from Cornwall acting as stakeholder.[116]

Wherever Cornish migrants went they rarely lost touch with Cornwall, but divided their attachments between their host communities and their native towns and villages, thereby creating dense transnational migration networks. Cornish migrants stayed in contact with friends and relatives in Cornwall through newspapers, letters, financial and social remittances, and the formation of Cornish societies in host communities. Contact with Cornwall was also maintained by the constant flow of migrants to and from Cornwall, which included Cornish wrestlers.[117] One of these was James Triggs, born in Helston, West Cornwall in 1873, who at the age of seventeen migrated to the USA in 1890 to work in the iron mines of Michigan. Whilst there he entered Cornish wrestling tournaments and was quite successful. In about 1900 he returned to Cornwall, becoming heavyweight champion in 1904. At some point thereafter, he travelled to South Africa, and in 1905 he defeated both Neilson, the champion of Australia, and Phil Mitchell the champion of South Africa, at the Stars and Stripes Hotel, Fordsburg, a suburb of Johannesburg, for a prize of £100. As a result of these two wins, his victory in Cornwall and his previous success against the American champion, a local South African newspaper proclaimed him the, 'champion of the four countries in the style of Cornish wrestling'.[118] In about 1907, Triggs returned to the USA, but following the First World War was back in Cornwall, becoming a founder member of the Cornwall County Wrestling Association in 1923.[119] A man of many parts, he was also reputed to have owned a mine in South Africa[120] and a saloon in Marquette, Michigan, as well as being a member of several mining syndicates.[121]

Conclusion

The evidence presented in this article indicates that wherever the Cornish went in Latin and North America, they clustered in distinct ethnic communities, projecting a strong sense of ethno-occupational identity inextricably entwined with hard-rock mining. Cornish wrestling played a small but significant role in this process, especially in the USA. The characteristics of the sport, whether it was a tournament or a challenge match, were broadly similar to those 'back home' in Cornwall. Competitions took place during the major holiday periods, which for tournaments often lasted for more than one day. Matches were usually held on land adjacent to a bar or hotel, and were promoted by entrepreneurial individuals, especially prominent businessmen, who possessed the necessary resources to raise the prize money and saw the opportunity to make a profit from a holiday crowd, which in some cases could be sizable. The prizes offered at tournaments were large enough to attract large entries, and the stakes laid down at challenge matches were substantial. Successful wrestlers were provided with the opportunity to gain a measure of prestige by becoming a 'champion' of their community or district.

There was also a number of notable differences between the manner in which Cornish wrestling was practised in Latin and North America, compared with 'back home' in Cornwall. Firstly, although tournaments in the USA and Canada may have occurred at different locations on the same day, they tended to be annual events, held (for example) on the Fourth of July or Labor Day, whereas in Cornwall they were often arranged on a weekly basis throughout the summer months, habitually coinciding with feast days. Consequently, as there were fewer matches held in the USA and Canada, the prize money that was offered was substantially larger than that in Cornwall, mainly because it would have been easier to raise the funds for an annual event. Secondly, in the USA, towards the end of the nineteenth century tournaments were largely replaced by challenge matches featuring prominent wrestlers, whereas in Cornwall the reverse was the case; both existed in the nineteenth century, but challenge matches never gained the same prominence in Cornwall and virtually disappeared by 1914. Thirdly, towards the end of the nineteenth century, Cornish wrestling became marginalized in the USA, becoming merely one of several different styles in which wrestlers participated, whereas in Cornwall other styles never emerged to challenge Cornish dominance. Fourthly, in the diaspora the sport enabled different immigrant groups to express their rivalries, not least the competition between the Irish and the Cornish, which was rarely an issue in Cornwall. Lastly, although Cornish wrestling has died out completely in Latin and North America, it has managed to survive in Cornwall.

Despite thriving for a relatively short period of time, Cornish style wrestling—through the efforts of individuals such as Jack Carkeek—played a small but not insignificant role in laying the foundations for the future of wrestling as a popular sport, especially the professional variety in the USA which developed apace in the second half of the twentieth century. Additionally, Cornish wrestling has re-emerged recently in North America as an icon of revived 'Cornishness', remembered fondly—and sometimes demonstrated enthusiastically—as an integral part of the continent's Cornish mining and cultural heritage.

Notes and references

1. See, for example, B. Deacon, *A Concise History of Cornwall* (Cardiff, 2007); P. Payton, *The Making of Modern Cornwall: Historical Experience and the Persistence of 'Difference'* (Redruth, 1992); P. Payton, *The Cornish Overseas* (Fowey, 1999); P. Payton, *Cornwall: A History* (Fowey, 2004).

2. Payton, *The Making of Modern Cornwall*, p. 107.

3. P. Payton, 'Cornish Emigration in Response to Changes in the International Copper Market in the 1860s' in P. Payton (ed.), *Cornish Studies: Three* (Exeter, 1995), pp. 60–82.

4. S. Schwartz, 'Cornish Migration Studies: An Epistemological and Paradigmatic Critique' in P. Payton (ed.), *Cornish Studies: Ten* (Exeter, 2002), p. 136, citing D. Baines, *Migration in a Mature Economy: Emigration and Internal Migration in England and Wales, 1861–1900* (Cambridge, 1985), p. 157.

5. R.M. James, 'Defining the Group: Nineteenth-Century Cornish on the North American Mining Frontier' in P. Payton (ed.), *Cornish Studies: Two* (Exeter, 1994), p. 32.

6. Ibid., p. 44.

7. Ibid.

8. *Barrier Miner*, 18 June 1904.

9. See, M. Tripp, 'The Persistence of Difference: A History of Cornish Wrestling', unpublished PhD thesis, University of Exeter, 2009; M. Tripp, 'Cornish Wrestling in Australia', *Sporting Traditions*, 28:1, (2011), pp. 21–37.

10. M. Dyreson, 'The United States of America' in S.W. Pope and J. Nauright (eds), *Routledge Companion to Sports History* (London, 2010).

11. H. Pascoe, 'Cornish Wrestling', *The Cornish Annual*, 1928, p. 64.
12. See, for example, *The West Briton and Cornwall Advertiser*, or *The Royal Cornwall Gazette* for this period.
13. See, for example, *Bell's Life in London*, 9 December 1827.
14. G. Jaouen and M.B. Nichols, *Celtic Wrestling The Jacket Styles: History of an Old Sport and Techniques of Cornu-Breton Wrestling* (Corsier-sur-Vevey, 2007).
15. Cornish Wrestling Association, 'The Rules of the Cornish Wrestling Association (as adopted at the 1994 AGM)', www.cornishwrestling.co.uk, accessed 15 December 2003.
16. J.G. Rule, 'The Labouring Miner in Cornwall c.1740–1870: A Study in Social History', unpublished PhD thesis, University of Warwick, 1971, p. 307.
17. Tripp, 'The Persistence of Difference'.
18. S. Schwartz, 'Migration Networks and the Transnationalization of Social Capital: Cornish Migration to Latin America, A Case Study' in P. Payton (ed.), *Cornish Studies: Thirteen* (Exeter, 2005), p. 267.
19. Payton, *The Cornish Overseas*.
20. S. Schwartz, 'Cornish Migration to Latin America: A Global and Transnational Perspective', unpublished PhD thesis, University of Exeter, 2003.
21. *West Briton*, 11 March 1825.
22. Ibid., 7 April 1826.
23. Ibid., 29 September 1826.
24. Ibid.
25. Schwartz, 'Migration Networks'.
26. *West Briton*, 14 July 1892.
27. M. Tangye, '"Schiller" Williams in Mexico', *Cornwall Today* 9, (1995), p. 39.
28. Ibid.
29. Ibid.
30. Ibid.
31. M. Tangye, 'The Wreck of the S.S. Schiller, 1875, and its Aftermath', *Cornwall Today* 8, (1995), p. 52.
32. Tangye, '"Schiller Williams"'.
33. G. Burke, 'The Cornish Diaspora of the Nineteenth Century' in S. Marks and P. Richardson (eds.), *International Labour Migration: Historical Perspectives*, (London, 1984), pp. 57–75.
34. Payton, *The Cornish Overseas*.
35. Payton, *Cornwall*.
36. Payton, *The Cornish Overseas*.
37. B. Deacon and S. Schwartz, 'Lives Across a Liquid Landscape: Cornish Migration and the Transatlantic World', Paper presented to the British World Conference, Auckland, New Zealand, 2005, p. 231 www.projects.exeter.ac.uk/documents, accessed 28 January 2011.
38. Ibid., p. 231.
39. Ibid.
40. Schwartz, 'Cornish Migration Studies', p. 143.
41. L.M.G. Rowe, 'Cornish Wrestling in Nevada County', *Nevada County Historical Society* 23:4 (1969), pp. 1–6.
42. Ibid.
43. *Grass Valley Daily Union*, 8 July 1873.

44. Ibid., 4 July 1879.

45. Ibid., 4 July 1882.

46. Rowe, 'Cornish Wrestling', www.theunion.com/article/20060309, accessed 29 May 2009.

47. *Grass Valley Daily Union*, 9 July 1868.

48. *Daily Alta California*, 9 July 1870.

49. *Grass Valley Daily Union*, 7 July 1876.

50. *Daily Alta California*, 8 July 1888.

51. *Grass Valley Daily Union*, 7 July 1876.

52. Ibid., 8 July 1882.

53. Ibid., 6 July 1884.

54. *Sacramento Daily Union*, 7 November 1859.

55. *Grass Valley Daily Union*, 9 July 1868.

56. Ibid., 9 July 1874.

57. Ibid., 16 June 1863.

58. Ibid., 6 July 1865

59. J. Rowe, *The Hard Rock Men: Cornish Immigrants and the North American Mining Frontier* (St Austell, 2004), citing the *Morning Union*, 5 September 1911.

60. Rowe, *The Hard Rock Men*, citing the *Morning Union*, 6 September 1921.

61. Ibid., citing the *Morning Union*, 2 September 1925.

62. R. Mann, 'The decade after the Gold Rush: Social Structure in Grass Valley and Nevada City', *The Pacific Historical Review* 41:4 (1972), p. 496.

63. *West Briton*, 15 November 1861.

64. Rowe, *The Hard Rock Men*, p. 178.

65. *Daily Alta California*, 15 June 1864.

66. *Sacramento Daily Union*, 11 May 1881.

67. Ibid., 1 April 1888.

68. J.S. McCormick, *The Gathering Place: An Illustrated History of Salt Lake City* (Salt Lake City, 2000).

69. *Salt Lake Herald*, 5 June 1884.

70. Ibid., 8 July 1884.

71. *Butte Daily Miner*, 16 May 1882.

72. Ibid., 27 May 1882.

73. W.D. Hand, 'The Folklore, Customs and Traditions of the Butte Miner', *California Folklore Quarterly* 5:2 (1946), p. 170.

74. *West Briton*, 24 August 1916.

75. Jaouen and Nichols, 'Celtic Wrestling', citing the *Portage Lake Mining Gazette*, 23 June 1870.

76. Rowe, *The Hard Rock Men*.

77. A.C. Todd, *The Cornish Miner in America: The Contribution to the Mining History of the US by Emigrant Cornish Miners—The Men Called Cousin Jack* (Truro, 1967), citing *The Mining Journal*, 2 April 1958.

78. *Minneapolis Journal*, 19 July 1902.

79. *Daily Journal*, 3 July 1903.

80. R.E. Lingenfelter, *The Hardrock Miners: A History of the Mining Labor Movement in the American West 1863–1893* (Berkeley, 1974).

81. James, 'Defining the Group', p. 37.

82. *Sacramento Daily Union*, 11 January 1868.

83. Ibid.
84. Jaouen and Nichols, *Celtic Wrestling*.
85. Todd, *The Cornish Miner*, p. 141.
86. Hand, 'The Folklore', p. 175 (footnote 54).
87. Tripp, 'The Persistence of Difference'.
88. *Grass Valley Daily Union*, 9 July 1867.
89. Todd, *The Cornish Miner*, p. 72, citing the *Grass Valley Daily Union*.
90. *Sacramento Daily Union*, 12 August 1876, citing the *Virginia Chronicle*, 8 August 1876.
91. Rowe, *The Hard Rock Men*, p. 274
92. *Sacramento Daily Union*, 14 January 1881.
93. Ibid., 11 May 1881.
94. Ibid., 1 September 1883.
95. Ibid., 21 March 1887.
96. *Bridgeport Herald*, 16 February 1902.
97. *West Briton*, 27 June 1887.
98. Ibid.
99. *West Briton*, 14 July 1887.
100. *Daily Alta California*, 5 November 1888.
101. Tripp, 'Cornish Wrestling in Australia'.
102. Ibid.
103. *Grass Valley Daily Union*, 3 July 1874.
104. Ibid., 8 July 1877.
105. *Bessemer Herald*, 31 July 1925.
106. Ibid., 10 August 1934.
107. Personal correspondence with Alison M. Wrynn, Professor and Associate Chair, California State University, Long Beach.
108. Personal correspondence with Philip Payton.
109. J. Arlott (ed.), *Oxford Companion to Sports and Games* (Oxford, 1976).
110. Personal correspondence with Gage Mckinney, January 2013.
111. Personal correspondence with Tommi O'Hagan, on behalf of the Cornish American Heritage Society, January 2012.
112. M. James-Korany, '"Blue Books" as sources for Cornish emigration history' in P. Payton (ed.), *Cornish Studies: One* (Exeter, 1993), pp. 31–45.
113. Payton, *Cornwall*.
114. Ibid. citing the *Daily British Colonist*, 28 December 1864.
115. *The Spokesman Review*, 4 September 1901.
116. M. Tangye, 'Sportsmen Cousin Jacks', *Cornwall Today* 2:2 (1995).
117. S. Schwartz, 'Bridging "The Great Divide": Cornish Labour Migration to America and the Evolution of Transnational Identity', paper presented at the *Race, Ethnicity and Migration: The United States in a Global Context Conference*, University of Minnesota, Minneapolis, 16–18 November 2000.
118. Jaouen and Nichols, *Celtic Wrestling*, p. 37
119. *West Briton*, 3 July 1924.
120. Ibid., 25 June 1925.
121. Ibid., 8 July 1926.

11

'The imprint of what-has-been'

Arthur Quiller-Couch, Daphne du Maurier and the writing of *Castle Dor*

Kirsty Bunting

Introduction

The year 2012 marked the fiftieth anniversary of the publication of Sir Arthur Quiller-Couch and Daphne du Maurier's *Castle Dor* (1962), an intricately plotted novel on the themes of time slippage, posthumous possession, inter-textuality and intersubjectivity. The story of the novel's production mirrors its complex plotting. Arthur Quiller-Couch began work on *Castle Dor* in the 1920s, yet it was still unfinished at his death in 1944. Daphne du Maurier was given the manuscript by his daughter Foy, and she completed and published the novel in 1962.

This article investigates the reasons why the novel received faint praise from reviewers in the 1960s and remains on the fringes of the du Maurier canon today, often overlooked by readers and critics despite the authors' continued celebrity, the plot's inventiveness and the insight the work offers into du Maurier and Quiller-Couch's shared love of Cornish landscape, heritage and myth making. This study argues that this neglect can be attributed to two factors: the first is the twentieth century's uneasy relationship with posthumous collaborations in fiction; the second is du Maurier's strategy of attempting to pre-emptively dispel this unease by exploiting readerly interest in the joint-authorship to her advantage. It was her intention to generate intrigue and ensure sales by, variously: inscribing the work with evidence of its double-handedness, giving insights into the collaborative method, and playing with notions of singularity and multiplicity in plotting and narrative. This study asks whether these strategies actually backfired, amplifying the unsettling effects of reading texts completed posthumously by a surviving author. It also asks what this strategic writing can tell us about du Maurier's troubled relationship with posthumous collaboration before examining what the recent critical and reception history of *Castle Dor* reveals about this century's attitude to such works.

Reading collaboration and the problem of posthumous completion of another's work *Castle Dor*'s neglect is not unusual: the literary results of collaborative endeavour have traditionally been overlooked in the projects of canonization and scholarly survey. Various critics have already explored and theorized the marginal status of collaborators (or of writing produced in collaboration) including Holly Laird, Wayne Koestenbaum, Jack Stillinger, Bette London, Marjorie Stone and Judith Thompson.[1] This article follows on from the groundwork laid by such critics. They have demonstrated that co-authorship has typically been received as, at best, a literary gimmick or a detective game of attribution resulting in readerly attempts at separating the work's individual hands or, at worst, collaboration was considered something less than true authorship, as though multiple voices result in the text's authority and integrity being compromised or diluted, rendering it imperfect, uncanny or even sordid and improper. Despite the profusion of collaboratively produced texts in the nineteenth and early twentieth centuries, their places in the literary tradition are yet undermined by the prevailing appeal of the uncomplicatedly solitary author-genius. This study argues that *posthumously* co-authored works were, and perhaps still are, received as *doubly* marginal and problematical.

It is evident that du Maurier understood the precarious position of *Castle Dor*. She accompanied its publication in 1962 with an article for the *Daily Telegraph* in which she revealed her conflicted feelings about her task, in particular musing on the status of the surviving, completing author.[2] She stated, '[t]he idea that one author can finish the work of another—and that other dead for many years—still seems to me presumptuous, and a bare-faced intrusion upon the silence of the grave'.[3] She states that attempting to imitate the dead author's style amounts to an act of 'pure bravado' akin to 'robbing the dead'.[4] Quiller-Couch himself had faced similar anxieties when he reluctantly completed the recently deceased Robert Louis Stevenson's novel *St. Ives: Being the Adventures of a French Prisoner in England* (1897).[5] A contemporaneous review entitled 'Stevenson's last legacy' in the *Illustrated London News* states: 'Mr Quiller-Couch was commissioned to take the pen that Stevenson might have held. He was brave enough to take it, to face the inevitable comparison in his disfavour and the inevitable allusion to his temerity'.[6] Although this reviewer found the novel satisfactory, it begins to establish the argument that the completing author of a posthumous novel has traditionally been viewed as audacious, and their posthumous literary venture brave or foolhardy.[7]

A periodical review of 1925 (this is around the time Quiller-Couch was laying aside *Castle Dor*, never to return to it) helps to further delineate twentieth-century attitudes to posthumous collaboration. Although the author discusses Joseph Conrad's unfinished novel, the fittingly named *Suspense*, it is clear that his assertions on the undesirability of posthumous completion apply to *all* unfinished literary works. It reads:

> There is something at once tragic and intriguing about a posthumous fragment of narrative from a famous pen. Personal regret, or disappointment that his work is left incomplete, is tempered by the thought that it provides an endless source of mental exercise, in the shape of the ever-fresh but ever-insolvable problem—how would it have developed, and what would have been the ending? [. . .] Nobody could even faintly guess how the story would have ended. [. . .] It is better that he did not give any outline, which he [a potential second author] might be tempted to fill in. As it is, I think there is little danger of such a proceeding, which is one devoutly to be deprecated.[8]

This pinpoints the chief difficulty for readers of posthumous collaborations: how to reconcile the feeling that the 'finished' book remains incomplete, compromised or subject to a curious split authorial subjectivity. There is an insurmountable feeling that an outline of the original book existed in full in the first author's imagination, now lost, the reader of the posthumously completed book experiences a mere impoverished and unsatisfactory 'alternative' ending sadly dissociated from its origins. These works take their place on the margins of each author's canon and in the far reaches of the literary canon. Why then did du Maurier take on this role? Her biographer Margaret Forster explains:

> In the circumstances, her great need was to plunge into another novel and for it to be a success in the old style; instead, she took on the task of completing *Castle Dor*, one of Sir Arthur Quiller-Couch's unfinished novels. Foy, her great friend, suggested it and, because she longed to be working on something and was honoured by the suggestion, she agreed. In many ways, though she did it well, and it gave her a real interest at a low point, it was a mistake. She worried terribly about how well she was doing it. [Du Maurier remarked]: 'it would be awful if they [. . .] said I had ruined his beautiful style'. It also tired her when she was feeling 'rather off'[. . .] struggling to match Q.'s fine English when she got home was not the best way to lift her spirits.[9]

Having begun to examine critical responses to posthumous collaboration in the twentieth century, we can now begin to understand du Maurier's anxieties and her authorial strategies in *Castle Dor*. Before outlining the ways in which du Maurier inscribed *Castle Dor* with an awareness of its double-handedness, a brief précis of the novel's plot is necessary. The action begins in the early 1840s with the birth of Linnet Lewarne and follows her adulterous relationship with French runaway Amyot Trestane. The plotting reworks strands of early Arthurian tradition as the narrative's temporal framework is fractured by flashbacks to a parallel romance between the mythical lovers Tristan and Iseult. Early medieval Tristan legends tell the story of the secret trysts between the married Queen Iseult and Tristan and the tragic events that follow the discovery of their affair by King Mark.[10] *Castle Dor* redoubles the potential for tragedy and romance as Linnet and Amyot find themselves 'mixed up in a tragedy of some thirteen hundred years ago' retracing the steps of Tristan and Iseult around the ancient earthworks of Cornwall's Castle Dor, reputed to be the hall of the sixth century Cornish chieftain Mark. The two couples' lives and love stories become so intertwined that by the story's conclusion Linnet feels unconsciously compelled to repeat Iseult's actions of centuries earlier and Amyot has become entirely immersed in the sensory experiences of his legendary counterpart Tristan. Linnet's physician, Doctor Carfax, with the help of one of his patients engages in researching the Cornish settings of the Tristan myths in an attempt to understand these ancient echoes:

His industrious patient [. . .] had drawn up a *résumé* of every known legend that had any bearing on the strange history of Tristan and Iseult, and the pattern of events, curiously intermingled as they were, followed a course uncannily similar to that which was happening on the same terrain today. Thought transference seemed the only possible explanation [. . .] the impressionable lad from Brittany and the impulsive young woman born at Castle Dor, had acted as mediums to a source of power which, if tapped, might revolutionize the whole conception of time in relation to the unconscious mind.[11]

Just as the two authors wrote about the overpowering possession of Amyot and Linnet by the mystic Arthurian forces which control them, the reader is invited to imagine *du Maurier's* autonomy and literary agency being overpowered by the posthumous influence of her old friend and mentor Quiller-Couch. Du Maurier achieves this by developing the theme of the palimpsestic nature of place, existence and personal experience which Quiller-Couch outlines in his opening passages in which he describes all that the ancient earthworks of Castle Dor have witnessed: 'memories [. . .] quarrel, ancient feud, litigation [. . .] All England is a palimpsest of such, scored over with writ of hate and love, begettings of children beneath the hazels, betrayals, appeals, curses, concealed travails'.[12] In so doing, Quiller-Couch creates an imaginative space in which the fixedness of the present can be elided in brief, ecstatic moments of connectedness to a remote past. The novel develops around this idea of residual historical memories having the ability to subvert linear temporal logic. It is at Castle Dor that the real historical Tristan and Iseult have 'escaped dimensions, to be universal; and yet just here—here, waiting' for Amyot and Linnet to encounter them.[13] Avril Horner and Sue Zlosnik's *Daphne du Maurier: Writing, Identity and the Gothic Imagination* explains, 'this concept of the palimpsestic nature of place would seem to underlie the appeal of Cornwall to du Maurier's imagination, deconstructing as it does the place/time binary'.[14] Du Maurier's memoir of her early years *Myself when Young* (first published in 1977 under the title *Growing Pains: The Shaping of a Writer*) demonstrates that she shared Quiller-Couch's investment in a palimpsestic sense of continuity, especially in significant places. In a passage notably similar to Quiller-Couch's opening passages of *Castle Dor*, quoted above, du Maurier explains her understanding of place, memory and return:

> Who can ever affirm, or deny, that the houses which have sheltered us as children, or as adults, and our predecessors too, do not have embedded in their walls, one with dust and cobwebs, one with the overlay of fresh wallpaper and paint, the imprint of what-has-been, the suffering, the joy? We are all ghosts of yesterday, and the phantom of tomorrow awaits us alike in sunshine or in shadow, dimly perceived at times, never entirely lost.[15]

Du Maurier develops this deconstructed imaginative space to intriguing effect in *Castle Dor* by hinting at a paratextual subplot in which she experiences a curious 'possession', akin to automatic writing, under the haunting influence of Quiller-Couch.

The influence of the man du Maurier described as her 'un-crowned king of Fowey, the famous Q', over her early career is well documented.[16] She often acknowledged how her reading diet had consisted chiefly of his works and that she had borrowed some of his ideas and imaginative constructions, including using the title of his short story *Frenchman's Creek* for her novel of 1941. Yet, du Maurier develops this commonplace type of literary influence in her writings about the completion of *Castle Dor* until Quiller-Couch is presented as a benign fortean presence with du Maurier as the mere conduit for his story. In her introduction to the 1979 edition of the novel she claimed that, 'by thinking back to conversations long forgotten' from 'happy evenings long ago when "Q" was host at Sunday supper' she found that she could take up the pen and 'fall into his mood' and 'recapture' and channel his literary voice.[17] Writing of *Castle Dor*, Raymond H. Thompson states, 'The love story gains its power from its sense of inevitability, of characters swept forward by emotions they cannot control'.[18] Just as the characters are haunted by the fatalistic sense of existing within the grooves of a narrative written down long ago in a barely accessible but curiously familiar past, du Maurier tells her readers that *she too* is 'swept forward' under the controlling influence of a deceased Other, her mentor 'Q'. *Castle Dor*'s Dr Carfax worries that when bringing Linette into the world, 'He [had] breathed into her his own sense of haunting tragedy, dooming her to unwilling repetition of a story that was not hers', whilst Amyot is described as being an 'unwilling participant in a struggle he did not understand'.[19] The performance of authorial unwillingness is a vital part of du Maurier's narrative strategy—she paints herself as the reticent and anxious surviving author, only half-conscious of the posthumous forces at work upon her. Just as du Maurier can 'fall into' the Quiller-Couch 'mood', Amyot can 'recapture' his historical counterpart Tristan: 'He hovered now in strange and sickening fashion on the threshold of another world. Whatever he said or did in the present time would only be repetition of a day gone by, and anyone who listened to his voice calling in the darkness would hear it as the voice of another, dead these thirteen hundred years'.[20] In making connections between the haunting of Amyot and Linette and the haunting of *Castle Dor* by the spectral Quiller-Couch, du Maurier asserts that the posthumous collaboration was no mere tribute or imitation but a kind of automatic writing in which the authors achieved the ultimate, ecstatic and perfect collaborative union with no fractures or deficit. In doing so, du Maurier is not only generating readerly intrigue and ensuring sales but also attempting to pre-empt accusations of collaborative imperfection, poor imitation or simply, failure in her task.

Du Maurier and *Castle Dor*'s publisher, J.M. Dent and Sons, revelled in the strange fact of the story's posthumous completion, inviting readers to share in the reading experience as literary 'detectives' looking for authorial liminality. This invitation extends from their advertising strategies to the novel's front matter. In fact, in her preface to the novel, Foy Quiller-Couch issues a challenge directly to the reader. She states, 'so cleverly has she woven her work into his, that I defy anyone to discover where the shuttle passed from his hand into hers'.[21]

My own research began in the Quiller-Couch archives of Trinity College Library, Oxford.[22] Here lies Quiller-Couch's contribution to *Castle Dor* and the answer to Foy's challenge. Quiller-Couch's half of the manuscript leaves off at chapter twenty-four. In the completed novel as it was first published in 1962, with Quiller-Couch's original chapter divisions reorganized, Du Maurier picks up the narrative at chapter nineteen, entitled 'An Encounter at Penquite'. As I have already stated, there was no concealment of the posthumous co-authorship; yet absolute secrecy was maintained about this moment of 'hand-over'. I argue that this is a deliberate marketing strategy. In keeping this secret, readers and critics are compelled to search for changes in tone, style or language; because surely no two authors could write so alike that their hands could really be indistinguishable? The clues, and some authorial 'red herrings', are scattered throughout the novel as it obliquely comments on its own creation and on its secret of 'who held the pen, and when?' These are most evident in its treatment of acts of investigation and the themes of writing and over-writing which can be read as a series of palimpsestic puzzles with the aim of exciting readers' curiosity about the work's authorial strategies. The novel is replete with knowing references to broken, unfinished or intertwined narratives and posthumous reconnections. The character Ledru, like his inventor Quiller-Couch, had been researching the geographical backdrops of the Cornish Tristan myths. On the eve of his death, Ledru comments that 'it is a curious coincidence that no poet, or shall we call him investigator, has ever lived to conclude this particular story. His work has always been finished by another'.[23] His acquaintance, Carfax, inherits Ledru's notes and takes up the dead man's quest. It is significant that, although these few lines fall within the first half of the novel, they are *not* evident in Quiller-Couch's manuscript; therefore these lines must be some of the very few inserted into his prose by du Maurier. Perhaps she hoped the reader (who at least knew that Quiller-Couch provided the early chapters) would think Quiller-Couch himself had experienced the uncanny prescience that he too would not live to complete the novel, thus inscribing the pages of *Castle Dor* with an atmosphere of personal tragedy and uncanny inevitability which parallels the fatalism of the Tristan story. Repeatedly, Du Maurier blurs the boundaries between the 'original' myth, *Castle Dor*'s plotting and the facts of the novel's authorship.

This is not the end of her playful narrative strategies. She concludes the novel with an 'epilogue' which takes the form of a poem, according to the narrator written by 'A local poet—a native of Troy who died young [and] left an imperfect poem in manuscript'.[24] Here then is a metatext, another incomplete manuscript within a once incomplete novel, and another mystery. Are we to read du Maurier's vague attribution as another element in the authorship challenge? Readers will no doubt wish to discover who wrote this poem. Was it Quiller-Couch? Famously he also wrote poetry *and* he was a native of 'Troy' (the name he invented for his thinly disguised, half-fictionalized Fowey). Or could this poem be the work of his son Bevil Quiller-Couch who died in a flu epidemic in occupied Germany in 1919 when he was in his late twenties? He too wrote poetry. Could inclusion of this poem be du Maurier's tribute to his memory thus introducing a third authorial voice in the *Castle Dor* manuscripts? Or, is this a du Maurier poem written either by herself when young, or created sometime around the novel's 1962 publication? The readership is again left in the dark with only du Maurier's intriguing clues and their guesswork.[25]

Castle Dor's critical reception

The unique challenges posed by *Castle Dor* meant that many contemporaneous critics and reviewers' reactions to the novel were not positive. They felt acutely the ambiguous and mocking textual merger of identities described above. Perhaps this is partly because the undeclared 'take over' upset their critical confidence. How can the experienced reviewer demonstrate their attuned reading skills if they are in the dark about attribution, and what does it mean for their credibility and even their pride if they incorrectly apportion literary labour? Privately, du Maurier revelled in the palimpsestic puzzle of *Castle Dor*'s posthumous completion and the readerly compulsion to separate the individual hands. Sheila Hodges, herself a collaborator of du Maurier's in her capacity as her editor, writes: 'I was not involved in the editing [of *Castle Dor*], since it was not published by Gollancz. In the copy, which she sent me, she wrote, "Spot the 'take-over'—towards the end of a chapter, but which??" When I got it wrong she wrote "Hurrah!" on a postcard'.[26]

Du Maurier's friend and biographer Judith Cook writes, 'It has never been divulged who wrote what, but it would seem from the text that "Q's" involvement finished less than halfway through'.[27] This reader, knowing du Maurier's writing style intimately, believed she could detect the take-over, saying, 'For a little while Daphne struggles to maintain his style, but then gradually moves into her own'.[28] For Cook the text is rendered imperfect 'simply because she had to finish a story begun by somebody else'. She states, 'It would have been far more interesting if "Q" had finished it and she had written a version of her own'.[29] Cook was not alone in thinking that the division of labour would show itself in the imperfect adoption of, or differentiation from, the Quiller-Couch style. E.D. O'Brien's review for the *Illustrated London News* reads:

> In her introduction to the book, Miss Quiller-Couch says [. . .] 'I defy anyone to discover where the shuttle passed from his hand to hers.' I accept this challenge and suggest that the break comes at Chapter XI. Until this point, both the language and the story are highly individual. Sir Arthur, if indeed he wrote so much, has told his story of the beautiful wife of a Cornish inn-keeper, falling in love with a roving Breton, very much within his chosen setting of the 1840s, touching fairly lightly on the Tristan-Iseult theme. From this point, the theme takes charge—sadly, I believe to the detriment of the book as a novel. Every "t" has to be crossed and every "i" dotted until we are left with a string of puppets deafening us with their clever archaeology.[30]

In fact, the heavy investment in the 'Tristan-Iseult theme' is Quiller-Couch's doing. Why might the critic attribute fastidious triteness and investigative fervour to du Maurier? Perhaps this relates to a common criticism levelled at co-authored works which was voiced most succinctly by Brander Matthews (1852–1927), author, critic and organizer of the American Copyright League, who stated that the co-authored text was at risk of being 'overworked' by the multiple hands who in their 'untiring pursuit of the idea into the remote fastnesses' create an 'over-sharpness of outline'.[31]

Leo Alfred Duggan's review for the *Times Literary Supplement* (13 April 1962) is perhaps the most cutting of all, regretting that the book was ever completed:

> Miss [Foy] Quiller-Couch explains that her father began this novel in the early 1920s [. . .] He laid it aside unfinished believing that "it would never be good enough to publish." In 1959 Miss Daphne du Maurier completed it, by request. She has done her work most skillfully, style and treatment are uniform throughout [. . .]. The book must have been great fun to write. It is not so much fun to read, for Q chose to copy the style of a romantic Victorian library novel [the reviewer goes on to demonstrate their point by quoting examples of Quiller-Couch's more florid passages]. Sir Arthur was a sound judge of prose. His verdict of the 1920s [that the book should have been left unpublished] stands.[32]

So even as Duggan finds the work is *not* fractured by a difference in style (he claims not to be able to detect the 'take over'), the book is still little more than a 'fun' experiment. Again co-authorship is relegated to the margins of the literary marketplace as mere hobby-writing, an amusing exercise or literary gimmick. For O'Brien this book could be no more than, 'a remarkably brave experiment' and in Cook's opinion it is merely an 'interesting exercise' and 'something of a disappointment'.[33] The process of marginalization by critics continued even after the initial reviews of 1962 as later critics and biographers began to discuss the novel's mode of writing.

Margaret Forster mentions *Castle Dor* only three times in her biography of du Maurier. In the first instance, Forster describes her decision to finish Quiller-Couch's novel as a 'mistake' motivated by her desire to be the 'bread-winner' in the face of high taxes and the upkeep of her home and family. Later, she states that *Castle Dor* had not been financially rewarding.[34] The biographer A.L. Rowse discusses the creation of *Castle Dor* in his study of his friend and University mentor, *Quiller-Couch: A Portrait of 'Q'* (1988).[35] Rowse paints a picture of Quiller-Couch in the 1920s as suffering from a waning celebrity and an inability to complete his current work: 'Sad and discouraged—no one to come to his *Poetics* class now, his name no longer in the publishers lists of forthcoming books [. . .] he was not getting on with the two books on the stocks that remained unfinished. He never spoke to me about *Castle*

Dore [sic] but I used to urge him to get on with his autobiography'.[36] Rowse did not see *Castle Dor* as a vital or significant work, Quiller-Couch's last masterpiece. He believed that if Quiller-Couch wanted to secure a lasting reputation into the mid-twentieth century he would achieve this through life-writing and memoirs. Perhaps the author followed his friend's counsel, as he laid the novel aside soon after. Rowse goes on to recount how Foy Quiller-Couch broke the news to him that she had sent her father's unfinished novel to du Maurier. According to Rowse, she wrote, 'I fear your censure over this'.[37] When critiquing the finished book, Rowse claims it is *begun* 'beautifully' and 'attractively' but he remains silent over du Maurier's contribution.

Raymond H. Thompson's study of the novel assumes that this story was '[b]egun by Sir Arthur Quiller-Couch [. . . and] completed from his notes by Daphne du Maurier'.[38] Throughout my archival studies I found no evidence that du Maurier was working from any form of notes or an early Quiller-Couch draft or plot outline. Du Maurier confirms she inherited the complicated, incomplete story 'with nothing solved'.[39] So why does Thompson credit Quiller-Couch with overall creative control of the novel from its inception to its posthumous completion? This division of the collaborative partnership into a traditional gendered economy of artistic creativity recurs frequently in writing about dyadic collaborative endeavour; typically in this model one member of the partnership is credited with overall creative control, whilst the other takes the role of assistant or helpmeet. Perhaps Thompson was seduced by du Maurier's claims to be writing under the influence of Quiller-Couch to the extent that her literary agency seems negligible? In this instance is she a victim of the success of her own playful authorial constructions and her claim to be an indistinguishable conduit to Quiller-Couch?

The 'Cornishness' of the novel may also have added to its marginality. How can the mythical proportions of the romance of Tristan and Iseult be played out amongst the pubs, country lanes and ancient earthworks of 1840's Cornwall? Judith Cook worried that because Quiller-Couch had 'made his protagonists not King, Queen and Knight, but publican, Breton onion seller, and publican's wife' du Maurier found herself 'left with a story which lacked the grandeur of myth, and she seems to have found real difficulty in blending all the ingredients of the original legend into a cohesive whole'.[40] A reviewer for the *Times* (5 April 1962) found the novel to be marred by its 'quaint' Cornishness, as well as its posthumous completion, having been written from the Celtic margins of popular fiction. It reads:

> Miss Daphne du Maurier agrees that it was 'not in any way an outstanding work of literature', but found the quaint, old-fashioned tale growing on her. Other readers may share the experience. [. . .] The tragedy never seems excessively sad; concept and manner are too artificial for that. The

book's charm lies rather in the contented country ways of Dr. Carfax, in its evocation of warm country evenings beneath a Cornish moon, and the scent and feel of the Cornish woods, dear both to Quiller-Couch and to Miss du Maurier.[41]

So ends this article's survey of *Castle Dor*'s reception history. We can safely conclude that the novel was not well received by critics despite, or perhaps partly because of, du Maurier's efforts to generate intrigue about the posthumous collaboration. Perhaps emphasizing this aspect of its authorship was a dangerous and ultimately unsuccessful strategy, and yet it was a strategy supported by the publishers. The following analysis of their publication tactics also reveals much about contemporaneous attitudes to posthumous collaborations and how to deal with the 'problem' of selling them to readers of popular fiction.

Selling *Castle Dor*

Castle Dor's first edition's gaudy dust jacket is boldly headed 'Sir Arthur Quiller-Couch', below this is the novel's title, and below this appears 'Daphne Du Maurier'. This communicates that Quiller-Couch was the book's originator and therefore, primary author. The centenary celebrations of Quiller-Couch's birth followed hard upon the novel's publication (which saw public events such as the unveiling of a plaque in his memory), so giving top-billing to Quiller-Couch also capitalizes on the timeliness of the publication. Foy's concern that the manuscript be completed may have been prompted by an awareness of this upcoming anniversary and the necessity of a tribute and continuation of her father's name in the publishers' lists of the mid-twentieth century.

In 1962 *The Times* ran Dent and Sons' advertisements for the recently released novel, headed 'A New Romance of Old Cornwall'. Both authors' names are printed in bold but Quiller-Couch again heads the page. It continues, 'A tumultuous story left half finished by 'Q' and completed with consummate artistry by Daphne du Maurier at the suggestion of Q's daughter'.[42] This tells us much about Dent's publication strategy. It instantly draws the readers' attention to the fact of its posthumous completion in order to generate interest, yet it tempers the arousal of any suspicions as to its literary value by immediately reassuring Quiller-Couch fans that he contributed a substantial 'half' of the novel and that du Maurier had done her work well. Crucially, it tells us that du Maurier's input is authorized and validated by the Quiller-Couch family. The legitimacy of the text is further emphasized by the decision to publish the book not with du Maurier's usual publisher,

Gollancz, but with Quiller-Couch's old publisher. This reassurance continues on the novel's flyleaf which reminds readers that Foy felt justified in getting another author to finish her father's book, that she would even have had his blessing in this endeavor as we are reminded that he himself had provided the final installments of Stevenson's *St. Ives*. Therefore, any fears about the quality of the book, its authority or du Maurier's role as co-author are allayed and the reader is enticed purely by the excitement of the 'tumultuous' romance, the myths of 'Old Cornwall' and any pleasurable interest generated by the fact of the collaboration.[43]

Conversely, when the *Virago Modern Classics* du Maurier series published its edition of 2004 (the first new edition of the novel since 1979), Quiller-Couch's name was entirely absent from the cover, only the back material explains his role. Clearly, this is done to complement the rest of the series, all of which are du Maurier titles without bothersome collaborative partners to acknowledge, and the decision may have been taken in the light of Quiller-Couch's lack of currency with readers of popular fiction in the twenty-first century. I suggest the decision to downplay the co-authorship may also highlight the continuing uncomfortable relationship that readers and publishers have with posthumous collaboration and with collaboration in general.

Reading *Castle Dor* today

Only a handful of recent studies have discussed the novel and most of these have also focused on the reworking of the Tristan myth, such as Raymond H. Thompson's *The Return from Avalon: A Study of the Arthurian Legend in Modern Fiction* (1985). Thompson calls *Castle Dor* '[t]he finest modern transposition of the Tristan and Iseult story' (22).[44] Peter G. Christensen offers a study of du Maurier's interpretation of the various Tristan tales in his essay, 'Daphne Du Maurier and Arthur Quiller-Couch's *Castle Dor*: History, Romance, and Recurrence'.[45] He also explores the transmittance of ancient Cornish and Breton legends and identifies the two novelists' source materials. Christensen's study also remarks upon the critical neglect of *Castle Dor*. Christopher Pittard's '"We are seeing the past through the wrong end of the telescope": Time, Space and Psychogeography in *Castle Dor*' discusses du Maurier's treatment of spatial liminality, 'with particular reference to psychogeography, the study of the influence of place on emotion'.[46] Pittard's study broadens out to consider the novel's constructions of gender as well as the 'characterisation of du Maurier as an author of nostalgic genre romance, and aligns her with a more postmodernist strand of Cornish fiction'.[47] Therefore, *Castle Dor* has received some serious critical attention, and yet it is more often overlooked by critics. For example, Richard Kelly does not list *Castle Dor* in his bibliography of du Maurier's works (1987), Michael S. Batt's 'Tristan and Isolde in Modern Literature: *L'eternel retour*' (1995) makes no mention of it, whilst many other major works of du Maurier and Quiller-Couch criticism and biography are either silent on the work, underestimate its significance, or lament its mode of production.[48] Helen Taylor's 'Rebecca's Afterlives: Sequels and Other Echoes' in *The Daphne du Maurier Companion* (2007) describes du Maurier's completion of *Castle Dor* as fitting into a recent tradition of modern sequels, parallel texts and companion novels in which writers draw 'on one another's stories, themes and characters', to create a complementary work, explaining that this has become a 'cottage industry' in recent decades:

> There is a growing fashion for finishing the incomplete fragment. In 1980 Charlotte Bronte's unfinished story "Emma" was completed and published by "Another Lady"; this was followed by the critically acclaimed version by Clare Boylan, *Emma Brown* (2003). And Jill Paton Walsh solved Dorothy L. Sayer's 1930s unfinished Lord Peter Wimsey mystery, *Thrones, Dominations* (1998). Du Maurier herself had led the way by completing Arthur Quiller-Couch's fragment, *Castle Dor*.[49]

The term 'fragment' seems too insubstantial a word to describe Quiller-Couch's drafts of continuous prose in the completed nineteen chapters left to du Maurier. Again, the collaboration is reduced to an echo of what would have been a 'true' novel had Quiller-Couch completed it. It is aligned with novels written in imitation of, or homage to, an earlier author. As the twenty-first century progresses and Sir Arthur Quiller-Couch and Daphne du Maurier's places in the literary tradition shift, is *Castle Dor* to continue to be relegated to the realms of the literary curiosity, alongside fragments, tributes, and other exercises or experiments in writing, or is it now possible to read the novel as novel?

This study demonstrated how *Castle Dor* obliquely commented on its own creation (and on its secret of 'who held the pen and when?') through its treatment of its characters' acts of investigation and writing and moments of time-slippage and liminal identities. By asking how du Maurier and her publishers generated intrigue by challenging readers and critics to detective games of attribution, I have thrown new light upon the negative critical response of the 1960s and the marginalization of this text in both the Quiller-Couch and du Maurier canon. The novel interrogates fears about authority and identity in interesting ways. Du Maurier enjoyed playing with her readers' concerns that her own, or Quiller-Couch's, voice, imagination or identity were being over-written, complicated, diluted or altered. Both authors ask questions about the fixedness of identity: how can Linette and Amyot so easily merge with Tristan and Iseult, and how can two authors merge so completely that the joins are undetectable? Far from shying away from the problems of the posthumous completion of another author's text, du Maurier, stating that 'the challenge was too great to dismiss', has co-authored a book which anticipates the readers' anxious or unconvinced responses and attempts to redirect these into pleasurable reading experiences.

By acknowledging the transcendental nature of reading and writing du Maurier may have suggested ways in which we might find a richer, more authentic sense of her literary identity, and our own identities as readers. *Castle Dor*'s challenging and subversive authorial and narrative methodologies may help to teach twenty-first century readers and scholars how to listen to textual multiplicity, by which I mean all of the fractured 'voices' and residual influences which contribute to our reading and writing experiences. *Castle Dor* suggests ways we can read authority as multiple, shared, conflicted, ecstatic, or defiant *without anxiety* since it actually represents a more accurate model of literary authority than that of the solitary author, divinely inspired, composing entirely alone. My question remains: will collaboratively authored texts always be read primarily as bearing the marks of difference from authorship that claims to be the product of solitary writing and inspiration? Du Maurier finished the novel with the following lines: 'From the minstrels down, poet after poet, had attempted to explain the genesis of love and had failed; still it loomed larger through their failures, asserting itself through them to be greater than any man's telling'.[50] After fifty years of reading *Castle Dor* as primarily a posthumous collaboration, perhaps it is time to read it as an epic romance, greater than its mode of telling.

Notes and references

1. H.A. Laird, *Women Co-Authors* (Urbana: Illinois, 2000); W. Koestembaum, *Double Talk: The Erotics of Male Literary Collaboration* (London, 1989); J. Stillinger, *Multiple Authorship and the Myth of Solitary Genius* (Oxford, 1991); B. London, *Writing Double: Women's Literary Partnerships* (Ithaca, 1999); M. Stone and J. Thompson, *Literary Couplings: Writing Couples, Collaborators and the Construction of Authorship* (Wisconsin, 2006).
2. *Sunday Telegraph*, April 1962. Later re-published as the introduction to the novel's 1979 edition, from which I quote here.
3. D. du Maurier, 'Introduction' to *Castle Dor* (London, 1979), p. 8.
4. Ibid., p. 9.
5. R.L. Stevenson and A. Quiller-Couch. *St. Ives: The Adventures of a French Prisoner in England. Pall Mall Magazine*, Nov. 1896–Nov. 1897. (Repr. New York/ London: Scribner's (1897) and Heinemann (1898).
6. 'Stevenson's last legacy', in *Illustrated London News*, 16 October 1897, p. 536.
7. Other examples of posthumously completed novels from the late nineteenth and early twentieth centuries include: *Blind Love* (1890) begun by Wilkie Collins

and concluded by Walter Besant; and *The Old Man's Youth* (1921), begun by William de Morgan and finished by his wife.

8. C.B.E. 'Books of the Day', in *Illustrated London News*, 3 October 1925, p. 624.

9. M. Forster, *Daphne du Maurier* (London, 1993), p. 316.

10. Many twelfth and early-thirteenth-century versions of the tale survive, written by the Anglo-Norman poet Thomas of Britain, Béroul, Eilhart von Oberge and Gottifried von Strassburg. These have been translated, retold and adapted throughout the centuries including Malory's 'Tale of Sir Tristram de Lyones' in his *Morte d'Arthur* and the operatic retelling by Wagner. According to Edith Ditmas, 'Only in Beroul's poem does one feel that the lovers are moving against a real Cornish background', perhaps this is why the Beroul poem is favoured by *Castle Dor's* literary historian characters (E.M.R. Ditmas, *Tristan and Iseult in Cornwall* (Gloucester, 1970), p. 12.

11. Quiller-Couch and D. du Maurier, *Castle Dor* (London, 1962), p. 199.

12. Ibid., p. 5.

13. Ibid., p. 5.

14. A. Horner and S. Zlosnik, *Daphne du Maurier: Writing, Identity and the Gothic Imagination* (Hampshire, 1998), p. 68.

15. D. du Maurier, *Myself When Young: The Shaping of a Writer* (London, 2004), p. 46.

16. 'Home is where the heart is', *The Times*, 30 April 1977.

17. D. du Maurier, 'Introduction' to *Castle Dor* (London, 1979), p. 9.

18. R.H. Thompson, *The Return from Avalon: A Study of the Arthurian Legend in Modern Fiction* (Connecticut, 1985), p. 31.

19. A. Quiller-Couch and D. du Maurier, *Castle Dor* (London, 1962), p. 199.

20. Ibid., p. 232.

21. Ibid., p. vii.

22. Manuscript of Castle Dor and draft chapters', NRA 34684. *Arthur Thomas Quiller-Couch, Correspondence and Papers*. Special Collections, Trinity College, Oxford, Library.

23. Ibid., p. 70.

24. Ibid., p. 239.

25. Perhaps a reader of *Cornish Studies* will hold the answer to this puzzle?

26. S. Hodges, 'Editing Daphne du Maurier', in *The Daphne du Maurier Companion* (ed.) Helen Taylor (London, 2007), pp. 25–47 (p. 36).

27. J. Cook, *Daphne: Portrait of Daphne Du Maurier* (London, 1991), p. 240.

28. Ibid.

29. Ibid.

30. E.D. O'Brien, 'Review of Castle Dor', *Illustrated London News*, 14 April 1962, p. 598.

31. B. Matthews, 'The Art and Mystery of Collaboration', in *With my Friends: Tales Told in Partnership* (London, 1891), p. 14.

32. L.A. Duggan, 'Review of Castle Dor', *Times Literary Supplement* 3137, 13 April 1962, p. 245.

33. E.D. O'Brien, p. 598, J. Cook, p. 240.

34. M. Forster, *Daphne du Maurier* (London, 1993), pp. 316, 319.

35. A.L. Rowse, *Quiller-Couch: A Portrait of 'Q'* (London, 1988), p. 23.

36. Ibid., p. 221.

37. Ibid., p.190.

38. R.H. Thompson, *The Return from Avalon: A Study of the Arthurian Legend in Modern Fiction* (Connecticut, 1985), p. 22.

39. D. du Maurier, 'Introduction' *Castle Dor* (1979), p. 8.

40. J. Cook, *Daphne: Portrait of Daphne Du Maurier* (London, 1991), p. 240.

41. 'Review of Castle Dor', *The Times* 55358, 5 April 1962, p. 13.

42. 'Advertisement for Castle Dor', *The Times* 55364, 12 April 1962, p. 19.

43. When *Castle Dor* was read in installments on BBC radio throughout the summer of 1977 both authors were credited in the radio listings.

44. R.H. Thompson, *The Return from Avalon: A Study of the Arthurian Legend in Modern Fiction* (Connecticut, 1985), p. 42. Thompson also usefully links each character in *Castle Dor* to their legendary or Arthurian counterparts. These are: Amyot = Tristan; Linnet = Iseult; Linnet's husband, the innkeeper Mark Lewarne = the cuckold King Mark; Linnet's housekeeper and barmaid Deborah Brangwyn = Brangäne the handmaid who betrays Iseult; Farmer Bosanko = King Hoel of Brittany who shelters Tristan during his banishment; Farmer Bosanko's children Mary and Johnny = Iseult of the White Hands and Kaedin or Kahedin; Dr Carfax = Tristan's friend Dinas; Ned Varcoe, the hunchback bartender = the spying dwarf (Ibid., p. 22–23).

45. P.G. Christensen, 'Daphne Du Maurier and Arthur Quiller-Couch's *Castle Dor*: History, Romance, and Recurrence' in *Tristania* 22 (2003), pp. 67–84.

46. C. Pittard, '"We are seeing the past through the wrong end of the telescope": Time, Space and Psychogeography in Castle Dor' in *Women: A Cultural Review* 20:1 (2009), pp. 57–73 (p. 58).

47. Ibid. p. 58.

48. R. Kelly, *Daphne du Maurier* (Boston, 1987); M.S. Batt, 'Tristan and Isolde in Modern Literature: L'eternel retour', in *Tristan and Isolde: A Casebook* (ed.) Joan Trasker Grimbert (New York, 1995), pp. 505–20.

49. H. Taylor, 'Rebecca's Afterlives: Sequels and Other Echoes', in *The Daphne du Maurier Companion* (ed.) Helen Taylor (London, 2007), pp. 75–92 (p. 76).

50. A. Quiller-Couch and D. du Maurier, *Castle Dor* (London, 1962), p. 242.

12

The 'Happy Chance' of Jack Clemo

Luke Thompson

En una noche oscura,
Con ansias, en amores inflamada
¡oh dichos aventura! . . .

(St John of the Cross)

Introduction

Jack Clemo (1916–1994) was a poet, novelist, autobiographer and short-story writer born on Goonamarris Slip near St Stephen-in-Brannel. He was the only surviving child of his war-widowed mother Eveline, who gave birth to Jack in the little clay-miner's cottage where he would live for nearly seventy years. Clemo left school at twelve, improbably determining to become a writer. His first significant success came with the novel *Wilding Graft* (1948), which he swiftly followed up with an autobiography, *Confession of a Rebel* (1949), and a collection of poems, *The Clay Verge* (1951). His religious convictions were best described in *The Invading Gospel* (1958), in which he claims to have been influenced by Karl Barth's type of 'neo-Calvinism', Charles Spurgeon, sex-mysticism, and 'American Hot Gospel'. Clemo's writing often explores ideas of election and predestation, and he seems to have believed that the Arminian idea of human redemption by means of our freedom to follow or to disregard Christ's salvation could be reconciled with the Calvinistic idea of predestined election.[1] That is to say, that freedom and predestination are compatible concepts in Clemo's theology. He shared his interests in predestination and fate with many of his favourite writers, such as T.F. Powys and Thomas Hardy, though it was chiefly his reading of Spurgeon in the 1930s and Barth in the 1940s that informed his own conclusions. Clemo never read beyond the beginning of Barth's enormous *Church Dogmatics*, but he found great inspiration in some of the shorter works, such as *Dogmatics in Outline* and Barth's essay in *Natural Theology*, as well as his celebrated *Epistle to the Romans*. Clemo was influenced equally by Spurgeon's *Sermons*. It is because of the influence of Spurgeon and Barth that Clemo so often called himself a Calvinist, though he would sometimes modify this to 'neo-Calvinism', by which he meant 'the positive side of Calvin's teaching without the negative distortions of Puritanism'.[2]

Clemo's diverse sources of inspiration led him to use the word 'pre-destination' in more than one way. On the one hand the term is used in the sense of predestination for election, which is the sense Barth and Spurgeon wrote about. On the other hand it is used to imply a divine plan or intention, God's methodology, a sense of which was always a part of Clemo's instincts[3] and was artistically supported by the novelistic structures of Hardy and Powys. Attention to this idea of predestination seems incompatible with the other idea, and Clemo's use of it in his early diaries sometimes appears to have more in common with Renaissance Hermeticism than the Methodism he was born into, or the Spurgeon and Barth-based new Calvinism with which he asso- ciated himself.

Within this divine plan Clemo observed more mundane patterns, paying attention to recurrent themes and dates, or temperaments similar to his own. Of particular significance was the kinship he felt with Robert Browning. While the work itself may not always owe very much to Browning, Clemo felt that they shared approaches to love and sexuality, and so close did he feel their affinity that he began paying apophenic attention to any similarities between them, their thoughts, words and biographies.

Marriage as divine vocation

Clemo married Ruth Peaty in 1968 and in 1984 moved out of Cornwall and the cottage in which he was born to his wife's hometown of Weymouth, where he died ten years later. The story of Jack Clemo's marriage is a central feature of the larger narrative of his life and writing. It is told several times in various works: in his own *Marriage of a Rebel*, in his mother Eveline Clemo's pamphlet *I Proved Thee at the Waters*, in Sally Magnusson's *Clemo: A Love Story*, and in his wife Ruth's notebooks.

Clemo considered marriage to be divine, and his destiny. In a letter to Charles Causley he wrote of his 'faith in my "election" for marriage'.[4] He had already touched on this in an article for *Unicorn* magazine eight years earlier, in 1961: 'What I have stressed in all my books is that within Christian redemption some men are predestined husbands and some women are predestined wives, and that the marriages of these "elect" lovers are different from ordinary marriages'.[5] Marriage would be the proof or confirmation of the kind of relationship he had with God. It was not only his desire to marry, but it was also God's promise to him that he would. Marriage, Clemo repeatedly wrote, was his 'vocation', a task set him by God. As 'vocation', it was not just a gift that would be given to him, but something that Clemo desired and would have to work for before it was achieved. The 'promise' Clemo perceived was that if he worked hard enough, looked out for the signs and kept his faith, then marriage would certainly be achieved. But the work would not be easy. Writing in *The Marriage of a Rebel*, Clemo explains, 'For twenty-five years I had been sustained and vitalised by the belief that God had destined me for marriage, and that for this very reason the devil had tried to make me un-marriageable'.[6]

By 'unmarriageable' Clemo is referring to his disabilities, being by this point both deaf and blind—physical qualities which placed him aside from usual experiences of the world and society just as much as his temperament always had. Nevertheless, long before he and Ruth Peaty first corresponded and fell in love, Jack believed in the battle over his destiny for marriage, a battle which he had to join. Constantly he would keep an eye out for signs from God, auguries, patterns in events that had personal significance. In particular he observed what he called the 'Browning Pattern', which was based on the conviction that he shared a particular affinity with the poet Robert Browning and that events in Browning's life would be paralleled in his own. Relevant here is the special conviction that Clemo would find his own Elizabeth Barrett. So when he received a letter in 1967 from Ruth Peaty, a woman in her mid-forties, some seven years younger than him, the date of its composition was excitedly observed, the 12th September, being also the wedding anniversary of Robert and Elizabeth Barrett Browning. After many false starts and mismatches, such a sign as this was potent and pleasing.

The story of how Ruth first came to write, and how the couple then met and married is central to the sense of predestination and realization in this narrative. The role of what appears to be luck is seen to be evidence (or 'proof', as the Clemos would write) of God's involvement, but it may be that an aspect of this story is not quite as it appeared to be.

A Letter from Ruth

Jack's own account of the story is told in *The Marriage of a Rebel* in 1980, his second autobiography after *Confession of a Rebel* which was published in 1949 in the wake of his successful and popular novel *Wilding Graft*. He sums up Ruth's first approach quite clearly:

> She wrote to me because a friend had told her about my books and she wanted further details; she also felt that I must be 'an interesting person'. I sent her a copy of *The Invading Gospel*, and its odd mixture of auto-biography, polemics, evangelism, poetry and literary criticism seemed to meet her need of a more complex approach than that of the average religious book.[7]

A few years earlier, Clemo's mother had published a pamphlet about having Jack Clemo for a son, called *I Proved Thee at the Waters*. Naturally, she too wrote an account of their convergence: 'In 1967, a lady from Weymouth wrote him saying how much she admired his book, "The Invading Gospel" . . . He was able to see from her letters that he was in touch with quite an unusual personality'.[8] The discrepancy between Jack's and his mother's order of events is a mistake attributable to the latter. It will be noticed that she tells how Ruth read *The Invading Gospel* before writing to Jack; yet that Jack says she had not read it when she first wrote. In fact she had not, but she was aware of the book and had expressed her interest[9], so that Jack sent her a copy.

In Sally Magnusson's version of their introduction and courtship, told in her *Clemo: A Love Story*, the importance of the belief in predestination is emphasized, Magnusson telling each aspect of the couple's story side by side; a section about Jack, one about Ruth, then another about Jack, and so on, until their individual stories coincide. She writes how Clemo 'believed that his destiny was to marry'[10], and that in spite of events making him appear 'unmarriageable', 'it arrived, just like that out of the blue—a letter dated 12 September, the anniversary of Browning's marriage. "Dear Jack," it began chattily, as if they had known each other for years. It was signed "Ruth (Peaty)".'[11] These aspects were clearly considered the most salient elements of the book's plot, being used as the hook for the back cover blurb. The idea of spontaneity, of the letter arriving 'out of the blue', is central to the sense of destiny or predestiny, of God's fulfilment of his 'promise' to Jack. Magnusson goes on to write that when Ruth:

> picked up her pen to write to Jack Clemo . . . he was simply a name passed on by one of her many correspondents who knew she was on the look-out for challenging books and interesting people. She was still struggling with questions such as why God allows tragedy, and the friend told her that *The Invading Gospel*, by a blind and deaf poet called Jack Clemo, had a whole chapter on just that problem.[12]

Magnusson received much of her information directly from the Clemos through Ruth, who put considerable work into the project, filling several note-books with information, ideas, directives and characters to include, as well as subjects for Magnusson to avoid. The skeleton of the above passage from *A Love Story* might be observed in Ruth's account from one of these: 'Heard of Jack through a correspondent Sept 1967 who informed me in a letter of a certain Jack Clemo (Blind + Deaf) who had written books on subjects I was interested in—The Cruelty of Nature—The Problem of Pain'.[13] Another biog-rapher, Michael Spinks, writes a similar story, but adds the name of Bernard Smith to it, writing that 'it was through him [Bernard Smith] and his wife Avril that a young disillusioned girl wrote Jack what she thought was to be a pen-letter from her home in Weymouth.'[14] Spinks goes on to say that the sub-sequent correspondence of Jack and Ruth after 'that first unlikely approach' 'grew and moved towards romance'. Bernard, then, is the 'correspondent' or 'friend' written of by Jack, Ruth and Eveline Clemo, and by Sally Magnusson. Indeed, Bernard had visited the Clemos in the early fifties, having read Jack's *Confession of a Rebel*. He followed Jack's work and made contact again some ten years later, a correspondence that came to have significance and was sustained until Jack's death.

But the story being developed here is quite clear: gaining the address from a mutual friend, Ruth wrote a letter of spiritual admiration to Jack on an auspicious date. Their correspondence developed into a romance. By divine contrivance, Ruth and Jack were pressed together, the element of unlikelihood and apparent chance evidencing predestination at every turn.

'The Christian Introduction Bureau'

However, this is not the full story. The mutual acquaintances, which Michael Spinks mentions, ran what was called 'The Christian Introduction Bureau', essentially a dating agency for Christians. Both Jack and Ruth submitted forms to the Bureau, including personal details like height and income, as well as statements of what they were looking for in a partner. In this last section both wrote 'Marriage', and enclosed their fees and photographs. Ruth seems to have considered this a last desperate attempt to find the relationship she was looking for. In correspondence with the 'Bureau' she wrote, 'the only way seems to resort to this',[15] significantly adding, 'one cannot expect God to work wonders for us while we just sit and wait'.

The importance of these documents to the biographer is several. In the first place, seeing Clemo describe himself and what he is looking for in such direct language is illuminating. In the second place, there is the question of why the couple did not want to mention the Bureau. Did they think that it harmed the mythopoeic quality of their marriage narrative, or did they fear the story was in some sense culturally taboo? In the third place, does it actually change anything?

The material itself is illuminating, and to some extent entertaining. In terms of trivial physical details there is some helpful information, such as both Ruth and Jack being 5' 6" tall. There are also interesting details to be found in comparing their responses to the same questions. For example, under 'Ambitions', Jack has written 'To continue Christian witness', while Ruth has written 'To be an interesting companion to someone'. A biographer or scholar might also find the ways in which Jack Clemo described himself on this form useful. Forced to distil his 'General Health' to a single line he writes: 'Good. Blind and partially deaf—people write on my palm'. Then, under 'General Appearance', he has: 'Medium build, grey-haired, large leonine head, rugged face'. The 'large leonine head' is an attractively odd inclusion. Most interesting might be this lovely description of what he is looking for in a woman:

> Any age under 40. About my own height or only an inch or two shorter; good powerful figure. Not fashionable or expensive in dress—simple and plain and perhaps untidy with long hair tumbling around her shoulders. Strong personality, serious and reliable but not solemn and stuffy—keen sense of fun and humour desired. Some taste for Christian literature. Must not smoke, drink, gamble or go to dance after marriage.[16]

Reading this, Ruth might have been concerned. She was forty-four, so she should have been too old for Jack. If Jack sent a photograph with his form it has not survived, but Ruth's has. She does not seem to have a 'good power-ful figure', but looks tall and slim. Her hair does not tumble anywhere, but is worn quite short. She must also have appeared disappointingly tidy.

Some of those demands might make us wince a little now, but Clemo's un-ashamed forthrightness is typical, and it is one of the qualities that can make his poetry and prose so unsettling, powerful and authentic. With that in mind, the question as to why this aspect of their relationship has been so deliberately avoided will be recalled. If Jack Clemo is as forthright as he so often appears to be, why is his own account of their getting together so misleading? It is clear from many letters held in the Special Collection archives at the University of Exeter that the Clemos were sensitive to gossip and perceived taboos. In response to an article about the causes of Jack's poor health, he complained that the 'clinical guesswork' was harmful and upsetting to his wife, writing, 'She feels that this irresponsible probing into private matters—some of it quite inaccurate—is damaging to us and might lose us friends'.[17] The concern for losing friends is repeated in a further correspondence with the same magazine, which adds support to this possibility. Again, in the earlier *Confession of a*

Rebel,[18] there is a passage where Clemo is taken to have a 'psycho-analytical test', apparently because of certain salacious gossip in the village. In this passage, Clemo seems to be describing how he did not reveal all to the analyst, not because he had any sense of guilt, but because he was distrustful of the analyst's conclusions. 'I had read enough books on sex and psychology', he wrote, 'to give intelligent answers to the psychiatrist's questions. I knew what he was talking about, what he was trying to get at'.[19]

That is, Clemo maintained his innocence to the reader just as he had to the analyst. But because he did not trust the psychiatric method or profession, he believes he has misled the analyst into accepting his own version of events. It is possible that the same sort of distrust that led him to manipulate the psychiatrist also led Clemo to censor his and Ruth's submissions to the 'Christian Introduction Bureau' in 1967, and to attempt to censor investigation into the causes of his ill-health. The point here is not to emphasize the malicious gossip concerning Clemo, but to try to understand his self-censorship of a key feature of a pivotal moment of his biography. The marriage of Ruth and Jack was a divine promise fulfilled; it was the end of decades of turmoil and profound frustration; and it marked a clear change in the man's poetry, outlook and attitude. So the importance of this relationship cannot be overlooked in any discussion of Clemo's life and work, and may hardly be overstated.

We can see now that where a taboo is perceived or an audience distrusted, Clemo was willing to avoid telling the truth in order to maintain a clearer view of the truth, so to speak. If an issue was clouded by controversy so thickly that one could not perceive it with sufficient clarity to distinguish the facts, then Clemo was willing to pretend that there was nothing to see anyway. The only doubt here might be that there *was* sufficient controversy around introduction agencies to justify this censorship. Perhaps it was rather the case that Jack or Ruth were somehow humiliated by the way they met. Or perhaps it was thought that the real story took something away from the magic of the personal myth they believed in and expounded. Did it fit the 'Browning Pattern'?

Re-writing the evidence

At first glance, the introduction of Ruth and Jack through an agency seems to detract from the sense of 'chance'. In one way this is true, but in another it is quite beside the point. It is true in the sense that an attempt was always made to present the likelihood of Jack and Ruth meeting as implausible, and signing up to an agency significantly detracts from the conjured sense of the supernatural. On the other hand, it has already been mentioned that Clemo considered this election and destiny to marry as a vocation, not as a simple gift. Destiny to him does not mean something that just happens and cannot be avoided. It is not the same sense of destiny that we might see toyed with in, say, Philip K. Dick's *Minority Report*, or more overtly in the *Final Destination* films. It is something that must be pursued, something to be attained. As Ruth's had opined in her letter to the Bureau: 'one cannot expect God to work wonders for us while we just sit and wait'.

Because of this formulation of destiny, a secular reader may well have trouble distinguishing Clemo's conception of destiny from the plainer observation that when one pursues something one is significantly more likely to achieve it. That Clemo found love and marriage after his relentless pursuit of them is seen by him as a 'proof' of God, and a 'proof' of his election for marriage. To the secular reader this is difficult to sympathize with. The fact that one looks hard for something that is presumed to exist, and as a consequence of one's efforts finds it eventually, is an utterly mundane formula. It does not seem much of a coincidence unless the conditions are extraordinary, and while in many other ways Jack Clemo's conditions were extraordinary (being a deaf-blind poet, for example), a fairly significant quantity of chance is taken away from Ruth and Jack's relationship by the fact of their signing up to an 'Introductions' company. Not only were they both looking hard for love and marriage, but they also employed help to find them.

Perhaps this is a reason for omitting the Bureau from accounts of their introduction; to maintain a stronger public sense of God's intervention in their relationship. If so, the motive is seriously questionable. There is some stronger evidence of this desire to rewrite the relationship in Jack Clemo's diaries of 1967 and 1968, the years during which Ruth and Jack began to correspond, became engaged and married. The rewriting, however, was not done by Jack, but by Ruth after Jack had died. According to Clemo's biographer, Michael Spinks,[20] Ruth began editing probably around 1995–96, and certainly by 2000, spending two mornings a week going through the manuscripts. Perhaps the most extensive work has been done on her early correspondence with Jack and on the diaries, tearing out entries she did not like, throwing away letters or cutting them up, scratching out, blacking out or 'tippexing' over words and phrases which she wanted to change, and annotating throughout. The period of their initial correspondence is one of the most heavily obfuscated, with twelve whole weeks cut out from the 1967 diary and the letters having been dramatically altered. A part of this process was doubtless Ruth's desire to be close again to Jack after he had died and to re-immerse herself in his life and in their life together, as well as to facilitate future studies of Clemo once the manuscripts were out of her hands and submitted to the archives at Exeter University. With this desire to help future Clemo readers, we might have a look at how the 1967 diary has been edited.

Jack in 1967 was suffering in the wake of a failed engagement to a woman acknowledged here as 'M.' He was profoundly despondent, feeling that his vocation had been spoiled not only by clashing personalities, but by supernatural forces too: 'I know it wasn't just her own personality I had to fight: there was a sinister inhuman power trying to destroy us both!'[21] This former fiancé was the closest he had come to a fulfilment of the divine promise he had received, and to the relief of his greatest personal longing. Many entries of this year reflect the anguish and despair he was suffering, marking anniversaries of memorable times they shared, reading her favourite books, and worrying that she might have been 'the only flower in my desert'. Among these 1967 entries, there are interesting hints at what is going on, such as 'Still waiting and wondering',[22] and 'Got a new photo album for my birthday. How soon will my wife's photo be in it?',[23] then 'Signed contract for *Cactus on Carmel*. I do pray my wife may be with me when it's published'.[24]

The sense in these entries is that Clemo is expecting something to arrive, specifically a letter from a woman who will say she wants to marry him within only a few months, the collection of poems which Clemo refers to, *Cactus on Carmel*, being published later that same year, in October. The writer is fifty-one years old at this time, so he must have had a reason for expecting a wife to appear in only a few months, and this reason is certainly the 'Christian Introduction Bureau'. Yet there is no direct reference to the Bureau in any diary entry. They have all been torn out.

Many changes have been made to these manuscripts, suggesting that Ruth wanted to build a picture of Clemo slightly skewed from the bare facts, but also that she wanted to perpetuate and develop the myth of their meeting. One such change is the way in which Ruth's annotations have created a dramatic tension in the record of Clemo's 'dark and fretted'[25] year of despondency. On the 14th August Clemo writes: 'Reading an anthology of Victorian Verse. I note that a dozen of the poets died before they were 51. God must have some purpose in sparing me—may it be clear soon'. Ruth has annotated: 'God did have a purpose—he married Ruth and produced 4 poetry books and auto-biographies'. Again, on the 19th of the same month, Jack writes of his 'awful loneliness', 'Yet there must be someone with a kindred stress'. Ruth responds: 'there was in the shape of Ruth who was a believer in God and loved poetry'.

This continues throughout the year, a dialogue between the despairing bachelor Jack in 1967 and the widowed Ruth some thirty years later. The drama is an interesting embellishment, creating a sense of this year as Jack's preparatory 'Dark Night' before the mystical consummation. It is possibly for this very effect that Ruth also steps out beyond her loving enthusiasm and makes a deliberately misleading statement. As it has been shown, Jack Clemo and Ruth Peaty entered into correspondence both aware that the other was looking for marriage from their relationship. They both stated this on the forms they submitted. So when Jack wrote 'I have neither hopes nor fears at this stage. M. is still the only woman who has loved me, and as long as this is so I'm bound to shrink from the thought of marrying someone else. God will adjust my emotions if he wants me to marry Ruth!'[26] He is being consistent and honest, but Ruth's commentary is not. She writes: 'Ruth was only writing about his work . . . It seems any contact with a woman caused J. to think of marriage!' The intention here is very clear. Ruth is claiming that she only contacted Jack about his work (though she has elsewhere stated that she had not read any), and she is also implying that she herself was not thinking about marriage at this stage, although it is now known that marriage certainly was her hope and intention when she contacted the Bureau, and that she wrote to Jack as a potential husband.

Conclusion

Ultimately, the Clemos' motive for the exclusion is unknown, but there still remains a good quantity of material in the archives at Exeter University to work through. The most likely reason seems to be the sense of humiliation, perceived especially by Ruth, though possibly by both. It will be recalled how Jack's letter to the magazine that tried to diagnose the cause of his blindness and deafness told the editors that the article hurt his wife's feelings. It may well be the case that Jack did not care very much whether anyone knew about the Bureau, but Ruth *did* care and did not want it known, so that the decision to withhold the real story was to protect Ruth's threatened sense of propriety. Nevertheless, it must not be forgotten that along with this anxiety to protect one another there was also a desire to present their coupling as supernaturally appointed, and the omission of the Bureau from the story does distort the sense of surprise or chance in their meeting.

That said, the couple were certainly very well suited. Both felt an urgent desire to marry. Both held traditional, to the point of unfashionable, Christian views and values. Both observed apparent coincidences and patterns in their experiences of the world to an extraordinary degree. It should also be noted that there cannot be many women who would consider so readily a deaf-blind poet living with his mother as a reasonable marriage prospect. There was the Dorset connection too, Ruth Peaty being from the county which linked some of Clemo's greatest influences, like Hardy and T.F. Powys. And there is still the excellent coincidence of the 12th September and Clemo's 'Browning Pattern'.

These, it might be argued, were no more unusual than any other fluke. But for Clemo coincidences are signs that we should all look out for and pay attention to. It is an idea he kept and developed from childhood, that such coincidences were the 'Revelation of God in life' and must be studied.[27] The idea links with others developed from his youth, such as the importance of 'experience' to religion, and perhaps also the almost solipsistic attitudes he held towards truth.

There is still a good deal of original research to be done on Clemo in almost every field, the poetry, novels, tales and religious writing, as well as the biography, landscape, context and politics. That this sensationalist biographical splinter comes from studying essentially a single file among thousands in the archives might give a sense of the amount there is still left to do.

Notes and references

1. For an excellent reference to these ideas see Clemo's letters to Victor Perry, EUL MS 375 in the University of Exeter's Special Collections.
2. UL MS 68/PERS/1/4/4. 'Notes for Sara Ramsden.'
3. See, for example, any of the early diaries of the 1930s, such as EUL MS 68/PERS/2/1, or 68/PERS/2/2, or 68/PERS/2/3, where this outlook is extraordinarily pronounced.
4. Letter to Charles Causley, 6 May 1969, in the University of Exeter's Special Collections archive, reference EUL MS 68/PERS/1/3/1.
5. 'Jack Clemo States His Case', *Unicorn Magazine* (1961).
6. Clemo is talking about the period of 1961, in his *The Marriage of a Rebel* (London, 1980), p. 112.
7. *The Marriage of a Rebel*, p. 128.
8. Eveline Clemo, *I Proved Thee at the Waters* (Derbyshire, 1976), p. 22.
9. 'I have not read your book: – "The Invading Gospel" but would like to do so.' Letter from Ruth, in EUL MS 68/PERS/1/2/5.
10. Sally Magnusson, *Clemo: A Love Story* (Tring, 1986), p. 10.
11. Ibid., p. 103.
12. Ibid., p. 105.
13. University of Exeter Special Collections archive, reference EUL MS 68/PERS/12/1/3.
14. In the 'London Cornish Association Newsletter', Summer 2009.
15. University of Exeter Special Collections archive, reference EUL MS 68/PERS/12/1/3.
16. While Ruth's form was handwritten in capitals, Jack's was typewritten. The occasional error was inevitable, and I have not edited them out.
17. EUL MS 68/12/1/3.
18. Jack Clemo, *Confession of a Rebel* (London, 1949).
19. Ibid., p. 193.
20. In correspondence with me, 22 March 2013.
21. EUL MS 68/PERS/2/30. 10 January.
22. Ibid., 3 February.
23. Ibid., 13 February.
24. Ibid., 7 April.

25. Ibid., 24 March.
26. Ibid., 15 September.
27. As described in an exchange of ideas between Clemo, Reverend J.R. Parkyn and Peter Dartnell in several issues of the *Cornish Guardian* through 1937.

13

Celtic Tradition and Regional Discontents
Cornish Nationalism Revisited

Peder Clark

Introduction

The Cornish are fortunate to be able to paint their regional discontents in the attractive colours of Celtic tradition, which makes them so much more viable.[1]

Eric Hobsbawm, in his landmark exploration of the development of the contemporary nation-state, made the above assertion as he turned his mind to the future development of European national consciousness, with the background of the Balkan conflict and that rapidly evolving situation fresh in his mind. Contemporary Cornwall belies the superficiality of the statement, and despite the slightly less tumultuous recent crises in British identity, Cornish nationalist movements have proved incapable over the last century of converting this perceived advantage into anything approaching self-determination.

Cornwall is stuck somewhere between being an English county and a Celtic nation, and this paradoxical dichotomy is becoming ever more acute in the age of devolution and localism. The Cornish mining historian A.K. Hamilton Jenkin, related a story from the nineteenth century that summarizes the situation as acutely now in the early twenty-first century as it did when he was writing in 1927:

'Hes Coornwall a nashion, hes a a Hiland, or hes a ferren country?', an old school dame, Peggy Combellack, would ask.

'He hedn't no nashon, he hedn't no highlan, nor he hedn't no ferren country,' the brightest of the scholars on one occasion answered.

'What hes a then?' asked Peggy.

'Why, he's kidged to a furren country from the top hand', was the reply.[2]

This perceived English cultural hegemony is felt keenly by Cornish nationalists, and indeed by Cornish historians as they have struggled to give what they see as the Cornish side of the story. It has resulted in a dual or hybrid Cornish identity, which, despite the peripherality of the area, both economically and geographically, has resulted in a certain Cornish reluctance to assert their case. Hobsbawm writes elsewhere that 'being a revolutionary in countries such as ours just happens to be difficult. There is no reason to believe that it will be less difficult in future than it has been in the past'.[3] There is a certain irony in applying this to Cornwall, but perhaps it just happens to be true. Either way, it is timely to review the current state of Cornish nationalism and to take account of its recent experience.

Cornwall's geography, demography and identity

Cornwall currently has a population of around 537,400 including the Isles of Scilly, but is amongst the fastest growing areas of the UK in demographic terms, with an expectation that the population will expand to 630,300 in the next decade.[4] This growth is primarily due to in-migration, although there has also been a recent trend for young people to stay in Cornwall, helping to further swell the population.[5] This growth in population, especially as a result of migration into the area, has been the subject of a good deal of disgruntlement. As in so many popular debates about migration elsewhere over the last decade, the raw statistics can happily be ignored or distorted. While the influx into Cornwall over the last half a century is mostly attributable to a younger, working-age demographic, 'stubborn myths of retirement migration' persist.[6] While Peter Mitchell eloquently debunks this misconception by looking at population trends since the end of the Second World War,[7] a popular view even amongst the well-informed indigenous population is that Cornwall is fast becoming 'a playground for people from elsewhere with money'.[8] This may well be the case, but the affluent that do settle are not necessarily the rich retired. Nonetheless, some of these mild prejudices are born out in the high number of second homes in Cornwall, resulting in house prices that correlate poorly with wages. Given the manner in which tourism has become the dominant industry, it is understandable that the Cornish might feel aggrieved. But to what extent might this reinforce, and be reinforced by, an already existing regional consciousness?

In the 2011 England and Wales census, 73,220 people in Cornwall self-identified as 'Cornish'.[9] This represents 13.8 per cent of the population, compared to a figure of 6.8 per cent in the 2001 census, following Cornwall Council's awareness-raising campaign, which gave guidance to people wishing to identify themselves as 'Cornish'.[10] Other surveys conducted in the last decade have demonstrated further evidence of a significant sense of Cornish identity. A study conducted by Morgan Stanley in 2004 asked people across Britain whether their primary identification was as European, British, English or to their county. Cornwall recorded the highest percentage of people relating to their local identity most strongly, with 44 per cent.[11] A postal survey conducted by the Council in the same year yielded 35 per cent of the 4,052 respondents opting for Cornish as their ethnicity.[12] On the results of the latter survey, Deacon rather optimistically posits that, as a result of in-migration, only about half the population of Cornwall were actually born and bred in the region, this response rate might equate to 'up to 70 per cent of the native-born population defining their primary identity as "Cornish"'.[13]

Three recent separate studies of Cornish identity—by Joanie Willett, Robert Dickinson and Kerryn Husk—look in more depth into what being 'Cornish' might signify. The first, by Willett, attempts to establish whether Cornish identity is no more than a 'vague notion', or if it can be classed as a 'social fact'. This is a sociological concept first introduced by Emile Durkheim, in which scientific empirical investigation can establish social phenomena as 'things by the same right as material things, although they differ from them in type'.[14] These social facts exist on a graduated scale, from being a 'morphological fact', fully integrated into the collective life of a community, through to 'institutionalized norms' or 'social currents', where the sociological concept is an established element of life, but not a primary identity. Finally, and most weakly, the lowest rung of the scale are 'transitory outbreaks', or momentary bouts of enthusiasm, which arguably might best describe the trips to Twickenham by Trelawny's Army in the early to mid-1990s (and again in 2013) when Cornwall repeatedly reached the final of the County Championship, a favoured point of reference for scholars of Cornish nationalism.[15] Willett attempts to apply these theories to the everyday concept of 'Cornishness' by surveying a small sample cross-section population across Cornwall, and concludes that Cornish identity is best described on Durkheim's spectrum as an 'institutionalised norm'. This seems a counterfactual conclusion, considering the evidence that there are few Cornish institutions per se. But her questionnaire and focus groups do identify that for those born and bred in Cornwall, the idea of being Cornish has significant relevance, although, interestingly, it is not necessarily exclusive of being British, or even

English.[16] Willett also believes her research demonstrates that Cornishness is 'dynamic, with newcomers socialized and assimilated into the identity'.[17] Yet this conclusion assertion is called into doubt by the attitudes of the indigenous Cornish described in Dickinson's work.

Dickinson attempts to research by empirical method what it means to be Cornish, 'inspired by and partly replicat[ing] a study of the contemporary Breton identity by Ronan Le Coadic'.[18] This inspiration is particularly interesting given the widely acknowledged link that Brittany and the Bretons share a common culture and linguistic roots with the Cornish. Dickinson's filter is to examine Cornish social representations; that is, the 'commonsense knowledge' that communities share and which gives them cohesion. He describes these as 'markers, products and regulators of identity',[19] and he undertakes semi-structured interviews with individuals in farming communities. These interviews raise some interesting points about Cornish identity, and how this relates to any expression of nationalism or regionalism. Consistent with the other studies, there was greater self-identification as 'Cornish' in West Cornwall rather than East, the physical distance from England seemingly linked to a cultural distance. Many interviewees expressed deeply entrenched ideas about Cornish identity, and what qualified an individual to describe oneself as Cornish: 'Jeremy put it vividly: "They say that to be accepted as Cornish you've got to have your grandfather in the graveyard, that's an old saying. You've got to be two or three generations before you're called Cornish".[20]

Despite these firm opinions, and the fact that all interviewees self-identified as Cornish (whether or not they complied with the strict criteria stated above), the majority were unwilling to paint themselves in Hobsbawm's 'attractive colours of Celtic tradition'. Although sometimes critical of 'the English' and worried about threats to cultural identity, most were reticent to engage with Cornish cultural or language groups, and were equivocal about the perhaps gaudier aspects of the last century's 'Cornish revival' such as the anachronistic Cornish tartan or even Kernow car-stickers. Unfortunately Dickinson does not explore the political views of the group, save for one interviewee mentioning the late Cornish MP David Penhaligon as the embodiment of Cornishness. Nonetheless, his study illustrates, even if only incidentally, that a firmly held identity might not readily translate into demonstrable or political expression.

Husk's paper is of interest primarily not for its function as a review of the literature on Cornish identity, nor even as an examination of socio-economic deprivation amongst the Cornish, but rather for the explicit connections that he makes to theories of nationalism. While Willett alludes briefly to the work of Anthony Smith and Benedict Anderson's 'imagined communities',[21] Husk examines his findings through Smith's idea of *ethnie*, described in his

1986 book *The Ethnic Origins of Nations*. Smith laments that the English language contains no word to describe an ethnic group or community, and so appropriates the French term, which he believes 'capture[s] the peculiar cultural individuality and shared historicity of ethnicity'.[22] He details the defining features of *ethnie* as comprising a collective name, a common myth of descent, a shared history, a distinctive shared culture, an association with a specific territory and a sense of solidarity.[23] Husk takes this conceptual framework and attempts to apply it to the Cornish, with the conclusion that they satisfy these criteria and can comfortably be described as a discrete *ethnie*: 'The group exists, and exists in significant numbers, highlighting the need to examine them in detail'.[24]

From this brief survey of the recent literature, 'Cornishness' appears to be a social fact, giving nationalist parties potentially a firm basis on which to build their ambitions. But what of the socio-economic conditions in which this group lives, and how might this impact upon any nationalist aspirations?

Cornwall's economy

For most of the twentieth century, Cornwall has suffered the after-effects of a protracted deindustrialization. In 1881, 31.4 per cent of the working population was involved in mining, with 40 per cent working in the service industry. One hundred years later, the proportion was 17.3 per cent and 74.9 per cent respectively, as Cornwall (and indeed Britain)'s mining industry was in its final throes.[25] While this process of deindustrialization was a gradual atrophying rather than a radical transformation, it has had a profound effect on Cornwall, and not just in economic terms. As graffiti daubed on South Crofty when it closed recounted:

> Cornish lads are fishermen
> And Cornish lads are miners, too.
> But when the fish and tin are gone
> What are the Cornish boys to do?[26]

Mining as a culture was deeply embedded in the Cornish consciousness. Indeed, the most immediate effect of deindustrialization in the nineteenth century, was mass emigration, a topic covered eloquently by Payton in *The Cornish Overseas*, resulting in strong Cornish diasporas that live on today in fevered debate on internet messageboards. Of course, throughout the latter half of the twentieth century the trend has been reversed, with significant in-migration into the area. The longer term impact of this industrial decline has been felt in both a changing landscape and employment patterns.

The decline of the china clay industry centred around the St Austell area acts as a concise illustration of the changing Cornish economy. The intensive mining around this area, which resulted in St Austell being a fairly well-off area in the nineteenth century and considered relatively prosperous until the 1960s, also created what are optimistically referred to as the Cornish Alps—hills created from the collateral product of china clay extraction. With the steady contraction of the industry since the 1960s, many of these pits and hills have lain barren and unused. Entrepreneur Tim Smit, having worked on a project to restore the Lost Gardens of Heligan, saw the potential in one 160-year-old clay pit, and created the Eden Project, an environmental and cultural centre that is now an international tourist attraction. It employs over six hundred local people and generates approximately £150 million per year for the local economy.[27] Meanwhile, St Austell continues to be a highly deprived town, with unemployment an enduring problem.

The contemporary Cornish economy can be typified by three features: seasonal tourism, second homes, and Objective One funding from the European Union. These three issues, all potentially grist to the nationalist mill, are briefly examined in turn. The Cornish tourist industry took off comparatively late, in the 1920s and 30s.[28] The 1950s and 60s represent a period of 'mass tourism', as 'the British seaside holiday became established as one of the aspirations, even expectations, of the working-class'.[29] Cornwall County Council estimated that visitors increased by over 50 per cent between 1954 and 1964 and this influx had a tangible impact upon local populations, with Newquay in particular experiencing a 13.6 per cent growth in hotels and guest houses during that decade.[30]

By 2010, over 4.1 million staying visitors were recorded in Cornwall, approximately eight times the local population, and worth an estimated £1.6 billion.[31] Tourism in Cornwall is seasonal by nature, with the visitors at season's peak in August (734,000), being almost nine times that in January (83,600).[32] As illustrated in the example of the St Austell area, some of this tourism has been built up from the ashes of old extractive industry, and Cornwall has successfully bid to UNESCO to have the Cornwall and West Devon Mining Landscape designated a World Heritage Site. Nonetheless, it is largely Cornwall's geography and natural environment that attracts visitors: 'the landscape can be seen as the real raw material of tourism; it can be regarded as the basic reason for the existence of tourism in Cornwall as well as its basic driving force'.[33]

It is also this natural beauty that makes property an attractive option for affluent people seeking a second home.[34] Small businessmen, for example, with high-speed internet connections, can as easily maintain their interests in Falmouth as they can in Farnham. While this particular development is not yet reflected in statistics, it is worth noting that 15.6 per cent of the working age population is self-employed, while 89.3 per cent of companies are classed as micro-businesses (0–9 employees).[35] The implication is that small businesses from outside can be competitive in the Cornish economy, and that a significant proportion may well be self-started. Payton describes this recent trend as potentially 'e-colonialism', especially if those with 'London-type salaries' add further 'to demand in a housing market where house prices are already high'.[36] It is too early to tell what the long-term impact of these movements might be, but the affordability of property has long been a concern to the indigenous Cornish. Currently (latest figures in 2011), the value of the lower quartile houses was 9.1 times the value of lower quartile wages.[37] This unaffordability of property is, to the Cornish mind, the fault of one thing: second homes. Many newspaper articles make reference to common graffiti about the issue,[38] and it is something that Mebyon Kernow (MK) has attempted to make political capital out of since the 1970s: 'posters bore such topical messages as "Cornish Wages: English Prices—Can YOU afford a mortgage?"' and "We are Fast Becoming Two Communities—the Cornish and the Prosperous".'[39]

There are approximately 13,000 second homes in Cornwall, representing 1 in 20 houses.[40] Thornton examines the problems of second homes, drawing on a study in Port Isaac. He elucidates the starkly different backgrounds of the second home owners and the local population, with evidence of 'social distance' and the resentment of the latter towards the former group. He also points to a 1975 study that noted that 'the potential for conflict remains high'.[41] Certainly, Cornwall Council has been sympathetic to this viewpoint, and succeeded in addressing one point of contention: Cornwall was the first area to ban second home owners from being on the electoral register.[42]

The status of Cornwall as a deprived part of the UK has never been in question, although the causes of this poverty cannot adequately be explained by any one factor. One further, and oft-quoted in nationalist circles, explanation is Kevin Cahill's controversial 2001 article in *Business Age* magazine (which curiously ceased publication the following year) entitled 'The Killing Of Cornwall', in which he gives his own, frank reason for Cornwall's predicament:

> One very simple and easily provable answer is because the Government in London is raping the county fiscally. Out of a tiny gross domestic product of £3.6 billion, the Government takes over £1.95 billion in taxes, and puts back into the county less than £1.65 billion, a gap of over £300 million. That latter sum, by itself, all but completely explains the increasing pace of impoverishment in Cornwall.[43]

Whatever the validity of this argument, (and Cornwall, in common with other remote and rural areas, appears to lose out in various government funding formulas), the European Union has acknowledged that Cornwall is sorely in need of investment. In 1999, Cornwall applied for and received Objective One funding from the EU, which gave approximately €350 million over six years to the region, in recognition of the fact that the Cornish Gross Domestic Product (GDP) per person is less than 75 per cent of the European average.[44] Interestingly, Cornwall had previously and unsuccessfully applied for the funding jointly with Devon. Since Objective One ended in 2006, Cornwall has further benefited from Convergence funding, to the tune of €458.1 million from 2007 to 2013.[45] While the investment has been welcome, it is, in the longer term, the symbolism of the funding that is most important. Objective One, and its successors, has given nationalists the encouragement that, even if Cornwall is not sufficiently recognized in Whitehall, Brussels sees the region as worthy of its attention and investment in its own right.

Cornwall's history, ethnomythology and historiography

If the Cornish complain that their socio-economic needs have been ignored by Whitehall, then they have equal cause for grievance with historians. Even despite the more recent trends in British history, which seek to adopt a less Anglo-centric perspective, Cornwall features only fleetingly in contemporary histories of the British Isles. Some parties view this omission as a conspiracy, and it is little wonder that Deacon describes Cornwall's historiography as a 'battleground' between the 'kernowcentric' and the 'kernowsceptic'.[46] In this loose typology, John Angarrack would stand proudly into the former category, modern British historians by default placed in the latter, with Mark Stoyle, Bernard Deacon and Philip Payton offering a more moderate middle ground, albeit one that is sensitive and sympathetic to Cornish viewpoints.

Of those in the allegedly kernowsceptic camp, Richard Weight and Hugh Kearney should be counted amongst the least culpable. Weight devotes a comparatively generous five pages to the Cornish in *Patriots*. In general he underplays Cornish distinctiveness. But he does note the rising strength of Cornish nationalism, which he attributes to the gradual but inexorable decline of the Cornish economy, the rediscovery of Celtic heritage, and the fact that successive UK governments have made little concession towards devolutionary measures for Cornwall.[47] In a shorter book covering a lengthier period, Kearney is careful in *The British Isles* to reference Cornwall and the Cornish at every stage, from its putative roots in the Cornouii tribe up until Norman times. But at that point he states rather perfunctorily that 'finally, Celtic-speaking

Cornwall . . . was incorporated into "England", governmentally if not culturally',[48] and that is last we hear of Cornwall. One can imagine why a kernowcentric historian might take umbrage.

Until the latter part of the twentieth century, then, there was little focus on Cornwall's history, or its history as a part of the British Isles. What historical literature there was, concentrated on the mining industry. One can understand why modern Cornish historians, both amateur and professional, have sought to redress the balance and offer a more detailed, comprehensive—and kernocentric—interpretation of Cornwall's history. Angarrack's *Our Future is History: Identity, Law and the Cornish Question* is perhaps the most unashamed attempt, a volume that Deacon pointedly describes as 'a story of a long and righteous struggle against English oppressors'.[49] Stoyle's work is more measured and scholarly, and concentrates on the period before and during the English Civil War, eloquently tracing what he perceives to be a palpable Cornish element to the region's participation in that conflict, and linking that with the rebellions of 1497 and 1549.[50] Deacon and Payton have both produced fine general histories of Cornwall, to which this article is deeply indebted.

But what of Cornwall's history itself, which plays so great a basis of identity in both Smith's idea of *ethnie* and Anderson's 'imagined communities'? Cornwall's history prior to the tenth century is open to conjecture. Nonetheless, there are a number of historical events that are important in Cornish nationalist rhetoric, and give the Cornish both the common myth of descent and the shared history of which Smith speaks. The first of these is Cornwall's Celtic past, and perceived association with the other Celtic nations: Wales, Scotland, Ireland, Brittany and the Isle of Man. This was a relationship often alluded to by MK in the 1960s and 70s, although emphasized less as the movement matured into the social democratic party of today. It was an association made forcefully by some of the more outspoken fringes of Cornish nationalism. Dr James Whetter, a prominent figure in Cornish politics and culture over the last half-century, was unequivocal: 'The Cornish people are a Celtic people. They have a right to fulfil themselves as an individual Celtic nation, as Cornish. Kernow is the homeland of the Cornish people, it has a right to be recognized as such at all levels'.[51]

Interestingly, Dick Cole, the current leader of MK, argued in an academic article in 1997 (before assuming the leadership) that in his view ethnic identities are social and not biological constructs. As he put it: 'the conclusion must be that our modern cultural and political identities were not formed through the mass migration of people but as a result of more complex and complicated factors such as assimilation, acculturation and accommodation'.[52] While one must acknowledge that Whetter and Cole were writing for different audiences, and with different motivations, it is clear that there is some distance between their views on what 'Celtic' means to the Cornish nationalist cause. For Whetter, 'Celtic' is primordial and essentialist—the root of Cornish nationality—but for Cole it is a dynamic term, constantly subject to renegotiation and not necessarily privileged in any imagining of the Cornish nation.

Payton similarly offers a careful analysis, furnishing a brief exposition of the terms 'Celt' and 'Celtic' from archeological and linguistic perspectives, before admitting that regardless of academic arguments, the 'Celtic influence has been of enduring significance, most notably in the Cornish language which developed from the Celtic dialect spoken in the peninsula, and has given us the vast majority of Cornish place names, many surnames, and a vernacular which survived until modern times'.[53] As Payton explains, for 'many modern observers, not least the Celtic revivalists of the twentieth and twenty-first centuries, it is with the dawn of the Iron Age that Cornwall begins to emerge from the murk of prehistory into the flowering and eventual full glare of Celtic civilization'.[54] This, in turn, was a prelude to the era when 'Cornwall begins to develop the territorial identity which marks it out geo-politically as the land apart'.[55] In this reading, the Cornish are a shadowy people, 'known to the English as the "West Welsh"',[56] with close maritime links to Brittany, still part of the western kingdom of Dumonia, yet relatively untouched by Roman influence. The subsequent history of Cornwall is especially opaque, until in the tenth century Athelstan annexed the territory as a separate but satellite entity to Wessex, setting the Tamar as the border.[57] A century later, having subdued southern England, William the Conqueror's forces marched into Cornwall, 'and put down all disturbances that arose'.[58] Charles Thomas, the first Director of the Institute of Cornish Studies, marks this as the firm end of any semblance of an independent Celtic nationhood:

> By the 11th century, the time of the great Domesday survey, Cornwall had on the face of it become a part of England. All our subsequent separatism or idiosyncrasies, whether remarked upon externally or boasted about internally, derive from the status and development of the peninsula in that millennium from 100 B.C. to A.D. 900.[59]

This complex period exerts an enduring influence over the Cornish nationalist imagination, with MK in 1968 declaring that 'Cornwall was England's first colony, conquered though not subdued, by Egbert and Athelstan of Wessex'.[60] The perceived antipathy towards the English is a persistent theme in this narrative, and is evident in the risings of 1497 and 1549, again popular points of reference for Cornish nationalists today. Similarly important in nationalist readings of Cornish history, is the Duchy of Cornwall.

As successor to the Earldom of Cornwall, the Duchy of Cornwall was created in 1337, 'with its revenues earmarked for the eldest son of the monarch',[61] a set of circumstances which has survived until the present day. Both Payton and Deacon are sceptical of the tendency amongst some kernowcentric observers to view this as straightforward evidence of Cornish quasi-autonomy, especially after A.L. Rowse's suggestion that the Duchy was 'a little government of its own'.[62] Deacon has also debunked some of the more outlandish ideas floated on internet messageboards,[63] concerning attempts by the Duchy's lawyers in the mid-nineteenth century to assert the Duchy's constitutional status (usually for economic gain).[64] Nonetheless, the distinctiveness lent to Cornwall by the Duchy continues to resound in the twenty-first century, informing debate about Cornwall's past, present and future. For example, the Stannary system, with its independent legal system of Stannary courts designed to regulate the tin industry, and the Stannary or Tinners' Parliament—with its theoretical power to disallow any Westminster statute—was an integral part of Duchy governance. In the nationalist imagination today, this is both evidence of Cornwall's historical quasi-autonomy and an extant legal model for a modern Cornish Assembly.

It is also important to note that the endowment of the Duchy of Cornwall to the Prince of Wales tied the future of Cornwall inextricably to the English (later British) royal family. It was a connection that both created and explained Cornwall's seemingly paradoxical, even contrary, behaviour in the centuries after the Duchy's creation—loyal Cornwall tied intimately by its distinctive institutions to the Crown; rebellious Cornwall jealously defending its particularism and independence. As Deacon put it, 'a very important link in the chain of Cornish history had been formed—one that produced that Cornish blend of conservatism and dependence (on the English crown) on the one hand and rebelliousness and independence on the other'.[65]

This mixture of rebelliousness and independence was to rear its head to most violent effect in 1497, with the Cornish rebellion of that year, led by St Keverne blacksmith Michael Angove and a lawyer from Bodmin, Thomas Flamank. Their frustrations were two-fold: the suspension of the Stannaries in 1496, and the level of taxation being demanded to fund Henry VII's conflict with a truculent Scotland supporting a pretender to the English throne, Perkin Warbeck. Despite reaching Blackheath, threatening the English state at its heart in Greenwich palace, Angove and Flamank's forces—some 10,000 strong—were speedily defeated, and the ringleaders executed. A subsequent landing in Cornwall by Warbeck also led to defeat. A humiliating reversal for the Cornish, this misadventure and its ensuing 'exhaustion kept the county quiet for half a century'.[66] Yet despite the short-term ignominy for the rebels, 1497 has in the longer-term excited the Cornish nationalist imagination, with the tiny 'terrorist' group An Gof (active in the closing decades of the twentieth century) naming itself after one of the leaders, and the current affairs and research group Cowethas Flamank formed in 1969 using the moniker of the other. In 1997 there was also a memorable march from St Keverne to Blackheath—'Keskerdh Kernow'—to commemorate the events of five hundred years before.

Likewise, the Prayer Book Rebellion of 1549 has also entered the nationalist repertoire. After initial clashes in 1548, when attempts had been made to remove certain 'popish' images from churches in Cornwall, a full-scale rebellion was launched the following year in response to the passing of the Act of Uniformity, in which church services were to be led from the Book of Common Prayer. The Cornish rejected this, drawing up a petition to King Edward VI declaring that 'we the Cornish men (whereof certain of us understand no English) utterly refuse this new English'.[67] From this emerges two important points, neither not lost on today's nationalists: firstly that there was still a considerable number of monoglot Cornish speakers, and secondly that the Cornish were once again resisting external intrusion into their affairs. If the rebellion of 1497 had been put down relatively leniently, the same was not true in 1548. There were several thousand Cornish casualties in the various engagements around Exeter, and the reprisals against the rebel clergy were brutal.[68] For some Cornish nationalists today, this amounts to genocide.[69]

Stoyle and Payton both point to a strong Cornish element in the English Civil War a century later. Payton attributes this in part to the wooing of the Cornish gentry by the Duchy of Cornwall,[70] while Stoyle emphasizes the quasi-nationalist element. He notes, for example, that in one of the final desperate stands of the war, the Royalist Sir Richard Grenville attempted to establish Cornwall as an autonomous region: 'in a letter written on 27 November [1646], he attempted to gain the Prince's support for an extraordinary plan, one which, if it had been carried out, would effectively have created a semi-independent Cornwall'.[71] Grenville's ruse was to ask the Prince, as the Duke of Cornwall, to seek a separate peace with Parliament for the area, using the devoted loyalty of the 'Cornish Army' that he had raised as a bargaining plea. Once again, there is that curious mix of loyalty to the Crown and a desire for autonomy that still haunts contemporary Cornwall, with its ambiguous relationship with the Duchy.

Although there is little historical evidence to suggest that the Cornish were prepared to rise in 1687 in protest against the imprisonment of Bishop Jonathan Trelawny by James II, the event has also assumed an important role in Cornish mythology, not least through the popularization of the Revd R.S. Hawker's nineteenth-century ballad 'The Song of the Western Men'—or 'Trelawny', as it is more often known. Celebrated as the unofficial Cornish national anthem, 'Trelawny' is sung wherever the Cornish gather—most notably at rugby matches—and is often viewed by nationalists as a metaphor for the rebelliousness of the early modern period, conflating the events of 1687 with those of 1497 and 1549. Indeed, Hawker's ballad might be seen as one of the first instances of the nineteenth-century romantic Celtic revival.[72]

Cornish language

Equally important as a metaphor, and again central to the mythology of Cornish nationalism, is the death in 1777 of Dolly Pentreath, variously described as the last native speaker or the last monoglot speaker of the Cornish language. As well as mourning the passing of Cornish as spoken vernacular, nationalists invest Pentreath's death with symbolic importance—a warning against allowing Cornish culture to decline or die out.[73]

Paradoxically, the revival of the Cornish language in the twentieth century both helps to explain the rise of the Cornish nationalist movement and accounts, at least in part, for its inability to gain popular momentum. Despite the supposed 'death' of the language, scholarly interest in the language had not disappeared.[74] The efforts of Henry Jenner and others towards the end of the nineteenth century had a galvanizing effect on this interest. Deacon, for example, notes the gathering of a larger than expected crowd in 1878 at the anniversary to mark Pentreath's passing.[75] Jenner's publication in 1904 of his *Handbook of the Cornish Language* coincided with his address to the Pan-Celtic Congress entitled 'Cornwall: A Celtic Nation', a title the Congress was in response happy to bestow upon the region.[76] His address linked explicitly the preservation of the language with Cornwall's avowed status as a Celtic nation:

If, however, you define a Celtic nation as one which, mainly composed of persons of Celtic blood and possessing Celtic characteristics, and having once had a separate national existence, has preserved a separate Celtic language and literature, I am not disinclined to agree; and I am prepared to show that Cornwall fulfils those conditions.[77]

The revival of the Cornish language continued throughout the twentieth century with the inauguration of the Cornish Gorsedd in 1928, 'a College of Bards who had been each admitted . . . on account of some outstanding contribution to Cornwall',[78] and through the efforts of Robert Morton Nance and A.S.D. Smith, and their respective *Cornish For All* (1929) and *Lessons in Spoken Cornish* (1931).[79] By the latter half of the last century, there was sufficient interest in the language to provoke heated discussions about which version of revived Cornish was the most 'authentic', leading eventually to the emergence of a 'Standard Written Form'.[80] It is important to note here the intimate relationship between language revival and the growth of nationalist movement, perceptible in Jenner's 1904 address and evident almost half a century later in the founding of MK (Sons of Cornwall) in 1951. As Thomas observed: 'The deliberate linguistic revival is central . . . because it has at all stages been intermingled with, and often used as the basis for, the other campaign to revive a Cornish national consciousness'.[81] Indeed, in the 1960s a movement to teach schoolchildren Cornish was also born, the aim of which was intrinsically political, a method of instilling in young people a sense of difference: 'they are in Kernow, and language is the summation of Cornish identity'.[82]

The roots of Cornish nationalism

From the very beginning, the revival of the Cornish language was linked to the fostering of national consciousness. Henry Jenner had asked himself why the Cornish should revive their language, and answered the question in his *Handbook of the Cornish Language*: 'Because they are Cornishmen . . . The reason why they should learn this language, the outward and audible sign of [their] separate nationality, is sentimental, and not in the least practical'.[83]

Nonetheless, the first revivalists were nothing if not sentimental, and it took a long time for the Cornish revival to harbour any political ambition. Royston Green, adopting a Marxian analysis of the 'national question', identifies three stages of the Cornish revival.[84] His chronology offers a useful model for considering the development of Cornish nationalism. Green's first phase relates to a period from the middle of the nineteenth century until 1914, when the alleged death of the language was challenged by a romantic, antiquarian Celtic revival. The second period relates to the institutionalization of the revival, with the formation of various organizations aiming to preserve Cornish cultural identity. The final period is from 1950 to the present, and relates to the formation of MK and its gradual politicization into the social democratic party that it is today.[85]

Both Green and Deacon are deeply critical of this first stage of revival. Deacon describes it as 'a largely ineffective and feeble movement',[86] and although Green begrudgingly identifies Jenner as 'in many ways the founder of modern Cornish', he critiques the revival itself. Jenner was 'the most pronounced exponent of this elitist and clerical trend', insists Green, 'Jenner and his followers cultivated feudal royalist politics at the same time as publishing much authentic Cornish material.[87] It was Jenner who, alongside L.C. Duncome-Jewell, played a major role in establishing Cowethas Kelto-Kernuak (CKK), a conduit for revivalist activity. Jewell, an eccentric anti-industrialist, was far more interested in Celtic mysticism than was his more pragmatic and scholarly colleague.[88] Amy Hale provides a detailed revisionist study of CKK, and reveals the proto-nationalist leanings of Duncombe-Jewell made plain in the latter's correspondence, when in 1901 he attempted to have Cornwall recognized as a Celtic nation by the other national members of the Celtic Association, the forerunner of the Congress. Hale describes Duncome-Jewell's efforts as 'not . . . eloquent or . . . well-organised . . . Yet it was the first time that the cultural components of Celtic-Cornwall were assembled, placed in a Pan-Celtic context, and presented to an international audience so forcefully'.[89]

Duncombe-Jewell's involvement with CKK seemingly came to an end in a squabble with the President and Irish representative of the Celtic Association, who questioned the veracity of Cornwall's Celtic literary heritage, a suggestion that Duncombe-Jewell took angry exception to. This left Jenner to take the reins of CKK, with markedly more success in a Pan-Celtic context in 1904.[90] Ultimately, it was the outbreak of hostilities in 1914 led to the dissolution of CKK. But Jenner's linguistic work had, in retrospect, accomplished far more than he could have imagined, or given his own political leanings, perhaps wished for. Thomas again:

> [T]he major achievement of Henry Jenner, Robert Morton Nance and their contemporaries, was the establishment of Cornishness, of national consciousness . . . had this overall Cornish Revival not been attempted, and accomplished, it would by now be quite impossible to construct the particular platform on which the linguistic, cultural, nationalistic, and environmental movements in Cornwall all perform'.[91]

The inter-war years, and Green's second period, tells the story, in Thomas' phrase, of the 'accomplishment' of the Cornish Revival. Inspired by the work of Jenner, a number of individuals set about developing and refining the Cornish language, simultaneously laying the groundwork for a cultural nationalism that would in time develop political concerns. It should be noted at this stage that Jenner himself was keen to highlight his purely cultural interest in Cornish matters, and studiously avoided reference to political nationalism. In 1924 Jenner pointedly remarked to an audience in Cornwall that the Revivalists had no intention of aping the slogan of Irish Republicans, Sinn Fein ('Ourselves Alone'), but preferred the far more inclusive Onen Hag Oll ('One and All').[92] Yet the work of the inter-war revivalists, with their promotion of the language, invented traditions such as the Cornish kilt, the use of St Piran's flag, and the establishment of the Gorsedd, stimulated a cultural nationalism that was inevitably 'political'.[93] These activities, for example, served to inspire a new, younger generation, that formed the quasi-political Tyr ha Tavas (Land and Language) organization in 1934.[94]

Tyr ha Tavas was a relatively short-lived organization but nonetheless was a small yet important step towards the politicization of the revivalist movement, lobbying local MPs on Cornish issues. Although Payton is critical of Tyr ha Tavas (the movement produced a magazine called *Kernow* which 'sold more copies outside of Cornwall than within'[95]), he concedes that this period lay the groundwork for a more full-throated nationalism in the post-war years. As he puts it: 'The triumph of the Cornish-Celtic revival was not the moving or the mobilising of the Cornish people (which it had singularly failed to achieve), but rather the credible "re-invention" of the Cornish identity in the face of industrial collapse and social paralysis.'[96] Garry Tregidga concurs, drawing comparisons between Tyr ha Tavas and the early development of the Welsh nationalist party:

development . . . was fairly similar to the early experience of Plaid Cymru: an initial concern with the language issue which was then extended to economic and political objectives . . . Tyr ha Tavas can be regarded as a bridge from the purely cultural and academic concerns of individuals like Jenner to the political objectives of Mebyon Kernow in the 1950s.[97]

Mebyon Kernow

MK's foundation in January 1951 was inspired by an outburst of Pan-Celtic consciousness and enthusiasm, following the previous year's extremely successful Celtic Congress, held in Truro. At least two of its founders were intent on emulating their colleagues in Wales. Richard Jenkin met with Professor Ambrose Bebb 'After the Congress was over . . . to discuss how Plaid Cymru had started, and to encourage us to go on and do the same'.[98] The chair of the new-found group was Helena Charles, a young nationalist markedly more focused on achieving political and socio-economic change for the Cornish than her predecessors had been. She highlighted similarities with Brittany and the Breton people, who she believed had suffered economically and culturally from the centralist policies of post-war France. Her analysis of the Cornish situation was peppered with anti-English rhetoric, arguing that 'the process of anglicisation and assimilation [was] proceeding fast'.[99] Charles met with early success, winning a seat in a by-election for Camborne-Redruth Urban District Council. However, her strident attitude had begun to cause fissures in the nascent party, not least amongst older members such as Robert Morton Nance, including those who had supported the politicization of Tyr ha Tavas in the 1930s. This infighting was such that Charles was poorly supported in her unsuccessful campaign to retain her seat, and eventually she resigned as Chair of MK in 1957.[100]

The appointment of Major Cecil Beer as leader in the same year marked the beginning of a period when MK slid back to the cultural nationalism of former times, and dropped its electoral pretensions until the following decade. The tone of MK's activities at this juncture is illustrated by an article in *New Cornwall* magazine, a publication that was either a de facto mouthpiece of MK or loosely associated with the group, depending on viewpoint. The article celebrated the party's tenth anniversary by stating limply that MK's role was 'to remind Cornish people of their unique culture and to develop it in every way and by every means',[101] with no mention of any constitutional or political objectives. Beer handed over to Robert Dunstone in 1960, but the noncommittal, cautious approach continued, with the typical MK executive meeting apparently taken up by discussion of 'calendars, Christmas cards, serviettes, Cornish language classes, and proposals for things like the Cornish kilt'.[102] In short, it was hardly the intense ideological debate of firebrands. Unsurprisingly, the membership in 1962 was said to number no more than 70 paying subscribers.[103]

This was to change by the end of the decade, a result of two external circumstances that provoked a reaction in MK and the wider Cornwall, and reinvigorated the movement to the extent that it began to receive recognition in the UK national press. The first of these was the successes at the ballot box of the other Celtic nationalist parties, Plaid Cymru and the Scottish National Party.[104] This stimulated the growth of MK as it developed branches across Cornwall, and the *Daily Telegraph* ran a story on MK in 1965 alongside other 'fringe groups', reporting that its membership had now swelled tenfold to around 700.[105] The second major event, which illustrates the generally reactive rather than proactive nature of Cornish nationalism, was what was dubbed 'Overspill'. This describes the policy pursued by the Greater London Council (GLC) in the mid-1960s to deal with the ever-expanding population of the capital city. The solution proposed was the building of new towns of up to 60,000 people. While the rumours of whole new conurbations in Cornwall were dismissed by the GLC, it continued to consider more modest Town Development Schemes, in which Cornish towns would receive the carrot of industrial development funding in exchange for providing housing for the 'overspill' from London. MK was vociferous in its opposition from the very start, a populist stance that won the group both increased membership and enhanced publicity. Ultimately, it gave MK its first seat on Cornwall County Council, when in 1967 Colin Murley narrowly defeated the incumbent Liberal councillor in the St Day and Lanner ward.[106]

Unsurprisingly, such relatively dramatic expansion resulted in growing pains for the group, resulting in two internal developments, which would have long-term strategic consequences for the future direction of the party. The first of these was the decision to turn MK from a pressure group to a more overtly political party. The current leader of MK, Councillor Dick Cole, describes the move as an act of 'bravery', ensuring that membership 'was no longer a badge of convenience for the self-interested politicians from London-centred parties'.[107] Perhaps the benefit of hindsight has enabled Cole to view events in such terms, but at the time MK remained assiduous in signing-up MPs from mainstream parties to their cause. Two Liberal MPs, John Pardoe in the North Cornwall constituency and Peter Bessell in Bodmin, joined MK and declared their support for Cornish self-government, whilst David Mudd, who was elected Conservative MP for Falmouth-Camborne in 1970, was also a member.[108] This dual membership was to cause frictions in 1967, and the subsequent decision to become more 'political' did little to assuage the more militant factions, resulting in a breakaway in 1969 to form the short-lived Cornish National Party (not to be confused with the later Cornish Nationalist Party). The popular anti-overspill stance of MK had given the illusion of a broader support base, a fact that the newly declared political party was cruelly reminded of in its weak performance in the 1970 general election.[109]

Nonetheless, under the new chairmanship of Len Truran from 1968, MK developed a far more efficient communications strategy, publishing a quarterly journal, *Cornish Nation*, which received contributions from across the Cornish community, including eminent writers such as A.L. Rowse and Daphne du Maurier. More importantly, among this new found willingness to engage in political debate, MK published what Deacon views as a 'ground-breaking document, anticipating later "mainstream" policies, such as renewable energy, more emphasis on "value-added" industries such as food processing rather than the primary industry of farming, a diversification of the economy, higher quality "cultural" tourism and a University for Cornwall'.[110]

The document was named, appropriately, *What Cornishmen Can Do*, and, as Deacon suggests, it was clear evidence of MK's more critical engagement with socio-economic conditions:

> Cornwall, we have always believed, is rich enough in both natural and human resources to be self-supporting; she pays far more in taxes and duties than she receives in social and economic benefits; she has an export potential which could easily encourage the Cornish to 'go it alone'. But Mebyon Kernow subscribes to no isolationist or chauvinist policies. We seek only a just provision for our own people in their own land, and believe that that provision will best be secured by goodwill and co-operation, rather than unrest and factitiousness.[111]

From this short extract one can perhaps find the twin sources of conflict that resulted in subsequent splits within MK. The first is the new-found concern with economic realities, rather than pre-occupation with a Celtic past, and a definite lurch towards socio-democratic principles rather than the emotional, right-wing appeals of some activists. The second is the realization that the future success of MK would depend on a realistic, collaborative approach with more mainstream politics, and a rejection of secessionist ideologies.

Despite MK's pragmatic attitude, Thomas saw the need in 1973 to clarify that MK was not 'as critics sometimes imagine, a kind of mad I.R.A.'.[112] This was prescient, for in the September of the following year *Cornish Nation* published a picture of the dead Irish hunger striker Michael Gaughan under the caption 'Celtic hero', an editorial decision that MK leaders were quick to distance themselves from.[113] Such clashes between militant elements and those who saw the party as a more moderate social democratic party, were to blight MK throughout the 1970s and produced a further division in the party when Whetter left to form the Cornish Nationalist Party (CNP) in 1975. Whetter had previously stood in two elections as an MK candidate, but was more interested in an ethnic nationalist approach. Although the split harmed MK in the short term, it brought about greater resolve to contest general elections (the party fielded three candidates in 1976), and a led to clearer articulation of its centre-left positioning. In 1977 Len Truran insisted that: 'The moderate views [of MK] are in the main shared by many and acclaimed by the majority in Cornwall. Indeed, other parties in Cornwall freely take certain of our policies and promote them as their own when they wish to appear representative of Cornwall'.[114]

The 1970s may have been largely a period of stasis, but for MK the decade ended on a positive note with a reasonably strong showing in the 1979 general election, contesting three seats and polling 4, 3 and 1.7 per cent in St Ives, Falmouth-Camborne and Bodmin constituencies respectively. This modest success was matched by the respectable 9,000 votes cast for the party in contemporaneous local elections, and the impressive 10,205 for the MK candidate Richard Jenkin in the European elections later that year.[115] Unfortunately for MK, these foundations were not built on into the 1980s, with further infighting leading to the resignation of Len Truran as chair in 1980, and with the party struggling to adapt to the harsher political climate of the Thatcher era. A succession of chairs came and went, and the party reached a low point in the 1987 general election, failing to field a candidate. The end of a miserable decade for the party was the resignation of the chair Loveday Carlyon in 1990, leaving MK in limbo and unsure of its future viability. An emergency meeting in 1990, ironically called by MK's London branch, did much to stop the internal rot, and in 1993 the party felt able once again to field nine candidates at local elections, and contest four out of five constituencies in the 1997 general election, when it published a thoughtful, centre-left manifesto, *Cornwall 2000—The Way Ahead*. In the event, the party fared poorly, polling only 1,906 votes between the candidates. In October that year, the latest stage in MK's development was ushered in with the election of Dick Cole to chair of the party.[116]

Cole's history of Mebyon Kernow (*Mebyon Kernow and Cornish Nationalism*, published in 2003), written collaboratively with Deacon and Tregidga, modestly ends shortly after this point, but he can take much of the credit for the comparatively uneventful years that have passed since then. His first months in office coincided with the closing of the South Crofty mine and attendant protests, supported by MK, but since then Cole has steered a steady course, with little internal wrangling. The party has slowly grown in electoral prowess, learning to make its impact locally rather than pinning its hopes on UK national ambitions, where under a first-past-the-post system MK continues to perform poorly (MK finished fifth in all constituencies bar one in 2010). MK currently has four members on Cornwall Council, and in the recent past has benefited occasionally from defections from other parties and independents. Cole has successfully professionalized the party; it has a slick website, articulate spokespeople, and clearly defined policies (in the 2010 general election these fell under the headings of prosperity for all, social justice, and sustainability)[117] that reflect the prevalent socio-economic conditions of Cornwall. There is little reference to a 'Celtic' ethnic nationalism in the party's rhetoric, and the party looks optimistically towards the next election when it hopes to reap the benefits from local disillusionment with the Liberal Democrats as a result of their Coalition with the Conservatives.

Other expressions of Cornish nationalism

If the story of Cornish nationalism since the Second World War is dominated by Mebyon Kernow, then there are various other groups that have sought to advance the nationalist cause, mostly through moderate means, although some through more violent methods.

Cornish Nationalist Party

The formation of the CNP, led by Whetter, arguably marked the point at which the ethnic nationalist elements in MK split away from the remaining civic nationalist main body. Payton asserts that the party's policy differed very little from MK, save that CNP was 'a vigorously pro-European organization . . . forging links with like-minded nationalist and regionalist groups in Europe',[118] but study of the mouthpiece of the party *Cornish Banner* (which Whetter still edits, and has now adopted a distinctly anti-European tone) or their manifestos reveals a definite 'Celtic' posture and a greater degree of militancy:

The CNP strives towards a federal Europe in which the Celtic countries are freed from their current imperialist overlords. The CNP works for Cornwall achieving the degree of autonomy that is necessary for her total fulfillment as a Celtic nation, for the total fulfillment of the Cornish people as a Celtic people. The CNP believes that healthy internationalism is based on strong nationalism.[119]

This harder line was matched by the apparent creation in 1976 of a uniformed youth wing known as the 'Greenshirts', swiftly disowned by the CNP leadership, and possibly the work of the rogue West Cornwall organizer who left the party later that year, complaining that it had been 'infiltrat[ed] by Communist elements'.[120] Like its divorced parent body, CNP performed weakly at the polling station, and was last seen in electoral action in 1985. In 2009 the CNP released a statement stating that it had reformed, although this was not followed by any further appearances on the electoral stage.[121]

An Gof

The most violent but also the most incompetent of the Cornish nationalist groups was the shadowy An Gof movement, named after the leader of the 1497 rebellion. In obvious imitation of IRA attacks, it claimed responsibility for the detonation of a bomb at the courthouse in St Austell in December 1980. Threatening telephone calls to newspapers and MK leaders followed throughout 1981, and an arson attack on a Redruth hairdresser's, mistaken for a Bristol and West Building Society branch, was also allegedly instigated by the group. An Gof aimed its vitriol as much at the perceived shortcomings of MK as its did against its supposedly English imperialist targets, and aside from further claims of a number of fires across the region in the mid 1980s, had disappeared from public view by the 1990s.[122] There were shades of such militancy in 2007, with reports in the UK national press of a group calling itself the Cornish National Liberation Army (CNLA) making firebomb threats to celebrity chefs Jamie Oliver and Rick Stein regarding their businesses near Newquay and in Padstow.[123]

Stannary Parliament

The Cornish Stannary Parliament movement surfaced in 1974, and has periodically been influential in nationalist circles since. A curious body, based on the premise that the Stannary 'Parliament and Law have never been formally repealed, though they have been unused since 1752 and 1896 respectively',[124] it has received scathing treatment from some observers.[125] Yet Deacon et al. ascribe a seriousness to the self-appointed Stannary Parliament not afforded by other commentators. They consider that the Stannary Parliament's arguments about Cornwall's constitutional status had important repercussions in the MK split of 1975, and point out that the Parliament's activities are illustrative of the continuing nostalgic, royalist bent in sections of the nationalist movement. Needless to say, the Duchy of Cornwall itself has studiously avoided making comment on the group's claims.[126]

Senedh Kernow/Cornish Constitutional Convention

A more realistic constitutional proposition is the cross-party campaign for a Cornish Assembly, launched in March 2000. As well as support from Conservative, Liberal Democrat, Independent and MK politicians, the movement gathered 50,000 signatures for a petition, which was handed to the then Prime Minister.[127] The group also produced policy documents outlining its arguments and suggested plans for an assembly, as well as jointly commissioning an independent report by the UCL Constitutional Unit about the future options for 'the Cornish question'.[128] The Convention's response to the White Paper on devolution in 2003 outlines its case for an assembly, as well as articulating the wider arguments for Cornish self-rule: Cornwall's status as an economic outlier, its geographic position as a peninsula, Cornish cultural and political distinctiveness, and Cornwall's 'special relationship with England, as a Celtic region that is both part of England and separate from it'.[129] This latter point is an important one; the Convention does not tub-thump about Cornwall's Celtic heritage, nor make accusatory statements about English imperialism, and so does not seek to alienate those residents of Cornwall (many of them in-migrants) who, as demonstrated in Dickinson and Willett's studies, can feel both Cornish and English, or at the very least 'British'. The Convention is candid, however, about the manner in which Cornwall is administrated:

> Cornwall suffers from what might be called 'institutional peripherality'. Many of the institutions that develop economic and social policy are located outside Cornwall. These include a myriad of quangos, government departments and agencies. Such bodies have neither the scope nor the remit to pursue policies specifically relevant to Cornwall. They seldom recognise Cornish strengths and special needs as a peripheral region . . . Furthermore, policy-making is fragmented since there is no single body to which these institutions are accountable.[130]

The Cornish Constitutional Convention outlines a pragmatic solution to these difficulties, with an assembly with devolved responsibilities overseen by 40–50 Assembly Members, and a First and deputy Minister. It also makes economic arguments, comparing itself to other devolved administrations: 'the Convention notes that if funding per capita were set at the same level that applies in Wales, it would result in an additional £101m p.a. being made available for the delivery of public services within Cornwall'.[131]

Ultimately the Convention's bid was unsuccessful in 2002, but campaigning by the non-partisan group (now styled Campaign for a Cornish Assembly) has continued throughout the last decade, taking an opportunistic approach to lobbying government Ministers on appropriate pieces of policy. The campaign appears to have built a reasonably effective cross-party collation that has mainstream appeal and a seriousness of purpose that, should political conditions become more favourable, gives Cornwall its best hope of future self-determination.

Liberal Democrats

Liberal concern with the national question in Cornwall can be traced back at least as far as 1910, long before the formation of MK, when the Liberal MP for St Austell, Thomas C. Agar Robartes remarked that the 'chief characteristic of Cornishmen is their love of independence. As a nation we dislike being trampled on'.[132] This sympathy has been evident throughout the subsequent century, expressed since the War by a succession of leading Liberals in Cornwall, notably the MPs John Pardoe, Peter Bessell, David Penhaligon, Paul Tyler and Matthew Taylor. Tregidga traces this long history, noting that the Liberals were the only party in 1959 to support Cornish devolution, on the basis that Cornwall was a 'separate nation'. Moreover, as Tregidga has pointed out, the Liberals/Liberal Democrats have been consistently successful in stealing MK's political clothes and in promoting themselves as the only credible 'centre-left and anti-metropolitan alternative to the Conservatives'. As Tregidga adds, the 'crucial point about the long-term development of ethno-regionalism in Cornwall was that until 1970 this process was mainly associated with the Liberals'.[133] It is a point seemingly accepted by MK, albeit tacitly, with its complaint (noted above) that 'other parties . . . freely take certain of our policies and promote them as their own when they wish to appear representative of Cornwall'.[134]

Today, Cornish interests are represented most strongly in Liberal Democrat circles, and thus at Westminster, by Andrew George and Dan Rogerson. Both MPs, elected in 1997 and 2005 respectively, opened their maiden speeches in the House of Commons in the Cornish language. George has written a book about his experiences of representing a Cornish constituency and his attempts to drag Cornish issues up the Westminster agenda, while Rogerson in particular has recently gone beyond the concerns of his constituency in representing wider Cornish issues. Rogerson is wary of the nationalist tag, but has learnt Cornish, is readily conversant in Cornish political and social history, and has held a St Piran's Day event in Parliament in recent years to educate other Members on the culture and prevailing socio-economic conditions of contemporary Cornwall.[135] More substantially, Rogerson tabled a 'Government of Cornwall Bill' in 2009, which was supported by all the then current Cornish MPs. This outlined a Cornish Assembly similar to that proposed by the Cornish Constitutional Convention, with a mandate to 'do anything which they consider appropriate to achieve the promotion or improvement of the economic, social and environmental well-being of Cornwall'.[136] The Bill lost out in the ballot for Private Member's Bills, and Rogerson speaks now of his frustration that his party's leadership 'don't get it.[137] Nonetheless, his advocacy adds further momentum to the campaign for an Assembly, and has demonstrated the common voice with which Cornish Liberal Democrat MPs speak, even in the sometimes uncomfortable Coalition with the Conservatives.

Gramsci and a 'mosaic of meaning'

Thus far, we have examined the origins of Cornish nationalism, taking our cue from Hobsbawm's well-known quip about 'Celtic tradition' and 'regional discontent', and have identified the Cornish as an ethnic group in terms of both Smith's *ethnie* and Durkheim's *social facts*. We have also attempted to penetrate the nationalist imagination, in particular its construction of Cornish history and identity, and to understand its varying motivations over time as it has evolved from predominantly 'ethnic' to broadly 'civic' in its outlook. But we have also observed that, despite this rich repertoire, Cornish nationalism has made only limited electoral impact, voters apparently unwilling to turn Cornish consciousness into political action, what nationalist potential there is being consistently usurped by the Liberal Democrats. Various factors, from the hybridity of Cornish identity to the disabilities of the UK first-past-the-post electoral system, help to explain this state of affairs. But before drawing conclusions, we should consider other perspectives.

Rob Burton, for example, provides a fresh perspective on Cornish identity, and provides perhaps the most compelling theoretical model to explain why Cornish nationalism is not as politically viable as Hobsbawm might have imagined. Burton looks at Cornish history through a Gramscian lens, and suggests that the 'cultural hegemony'—to employ the phrase made famous by Antonio Gramsci, the Marxist thinker—that has been visited upon the Cornish by the English nation and state throughout history has resulted in a duality of identity. As Burton explains it, this is a duality between 'the "official" conception, or dominant English viewpoint' and 'the "popular" conception of the world, i.e. a Cornish conception which, despite the dominance of the English viewpoint, has its own vigour and its own spontaneous life'.[138]

This duality is akin to the hybridity detected by Willett and Dickinson. But Burton makes the additional point that the Cornish live within a 'mosaic of meaning', in which tiny pieces of different identities make up the whole, often in an incoherent or paradoxical fashion: 'The pasty, brass bands, bards, piskeys, Trelawny's Army, the tartan, Cornish Rebellion beer and so on, form, all in their own ways, a cultural "text"—a complex and often paradoxical text wherein lies the roots of Cornish identity'.[139] Burton also astutely observes that for Gramsci, cultural hegemony is never static. It is, as Adamson has explained: 'a process of continuous creation, which, given its massive scale, is bound to be uneven in the degree of legitimacy it commands and to leave some room for antagonistic cultural expressions to develop.[140] This is an 'uneven legitimacy' and space 'for antagonistic cultural expression' to which the Cornish have responded, albeit in an often inchoate and fragmented manner, creating that curious meld of loyalty on the one hand and rebelliousness on the other.

Rob Burton and the writer Frank Halliday might seem unlikely bed-fellows, but F.E. Halliday's suggestion that 'Cornish nationalism was merged, but never submerged, in a greater English nationalism' may have a greater degree of truth than Cornish nationalists themselves care to admit.[141] Halliday was no Gramscian but his observation seems to be one of the most accurate and sensitive portrayals of Cornish nationalism; not denying that it exists, but suggesting that perhaps its strength has been fragmented and refracted among other competing identities.

Payton and peripheralism

Interestingly, Philip Payton concludes *The Making of Modern Cornwall* (1992), in which he explores the nature of Cornish 'distinctiveness', by arguing that throughout Cornwall's past there have been what he describes as 'constants of peripherality', which together account for Cornwall's enduring isolation from the 'centre' of the UK state.[142] However, Payton argues, 'peripherality' is itself dynamic. Borrowing Tarrow's typology, he postulates 'phases of peripherality', moving from an 'Older Peripheralism' of territorial and cultural isolation in the medieval period, to the 'Second Peripheralism' of industrialization and de-industrialization, and a post-Second World War 'Third Peripheralism' of rapid socio-economic change. This latter period, Payton argues, has not only perpetuated Cornwall's deleterious peripheral condition but has added new vitality to the Cornish identity, as Cornwall reaches for new cultural markers to deploy in protest against the negative impact of socio-economic change.[143] This 'persistence of difference' model provides a coherent historical framework in which we might understand the otherwise perplexing mechanics of Gramscian resistance to cultural hegemony. But perhaps it also adds to the puzzle of why this enduring but dynamic sense of Cornish identity has not resulted in a greater degree of popular support for more political autonomy from the 'centre'.

As Bernard Deacon reminds us, in an important but sobering gloss on Smith's *ethnie* theory, 'a host of *ethnies* existed in the past which never acquired the status of nation'.[144] The Cornish, as we have seen, appear readily to meet all the criteria of an *ethnie*. Yet, as Deacon argues, they 'can productively be viewed as an example of a people who created their own ethno-history but were unable and/or unwilling to transform themselves into a nation'.[145] This, in turn, helps to explain the relative weakness of Cornish nationalism. As Deacon emphasizes, it is a mistake to imagine that an apparently strong Cornish identity will lead automatically to a strong nationalist movement. As he puts it succinctly, one must 'distinguish between the articulate expression of a minority twentieth century Cornish nationalism and a less articulate popular Cornishness'.[146]

The timidity of political nationalism

As we have seen, political nationalism in Cornwall has been weak, despite the apparently solid foundations on which to build: a Celtic ethno-history, socio-economic conditions that demonstrate neglect by successive central governments, and a firmly held popular Cornish identity. Yet despite an enduring peripherality, the Cornish *ethnie* has never been able to imagine itself unequivocally as a nation. Instead, Cornishness has settled into a dual or hybrid identity, albeit one with periodic 'Gramscian flashes' in which there are incoherent and fragmented exhibitions of resistance. As a result, political nationalism has been unable to build a strong core of support. It has also made Cornish nationalism appear disorganized and hesitant, notwithstanding Cole's recent efforts to professionalize MK.

The ambiguity of hybrid identity has also fed the wider timidity and nostalgia of the Cornish nationalist movement. The Stannary Parliament, with stunning inability to engage with the socio-economic conditions affecting ordinary Cornish people, bases its strategy on obscure legal arguments dating back to the medieval period. It is little surprise that it fails to attract wider support outside its small band of devotees. Extensive in-migration has also lent a new dimension to Cornish hybridity, creating an environment in which a strident Celtic ethno-nationalism, such as that advocated by the CNP, is likely to have little general appeal. It is no accident that MK has distanced itself from ethno-nationalism, adopting instead a far more inclusive 'civic' policy. As early as 1977 the party was keen to stress that it campaigned for 'social justice, prosperity and an independent voice to all those who would call themselves Cornish in Cornwall, whether by birth, descent or identification with the Country that they have adopted'.[147] Yet in eschewing more strident positions, MK has sometimes appeared unduly deferential, falling back on the loyalist and Royalist traditions of the Cornish. Deacon et al. note that the MK general election manifesto in 1970 stressed that the movement was 'loyal to Her Majesty', and in 1977 the MK AGM voted by a margin of two to one to send the Queen jubilee greetings (albeit in Cornish).[148] This peculiar mix of 'conservative rebelliousness'[149] is matched by those who insist on seeing debates about the constitutional status of the Duchy of Cornwall as a plausible route to Cornish self-determination.

The Liberal Democrats have been the main beneficiary of the weakness of Cornish nationalism,[150] with Andrew George and Dan Rogerson both providing strong Cornish voices in the current parliament. However, it remains to be seen what the effect of their Coalition with the Conservatives in government—viewed with distaste by many Liberal Democrat activists and supporters in Cornwall—will be in the next general election.[151]The embarrassment experienced by Cornish Liberal Democrat MPs over the proposed redrawing of constituency boundaries (with the possibility that one might straddle the River Tamar, creating a so-called Devonwall seat) has also been unsettling. Prime Minister David Cameron's glib opinion that 'it's the Tamar, not the Amazon',[152] demonstrates the uphill battle that Rogerson and his colleagues have in persuading the Coalition government to 'get it' as far as Cornwall is concerned.

Conclusion: Following in the footsteps of Plaid Cymru and the SNP?

As the Liberal Democrats experience discomfort in Coalition, perhaps there is at last an opportunity for MK? Certainly, the ripples emanating from the forthcoming Scottish referendum on independence have been felt in Cornwall. In March 2012 *The Times* ran a feature on Cornish nationalism, with a *T2* front-page headline: 'Could Cornwall go the same way as Scotland?'.[153] A reduction of the issue, it nonetheless suggests a natural link. Payton reports similar increased interest from a number of UK national newspapers in the past year, and poses the question:

If Scotland becomes independent, then what is Cornwall? How does it fit into the remnant? Cornwall will look even more 'different', in a rump UK without Scotland ... Is it more like Wales, is it part of England? At that time, people in Cornwall who have been quite happy in a blurred identity, with the St Piran's flag and the Union flag flying side by side, may have to make some choices about identity.[154]

Indeed, Deacon et al. note that the debates around Home Rule in Ireland in the 1880s 'can be regarded as a catalyst for the rise of nationalism in both Scotland and Wales'.[155]

It may be that Cornish nationalism now finds itself in a similar situation, benefiting from the recent devolution of power to Wales and Scotland (and possibly the prospect of Scottish independence). After all, during its first twenty years of existence Plaid Cymru 'struggled to develop a secure niche in Welsh politics'.[156] As Payton puts it, MK's current position 'reflects Plaid Cymru in the 1970s'.[157] From this perspective, MK's encouraging recent local electoral performances, alongside the increasing professionalism under Cole's leadership, could see the party emulating Plaid Cymru and SNP's model of success in years to come.

Yet the inherent disabilities of Cornish nationalism remain. Despite an apparently promising base, the ambiguity of Cornwall's hybrid identity has combined with in-fighting, uncertainty, and a timid and deferential attitude to ensure that the movement has consistently lacked credibility. Objectively, the popular and cross-party support for a Cornish Assembly is probably the most significant step yet in a long journey, and likely to be Cornwall's best hope for a measure of self-determination. Contrary to Hobsbawm's analysis, it is not the 'attractive colours of Celtic tradition' —or crude ethno-nationalism —but the 'regional discontents' themselves, articulated in a forthright civic nationalism of the type projected by Dick Cole, that might just make Cornish nationalism viable in future times.

Notes and references

1. E. Hobsbawm, *Nations and Nationalism since 1780: Programme, Myth, Reality* (Cambridge, 1992), p. 178.
2. A.K. Hamilton Jenkin, *The Cornish Miner* (London, 1927), pp. 274–75.
3. E. Hobsbawm, *Revolutionaries* (London, 2007), p. 18.
4. Cornwall Council, *Cornwall's economy at a glance* (Truro, 2012), p. 6.
5. Cornwall Council, *Understanding Cornwall 2010–11: People—An overview of demographic issues* (Truro, 2010), p. 2.
6. B. Deacon, *Cornwall: A Concise History* (Cardiff, 2007), p. 207.

7. P. Mitchell, 'The Demographic Revolution' in P. Payton (ed.), *Cornwall Since The War: The Contemporary History of a European Region* (Redruth, 1993), pp. 142–49.

8. Interview with Philip Payton, 26 March 2012.

9. Cornwall Council, 2011 Census: An overview of the headline figures for Cornwall (Truro, 2013), p. 5.

10. Cornwall Council, *Call yourself Cornish?* (Truro, 2011).

11. BBC News, 'Welsh are "more patriotic"', http://news.bbc.co.uk/1/hi/wales/3527673.stm, accessed 9 August 2012.

12. Cornwall Council, *Quality of Life Survey* (Truro, 2007).

13. B. Deacon, 'Peggy Combellack's conundrum: locating the Cornish identity', unpublished paper, available at www.projects.ex.ac.uk/cornishcom/documents/conundrum.pdf, accessed 6 July 2012, p. 6.

14. E. Durkheim, *Selected Writings* (Cambridge, 1972), p. 58.

15. B. Deacon, 'And shall Trelawny die? The Cornish Identity' in P. Payton (ed.), *Cornwall Since The War: The Contemporary History of a European Region* (Redruth, 1993), pp. 207–9.

16. J. Willett, 'Cornish Identity: Vague Notion or Social Fact' in P. Payton (ed.), *Cornish Studies: Sixteen* (Exeter, 2008), pp. 193–99.

17. Ibid., p. 199.

18. R. Dickinson, 'Meanings of Cornishness: A Study of Contemporary Cornish Identity' in P. Payton (ed.), *Cornish Studies: Eighteen* (Exeter, 2010), p. 70.

19. Ibid., p. 75.

20. Ibid., p. 77.

21. Willett, 'Cornish Identity', p. 186.

22. A.D. Smith, *The Ethnic Origins of Nations* (Oxford, 1986), p. 22.

23. Ibid., pp. 22–30.

24. K. Husk, 'Ethnicity and Social Exclusion: Research and Policy Implications in a Cornish Case Study', *Social and Public Policy Review* 5:1 (2011), p. 20.

25. M. Havinden, J. Quéniart, J. Stanyer (eds), *Centre and Periphery: Brittany and Cornwall & Devon Compared* (Exeter, 1991), p. 81.

26. R. Weight, *Patriots: National Identity in Britain, 1940–2000* (London, 2003), p. 602.

27. T. Kendle, 'The Eden Project and Regional Regeneration', *Journal of the Royal Agricultural Society of England* 164 (2003), p. 2.

28. P. Thornton, 'Cornwall and Changes in the "Tourist Gaze"' in P. Payton (ed.), *Cornish Studies: One* (Exeter, 1993), pp. 80–96.

29. A. Williams and G. Shaw, 'The Age of Mass Tourism' in P. Payton (ed.), *Cornwall Since The War*, p. 87.

30. Cornwall County Council, *Survey of the Holiday Industry* (Truro, 1966), p. 25.

31. South West Research Company, *Value of Tourism 2010: Cornwall* (Truro, 2010), p. 2.

32. Ibid., p. 6.

33. The Objective One Partnership for Cornwall and Scilly, *Objective One Tourism Proposal*, 2001, p. 19. Available at www.objectiveone.com/ob1/pdfs/tourism.pdf, accessed 29 April 2013.

34. P. Thornton, 'Second Homes in Cornwall' in P. Payton (ed.), *Cornish Studies: Four* (Exeter, 1996), p. 156.

35. Cornwall Council, *Cornwall's economy at a glance*, p. 2.

36. Interview with Philip Payton, 26 March 2012.

37. Cornwall Council, *Cornwall's economy at a glance*, p. 6.

38. M. White, 'Cornish nasties', *The Guardian*, 14 June 2007. www.guardian.co.uk/commentisfree/2007/jun/14/cornishnasties, accessed 23 August 2012.

39. C. Thomas, *The Importance of Being Cornish in Cornwall: An Inaugural Lecture* (Redruth, 1973), p. 15.

40. R. Alleyne, 'Second home owners banned from voting in Cornwall elections', *The Telegraph*, 9 September 2011. www.telegraph.co.uk/news/politics/8750278/Second-home-owners-banned-from-voting-in-Cornwall-elections.html, accessed 23 August 2012.

41. Thornton, 'Second Homes in Cornwall', pp. 155–56.

42. Alleyne, 'Second home owners banned from voting in Cornwall elections'.

43. K. Cahill, 'The Killing of Cornwall', *Business Age Magazine* 18 (2001), p. 18.

44. Cornwall Council, 'Guide to European Funding 2007–2013' website www.cornwall.gov.uk/default.aspx?page=4643, accessed 3 September 2012.

45. European Regional Development Fund, *Convergence Programme for Cornwall and the Isles of Scilly: Operational Programme 2007–2013* (Truro, 2007), p. 2. www.cornwall.gov.uk/PDF/ERDF%20Operational%20Programme.pdf

46. Deacon, *Cornwall*, p. 1.

47. Weight, *Patriots*, pp. 598–603.

48. H. Kearney, *The British Isles: A History of Four Nations* (Cambridge, 1989), p. 70.

49. Deacon, *Cornwall*, p. 2.

50. M. Stoyle, *West Britons: Cornish Identities and the Early Modern British State* (Exeter, 2002), pp. 4–5.

51. J. Whetter, *A Celtic Tomorrow* (St Austell, 1973), p. 81.

52. D. Cole, 'The Cornish Identity and Genetics—An Alternative View' in P. Payton (ed.) *Cornish Studies: Five* (Exeter, 1997), p. 28.

53. P. Payton, *Cornwall: A History* (2nd edn) (Fowey, 2004), p. 40.

54. Ibid., p.35.

55. Ibid., p. 49.

56. Deacon, *Cornwall*, p. 4.

57. Payton, *Cornwall*, p. 69.

58. Deacon, *Cornwall*, p. 22.

59. Thomas, *The Importance of Being Cornish in Cornwall*, pp. 6–7.

60. Mebyon Kernow, *What Cornishmen Can Do: The Economic Possibilities Before Cornwall* (Truro, 1968), p. 3.

61. Deacon, *Cornwall*, p. 36.

62. A.L. Rowse, *Tudor Cornwall* (St Agnes, 2005), p. 82.

63. These arguments are in part repeated in Payton, *Cornwall*, p. 79.

64. Deacon, *Cornwall*, p. 37.

65. Deacon, *Cornwall*, p. 38.

66. Rowse, *Tudor Cornwall*, p. 140.

67. Quoted in Payton, *Cornwall*, p. 123.

68. Ibid., pp. 122–26.

69. Deacon, *Cornwall*, p.76.

70. Ibid., p. 131.

71. Stoyle, *West Britons*, p. 104.

72. Deacon, *Cornwall*, p. 149.

73. Payton, *Cornwall*, pp. 175–76.
74. Thomas, *The Importance of Being Cornish in Cornwall*, p. 8.
75. Deacon, *Cornwall*, p. 187.
76. Payton, *The Making of Modern Cornwall*, p. 134.
77. H. Jenner, 'Cornwall: A Celtic Nation', *The Celtic Review* 1:3 (1905), p. 238.
78. Payton, *The Making of Modern Cornwall*, p. 134.
79. B. Deacon and P. Payton, 'The Ideology of Language Revival', in Payton (ed.), *Cornwall Since The War*, p. 273.
80. K. MacKinnon, 'Cornish at its Millennium: An Independent Study of the Language Undertaken in 2000' in P. Payton (ed.), *Cornish Studies: Ten* (Exeter, 2002), p. 268.
81. Thomas, *The Importance of Being Cornish in Cornwall*, pp. 9–10.
82. J. Whetter, 'Reasons for Learning the Cornish Language', *Cornish Nation* 2 (1970), p. 2.
83. J. Parry 'The Revival of Cornish: An Dasserghyans Kernewek', *PMLA* 61:1 (1946), pp. 259–60.
84. R. Green, *The National Question in Cornwall: A Historical Review* (London, 1981).
85. Ibid., pp. 22–23.
86. Deacon, *Cornwall*, p. 186.
87. Green, *The National Question in Cornwall*, p. 23.
88. Payton, *Cornwall*, p. 261.
89. A. Hale, 'Genesis of the Celto-Cornish Revival?': L.C. Duncombe-Jewell and the Cowethas Kelto-Kernuak' in P. Payton (ed.), *Cornish Studies: Five* (Exeter, 1997), p. 106.
90. Ibid., pp. 108–9.
91. Thomas, *The Importance of Being Cornish in Cornwall*, p. 9.
92. Payton, *Cornwall*, p. 266.
93. Ibid., p. 263.
94. Ibid., p. 267.
95. Payton, *The Making of Modern Cornwall*, p. 135.
96. Payton, *Cornwall*, p. 267.
97. G. Tregidga, 'The Politics of the Celto-Cornish Revival 1886–1939' in Payton (ed.), *Cornish Studies: Five*, p. 146.
98. Deacon et al., *Mebyon Kernow and Cornish Nationalism*, p. 32.
99. Ibid., p. 33.
100. Ibid., p. 32–37.
101. Ibid., p. 38.
102. Ibid., p. 46.
103. Ibid., p. 45.
104. Payton, *The Making of Modern Cornwall*, pp. 24–25.
105. Deacon et al., *Mebyon Kernow and Cornish Nationalism*, p. 48.
106. Ibid., pp. 49–50.
107. Dick Cole speech at Mebyon Kernow Annual Conference, 24 November 2011, available at www.youtube.com/watch?v=kg65TDlGcjk, accessed 23 September 2012.
108. Payton, *The Making of Modern Cornwall*, p. 25.
109. Deacon et al., *Mebyon Kernow and Cornish Nationalism*, pp. 55–57; Payton, *The Making of Modern Cornwall*, pp. 25–26.

110. Deacon, *Cornwall*, p. 210.
111. Mebyon Kernow, *What Cornishmen Can Do*, p. 27.
112. Thomas, *The Importance of Being Cornish in Cornwall*, p. 14.
113. Deacon et al., *Mebyon Kernow and Cornish Nationalism*, p. 63.
114. L. Truran, *For Cornwall: A Future!* (Redruth, 1977), p. 3.
115. Deacon et al., *Mebyon Kernow and Cornish Nationalism*, p. 71.
116. Ibid., p. 96.
117. Mebyon Kernow, 'A Party Political Broadcast by Mebyon Kernow—The Party for Cornwall' (2009), available at www.youtube.com/watch?v=bYIgzI6Rl4c, accessed 20 September 2012.
118. Payton, *The Making of Modern Cornwall*, p. 200.
119. Cornish Nationalist Party, *Program an Party Kenethlgek Kernow—Programme of the Cornish Nationalist Party* (St Austell, 1977).
120. Deacon et al., *Mebyon Kernow and Cornish Nationalism*, p. 67.
121. This is Cornwall, 'Cornish Nationalist Party regroups to contest elections', 6 April 2009, available at www.thisiscornwall.co.uk/Cornish-Nationalist-Party-regroups-contest-elections/story-11420903-detail/story.html, accessed 28 September 2012.
122. Deacon et al., *Mebyon Kernow and Cornish Nationalism*, pp. 67–68; *The Making of Modern Cornwall*, p. 202.
123. R. Savill, 'Cornish firebomb threat to top chefs', *The Telegraph*, 14 June 2007. www.telegraph.co.uk/news/uknews/1554444/Cornish-firebomb-threat-to-top-chefs.html, accessed 26 September 2012.
124. M. Sandford, *The Cornish Question: Devolution in the South-West Region* (London, 2002), p. 38.
125. Interview with Payton, 26 March 2012.
126. Deacon et al., *Mebyon Kernow and Cornish Nationalism*, pp. 65–66.
127. Senedh Kernow, *Devolution for One and All: Governance for Cornwall in the 21st Century* (Truro, 2002), p. 2.
128. Sandford, *The Cornish Question*.
129. Senedh Kernow, *Your Region: Your Choice—the Case for Cornwall: Cornwall's response to the Government's Devolution White Paper* (Truro, 2003), p. 5.
130. Senedh Kernow, *Devolution for One and All*, p. 5.
131. Ibid., p. 7.
132. Deacon et al., *Mebyon Kernow and Cornish Nationalism*, p. 18.
133. G. Tregidga, 'Devolution for the Duchy: The Liberal Party and the Nationalist Movement in Cornwall', *Journal of Liberal Democrat History* 22 (1999), p. 23.
134. Truran, *For Cornwall*, p. 3.
135. Interview with Dan Rogerson MP, 4 September 2012.
136. House of Commons, *Government of Cornwall Bill* (London, 2009), p. 15.
137. Interview with Rogerson, 4 September 2012.
138. R. Burton, 'A Passion to Exist: Cultural Hegemony and the Roots of Cornish Identity' in Payton (ed.), *Cornish Studies: Five*, p. 152.
139. Ibid., p. 161.
140. W. Adamson, *Hegemony and Revolution: A Study of Antonio Gramsci's Political and Cultural Theory* (Berkeley, 1980), p. 174.
141. F. Halliday, *A History of Cornwall* (London, 1959), p. 184.
142. Payton, *The Making of Modern Cornwall*, p. 240.
143. Ibid.

144. Deacon, 'Peggy Combellack's conundrum', p. 12.
145. Ibid., p. 12.
146. Ibid., p. 10.
147. Truran, *For Cornwall*, p. 4.
148. Deacon et al., *Mebyon Kernow and Cornish Nationalism*, p. 70.
149. Deacon, 'Peggy Combellack's conundrum', p. 22.
150. Payton, *The Making of Modern Cornwall*, p. 228.
151. Interview with Payton, 26 March 2012.
152. S. de Bruxelles, 'All Quiet On The Southwestern Front?', *The Times: T2*, 5 March 2012, p. 5.
153. Ibid., p. 1.
154. Interview with Payton, 26 March 2012.
155. Deacon et al., *Mebyon Kernow and Cornish Nationalism*, p. 17.
156. Ibid., p. 17.
157. Interview with Payton, 26 March 2012.

14

Betjeman's Badge

Postscript for a Pan-Celtic Nationalist

Philip Payton

Introduction

One of the occupational hazards of the biographer—and indeed any writer of serious non-fiction—is the discovery after publication of new evidence that would have measurably supported the principal arguments or thesis of the book. Such was the case of *John Betjeman and Cornwall: 'The Celebrated Cornish Nationalist'*, published in 2010.[1] Put simply, the biography suggested that, despite appearing 'quintessentially English', Betjeman—who had been taunted as a schoolboy for his German surname—doubted his own Englishness and searched instead for an alternative Celtic identity. A Welsh twig in his family tree served to authenticate this identity (he even acquired a smattering of Welsh and later learned Irish) but he rooted it in Cornwall, especially in North Cornwall where he had holidayed as a child, finding inspiration in its 'Celtic Christianity' and Anglo-Catholic tradition. Cornwall was a place of 'liberation', where Betjeman could find relief from the conflicting pressures of everyday life. But his engagement with Cornwall was active and at times combative, insisting that the Duchy (as he termed it) was a Celtic nation apart from England, and championing an environmentalism that anticipated today's obsession with 'sustainability'.

Betjeman also affected a strident Cornish nationalism, from advocating study of the Cornish language to supporting the nationalist party Mebyon Kernow (MK) in its opposition to the Beeching railway cuts. He likewise expressed more than a passing sympathy for other Celtic nationalisms. In Ireland during the war, for example, he had explained Irish neutrality to a doubtful British public, and developed a keen regard for Eamon de Valera as well as deciding that the partition of the island had been a huge mistake. In characteristic Betjemanesque style, partly but not entirely tongue in cheek, he had cultivated his own Celtic personas. There was Jan Trebetjeman ('the celebrated Cornish nationalist'), Sean (and occasionally Deirdre) O'Betjeman (Irish), Ewen Quetjeman (Manx), and Iain MacBetjeman (Scots). For those who imagined that he was only larking about, there was his chastening BBC radio broadcast in February 1943 in which he insisted that 'When people talk to me about "the British", as though they were all the same, I give up'.[2] At the height of the war, and with victory not yet in sight, this was highly subversive (even J.B. Priestley had been persuaded to substitute 'Britain' for 'England' in his wartime broadcasts) but it reflected Betjeman's deeply held conviction about the inherent diversity of these islands, with their multiple national identities.

In considering Betjeman's connections with Mebyon Kernow, the biography noted his support for several of the party's policy objectives, although observing that (unlike Daphne du Maurier, for instance) he apparently stopped short of joining the movement. Indeed, the book detected a degree of hostility towards Betjeman in some nationalist circles, citing in particular Victor Elphick's hard-hitting parody of his own poem 'Trebetherick', which had appeared in the MK magazine *Cornish Nation* in March 1973. Among several verses was the shocking stanza:

They it was who had laid the golf courses, invented
Surfing at Newquay, made gift-shops popular, rented
Cottages, cashed in on brass piskies and Joans-the-Wad
Made in darkest Birmingham. Then Saxon feet, rough-shod,
Trampled Kernow's landscape, where Piran's flag had flown.
Hengist and Horsa rape while Betjeman holds her down.[3]

There was also the embittered chorus:

Forgotten is St Enodoc, the wave is any wave,
Concrete covers springy turf. What did we pray to thee?
That our children should lose all the happy days you gave,
To Tom, Dick and Harry and London-by-the-sea.[4]

The biography doubted whether Betjeman had actually seen Elphick's composition, but speculated that—if he had—he might have agreed that Elphick had a point. Betjeman was alive to his own role in precipitating the despoliation of Cornwall, as he saw it, and was candid enough to confess his own complicity and guilt.

Summoned by Bells

There the story remained, until a routine re-viewing (for teaching purposes) of Jonathan Stedall's classic television film version of John Betjeman's blank verse biography *Summoned by Bells* revealed the existence of 'Betjeman's badge'.[5] In the two sequences showing Betjeman in Cornwall, he is wearing a badge on the left lapel of his tweed jacket. The badge is observed best in the frames where Betjeman is stooping at the holy well at St Enodoc. It is a white enamel button badge, with a Cornish (St Piran's) flag in the centre and the bilingual slogan 'Kernow Kensa—Cornwall First' printed in black around the outside circle rim. Produced exclusively for MK and advertised in *Cornish Nation*, this lapel badge—and its equivalent depicting in red a map of Cornwall with the slogan 'Kernow bys Vyken—Cornwall Forever'—was available only by post from the 'Mebyon Kernow Shop'. The initial advertisement appeared in the March 1972 edition of *Cornish Nation*, was repeated in the June issue, and then reproduced again in September and in the December—the latter two issues actually illustrating the badges in question. The advertisement reappeared once thereafter, in March 1973, in the same issue as Victor Elphick's poem, although no longer illustrated. At 2 ½ pence each (or 28p for ten post free [five of each]), the badges proved immensely popular, with high demand from across Cornwall and beyond—even in distant Sussex, where an enthusiastic schoolboy managed a roaring trade in selling them on to bemused classmates.

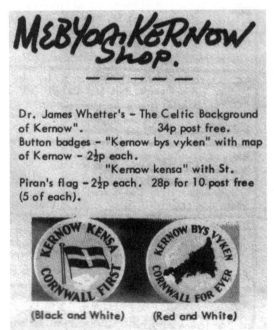

Figure 1.   'Mebyon Kernow Shop' advertisement for enamel lapel 'button badges'

Figure 2. 'Betjeman's Badge' plainly visible on his lapel as John Betjeman stoops at St Enodoc's well (from *Summoned by Bells*, produced and directed by Jonathan Stedall in 1976)

Indeed, so successful were the badges that they were soon sold out. It is not clear why there was not a second production run, but after the March 1973 edition of *Cornish Nation* they disappeared from the MK sales list, never to appear again. Those who had acquired these attractive badges began to appreciate their rarity value, and among those who continued to sport them with pride was John Betjeman himself. It is not known how Betjeman obtained his example—perhaps from contacts in Padstow, where there were prominent MK members, or possibly by spotting the advertisement in *Cornish Nation* and sending off for one to the 'Mebyon Kernow Shop'. This raises the intriguing possibility that he may, after all, have consulted the pages of *Cornish Nation* from time to time, pursuing his interest in Cornish nationalism—in which case he may well have seen Victor Elphick's angry poem.

The film version of *Summoned by Bells* was made in 1976. First mooted in 1972, the idea was initially resisted by Betjeman. He thought it too intimate, and did not relish bringing back old and painful memories. But later he was persuaded to take the plunge, to celebrate his 70th birthday. Despite his close friendship with Jonathan Stedall, he did not enjoy making the film, and all his earlier misgivings resurfaced.[6] Although not yet quite in his twilight years, Betjeman in *Summoned by Bells* appears reflective and often sad, giving the film the melancholy and pathos so appreciated by admiring audiences. When it was first broadcast it was recognized as a triumph, affording viewers a penetrating insight into the 'real' Betjeman, discomforting though this was for him personally.

Given Betjeman's mixed feelings and uneasiness about the film, it is interesting that he thought to wear his 'Kernow-Kensa—Cornwall First' badge. Produced by Mebyon Kernow, depicting St Piran's flag, and with a bilingual political message, the badge was an unequivocal expression of Cornish nationalist sympathies. It was, moreover, a sympathy that Betjeman sought to display to his global audiences, or at least to discerning and observant viewers alert to such subtleties. Here, alas, was important evidence that would elude *John Betjeman and Cornwall: 'The Celebrated Cornish Nationalist'*, although it was no doubt spotted by those paying closer attention to detail in the film. Victor Elphick had imagined St Piran's flag obliterated at the hands of Betjeman and his ilk, yet here, ironically, was that very device depicted at the centre of 'Betjeman's badge'. It may be going too far to suggest that this irony, apparent to those readers of Elphick's poem who were also careful viewers of *Summoned by Bells*, was deliberate, a product of Betjeman's self-deprecating and sometimes contrary humour. But it does evidence commitment in the face of criticism, a determination on Betjeman's part to claim common cause with Cornwall and the spirit of Cornish nationalism, together with his yearning 'to belong'—to acquire a veneer of Cornishness within his alternative Pan-Celtic identity.

'Celtic Nationalists'

No sooner had *John Betjeman and Cornwall: 'The Celebrated Cornish Nationalist'* been published, than Horace Liberty—editor of *The Betjemanian: The Journal of the Betjeman Society*—wrote to draw attention to a letter in his private collection from John Betjeman to Revd Dr Peter Moore, dated 1958.[7] Written a decade or so after his return from Ireland, and little more than half-a-dozen years since the foundation of Mebyon Kernow, Betjeman's letter revealed him at the height of his Pan-Celtic enthusiasms. In 1958 Peter Moore was vicar of the Worcestershire parish of Alfrick with Lusley, and later, after a varied career, became Dean of St Albans. A High Churchman with a strong interest in architecture, he was exactly the kind of clergyman likely to appeal to Betjeman. This was reflected in the informality of their correspondence, especially in Betjeman's multiple Celtic Nationalist signatures—including a Welsh version, Evan ap [B]etjeman. He explained that the possibly obscure designation 'Ewan Quetjeman' was Manx, but left Moore to struggle with 'Writers to the Cygnet'. In Scots law, a 'writer to the signet' is the traditional term for a solicitor, so here, perhaps, was another 'Celtic' allusion, albeit one that also suggested a self-deprecating 'ugly duckling' persona.

In 1957, the year before the Moore correspondence, the writer Gladys Bertha Stern—known invariably to her friends as 'Peter'—had published her collection . . . *and did he speak to you?*, a series of essays about her literary acquaintances. Among those friends was John Betjeman, the subject of one of her chapters. Betjeman thought her a 'sweet . . . generous and encouraging critic', writing in 1954 that 'I *am* lucky in getting the attention of writers like you, dear Peter, whom I admire'.[8] As Paul Robinson notes in a recent (2013)

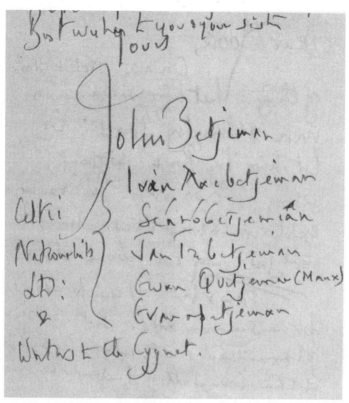

Figure 3. John Betjeman's Celtic Nationalist signatures
in his letter to the Revd Dr Peter Moore in 1958

article, Betjeman had given Peter Stern a copy of his volume, *A Few Late Chrysanthemums* (1954), inscribing it to her 'from Her Berkshire choms'– the 'Celtic Nationalists'– and listing all five supposed Celtic variants of his name.[9] Again, he explained that Ewen Quetjeman was Manx, in case she could not guess. It was an inscription that Stern remembered fondly in her own book. 'Mine eyes dazzle', she wrote, 'and fall on the fly leaf opposite, where this same man of erudition and scholarship has chosen to inscribe my volume'.[10] Alas, it was another important shred of evidence that had been missed in the biography.

Further overlooked material was another important inscription, this time to Joan Kunzer (née Larkworthy) in a complimentary copy of Betjeman's book *First and Last Loves* (1952). Now in the private collection of Phil Richardson, this inscription is tribute to the enduring friendship of John Betjeman and Joan Kunzer, or Larkworthy as she was when they first met in Cornwall in

1910. She was four years old and Betjeman five, and together they forged a relationship that would last for the rest of their lives. 'Inscribed For My Oldest Friend Joan Kunzer by Her Oldest Friend', Betjeman wrote, again attributing the inscription to his 'Celtic Nationalist' personae and listing the familiar variants: Irish, Cornish, Manx, Scottish, Welsh. But there was one additional form: 'John Betjeman (Vague)'.[11] In this telling appellation, Betjeman admitted the rootlessness, as he saw it, of his own name and personal identity. Maybe German—or Dutch, as his mother insisted—or English (or not), or possibly Welsh, Cornish, or Irish (by tortuous descent or intimate association), he revealed the deep ambiguities and uncertainties of who he was. To be simply John Betjeman was merely 'Vague', an admission of not really belonging anywhere. Indeed, he had been born 'John Betjemann', only abandoning the tell-tale double *nn* after its apparent German-ness had become too much to bear during the Great War, replacing it with the more acceptable but bland alternative 'Betjeman'. It was a vagueness of identity that ultimately drove him to develop his multiple and fondly held—and oft-repeated—Celtic allegiances. That these existed alongside his equally passionate celebration all things English ('at some visceral level he spoke for England',[12] according to A.N. Wilson), merely accentuates the ambiguity.

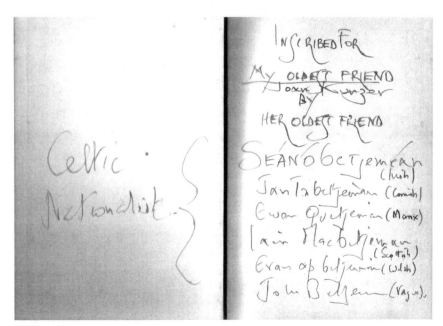

Figure 4.   John Betjeman's inscription of Joan Kunzer's copy
of *First and Last Loves* (1952)

Conclusion

The obvious point here is that the biographer's work is never done, and that—unless he or she intends to emulate those never-to-be-published local historians (so despised by A.L. Rowse) who refuse to write up their research for fear of missing undiscovered 'facts'—it is inevitable that new, sometimes important, material will only come to light after the finished volume has graced the shelves of bookshops. In this particular case, there is the perhaps more important observation—that evidence that has emerged since the publication of *John Betjeman and Cornwall: 'The Celebrated Cornish Nationalist'* has served to bolster the principal themes of the book (the identification with Cornish nationalism, the cultivation of alternative Celtic identities) in new and significant ways. 'Betjeman's badge' and the detailed signatures and inscriptions penned for close friends, were part of Betjeman's strategy to make plain his sympathies and allegiances, part of his public and private response to the continuing ambiguity and uncertainty of his personal identity.

Acknowledgements

I am indebted to Horace Liberty for extensive help with this article, and to Rachel Moseley for her technical assistance and great enthusiasm for the subject. I also thank Jonathan Stedall for his permission to reproduce the image of John Betjeman at the holy well of St Enodoc.

Notes and references

1. Philip Payton, *John Betjeman and Cornwall: The Celebrated Cornish Nationalist* (Exeter, 2010).
2. John Betjeman, 'Coming Home', BBC Home Service, 15 February 1943; published in the *Listener*, 11 March 1943.
3. *Cornish Nation*, March 1973.
4. Ibid.
5. *Summoned by Bells*, BBC 1976.
6. William S. Peterson, *John Betjeman: A Bibliography* (Oxford, 2006), p. 374; Bevis Hillier, *Betjeman: The Bonus of Laughter* (London, 2004), p. 443.
7. Letter from Horace Liberty to Philip Payton, 31 December 2010.
8. Candida Lycett Green (ed.), *John Betjeman: Letters—Volume Two: 1951–1984* (London, 1995), p. 69.
9. Paul Robinson, 'G.B. Stern on John Betjeman', *The Betjemanian: The Journal of the Betjeman Society*, Vol. 24, 2012/2013, p. 73.
10. cited in ibid., p. 72.
11. I am indebted to Horace Liberty for this information.
12. A.N. Wilson, *Betjeman* (London, 2006), p. 11.

Philip Payton: Bibliography

2013

(with Helen Doe and Alston Kennerley) (eds), *The Maritime History of Cornwall*, University of Exeter Press, 2013.

(ed.), *Cornish Studies: Twenty One—Coming of Age?*, University of Exeter Press, 2013, x + 337pp.

'Betjeman's Badge: Postscript for a Pan-Celtic Nationalist', in P. Payton (ed.), *Cornish Studies: Twenty-One—Coming of Age?*, University of Exeter Press, pp. 321–28.

Review of Cathryn Pearce, *Cornish Wrecking 1700–1860: Reality and Popular Myth*, Brewer & Boydell, Woodbridge, 2010, in *Mariners' Mirror*, Vol. 99, No. 2, pp. 247–49.

2012

Regional Australia and the Great War: 'The Boys from Old Kio', University of Exeter Press, 2012, xviii + 244pp.

(ed.), *Cornish Studies: Twenty—Essays in Honour of Bernard Deacon*, University of Exeter Press, 2012, viii + 264pp.

'Bernard Deacon', in P. Payton (ed.), *Cornish Studies: Twenty*, University of Exeter Press, 2012, pp. 9–12.

'Conflict and Consensus in the Cornish Language Revival', in Liam MacAmhlaigh and Brian O'Curnain, *A Festschrift Honour of Nicholas Williams*, Arlen House, Dublin, 2012, pp. 158–72.

2011

(ed.), *Cornish Studies: Nineteen*, University of Exeter Press, 2011, ix + 241pp.

'Diversity and Complexity in Twentieth-century Cornish Identities': Review article: Reviews of Gage McKinney, *The 1930s: No Depression Here*, Comstock Bonanza

Press, Grass Valley (California), 2009, and Kevin J. Gardner, *Betjeman and the Anglican Imagination*, SPCK, London, 2010, in P. Payton (ed.), *Cornish Studies: Nineteen*, University of Exeter Press, 2011, pp. 235–41.

2010

John Betjeman and Cornwall: 'The Celebrated Cornish Nationalist', University of Exeter Press, 2010, xx + 258pp.

(ed.), *Cornish Studies: Eighteen*, University of Exeter Press, 2010, xi + 244pp.

'Competing Celticities: Cornish and Irish Constructions of Australia', in Pamela O'Neill (ed.), *Celts in Legend and Reality*, Sydney Series in Celtic Studies 9, University of Sydney, 2010, pp. 463–83.

2009

(with Shelley Trower) (eds), *Cornish Studies: Seventeen*, University of Exeter Press, 2009, xi + 222pp.

D.H. Lawrence and Cornwall, Truran, St Agnes, 2009, 48pp.

'Cornish', in Josep R. Guzman and Joan Verdegal (eds), *Minorized Languages in Europe: State and Survival*, Mararyk University Press (Czech Republic) and Compostella Group of Universities, 2009, pp. 68–78.

2008

(ed.), *Cornish Studies: Sixteen*, University of Exeter Press, 2008, x + 243pp.

'Preface', in Alan M. Kent and Gage McKinney (eds), *The Busy Earth: A Reader in Global Cornish Literature 1700–2000*, Cornish Hillside, St Austell, 2008, pp. 12–14.

2007

Making Moonta: The Invention of 'Australia's Little Cornwall', University of Exeter Press, 2007, xiii + 269pp.

(ed.), *Cornish Studies: Fifteen*, University of Exeter Press, 2007, viii + 263pp.

'"The Man with the Donkey": Private Simpson, the ANZAC myth, and Civic Education in Australian Primary Schools in the 1950s and 1960s', *Australian Studies*, Vol. 20 1&2, 2007, pp. 265–89.

'"A Duchy in every respect un-English": Discourses of Identity in Late Modern Cornwall', in Bill Lancaster, Diana Newton and Natasha Vall (eds), *An Agenda for Regional History*, Northumbria University Press, Newcastle-upon-Tyne, 2007, pp. 317–31.

Review Article: Review of Barry McGowan, *Fool's Gold: Myths and Legends of Gold-seeking in Australia*, Lothian Books, Sydney, in *Journal of Australasian Mining History* 5, September 2007, pp. 178–80.

'John Betjeman and the Holy Grail: One Man's Celtic Quest', in P. Payton (ed.), *Cornish Studies: Fifteen*, University of Exeter Press, 2007, pp. 185–208.

2006

(ed.), *Cornish Studies: Fourteen*, University of Exeter Press, 2006, vi + 247pp.

'Making Moonta: The Invention of Australia's Little Cornwall', in *Journal of Australasian Mining History* 4, September 2006, pp. 47–67.

'Cornish', in Josep R. Guzman (ed.), *Llengues no Romaniques Minoratizades Europa*, Universitat Jaume II, Castello de la Plana (Spain), 2006, pp. 113–20.

2005

A.L. Rowse and Cornwall: A Paradoxical Patriot, University of Exeter Press, 2005, xii + 324pp .

The Cornish Overseas: A History of Cornwall's Great Emigration, Cornwall Editions, Fowey, 2005, 466pp.

(ed.), *Cornish Studies: Thirteen*, University of Exeter Press, 2005, vi + 314pp.

'Bridget Cleary and Cornish Studies: Folklore, Story-telling and Modernity', in P. Payton (ed.), *Cornish Studies: Thirteen*, University of Exeter Press, 2005, pp. 194–215.

'Maritime History and the Emigration Trade: The Case of Mid Nineteenth-Century Cornwall', *History Focus* (Institute of Historical Research), 2005.

'Cornish', in Keith Brown (ed.), *The Encyclopedia of Languages and Linguistics*, Elsevier, London, 2nd edn, 2005.

'Introduction', in A.L. Rowse, *Tudor Cornwall: Portrait of a Society*, new edn, Cornish Classics/Truran Books, Truro, 2005, pp. i–vi.

Review of J.P.D. Cooper, *Propaganda and the Tudor State: Political Culture in the Westcountry*, Oxford University Press, 2003, in *Journal of British Studies*, Vol. 44, No. 3, July 2005, pp. 644–45.

2004

Cornwall: A History, Cornwall Editions, Fowey, 2004, x + 326pp.

(ed.), *Cornish Studies: Twelve*, University of Exeter Press, 2004, iv + 314pp.

'John Basset (1791–1843)', in Christopher Matthews (ed.), *The New Oxford Dictionary of National Biography*, Oxford University Press, Vol. 4, 2004, pp. 264–65.

'Robert Were Fox (1754–1818)', in Matthews (ed.), *The New Oxford Dictionary of National Biography*, Oxford University Press, Vol. 20, 2004, pp. 676–77.

'Richard Trevithick (1771–1833)', in Christopher Matthews (ed.), *The New Oxford Dictionary of National Biography*, Oxford University Press, Vol. 55, 2004, pp. 354–58.

'Arthur Woolf (1766–1837)', in Christopher Matthews (ed.), *The New Oxford Dictionary of National Biography*, Oxford University Press, Vol. 60, 2004, pp. 252–53.

2003

(ed.), *Cornish Studies: Eleven*, University of Exeter Press, 2003, vi + 330pp.
'"I was before my time, caught betwixt and between": A.L. Rowse and the Writing of Cornish and British History', in P. Payton (ed.), *Cornish Studies: Eleven*, University of Exeter Press, 2003, pp. 11–39.

2002

A Vision of Cornwall, Alexander Associates, Fowey, 2002, vii + 226pp.
Cornwall's History: An Introduction, Tor Mark Press, Redruth, 2002, 58pp.
(ed.), *Cornish Studies: Ten*, University of Exeter Press, 2002, vi + 306pp.
'Industrial Celts? Cornish Identity in the Age of Technological Prowess', in P. Payton (ed.), *Cornish Studies: Ten*, University of Exeter Press, 2002, pp. 116–35.
'The Cornish', in James Jupp (ed.), *The Australian People*, Cambridge University Press, 2002.

2001

(ed.), *Cornish Studies: Nine*, University of Exeter Press, 2001, vii + 328pp.
'Cousin Jacks and Ancient Britons: Cornish Immigrants and Ethnic Identity', *Journal of Australian Studies* 68, 2001, pp. 54–64.
'Cousin Jacks and Ancient Britons: Cornish Immigrants and Ethnic Identity', in Wilfred Prest and Graham Tulloch (eds), *Scatterlings of Empire*, University of Queensland Press, 2001, pp. 54–64.
'"Vote Labor, and Rid South Australia of a Danger to the Purity of Our Race": The Cornish Radical Tradition in South Australia, 1900–1939', in P. Payton (ed.), *Cornish Studies: Nine*, University of Exeter Press, 2001, pp. 173–203.

2000

(with Amy Hale) (eds), *New Directions in Celtic Studies*, University of Exeter Press, 2000, x + 235pp.
(ed.), *Cornwall For Ever! The Millennium Book for Cornwall*, Cornwall Heritage Trust, Lostwithiel, 2000, 248pp.
(ed), *Cornish Studies: Eight*, University of Exeter Press, 2000, vii + 256pp.
'Cornish', in Jan Wirrer (ed.), *Minderheiten-Und Regionalsprachen in Europa*, Westedeutscher Verlag, Wiesbaden, 2000, pp. 97–104.
'Cornish', in Glanville Price (ed.), *Languages in Britain and Ireland*, Blackwell, Oxford, 2000, pp. 109–19.
'Local and Regional History: The View from Cornwall', *Locality* (Centre for Community History UNSW), Vol. 11, No. 3, 2000, pp. 18–22.
'Re-inventing Celtic Australia', in Amy Hale and Philip Payton (eds), *New Directions in Celtic Studies*, University of Exeter Press, 2000, pp. 108–25.

1999

The Cornish Overseas, Alexander Associates, Fowey, 1999, xii + 420pp.

(ed.), *Cornish Studies: Seven*, University of Exeter Press, 1999, vii + 237pp.

'The Ideology of Language Revival in Modern Cornwall', in Ronald Black, William Gillies and Roibeard O'Maolaliagh (eds), *Celtic Connections: Proceedings of the 10th International Congress of Celtic Studies Vol.1*, Tuckwell, Edinburgh, 1999, pp. 395–424.

'Ethnicity in Western Europe Today', in Karl Cordell (ed.), *Ethnicity and Democratisation in the New Europe*, Routledge, London, 1999, pp. 24–36.

'The Retreat of Cornish', in Roger Kain and William Ravenhill (eds), *Historical Atlas of South West England*, University of Exeter Press, 1999, pp. 267–68.

1998

(ed.), *Cornish Studies: Six*, University of Exeter Press, 1998, vii + 210pp.

'Cornish', in Glanville Price (ed.), *Encyclopedia of European Languages*, Blackwell, Oxford, 1998, pp. 99–103.

Review of Gage McKinney, *A High and Holy Place: A Mining Camp Church at New Almaden*, New Almaden County Quicksilver Association, New Almaden (California), 1997, in P. Payton (ed.), *Cornish Studies: Six*, University of Exeter Press, 1998, p. 202.

Review of Richard Dawe, *Cornish Pioneers in South Africa: 'Gold and Diamonds, Copper and Blood'*, Cornish Hillside Publications, St Austell, 1998, in P. Payton (ed.), *Cornish Studies: Six*, University of Exeter Press, 1998, p. 203.

Review of Geoffrey Cubitt (ed.), *Imagining Nations*, Manchester University Press, 1998, in P. Payton (ed.), *Cornish Studies: Six*, University of Exeter Press, 1998, pp. 204–5.

'The Cornish and the Dominions: A Case Study in Sub-state Imperial Contact', in Fred Nash and Jim Bulpitt (eds), *The Dominion Concept Conference, University of Warwick, July 1998*, Political Studies Association/British International Studies Association, 1998 (CD).

1997

(ed.), *Cornish Studies: Five*, University of Exeter Press, 1997, vii + 193pp.

'Re-inventing Celtic Australia: Constructions of Identity from the Colonial Period to the Era of Multiculturalism', *Australian Studies*, Vol. 12, No. 2, Winter 1997, pp. 78–90.

'Identity, Ideology and Language in Modern Cornwall', in Hildegard L.C. Tristram (ed.), *The Celtic Englishes*, Universitsverlad C. Winter, Heidelberg, 1997, pp. 100–22.

'Cornwall in Context: The New Cornish Historiography', in P. Payton (ed.), *Cornish Studies: Five*, University of Exeter Press, 1997, pp. 9–20.

(with F. Roff Rayner and F.L. Harris), 'Cornwall Education Week: Seventy Years On', in P. Payton (ed.), *Cornish Studies: Five*, University of Exeter Press, 1997, pp. 180–87.

'Paralysis and Revival: The Reconstruction of Celtic-Catholic Cornwall 1890–1945', in Ella Westland (ed.), *Cornwall: The Cultural Construction of Place*, Patten Press, Penzance, 1997, pp. 25–39.

'"An English Cross-country Railway": Rural England and the Cultural Reconstruction of the Somerset and Dorset Railway', in Colin Dival (ed.), *Railway, Place and Identity: Working Papers in Railway Studies No.2*, Institute of Railway Studies, University of York, 1997, pp. 17–24.

'The Cornish Problem: Prospects for Devolution in the Duchy', *Proceedings of the ECTARC Conference on Regionalism in Europe*, European Centre for Traditional and Regional Cultures, Llangollen, 1997, 4pp.

1996

Cornwall, Alexander Associates, Fowey, 1996, viii + 310pp.

(with Nicholas Johnson and Adrian Spalding) (eds), *The Conservation Value of Metalliferous Mine Sites in Cornwall*, Institute of Cornish Studies/Cornwall Archaeological Unit, Truro, 1996, viii + 54pp.

(ed.), *Cornish Studies: Four*, University of Exeter Press, 1996, vii + 190pp.

'Inconvenient Peripheries: Ethnic Identity and the United Kingdom Estate—The Cases of Protestant Ulster and Cornwall', in Iain Hampsher-Monk and Jeffrey Stanyer (eds), *Contemporary Political Studies*, Political Studies Association of the UK, Belfast, 1996, pp. 395–408.

'Which Cornish? Ideology and Language Revival in Post-War Cornwall', in Máireád Nic Craith (ed.), *Watching One's Tongue: Aspects of Romance and Celtic Languages*, Liverpool University Press, 1996, pp. 111–35.

'Derelict Land and Cultural Identity: The Case of Cornwall', in Philip Payton, Nicholas Johnson and Adrian Spalding (eds), *The Conservation Value of Metalliferous Mine Sites in Cornwall*, Institute of Cornish Studies/Cornwall Archaeological Unit, Truro, 1996, pp. 9–14.

'Royal Naval Engineering College: A History', in Steven Haines and Richard Clarke (eds), *The Royal Naval Engineering College, Manadon: A Commemoration*, Institute of Marine Engineers, London, 1996, pp. 26–60.

'Reforming Thirties and Hungry Forties: The Genesis of Cornwall's Emigration Trade', in P. Payton (ed.), *Cornish Studies: Four*, University of Exeter Press, 1996, pp. 107–27.

Review of Anne Duffin, *Faction and Faith: Politics and Religion of the Cornish Gentry before the Civil War*, University of Exeter Press, 1996, in P. Payton (ed.), *Cornish Studies: Four*, University of Exeter Press, 1996, pp. 182–85.

'Introduction' to John Rowe, *Changing Times and Fortunes: A Cornish Farmer's Life 1828–1904*, Cornish Hillside, St Austell, 1996, pp. v–vii.

'Foreword', in Daniel Mason, *Cousin Jack*, Alexander Associates, Fowey, 1996, p. 5.

1995

(ed.), *Cornish Studies: Three*, University of Exeter Press, 1995, vi + 218pp.

(with Paul Thornton), 'The Great Western Railway and the Cornish-Celtic Revival', in P. Payton (ed.), *Cornish Studies: Three*, University of Exeter Press, 1995, pp. 83–103.

'Cornish Emigration in Response to Changes in the International Copper Market in the 1860s', in P. Payton (ed.), *Cornish Studies: Three*, University of Exeter Press, 1995, pp. 60–82.

Review article: Mark Stoyle, *Loyalty and Locality: Popular Allegiance in Devon During the English Civil War*, University of Exeter Press, 1994, in P. Payton (ed.), *Cornish Studies: Three*, University of Exeter Press, 1995, pp. 206–11.

Review of P.A.S. Pool, *The Second Death of Cornish*, Dyllansow Truran, Redruth, 1995, in P. Payton (ed.), *Cornish Studies: Three*, University of Exeter Press, 1995, pp. 211–13.

Review of Bernard Susser, *The Jews of South-West England: The Rise and Decline of Their Medieval and Modern Communities*, University of Exeter Press, 1993, in *Albion*, Vol. 27, No. 3, Fall 1995, pp. 464–66.

1994

(ed.), *Cornish Studies: Two*, University of Exeter Press, 1994, vi + 173pp.

'Ethnic Consciousness', in Michael Foley (ed.), *Ideas That Shape Politics*, Manchester University Press, 1994, pp. 172–80.

'Naval Education and Training', in Michael Duffy, Stephen Fisher, Basil Greenhill, David Starkey and Joyce Youings (eds), *The New Maritime History of Devon Vol.II*, Conway, London, 1994, pp. 191–203.

'Labour Failure and Liberal Tenacity: Radical Politics and Cornish Political Culture, 1880–1939', in P. Payton (ed.), *Cornish Studies: Two*, University of Exeter Press, 1994, pp. 83–95.

(with Allen Ivey), 'Towards a Cornish Identity Theory', in P. Payton (ed.), *Cornish Studies: Two*, University of Exeter Press, 1994, pp. 151–63.

1993

(ed.), *Cornish Studies: One*, University of Exeter Press, 1993, vi+ 161pp.

(ed.), *Cornwall Since the War: The Contemporary History of A European Region*, Institute of Cornish Studies/Dyllansow Truran, Redruth, 1993, xii + 312pp.

(with Leonard Truran) (eds), Cyril Noall's *St Ives Mining District: Vol II*, Dyllansow Truran, Redruth, 1993, xxvii + 157pp.

'Post-War Cornwall: A Suitable Case for Treatment?', in Philip Payton (ed.), *Cornwall Since the War: The Contemporary History of a European Region*, Institute of Cornish Studies/Dyllansow Truran, Redruth, 1993, pp. 6–21.

'Territory and Identity', in Philip Payton (ed.), *Cornwall Since the War: The Contemporary History of a European Region*, Institute of Cornish Studies/Dyllansow Truran, Redruth, 1993, pp. 224–52.

(with Bernard Deacon), 'The Ideology of Language Revival', in Philip Payton (ed.),

Cornwall Since the War: The Contemporary History of a European Nation, Institute of Cornish Studies/Dyllansow Truran, Redruth, 1993, pp. 271–90.

(with Bernard Deacon), 'Re-inventing Cornwall: Culture Change on the European Periphery', in P. Payton (ed.) *Cornish Studies: One*, University of Exeter Press, 1993, pp. 62–79.

'". . . a concealed envy against the English": A Note on the Aftermath of the 1497 Rebellions in Cornwall', in P. Payton (ed.), *Cornish Studies: One*, University of Exeter Press, 1993, pp. 241–48.

1992

The Making of Modern Cornwall: Historical Experience and the Persistence of 'Difference', Dyllansow Truran, Redruth, 1992, xii + 272pp.

(with Victoria Syme), 'Eastern Europe: Economic Transition and Ethnic Tension', in Michael Pugh (ed.), *European Security: Towards 2000*, Manchester University Press, 1992, pp. 86–103.

'The Great Migration', in *Cornish Studies for Schools*, Cornwall County Council, Truro, 1992, pp. 58–59.

'Quarrying: Granite and Slate', in *Cornish Studies for Schools*, Cornwall County Council, Truro, 1992, pp. 67–69.

'On Centre and Periphery', *Journal of Interdisciplinary Economics*, Vol. 4, No. 3, 1992, pp. 207–11.

'Socio-economic Change in Post-War Cornwall', *Journal of Interdisciplinary Economics*, 4:3, 1992, pp. 241–48.

Review of H.A. Havinden, J. Queniart and J. Stanyer (eds), *Centre and Periphery: Brittany and Devon & Cornwall Compared*, University of Exeter Press, 1991, in *Journal of Interdisciplinary Economics* 4:3, 1992, pp. 296–97.

1991

Review of Louis Le Bailey, *The Man Around the Engine: Life below the Waterline*, Kenneth Mason, Emsworth, 1990, in *Mariners' Mirror*, Vol. 77, No. 2, May 1991, pp. 208–9.

Review of Colin H. Williams and Eleonore Kofman (eds), *Community Conflict, Partition and Nationalism*, Routledge, London, 1989, in *Journal of Strategic Studies*, Vol. 14, No. 1, March 1991, p. 125.

1989

(ed.), Cyril Noall's *Cornish Mine Disasters*, Dyllansow Truran, Redruth, 1989, vii + 194pp.

1988

Tregantle and Scraesdon: Their Forts and Railway, Dyllansow Truran, Redruth, 1988, iv + 48pp.

'The Cornish', in James Jupp (ed.), *The Australian Peoples: An Encyclopedia of the Nations, Its Origins and Peoples*, Australian National University/Angus Robertson, Sydney, 1988, pp. 326–34.

1987

The Cornish Farmer in Australia, Dyllansow Truran, Redruth, 1987, xvi + 143pp.

1984

The Cornish Miner in Australia: Cousin Jack Down Under, Dyllansow Truran, Redruth, 1984, xii + 242pp.

Cornish Carols From Australia, Dyllansow Truran, Redruth, 1984, xvi + 26pp.

1983

The Story of HMS Fisgard, Dyllansow Truran, Redruth, 1983, x + 56pp.

1978

Pictorial History of Australia's Little Cornwall, Rigby, Adelaide, 1978, 94pp.

(in preparation)

Philip Payton, *A History of Sussex*, Carnegie, Lancaster, forthcoming 2014.

Philip Payton, *'Australia will be there!': Australia and the First World War*, Robert Hale, London, forthcoming 2014.